# COMPASITO

Manual on human rights education for children

## Edited and co-written by:

Nancy Flowers

## Contributors

Maria Emília Brederode-Santos
Jo Claeys
Rania Fazah
Annette Schneider
Zsuzsanna Szelényi

## Coordination and final editing

Zsuzsanna Szelényi

## Illustration

Diána Nagy

All correspondence related to this publication or the reproduction or translation of all or part of it should be addressed to:

Council of Europe, Directorate of Youth and Sport

European Youth Centre Budapest

H – 1024 Budapest, Zivatar utca 1-3

e-mail: eycb.secretariat@coe.int

Design: Daniel Horvath, http://danielhorvath.com

Proofreading: Rachel Appleby

© Council of Europe, November 2007

Published by the Directorate of Youth and Sport of the Council of Europe

ISBN: 978-92-871-6369-1

Printed in Hungary

# CONTENTS

Acknowledgements . . . . . . . . . . . . . . . . . . . . . . . . . . . . . . . . . . . . 6
Preface . . . . . . . . . . . . . . . . . . . . . . . . . . . . . . . . . . . . . . . . . . . . . 7

## INTRODUCTION . . . . . . . . . . . . . . . . . . . . . . . . . . . . . . . . . . . . . . . . . 9

Welcome to COMPASITO – a manual on human rights education for children! . . . . . . . . . 9
What is human rights education with children? . . . . . . . . . . . . . . . . . . . . . . 9
Human rights education and education for democratic citizenship . . . . . . . . . . . . . . 10
    Whom is COMPASITO for? . . . . . . . . . . . . . . . . . . . . . . . . . . . . . . . . 10
What is in COMPASITO? . . . . . . . . . . . . . . . . . . . . . . . . . . . . . . . . . . . . 11
    The organisation of COMPASITO . . . . . . . . . . . . . . . . . . . . . . . . . . . 12
    COMPASITO in the framework of the Human Rights Education Youth Programme . . . . . . . 12

## I. INTRODUCING HUMAN RIGHTS . . . . . . . . . . . . . . . . . . . . . . . 15

1. What are human rights? . . . . . . . . . . . . . . . . . . . . . . . . . . . . . . . . . 15
    Precursors of twentieth century human rights . . . . . . . . . . . . . . . . . . . 15
    The Universal Declaration of Human Rights . . . . . . . . . . . . . . . . . . . . 16
    The human rights framework . . . . . . . . . . . . . . . . . . . . . . . . . . . . 16
    The commitment of ratification . . . . . . . . . . . . . . . . . . . . . . . . . . . 17
    The evolution of a human rights convention . . . . . . . . . . . . . . . . . . . . 18
    Regional human rights conventions . . . . . . . . . . . . . . . . . . . . . . . . . 19
    Human Rights mechanisms of the Council of Europe . . . . . . . . . . . . . . . 20
2. What are children's rights? . . . . . . . . . . . . . . . . . . . . . . . . . . . . . . . 21
    General principles of the Children's Convention . . . . . . . . . . . . . . . . . 22
    Monitoring the Convention on the Rights of the Child . . . . . . . . . . . . . . 22
    Promoting the Convention on the Rights of the Child . . . . . . . . . . . . . . 23

## II. WHAT IS HUMAN RIGHTS EDUCATION? . . . . . . . . . . . . . . . . 25

1. Introducing human rights education . . . . . . . . . . . . . . . . . . . . . . . . . 25
    Human rights education for children . . . . . . . . . . . . . . . . . . . . . . . . 25
    Knowledge, skills and attitudes . . . . . . . . . . . . . . . . . . . . . . . . . . . 26
    Methodologies for human rights education . . . . . . . . . . . . . . . . . . . . 27
    Non-formal education . . . . . . . . . . . . . . . . . . . . . . . . . . . . . . . . 28
    Introducing human rights education in work with children . . . . . . . . . . . . 28
    The right to human rights education . . . . . . . . . . . . . . . . . . . . . . . . 29
    Human rights education and other educational fields . . . . . . . . . . . . . . . 29
2. Human Rights Education in an international context . . . . . . . . . . . . . . . . 30
    United Nations . . . . . . . . . . . . . . . . . . . . . . . . . . . . . . . . . . . . . 30
    UNESCO . . . . . . . . . . . . . . . . . . . . . . . . . . . . . . . . . . . . . . . . 31
    UNICEF . . . . . . . . . . . . . . . . . . . . . . . . . . . . . . . . . . . . . . . . . 31
    Council of Europe . . . . . . . . . . . . . . . . . . . . . . . . . . . . . . . . . . . 32
    Non-governmental organisations . . . . . . . . . . . . . . . . . . . . . . . . . . 33

## III. HOW TO USE COMPASITO . . . . . . . . . . . . . . . . . . . . . . . . . . . 37

Getting started with COMPASITO . . . . . . . . . . . . . . . . . . . . . . . . . . . . . . 37
The goal of COMPASITO . . . . . . . . . . . . . . . . . . . . . . . . . . . . . . . . . . . 38

Experiential learning . . . . . . . . . . . . . . . . . . . . . . . . . . . . . . . . . . . . . . . 38
   Experiencing . . . . . . . . . . . . . . . . . . . . . . . . . . . . . . . . . . . . . . . . 39
   Reporting . . . . . . . . . . . . . . . . . . . . . . . . . . . . . . . . . . . . . . . . . . . 39
   Reflecting . . . . . . . . . . . . . . . . . . . . . . . . . . . . . . . . . . . . . . . . . . . 39
   Generalising . . . . . . . . . . . . . . . . . . . . . . . . . . . . . . . . . . . . . . . . . 39
   Applying . . . . . . . . . . . . . . . . . . . . . . . . . . . . . . . . . . . . . . . . . . . . 39
Facilitation . . . . . . . . . . . . . . . . . . . . . . . . . . . . . . . . . . . . . . . . . . . . . . . . 40
Thinking and learning styles . . . . . . . . . . . . . . . . . . . . . . . . . . . . . . . . . 41
   Which is your thinking style? . . . . . . . . . . . . . . . . . . . . . . . . . . . 41
   Which is your favorite or dominant learning style? . . . . . . . . . 41
Children's developmental levels . . . . . . . . . . . . . . . . . . . . . . . . . . . . . . 42
What is in a COMPASITO activity? . . . . . . . . . . . . . . . . . . . . . . . . . . . . . 44
The Convention on the Rights of the Child as foundation . . . . . . . . . 45
Selecting activities . . . . . . . . . . . . . . . . . . . . . . . . . . . . . . . . . . . . . . . . . . 46
Adapting activities . . . . . . . . . . . . . . . . . . . . . . . . . . . . . . . . . . . . . . . . . . 47
Tips for promoting participation . . . . . . . . . . . . . . . . . . . . . . . . . . . . . . 48
Tips for facilitation . . . . . . . . . . . . . . . . . . . . . . . . . . . . . . . . . . . . . . . . . 48
   Icebreakers / Warm-ups / Starters . . . . . . . . . . . . . . . . . . . . . . . 49
   Energizers . . . . . . . . . . . . . . . . . . . . . . . . . . . . . . . . . . . . . . . . . . 49
   Evaluation and Reflection Opportunities . . . . . . . . . . . . . . . . . 50
   Managing Conflict . . . . . . . . . . . . . . . . . . . . . . . . . . . . . . . . . . . 50
Practising human rights education . . . . . . . . . . . . . . . . . . . . . . . . . . . . 51

## IV. ACTIVITIES

 . . . . . . . . . . . . . . . . . . . . . . . . . . . . . . . . . . . . . . . . . . . . . . . . . . . . . . . . . . 52

Summary of Activities . . . . . . . . . . . . . . . . . . . . . . . . . . . . . . . . . . . . . . . 52
  1. A Body of Knowledge . . . . . . . . . . . . . . . . . . . . . . . . . . . . . . . . . 53
  2. A Constitution for Our Group . . . . . . . . . . . . . . . . . . . . . . . . . . 56
  3. A Human Rights Calendar . . . . . . . . . . . . . . . . . . . . . . . . . . . . . 60
  4. Advertising Human Rights . . . . . . . . . . . . . . . . . . . . . . . . . . . . . 64
  5. Blindfolded . . . . . . . . . . . . . . . . . . . . . . . . . . . . . . . . . . . . . . . . . 67
  6. Board Games . . . . . . . . . . . . . . . . . . . . . . . . . . . . . . . . . . . . . . . . 70
    6a, Do You Know Your Rights? . . . . . . . . . . . . . . . . . . . . . . . . 70
    6b, Moksha-Patamu . . . . . . . . . . . . . . . . . . . . . . . . . . . . . . . . 77
  7. Boys Don't Cry! . . . . . . . . . . . . . . . . . . . . . . . . . . . . . . . . . . . . . . 82
  8. Bullying Scenes . . . . . . . . . . . . . . . . . . . . . . . . . . . . . . . . . . . . . . 85
  9. Capture the Castle . . . . . . . . . . . . . . . . . . . . . . . . . . . . . . . . . . . 89
  10. COMPASITO Reporter . . . . . . . . . . . . . . . . . . . . . . . . . . . . . . . 92
  11. Cookie Monster . . . . . . . . . . . . . . . . . . . . . . . . . . . . . . . . . . . . . 95
  12. Dear Diary . . . . . . . . . . . . . . . . . . . . . . . . . . . . . . . . . . . . . . . . . 99
  13. Every Vote Counts . . . . . . . . . . . . . . . . . . . . . . . . . . . . . . . . . 103
  14. From Bystander to Helper . . . . . . . . . . . . . . . . . . . . . . . . . . . 108
  15. Human Rights in the News . . . . . . . . . . . . . . . . . . . . . . . . . . 110
  16. Modern Fairytale . . . . . . . . . . . . . . . . . . . . . . . . . . . . . . . . . . 113
  17. Most Important for Whom? . . . . . . . . . . . . . . . . . . . . . . . . . . 118
  18. My Universe of Rights . . . . . . . . . . . . . . . . . . . . . . . . . . . . . . 122
  19. Once Upon a Time... . . . . . . . . . . . . . . . . . . . . . . . . . . . . . . . . 125
  20. Picture Games . . . . . . . . . . . . . . . . . . . . . . . . . . . . . . . . . . . . 130
    20a. Part of the Picture . . . . . . . . . . . . . . . . . . . . . . . . . . . . . 130
    20b. Captions . . . . . . . . . . . . . . . . . . . . . . . . . . . . . . . . . . . . 131

20c. Speech Bubbles . . . . . . . . . . . . . . . . . . . . . . . . . . . . . . . . . . . . . . 132
21. Picturing Ways Out of Violence . . . . . . . . . . . . . . . . . . . . . . . . . . 133
22. Puppets Tell the Story . . . . . . . . . . . . . . . . . . . . . . . . . . . . . . . . . . 135
23. Putting Rights on the Map . . . . . . . . . . . . . . . . . . . . . . . . . . . . . . 138
24. Rabbit's Rights . . . . . . . . . . . . . . . . . . . . . . . . . . . . . . . . . . . . . . . . 141
25. Red Alert . . . . . . . . . . . . . . . . . . . . . . . . . . . . . . . . . . . . . . . . . . . . . 143
26. Rights Mobile . . . . . . . . . . . . . . . . . . . . . . . . . . . . . . . . . . . . . . . . . 148
27. Sailing to a New Land . . . . . . . . . . . . . . . . . . . . . . . . . . . . . . . . . 152
28. Silent Speaker . . . . . . . . . . . . . . . . . . . . . . . . . . . . . . . . . . . . . . . . 160
29. Take a Step Forward . . . . . . . . . . . . . . . . . . . . . . . . . . . . . . . . . . . 163
30. The Battle for the Orange . . . . . . . . . . . . . . . . . . . . . . . . . . . . . . 169
31. The Invisibles are Coming . . . . . . . . . . . . . . . . . . . . . . . . . . . . . . 171
32. Waterdrops . . . . . . . . . . . . . . . . . . . . . . . . . . . . . . . . . . . . . . . . . . . 176
33. We are Family . . . . . . . . . . . . . . . . . . . . . . . . . . . . . . . . . . . . . . . . 180
34. What a Wonderful World . . . . . . . . . . . . . . . . . . . . . . . . . . . . . . 182
35. What I Like and What I Do . . . . . . . . . . . . . . . . . . . . . . . . . . . . . 185
36. What if … . . . . . . . . . . . . . . . . . . . . . . . . . . . . . . . . . . . . . . . . . . . . 187
37. Where do you stand? . . . . . . . . . . . . . . . . . . . . . . . . . . . . . . . . . . 192
38. Who's Behind Me? . . . . . . . . . . . . . . . . . . . . . . . . . . . . . . . . . . . . 195
39. Who Should Decide? . . . . . . . . . . . . . . . . . . . . . . . . . . . . . . . . . . 198
40. Words that Wound . . . . . . . . . . . . . . . . . . . . . . . . . . . . . . . . . . . . 202
41. World Summer Camp . . . . . . . . . . . . . . . . . . . . . . . . . . . . . . . . . . 205
42. Zabderfilio . . . . . . . . . . . . . . . . . . . . . . . . . . . . . . . . . . . . . . . . . . . 209

## V. THEMES <span></span> . . . . . . . . . . . . . . . . . . . . . . . . . . . . . . . . . . . . 213

1. Citizenship . . . . . . . . . . . . . . . . . . . . . . . . . . . . . . . . . . . . . . . . . . . 213
2. Democracy . . . . . . . . . . . . . . . . . . . . . . . . . . . . . . . . . . . . . . . . . . . . 219
3. Discrimination . . . . . . . . . . . . . . . . . . . . . . . . . . . . . . . . . . . . . . . . 224
4. Education and Leisure . . . . . . . . . . . . . . . . . . . . . . . . . . . . . . . . . . 231
5. Environment . . . . . . . . . . . . . . . . . . . . . . . . . . . . . . . . . . . . . . . . . . 236
6. Family and Alternative Care . . . . . . . . . . . . . . . . . . . . . . . . . . . . . 240
7. Gender Equality . . . . . . . . . . . . . . . . . . . . . . . . . . . . . . . . . . . . . . . 245
8. Health and Welfare . . . . . . . . . . . . . . . . . . . . . . . . . . . . . . . . . . . . 251
9. Media and Internet . . . . . . . . . . . . . . . . . . . . . . . . . . . . . . . . . . . . 257
10. Participation . . . . . . . . . . . . . . . . . . . . . . . . . . . . . . . . . . . . . . . . . 262
11. Peace . . . . . . . . . . . . . . . . . . . . . . . . . . . . . . . . . . . . . . . . . . . . . . . 269
12. Poverty and Social Exclusion . . . . . . . . . . . . . . . . . . . . . . . . . . . 275
13. Violence . . . . . . . . . . . . . . . . . . . . . . . . . . . . . . . . . . . . . . . . . . . . . 280

## VI. APPENDICES <span></span> . . . . . . . . . . . . . . . . . . . . . . . . . . . . . . . . 289

Universal Declaration of Human Rights (Child-Friendly Version) . . . . . . . . . . . 289
Universal Declaration of Human Rights . . . . . . . . . . . . . . . . . . . . . . 291
The European Convention on Human Rights (Child-Friendly Version) . . . . . . . . 294
Convention on the Rights of the Child (CRC) (Child-Friendly Version) . . . . . . . 296
Convention on the Rights of the Child . . . . . . . . . . . . . . . . . . . . . . . 299
Human Rights Glossary . . . . . . . . . . . . . . . . . . . . . . . . . . . . . . . . . . 308
Useful Resources . . . . . . . . . . . . . . . . . . . . . . . . . . . . . . . . . . . . . . . 312
Status of Ratification of Major International Human Rights Instruments . . . . . . . 314

# Acknowledgements

This guide is the result of the work and contributions of several experts and practitioners to which *Nancy Flowers* in particular has lent consistency, professionalism and soul.

We would like to thank *Annette Schneider* for her professional contribution to the educational steadiness and quality of the manual.

Special thanks go to *Rui Gomes*, editor of 'COMPASS – a manual on human rights education with young people', who represented the continuation of the concept of 'COMPASS', participated in the shaping of the concept of this manual, and followed the entire production process with invaluable comments and critical observations.

It was *Laura De Witte* who convinced us of the importance and feasibility of producing such a manual for children, came up with the title and shared with us her comments on the activities.

We would like to thank *Katalin Lerch*, *Merit Ulvik* and *Jiri Tomcala* for their contribution to the formulation of the content of the manual as members of the Development Team.

Thanks to *Iris Bawidamann* and *Nadine Lyamouri-Bajja* for their feedback, contributions and educational support to the activities of the manual.

The activities of the manual were tested by several highly committed colleagues: *Burcu Meltem Arik, Paola Bortini, Mario D'Agostino, Gabriele Cespa, Caroline Gebara, Mara Georgescu, Ilona Hudák, Giorgi Kikalishvili, Sasho Kochankovski, Anna Lechowska, Anabela Moreira, Bijana Temelkova and Anne Thiemann.*

### We would also like to thank the following:

- All those who participated in the first Consultative meeting on 'COMPASITO' in November 2005, for their work on designing the concept.
- *Tamara Kafkova, Nicoleta Dumitru* and *Ali Oktay Koc*, the EYCB trainees in the production process, for their work in compiling and checking references and useful resources.
- *Antje Rothemund, Anikó Kaposvári*, and *Eva B. Nagy* for their supportive remarks and useful suggestions.
- Colleagues from different sections of the Council of Europe:
  - *David Crowe*, General Directorate of Human Rights, and
  - *Ólöf Ólafsdóttir*, Directorate of School, Out-of-School and Higher Education for their expert opinions;
  - *Elda Moreno*, Secretary of the Programme 'Building a Europe for and with Children', for motivation and support during the production process.
- *Gabriella Tisza*, information officer of the EYCB, without whose committed work the entire interactive communication process would not have taken place.
- *Rachel Appleby*, for being more than a proofreader.
- *Dániel Horváth* and *Diána Nagy* for their creativity and flexibility in producing the design and illustration to this manual.

We apologise for any omission and regret that we were not able to include all materials and suggestions received.

# Preface

The ability to live together in a democracy does not come naturally. The knowledge, skills and values that are the preconditions of living in a democracy should be learnt and nurtured throughout life. While key concepts of democracy and human rights should be understood by children, values such as dignity, tolerance and respect for others, and skills such as cooperation, critical thinking and standing up for one's rights cannot be taught in traditional ways. They should be learnt through experience and practise, by living and acting in a democratic environment and from the earliest possible age. This is what human rights education is about and this is what 'COMPASITO – manual on human rights education for children' is for.

The Council of Europe's commitment to human rights dates back to its very foundation. The Europe we want to build, based on a culture of peace and human rights, can only be pursued with everyone being actively involved.

Since the adoption of the Convention of the Rights of the Child, a fundamental change in paradigm has taken place in working with children, and this is the right for children to be consulted and to be heard on decisions concerning them. However, a meaningful participation of children is only possible if adults accept children as partners in issues that concern them. Making this a reality, and thus safeguarding the dignity of children, however, is a real challenge for adults; and the way adults deal with children reflects how society sees the future. Human rights and human rights education is a common learning process that concerns not only children, but adults as well.

The Council of Europe has launched the project 'Building a Europe for and with children' to focus on the respect for children's dignity across Europe: to promote children's rights and eradicate violence against children. The participation of children is essential in both dimensions. COMPASITO has an important role to play in this process. Based on the experiences of the highly acclaimed Human Rights Education Youth Programme of the Council's youth sector, and the success of 'COMPASS, the manual on human rights education with young people', COMPASITO provides children, educators, teachers and parents with activities and methods to introduce children to human rights in creative and attractive ways. This manual is a starting point: COMPASITO provides directions, but it is up to the children and those working with them to use it, and to use it in the best ways possible.

It is by knowing their rights that children are able to best denounce and reject abuse; it is by committing themselves to human rights that children contribute to a better world, for today and tomorrow; and it is by working with children for human rights that adults become credible in children's eyes.

This manual is an invaluable contribution to supporting children and upholding children's human rights across Europe.

*Maud de Boer- Buquicchio*
Deputy Secretary General of the Council of Europe

# INTRODUCTION

*The States Parties agree that the education of the child shall be directed to (a) the development of the child's personality, talents and mental and physical abilities to their fullest potential (b) the development of respect for human rights and fundamental freedoms...*

Article 29, Convention on the Rights of the Child, 1989

## Welcome to COMPASITO – a manual on human rights education for children!

We hope that this manual will provide you with ideas, inspiration and practical help to explore human rights with children. Living among other people in their families, communities and society, children become aware from a very early age of questions related to justice and seek for the meaning of the world. By fostering an understanding of human rights, shaping opinions and developing attitudes, human rights education strongly supports this natural interest and learning process.

Children are often considered people who are 'not yet adult' and therefore dependent, inexperienced, undisciplined and in need of order or guidance. COMPASITO builds on another concept explained well by Lothar Krappmann, German sociologist and educationalist: children live 'here and now', "they generate their views on problems and construct competent solutions".[1] COMPASITO looks at children as young citizens of the present and as rights-holders who are competent in many issues related to their life. It builds on children's motivations, experiences and search for solutions.

> Children are strong, rich and capable. All children have preparedness, potential, curiosity, and interest in constructing their learning, negotiating with everything their environment brings to them.
>
> *Loris Malaguzzi*

COMPASITO was inspired by 'COMPASS – a manual on human rights education with young people', which was developed by the Council of Europe in 2002. More than expected, 'COMPASS' is used with younger people of secondary school age and in school environments in many European countries. The expectations of users of 'COMPASS' for a training manual directed specifically at children matched our own convictions that human rights education should start at the earliest possible age.

COMPASITO builds on the philosophy and educational approaches of 'COMPASS'. As with 'COMPASS', it uses a non-formal educational methodology and a structure that provides theoretical and practical support to users of the manual. However, while 'COMPASS' addresses young people themselves, COMPASITO addresses adult educators who work with children. It provides them with theoretical and methodological information and substantial discussion of the book's human rights themes. COMPASITO also encourages educators to adapt material to reflect their own and their children's reality. Although the practical activities are designed to play with children, most activities need the proper facilitation of an educational expert.

## What is human rights education with children?

Human rights education is a process that aims to establish a culture of human rights. The educational process builds on children's active participation by which they learn about human rights and under-

stand human rights issues, acquire skills and abilities to be able to defend human rights and develop attitudes of respect of equality and dignity.

Human rights education, therefore, should have a key role in any educational processes. The United Nations **Convention of the Rights of the Child** (CRC) provides an invaluable tool to introduce human rights for children. The CRC specifies those human rights that are relevant to children. Learning and experiencing children's rights therefore help children to understand what human rights are about, to understand that they are rights-holders themselves and to adapt and apply these rights in their specific context. This is the key aim of human rights education with children. In COMPASITO, moreover, children's rights are presented within the wider picture of human rights as a whole. Thus, universal human rights and children's rights are jointly elaborated to provide opportunities in such a way that while understanding their own rights children also understand that all human beings have human rights.

> The States Parties agree that the education of the child shall be directed to ... (d) the preparation of the child for responsible life in a free society, in the spirit of understanding, peace, tolerance, equality of sexes, and friendship among all peoples, ethnic, national and religious groups and persons of indigenous origin.
>
> *Article 29, Convention on the Rights of the Child, 1989*

# Human rights education and education for democratic citizenship

Human rights are essential to democratic development and to citizenship education. Several recent social and political developments both in Europe and in other places of the world, such as economic interdependence, racism, terrorism, political apathy, growing social gaps or the mediatisation of politics, challenge the foundations of a culture of peace and human rights and thus, endanger democratic stability. This is why human rights education and education for democratic citizenship have become key priorities of governments and even more non-governmental organisations in the last decade.

Human rights education and education for democratic citizenship go hand in hand as both aim at education for democracy. Both forms of education lead young people to acquire knowledge, set core values and develop skills. Education for democratic citizenship puts the 'child citizen' into the focus and aims to educate children to be active and responsible members of their communities. Human rights education, on the other hand, emphasizes the human being promoting equality, human dignity, participation and empowerment for everyone. Human rights education includes citizenship as one of its key themes, and education for democratic citizenship builds on human rights values. Whatever their differences, both approaches serve the development of democracy, human rights and peace.

## Whom is COMPASITO for?

COMPASITO primarily was designed for educators and trainers working with children, teachers, caretakers and parents as well, especially those who are interested in human rights education with children and who are looking for practical tools to discuss values and social issues with children. The activities are designed for children from six to thirteen years.

COMPASITO builds on both the child and the facilitator's existing knowledge and experience. The activities can be used with children wherever they spend the greatest part of their daily life: in schools, in childcare centres, afternoon-schools, leisure centres, children's organisations, or children's camps, and some of them even in the family environment. While children do not need to have any special skills to participate in most of the activities, facilitators do have to possess experience and skills in using non-formal educational methodology to run the activities successfully.

# What is in Compasito?

In the last decade several high-quality, child-related training materials on human rights and children's rights have been produced in Europe and internationally. The Compasito development team built on these experiences and tried to complement them in a European context. The manual provides specific content on human rights education, a non-formal educational methodology and an intercultural approach.

## Themes related to human rights

Compasito is based on the same philosophical and educational approaches as 'Compass', and several parts, especially on conceptual topics, are drawn directly from the text of 'Compass'. The core of the manual is its educational activities designed for children. The activities in Compasito are organised around thirteen selected themes: Citizenship, Democracy, Discrimination, Education and leisure, Environment, Family and alternative care, Gender equality, Health and welfare, Media and Internet, Participation, Peace and conflict, Poverty and social exclusion, Violence. In order to bring human rights issues closer to everyday reality and children's personal experiences, these themes focus broadly on values and social issues rather than on formal rights as laid down in conventions. The development team selected them carefully from dozens of ideas in the belief that they cover human rights fields of key importance for children, even if this manual doesn't have the means to list all important subjects. Some themes also address issues that are relevant but seldom elaborated in other manuals, such as Education, Health, or Gender Equality. In addition to these selected themes, a category of general human rights was also introduced to provide children with an understanding of the concept of rights and how to adapt and apply them in their daily context.

## Non-formal educational methodology

Compasito follows non-formal educational methodologies, building on the active participation and personal experiences of children. Participation and cooperation of children helps to build group cohesion and reduce biases between group members. It furthers understanding of complex concepts, improves problem solving skills and facilitates creativity and practicality: all important aims of human rights education. Adults should not fall into the trap of assuming that we, the educators, possess the ultimate truth. Children will bring to the educational process their experiences, which must be actively drawn upon to ensure their interest and effective development. Questions and even conflicts should be regarded as fundamental educational resources, which can be assessed in a positive manner.

## An intercultural and participatory approach

While children are very much engaged in their own neighbourhood, cultures and friendship groups, they are curious of the world: other cultures, regions and people. Compasito uses stories and situations from various regions and cultural backgrounds. This rich variety offers children an opportunity to reflect on various cultures and build a stable identity on these reflections. As Reva Klein, a British educationalist, explains, children do not simply learn about other children's lives, but they form empathy and solidarity and understand their role in taking action on a more global scale.[2]

Compasito supports this context and approach through an intercultural and inclusive development process. In late 2005 a consultative meeting of practitioners working directly with children outlined the concept of the manual, which was than closely followed by the international development team, which came together as a result of an open call. This international team found it essential to produce Compasito in close cooperation with potential users and children themselves. For this purpose an international reference group of practitioners was established and consulted during the development process. This reference group tested and evaluated the activities proposed to be included in Compasito and provided feedback on the theoretical parts.

## The organisation of Compasito

**Chapter I.** familiarizes the reader with what we mean by human rights and children's rights and describes the main international human rights mechanisms.

**Chapter II.** explains the aims and outcomes of human rights education and puts it into both European and international perspectives.

**Chapter III.** gives information and practical tips on how Compasito can be used in various formal and non-formal educational settings and how to get the best out of its educational approaches. The tips for facilitators provides ideas on how to start human rights activities with children and how to follow them up including concrete actions.

**Chapter IV.** collects 42 practical activities for different age groups and at different levels of complexity related to the selected themes of human rights. Children do not need to have any special skills to be involved in most Compasito activities. Users of the manual are encouraged to use the activities in a creative way either in a sequence or individually.

**Chapter V.** provides essential background information on the thirteen selected themes. Facilitators are encouraged to read the relevant themes before starting an activity. Questions included in these texts are intended to help readers to reflect on their own knowledge and attitudes and to be able to put the themes in a personal or local context.

The **Appendices** contain essential information on legal documents that have key relevance for children in a European context. The text of the European Convention of Human Rights, the Universal Declaration of Human Rights and the United Nations Convention of the Rights of the Child can be found here also in child-friendly format. The Human Rights Glossary contains the explanation of the key legal terms appearing in the manual. The terms in the glossary are found in bold in the text of Compasito.

## Compasito in the framework of the Human Rights Education Youth Programme

Compasito is published in the framework of the Council of Europe's Youth Programme on Human Rights Education and Intercultural Dialogue. The Programme seeks to involve young people in human rights issues, reaching beyond those already active and motivated to reach a wider public and bring human rights closer to their daily reality. Since being launched in 2000 the Programme has reached thousands of young people and resulted in a cascading effect in the development of human rights educational programmes and human rights projects all over Europe. An important educational resource of the Council of Europe's Youth Programme on Human Rights Education and Intercultural Dialogue is 'Compass – a manual on human rights education with young people', which has been translated into more than twenty different languages since its publication in 2002. This very successful manual has motivated and guided young people and their organisations to deal with issues such as democracy, social justice or gender equality.

The Council of Europe's Youth Programme on Human Rights Education and Intercultural Dialogue reflects and supports the United Nation's World Programme for Human Rights Education (2005 ongoing). This worldwide Programme seeks to help make human rights a reality in every community by promoting a common understanding of the basic principles and methodologies of human rights education. The Action Plan of the World Programme for 2005-2007 focuses on primary and secondary education systems and proposes a concrete strategy and practical ideas for implementing human rights education nationally.

...........................
**Useful resources**

Gandini, Lella, Edward, Carolyn, Forman, George, eds., *The Hundred Languages of Children: The Reggio Emilia Approach Advanced Reflections*: Ablex/Greenwood, 1998.

Kein, Reva, *Citizens by Right, Citizenship education in primary schools*: Trentham Books and Save the Children, 2001.

Krappmann, Lothar, *'The Rights of the Child as a Challenge to Human Rights Education"* in Journal of Social Science Education: Bielefeld, 2006: www.jsse.org/2006-1/krappmann_child-rights.htm

.................
**References**

1    Krappmann, Lothar, *'The Rights of the Child as a Challenge to Human Rights Education'* in Journal of Social Science Education: Bielefeld, 2006: www.jsse.org/2006-1/krappmann_child-rights.htm
2    Kein, Reva, *Citizens by Right, Citizenship education in primary schools*: Trentham Books and Save the Children, 2001, p. 53.

# I. INTRODUCING HUMAN RIGHTS

*[R]ecognition of the inherent dignity and of the equal and inalienable rights of all members of the human family is the foundation of freedom, justice and peace in the world.*

Preamble, Universal Declaration of Human Rights

## 1. What are human rights?

- Human rights are held by all persons equally, universally and forever.
- Human rights are **universal**: they are always the same for all human beings everywhere in the world. You do not have human rights because you are a citizen of any country but because you are a member of the human family. This means children have human rights as well as adults.
- Human rights are **inalienable**: you cannot lose these rights any more than you can cease to be a human being.
- Human rights are **indivisible**: no-one can take away a right because it is 'less important' or 'non-essential'.
- Human rights are **interdependent**: together human rights form a complementary framework. For example, your ability to participate in local decision making is directly affected by your right to express yourself, to associate with others, to get an education and even to obtain the necessities of life.
- Human rights reflect basic human needs. They establish basic standards without which people cannot live in dignity. To violate someone's human rights is to treat that person as though he or she were not a human being. To advocate human rights is to demand that the human dignity of all people be respected.
- In claiming these human rights, everyone also accepts responsibilities: to respect the rights of others and to protect and support people whose rights are abused or denied. Meeting these responsibilities means claiming solidarity with all other human beings.

### Precursors of twentieth century human rights

Many people regard the development of human rights law as one of the greatest accomplishments of the twentieth century. However, human rights did not begin with law or the United Nations. Throughout human history societies have developed systems of justice and propriety that sought the welfare of society as a whole. References to justice, fairness and humanity are common to all world religions: Buddhism, Christianity, Confucianism and Islam. However, formal principles usually differ from common practise. Until the eighteenth century no society, civilisation or culture, in either the Western or non-Western world, had a widely endorsed practise or vision of inalienable human rights.

Documents asserting individual rights, such as the Magna Carta (1215), the English Bill of Rights (1689) the French Declaration on the Rights of Man and Citizen (1789) and the US Constitution and Bill of Right (1791) are the written precursors to many of today's human rights instruments. Yet most of these influential landmarks excluded women, many minorities and members of certain social, reli-

gious, economic and political groups. None reflects the fundamental concept that everyone is entitled to certain rights solely by virtue of their humanity.

Other important historical antecedents of human rights lie in nineteenth century efforts to prohibit the slave trade and to limit the horrors of war. For example, the **Geneva Conventions** established bases of international **humanitarian law,** which covers the way that wars should be fought and the protection of individuals during armed conflict. They specifically protect people who do not take part in the fighting and those who can no longer fight (e.g. wounded, sick and shipwrecked troops, prisoners of war).

Concern over the protection of certain vulnerable groups was raised by the League of Nations at the end of the First World War. For example, the **International Labour Organisation** (ILO, originally a body of the League of Nations and now a UN agency) established many important conventions setting standards to protect working people, such as the Minimum Age Convention (1919), the Forced Labour Convention (1930) and the Forty-hour Week Convention (1935).

Although the international human rights framework builds on these earlier documents, it is principally based on United Nations documents.

## The Universal Declaration of Human Rights

Two major influences in the mid-twentieth century propelled human rights onto the global arena and the awareness of people around the world. The first was struggles of colonial people to assert their independence from foreign powers, claiming their human equality and right to self-determination. The second catalyst was the Second World War. The extermination by Nazi Germany of over six million Jews, Roma people, homosexuals and persons with disabilities horrified the world. Calls came from across the globe for human rights standards to bolster international peace and protect citizens from abuses by governments. These voices played a critical role in the establishment of the United Nations in 1945 and are echoed in its founding document, the UN Charter.

Rights for all members of the human family were first articulated in the United Nations **Universal Declaration of Human Rights** (UDHR), one of the first initiatives of the newly established United Nations. Its thirty articles together form a comprehensive statement covering economic, social, cultural, political, and civil rights. The Declaration is both universal (it applies to all people everywhere) and indivisible (all rights are equally important to the full realization of one's humanity). See APPENDICES, P. 289, for both the complete text and a child-friendly version of the UDHR.

## The human rights framework

Although the Universal Declaration has achieved the status of customary international law in its more than sixty years, as a **declaration** it is only a statement of intent, a set of principles to which United Nations member states commit themselves in an effort to provide all people a life of human dignity. For the rights defined in a declaration to have full legal force, they must be written into documents called **conventions** (also referred to as **treaties** or **covenants**), which set international norms and standards.

Immediately after the Universal Declaration was adopted, work began to codify the rights it contained into a legally binding convention. For political and procedural reasons, these rights were divided between two separate covenants, each addressing different categories of rights. The **International Covenant on Civil and Political Rights (ICCPR)** articulates the specific, liberty-oriented rights that a state may not take from its citizens, such as freedom of expression and freedom of movement. The **International Covenant on Economic, Social, and Cultural Rights (ICESCR)** addresses those articles in the UDHR that define an individual's rights to self-determinations as well as basic necessities, such as food, housing and health care, which a state should provide for its citizens, in so far as it is able. The UN General

Assembly adopted both covenants in 1966. See APPENDICES, P. 289, for a list of countries that have ratified the Covenants.

Since its adoption in 1948, the Universal Declaration has served as the foundation for the twenty major human rights conventions. Together these constitute the human rights framework, the evolving body of these international documents that define human rights and establish mechanisms to promote and protect them.

---

**Principal United Nations Human Rights Conventions**

Convention on the Prevention and Punishment of the Crime of Genocide, 1948

Convention Relating to the Status of Refugees, 1951

Slavery Convention of 1926, Amended by Protocol, 1953

International Covenant on Civil and Political Rights, 1966

International Convention on the Elimination of all forms of Racial Discrimination, 1966

Convention on the Non-Applicability of Statutory Limitations to War Crimes and Crimes Against Humanity, 1968

Convention on the Elimination of all Forms of Discrimination against Women, 1979

Convention against Torture and other Cruel, Inhuman, or Degrading Treatment or Punishment, 1984

Convention on the Rights of the Child, 1989

Convention on the Rights of Migrant Workers and the Members of their Families, 1990

Convention on the Rights of Persons with Disabilities, 2006.

Note: Date refers to the year the UN General Assembly adopted the convention.

---

## The commitment of ratification

**Ratification** of a convention is a serious, legally binding undertaken by a government on behalf of a state. Every convention contains articles that establish procedures for monitoring and reporting how ratifying governments are complying with the convention. When a government ratifies a convention, it accepts the procedures it defines, which may include these commitments:

- to uphold the convention, respecting, promoting, and providing for the rights it establishes, and not to take any action the treaty prohibits;
- to change any law in the country that contradicts or does not meet the standards set by the convention;
- to be monitored by a designated authority to see that it is, in fact, keeping its commitments;
- to report at regular intervals on its progress in making these human rights real in the lives of its citizens.

Once a country ratifies a convention, its citizens have a powerful advocacy tool. They can hold their government accountable if it fails to respect the human rights to which it has committed itself. For this reason citizens need to know which human rights conventions their country has promised to uphold. For example, the **Convention on the Rights of the Child** (CRC) establishes very specific standards for the humane treatment of children who are detained by police. If cases of mistreatment arise, such as children being imprisoned with adults, child advocates can demand that the government meet the standards to which it is legally committed.

The human rights framework is dynamic. As the needs of certain groups of people are recognized and defined and as world events point to the need for awareness and action on specific human rights issues, international human rights law continuously evolves in response. For example, when the Universal Declaration was written in 1948, few people recognized the dangers of environmental degradation; therefore this document does not mention the environment. At the beginning of the twenty-first century,

however, activists and governments are working to draft a new convention linking human rights to a safe and healthy environment.

Today many human rights conventions have **entered into force** as international law; some are still in the process of ratification. Others, such as a convention on the rights of indigenous peoples and a convention on environmental rights, are currently being drafted through the collaborative efforts of governments and non-governmental organisations.

Although such evolution in human rights emerges at the UN level, they are increasingly initiated at the grassroots level by people struggling for justice and equality in their own communities. Since the founding of the United Nations, the role of **non-governmental organisations** (NGOs) has grown steadily. It is NGOS, both large and small, local and international, that carry the voices and concerns of ordinary people to the United Nations. Although the General Assembly, which is composed of representatives of governments, adopts a treaty and governments ratify it, NGOs influence governments and UN bodies at every level. Not only do they contribute to the drafting of human rights conventions, they play an important role in advocating for their ratification and monitoring to see that governments live up to their obligations.

QUESTION: *Are there non-governmental organisations in your country that monitor and advocate for human rights? Do any especially work on children's rights? What do they do? Are they effective?*

Like all human endeavors, the United Nations and the human rights framework that has evolved under its auspices is imperfect. Many critics say the world does not need more human rights conventions but instead the full implementation of those already established. Others believe that the UN system is so flawed that the high ideals and standards it seeks to establish lack credibility. However, in the scope of human history, both the UN and human rights framework are in their infancy. The challenge to citizens of all countries is to work towards evolving more effective UN institutions without compromising the high ideals on which the UN was founded.

## The evolution of a human rights convention

The creation of a human rights convention involves the collaborative efforts of many individuals and institutions. The starting point is always a perceived need, a human rights problem that needs to be addressed by the international community. It may be a general need to codify basic rights, such as those in the Covenants, or a specific global concern, such as the proliferation of land mines or the trafficking of persons.

The Convention on the Rights of the Child provides an example of the process by which a human rights convention evolves and the role of NGOs in its creation.

1. **Identification of a problem:**

   Efforts to protect children from abuse and exploitation date back to the nineteenth century, when children were generally regarded as the property of their parents until they reached the age of maturity, generally twenty-one. Reformers focused on child labour and abuse of homeless or orphaned children. In 1923 Eglantine Jebb drafted The Declaration on the Rights of the Child, which was adopted by the League of Nations in 1924.

   However, neither the UDHR nor the conventions that evolved as the UN human rights framework made any specific notice of the rights of children. These documents tacitly generalised that like every human being, children had human rights, but they failed to recognize children as rights-bearing individuals.

2. **A statement of general principles:**

   The first step toward the Children's Convention was the UN **Declaration on the Rights of the**

**Child.** In 1959 a working group drafted ten principles setting forth the basic rights to which all children should be entitled. However, as a declaration, these principles were not legally binding on governments.

3. **The drafting process:**

These principles then needed to be codified in a convention. The formal drafting process for the Children's Convention lasted nine years, during which representatives of governments, intergovernmental agencies, such as UNICEF and UNESCO, and nongovernmental organisations large (e.g. Save the Children, the International Red Cross, Oxfam) and small (e.g. national organisations working on specific issues such as child labour, health, education or sports) worked together to create consensus on the language of the convention.

4. **Adoption:**

The Children's Convention was adopted by the UN General Assembly in 1989.

5. **Ratification:**

The Children's Convention was immediately signed and ratified by more nations in a shorter period of time than any other UN convention.

6. **Entry into force:**

As a result of its rapid ratification, the Children's Convention entered into force as international law in 1990, only a few months after its adoption. Furthermore, the total number of member states that have ratified the Children's Convention has surpassed that of all other conventions. So far only two member states have not ratified it: Somalia and the United States.

7. **Implementation, Monitoring and Advocacy:**

As with all human rights conventions, the Children's Convention provides individuals, NGOs and international organisations with a legal basis for their advocacy on behalf of children. They can motivate a government to ratify a treaty and monitor how they keep their treaty obligations. When a government fails to meet these commitments and violates the rights of children, NGOs can call them to account. In cases of systematic abuse, individuals and NGOs can bring a case before the Committee on the Rights of the Child.

# Regional human rights conventions

While the rights covered in the UN human rights framework are universal, complementary human rights systems have been developed that apply to the people living in specific parts of the world. These regional human rights conventions are meant to reinforce UN Conventions, which remain the framework and minimum standard in all parts of the world.

Examples are:

- **European Convention for the Protection of Human Rights and Fundamental Freedoms** (ECHR, also known as the **European Convention on Human Rights**), adopted in 1950 by the Council of Europe and now ratified by its 47 member states;
- **The European Convention for the Prevention of Torture and Inhuman or Degrading Treatment or Punishment**, adopted in 1987 by the Council of Europe in 1987;
- **The European Social Charter**, adopted by the Council of Europe in 1961 and revised in 1996;
- **The American Convention on Human Rights,** adopted in 1969 by the Organisation of American States (OAS), applies to ratifying governments in North, Central and South America;
- **The African Charter on Human and People's Rights,** adopted in 1981 by the Organisation of African Unity (OAU).

# Human Rights mechanisms of the Council of Europe

**The European Convention on Human Rights** is the oldest and strongest of these regional human rights systems with standards for Europe that sometimes surpass those of international human rights conventions. The twenty-seven states belonging to the European Union are also members of the Council of Europe and thus legally obliged to recognize and respect human rights through their national legislation, resorting to international mechanisms as a kind of 'last resort' when domestic remedies prove ineffective. Within the Council of Europe the European Convention is implemented by the Committee of Ministers and the European Court of Human Rights, located in Strasbourg, France.

The European Court of Human Rights is a permanent judicial body that hears and decides on individual complaints concerning violations of the European Convention by anyone residing in the territory of the member states. It complements the human rights guaranties that exist at national level.

While the European Convention and the European Court on Human Rights remain key in the Council of Europe's work on human rights, the organisation has developed several non-judicial means to monitor and develop the realisation of human rights in its members states. For example the European Commission against Racism and Intolerance (ECRI) is an independent body of experts. The Commission monitors racism, xenophobia, antisemitism and intolerance at the level of greater Europe and makes recommendations to governments on how to combat them. The ECRI works in close cooperation with NGOs.

The **European Social Charter** (ESC, adopted 1961, revised 1996) guarantees **social and economic human rights** such as adequate housing, accessible health care, free primary and secondary education and vocational training, non-discriminative employment and safe work conditions, legal and social protection, fair treatment of migrant persons and non-discrimination in every sphere of society. It establishes a supervisory mechanism to ensure that states that have ratified the Charter implement these rights. They must also report annually to the European Committee of Social Rights on their progress.

The Commissioner for Human Rights, an independent institution within the Council of Europe, is mandated to promote the awareness of and respect for human rights in the member states. The Commissioner identifies possible shortcomings in human rights law and practise, raises awareness and encourages reform measures to achieve tangible improvement in the area of human rights promotion and protection.

There is an important distinction between the Court and the Commissioner. The Court is reactive: it can respond only to complaints laid before it by individuals or by the member states themselves. The Commissioner, on the other hand, may be proactive, conducting investigations on how human rights are safeguarded in different European countries. However, only the Court has the power to take decisions – in the form of judgments – which are binding on the member states.

# 2. What are children's rights?

*The UN Convention on the Rights of the Child marked a turning point, recognising worldwide that children are not only subjects of protection but also holders of civil and political rights.*

Maud de Beur-Buquicchio,
Deputy Secretary General, Council of Europe[1]

The UN Convention on the Rights of the Child (CRC) provides an ideal approach for children to learn about their human rights. Because it specifies human rights especially relevant to children, everyone, but especially children, parents and adults who work with children, should be familiar with this important component of the international human rights framework. COMPASITO frames children's rights within the broader context of human rights as a whole and seeks to help children understand that along with all other members of the human family, they too are rights-holders.

The UN General Assembly adopted the Convention on the Rights of the Child in 1989 after nearly a decade of compromise and negotiation among member states and wide consultations with NGOs. Since then more countries have ratified the so called Children's Convention than any other human rights treaty and with fewer **reservations**, which are formal exceptions taken to parts with which a state may not agree.

The Convention on the Rights of the Child (also called the **Children's Convention**) defines a child as anyone below the age of eighteen and affirms the child as fully possessed of human rights. It contains 54 articles of children's rights that can be divided into three general categories, sometimes known as the 'three *Ps*':

- **Protection**, guaranteeing the safety of children and covering specific issues such as abuse, neglect, and exploitation;
- **Provision**, covering the special needs of children such as education and health care;
- **Participation**, recognising the child's **evolving capacity** to make decisions and participate in society as he or she approaches maturity.

The Convention contains several groundbreaking approaches to human rights. Children's right to participation constitutes an area not previously addressed in the UDHR (1948) or the Declaration on the Rights of the Child (1959). Another innovation of the Convention is the use of the pronouns *he* and *she* rather than the generic *he* to include both males and females.

The Convention strongly emphasizes the primacy and importance of the role, authority and responsibility of the child's family. It affirms the child's right not only to the language and culture of the family, but also to have that language and culture respected. The Convention also exhorts the state to support families are not able to provide an adequate standard of living for their children.

While acknowledging the importance of family to a child's well-being, the Children's Convention also recognizes children as right-bearing individuals, guaranteeing them, as appropriate to their evolving capacity, the right to identity, to privacy, to information, to thought, conscience, and religion, to expression, and to association.

The Convention has had enormous worldwide impact. It has intensified the child-rights efforts of UN agencies such as UNICEF and the International Labour Organisation (ILO); it has affected subsequent child-rights treaties (e.g. *Hague Convention on Inter country Adoption,* which speaks of a child's right to a family rather than a family's right to a child, and the *Convention on the Rights of Persons with Disabilities*); it has focused international movements to stamp out pervasive forms of child abuse such as child prostitution and child soldiers, both of which are now the subjects of **optional protocols** (amendments to the CRC).

## General principles of the Children's Convention

Children's rights in the CRC reflect four general principles:

1. **Non-discrimination** (Article 2): All rights apply to all children without exception. The state has an obligation to protect children from any form of discrimination.

2. **The child's best interest** (Article 3): The determining factor in all actions dealing with any child should be his or her best interest. In all cases, the best interests of the child take precedence over the interests of the adults concerned (e.g. parents, teachers, guardians). However, the question of how to decide on the best interests of the child remains difficult to determine and open to discussion.

3. **The rights to life, survival and development** (Article 6): the right of the child to life is inherent, and it is the state's obligation to ensure the child's survival and development. This means that children cannot be subject to the death sentence or to termination of life.

4. **Respect for the views of the child** (Article 12): The child has the right to express an opinion and to have that opinion taken into account in any matter affecting him or her.

**QUESTION:** *The child's best interest is a fundamental principle of the Children's Convention. However, who decides what is best for a child? What happens when parents, teachers, authorities or the child have conflicting opinions about what is 'best' for the child?*

The Children's Convention is a powerful instrument, which by its very nature engages young people in an examination of their own rights. It is also an effective tool to assist people of all ages in identifying the complex responsibilities that go with ensuring these rights for children. Using the convention in this way will teach children how to advocate on their own behalf.

## Monitoring the Convention on the Rights of the Child

Like all human rights treaties, the Convention on the Rights of the Child contains articles that establish how governments' compliance with the treaty will be monitored. Part II, Articles 42-45, of the Convention sets up these procedures and requirements:

- It requires that governments make the rights in the Convention widely known to both adults and children (Article 42);
- It establishes the Committee on the Rights of the Child, an body of independent experts that monitors implementation of the Convention on the Rights of the Child by its State parties (Article 43);
- It requires states to report every five years on their efforts to implement the Convention (Article 44).
- It encourages international cooperation in the implementation of the Convention, especially with specialized UN agencies such as UNICEF (Article 45).

These mandatory reports, usually prepared by a government agency specializing in children's issues, indicate who is not enjoying which rights, identify the constraints and obstacles to realising the rights and what the government intends to do to overcome these challenges. The report is presented to the Committee on the Rights of the Child in Geneva, where the Office of the United Nations' High Commissioner for Human Rights is based, which reviews it and makes recommendations for future action.

**QUESTION:** *What government agency prepares the report on implementation of the Children's Convention in your country? How do they acquire their information?*

QUESTION: *Has your country reported regularly on its implementation of the Convention on the Rights of the Child?*

The monitoring and reporting process also provides an opportunity for civil society institutions, NGOs, specialist agencies, children and young people, and other people dealing with children, to participate actively. They may produce an alternative or **shadow report** that challenges government claims or raises issues that may have been missed in the official report.[2]

QUESTION: *Have alternative or shadow reports been submitted from your country? If so, who made them? On what issues did they differ from the government?*

## Monitoring children's rights

The UN often appoints an expert to serve as a **Special Rapporteur** to gather information on a critical issue or country. In response to international concern about the growing commercial sexual exploitation and the sale of children, in 1990 the UN General Assembly created the mandate for a rapporteur to gather information and report on the sale of children, child pornography and child prostitution.

A number of non-governmental organisations also monitor how the Children's Convention is being implemented. Some of these are large international children's advocacy organisations such as Save the Children and Child Rights Information Network (CRIN). Others operate at the regional and national levels. In Europe, for example, the European Network of Ombudsmen for Children (ENOC) investigates, criticises and publicises administrative actions that might be violating the CRC. The ombudsman can intervene separately from legal representatives, parents or guardians to represent the child's rights in a variety of civil or criminal cases where children are directly or indirectly involved. The Network includes representatives from Austria, Belgium, Denmark, Finland, France, Hungary, Iceland, Ireland, Lithuania, the former Yugoslav Republic of Macedonia, Norway, Portugal, the Russian Federation, Spain, Sweden and Wales.[3]

## Promoting the Convention on the Rights of the Child

Civil society, children, teachers, parents and other agencies can play a major role in awareness raising and lobbying for action to promote child rights. To ensure that everyone who works with children as well as children themselves are aware of these rights, the Convention on the Rights of the Child should be available in school libraries and read and discussed in classrooms and with parents.

One of the most important ways to promote the Convention is through systematic human rights education, beginning in the early years of childhood. Every child has a right to know his or her rights and those of others!

...........................

### Useful resources

- Eide, Asbjørn and Alfredsson, Guthmundur, *The Universal Declaration of Human Rights:* A common standard of achievement: Martinus Nijhof, 1999.
- Franklin, Bob, *Handbook of Children's Rights:* Routledge, 2001.
- Hodgkin, Rachel and Newell, Peter, *Implementation Handbook for the Convention on the Rights of the Child:* UNICEF, 2002.

### Useful websites

- Amnesty International: www.amnesty.org
- Children's Rights Information Network: www.crin.org
- Council of Europe: www.coe.int
- Democracy and Human Rights Education in Europe:
- www.dare-network.org
- European Children's Network (EURONET): www.europeanchildrensnetwork.org
- European Network of Ombudspersons for Children: www.ombudsnet.org/enoc/
- Human Rights Watch: www.hrw.org
- UNESCO: www.unesco.org
- UNICEF: www.unicef.org
- United Nations High Commissioner for Human Rights: www.ohchr.org/english

### References

1  Speech made at the Conference on International Justice for Children, 17 September 2007.
2  Action for the Rights of Children (ARC), CD by UNICEF & Save the Children Alliance, 2003.
3  See www.ombudsnet.org

# II. WHAT IS HUMAN RIGHTS EDUCATION?

*... [E]very individual and every organ of society ... shall strive by teaching and education to pro-mote respect for these rights and freedoms...*

Preamble, Universal Declaration of Human Rights

## 1. Introducing human rights education

No single definition for human rights education will serve the many ways in which people young and old come to understand, practise and value their rights and respect the rights of others. The Council of Europe's Human Rights Education Youth Programme defines human rights education as:

*...educational programmes and activities that focus on promoting equality in human dignity, in conjunction with programmes such as those promoting intercultural learning, participation and empowerment of minorities.*

The telling phrase in this definition is "in conjunction", for human rights education is rarely undertaken outside of a specific context, ideally based on the needs, preferences, abilities and desires of the learners.

The key to defining human rights education is its purpose, for no matter what the methodology or context, its aim is always the development of a culture of human rights. The essential elements of such a culture can provide general objectives for human rights education:

- to strengthen respect for human rights and fundamental freedoms
- to value human dignity and develop individual self-respect and respect for others
- to develop attitudes and behaviours that will lead to respect for the rights of others
- to ensure genuine gender equality and equal opportunities for women and men in all spheres
- to promote respect, understanding and appreciation of diversity, particularly towards different national, ethnic, religious, linguistic and other minorities and communities
- to empower people towards more active citizenship
- to promote democracy, development, social justice, communal harmony, solidarity and friendship among people and nations
- to further the activities of international institutions aimed at the creation of a culture of peace, based upon universal values of human rights, international understanding, tolerance and non-violence.

### Human rights education for children

Childhood is the ideal time to begin lifelong learning about and for human rights. And the far reaching objectives of general human rights education can be interpreted to fit the world of the young child in more concrete terms of personal experience in the community, in the family and in the personal relationships the child encounters everyday with adults and other children. Human rights learning seeks to foster feelings of confidence and social tolerance, the fundamental bases for the whole culture of human rights:

- to value self and others

- to recognize and respect human rights in everyday life
- to understand one's own basic rights and be able to articulate them
- to appreciate and respect differences
- to acquire attitudes to address conflicts in non-violent ways that respect the rights of others
- to develop children's confidence in their ability to take action and their skills to defend and promote human rights.

Although they are at the beginning of their formal education, children possess a wealth of knowledge about their world and the people in it. As far as possible, human rights learning should connect with and enlighten what children already know. For example, although they may not use words like *justice*, *equality* or *discrimination*, by the age of seven or eight most children have a strong sense of what is 'fair'.

## Knowledge, skills and attitudes

### Knowledge: Learning about human rights:

What type of knowledge do children need to understand human rights in their daily lives? What skills and attitudes do they need to develop and sustain a real-life culture of human rights? COMPASITO seeks to answer these questions in both the background information it provides for facilitators and the activities it recommends for children's human right learning. Together they form a holistic approach that includes learning *about* human rights, learning *for* human rights and learning *in* human rights.

Although knowledge *about* human rights necessarily varies with the maturity and capacity of the child, in general it includes these essential concepts:

- Human rights provide standards of behaviour in the family, in school, in the community and in the wider world;
- Human rights standards are universal, although there may be different ways of interpreting and experiencing them;
- Every child has human rights and also the responsibility to respect the rights of others. These include the right for protection, provisions and the right to participation, such as to express opinions in matters that concern oneself. These rights are set down in the **Convention of the Rights of the Child**;
- Other international documents also exist to implement the protection of human rights, such as the **United Nations Declarations on Human Rights** (UDHR) and the **European Convention on Human Rights** (ECHR).

### Skills: learning for human rights:

Children need to acquire the skills that will enable them to participate in a democracy and contribute to building a culture of human rights. Skills *for* human rights include:

- Active listening and communication: being able to listen to different points of view, to express one's own opinions and evaluate both;
- Critical thinking: distinguishing between fact and opinion, being aware of prejudices and pre-conceptions, recognising forms of manipulation;
- Cooperating in group work and addressing conflict positively;
- Consensus building;
- Participating democratically in activities with peers;
- Expressing oneself with self-confidence;
- Problem solving.

**Attitudes: Learning in human rights:**

Human rights are not just legal documents that bind states. They are also principles for how children and all people should live together. Yet because they are intangibles principally expressed through the actions they inform, human rights values and attitudes are both the most difficult and the most long-lasting form of human rights education. Children learn as much or more from unspoken examples as they do from overt lessons, and they have a keen sense of hypocrisy. It is incumbent on everyone who works with children to model the human rights values they wish to impart.

Attitudes to be learned in human rights include:

- Respect for self and others;
- A sense of responsibility for one's own actions;
- Curiosity, an open mind and an appreciation of diversity;
- Empathy and solidarity with others and a commitment to support those whose human rights are denied;
- A sense of human dignity, of self-worth and of others' worth, irrespective of social, cultural, linguistic or religious differences;
- A sense of justice and social responsibility to see that everyone is treated justly;
- The desire to contribute to the betterment of the school or community;
- The confidence to promote human rights both locally and globally.

# Methodologies for human rights education

Because participatory methodologies assume that everyone has the right to an opinion and respects individual differences, they have proven especially effective for human rights education. Going beyond factual content to include skills, attitudes, values and action requires an educational structure that is 'horizontal' rather than 'hierarchical'. Its democratic structure engages each individual and empowers her or him to think and interpret independently. It encourages critical analysis of real-life situations and can lead to thoughtful and appropriate action to promote and protect human rights. In other words, to be effective, human rights education must provide children with a supportive framework where the rights of every individual child are respected.

The methodologies described below are used in a great variety of learning environments, both formal and non-formal, with a limitless number of topics. However, they have in common certain features that make them especially appropriate for people of all ages to learn about human rights:

- Respect for children's experience and recognition of a variety of points of view;
- Promotion of personal enrichment, self-esteem, and respect for the individual child;
- Empowerment of children to define what they want to know and to seek information for themselves;
- Active engagement of all children in their own learning with a minimum of passive listening;
- Encouragement of non-hierarchical, democratic, collaborative learning environments;
- Encouragement of reflection, analysis, and critical thinking;
- Engagement of subjective and emotional responses, as well as cognitive learning;
- Encouragement of behavioral and attitudinal change;
- Emphasis on skill building and practical application of learning;
- Recognition of the importance of humor, fun, and creative play for learning.

The activities in COMPASITO combine a variety of methods and techniques with these characteristics. Facilitators should always be aware that some methods may be inappropriate for some groups of

mixed cultural backgrounds or special needs (e.g. physical contact, graphic arts) or require unfamiliar or unavailable resources (e.g. access to Internet or library resources). Every activity should be approached with the expectation that the facilitators will adapt the methodologies to meet the needs of the children and the cultural and social environment in which they live.

## Non-formal education

Many of the choices and adaptations a facilitator makes depends on the makeup of the group, the age of the children, the skills of the facilitator and the context in which they live and work. An important consideration is whether the setting for human rights education is formal, non-formal or informal.

**Formal education** refers to the structured education system that runs from primary to tertiary education, and can also include specialised programmes for technical and professional training. The main actors are schools and a range of higher education institutions. The Universal Declaration and the Convention on the Rights of the Child mandate that all children should have at least an elementary formal education.

**Non-formal education** refers to any intentional, voluntary and planned programme of personal and social education that aims to convey and practise values and develop a wide range of skills and competencies for democratic life. Non-formal education for children might include out-of-school activities, extra-curricular activities in schools, summer camps and leisure centres. Non-formal education emphasises a participative approach to learning.

**Informal education** refers to the unintentional lifelong process whereby everyone acquires attitudes, values, skills and knowledge from the educational influences and resources in his or her own environment and from daily experience (e.g. family, neighbours, library, mass media, work, play).

Formal, non-formal and informal education are complementary and mutually reinforcing elements of a lifelong learning process. The activities in COMPASITO have been designed to be flexible enough for use in all such contexts: in the school, in children's organisations, in youth clubs, in summer camps in settings of social work and in the family.

## Introducing human rights education in work with children

Just as human rights are a part of everyone's daily life experience, so human rights education should be integrated into children's ongoing learning. COMPASITO is not intended or recommended as a 'course' on human rights, but as a resource for raising children's awareness and understanding of human rights in the context of their lives. Look for opportunities to relate human rights to what is happening in the school, the community and the group of children you work with: a conflict on the playground, negative attitudes toward minorities or sexist exclusion of girls from certain activities. On the other hand, avoid approaching human rights only from the perspective of violations. Emphasize that we enjoy some human rights every day.

One primary aim of human rights education is action on behalf of human rights. Encourage and develop children's ability to take appropriate and meaningful action to address human rights issues. For children this action may be between individuals, such as resolving conflicts within the group or the family, perhaps changing behaviour toward siblings. Action may also take place in the wider community, such as organizing a celebration for International Human Rights Day or putting on an exhibiting of human rights-related artwork. The younger the children, the more they will rely on the facilitator's support in initiating and executing more complex projects.

# The right to human rights education

Education in human rights is itself a fundamental human right and also a responsibility: the Preamble to the UDHR exhorts "every individual and every organ of society" to "strive by teaching and education to promote respect for these rights and freedoms." Article 26.2 of the UDHR states that –

> *Education shall be directed … to the strengthening of respect for human rights and fundamental freedoms. It shall promote understanding, tolerance and friendship among all nations, racial or religious groups, and shall further the activities of the United Nations for the maintenance of peace.*

The **International Covenant on Civil and Political Rights** (ICCPR) declares that a government "may not stand in the way of people learning about [their rights]."

People who do not know their rights are more vulnerable to having them abused and often lack the language and conceptual framework to effectively advocate for them. All the more reason for introducing human rights education to children!

Growing consensus around the world recognizes education for, about and in human rights as essential to a quality education. It can contribute to the building of free, just and peaceful societies. Human rights education is also increasingly recognized as an effective strategy to prevent human rights abuses.

# Human rights education and other educational fields

COMPASITO is structured around thirteen human rights-related themes, each of which relates directly to one or more concrete human rights (See CHAPTER V., P. 213, for a discussion of these themes):

- Citizenship
- Democracy
- Discrimination
- Education and leisure
- Environment
- Family and alternative care
- Gender equality
- Health and welfare
- Media and Internet
- Participation
- Peace and human security
- Poverty and social exclusion
- Violence

None of these themes is more important than another. Indeed, they are so interrelated that addressing any one of them provides a common link with any other. This is a direct consequence of the fact that human rights are **indivisible**, **interdependent** and interrelated: they cannot be treated in isolation, because all are connected to one another in various ways.

The diagram below provides one illustration of this interdependence. The issues in the outer circle blend into one another, just as the educational spheres in the central circle merge together. Even the distinction between **first, second and third generation rights** are not clear-cut. Education, for example, is traditionally classed as a second generation right, but education is just as necessary for participation (first generation right) as it for sustainable development (a third generation right). Accordingly, the following analysis should be seen as just one description among many, but it should help to illustrate the ways in which the various themes are relevant to many of the current educational fields and how these fields overlap with one another.

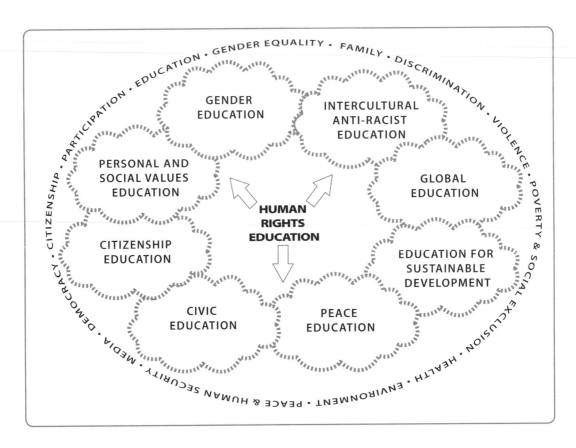

# 2. Human rights education in an international context

*...democracy is not fixed and immutable, but rather that it must be built and rebuilt every day in every society.*

The Dakar Framework for Action

Human rights education has emerged as one of the most important means for developing a human rights culture. Although since 1948 human rights legislation has been increasingly elaborated on at both the international and European levels, and most human rights documents endorse human rights education, the potential of human rights education has so far remained unrealised. Insufficient political will, lack of resources and inadequate teaching materials have limited the effectiveness of human rights education. However, the development of human rights-related non-governmental organisations in the last decades and the democratic transition in dozen s of countries in Central and Eastern Europe have given the human rights education movement a vital impetus. International organisations have played an essential role in developing more effective and consistent human rights education strategies at the national level.

## United Nations

### United Nations World Programme for Human Rights Education

In December 1994 the UN General Assembly proclaimed 1995-2004 the United Nations Decade for Human Rights Education. The official recommendation recognizes human rights education as key for

the promotion and achievement of stable and harmonious relations among communities and for the fostering of mutual understanding, tolerance and peace. It calls on all states and institutions to include human rights, humanitarian law, democracy and the rule of law as subjects in the curricula of all learning institutions in formal and non-formal settings.[1]

As a follow-up to the Decade in December 2004 the UN General Assembly proclaimed a World Programme for Human Rights Education (2005-ongoing). Building on the achievements of the United Nations Decade for Human Rights Education, this worldwide programme seeks to help make human rights a reality in every community. The Action Plan of the World Programme for 2005-2007 focuses on the primary and secondary education systems and proposes concrete strategies and practical ideas for implementing human rights education on national level.[2]

### The UN Decade of Education for Sustainable Development

The UN Decade of Education for Sustainable Development (2005-2014) links environmental development and human rights education, emphasizing that education is essential for people to have the skills and capacities they need to address environment and development issues.[3]

### CyberSchoolbus: A special UN project for children

CyberSchoolBus is a global web-based teaching and learning project of the United Nations that aims to engage children in human rights issues. The CyberSchoolBus collects inspiring stories of classes or schools defending and promoting human rights in their own communities, neighbourhoods and cities. These stories become part of a global atlas of student actions compiled and published on the Internet by the UN CyberSchoolBus.

## UNESCO

UNESCO, the United Nations Educational, Scientific and Cultural Organization, had a key role in the development, implementation and evaluation of the projects foreseen during the UN Decade for Human Rights Education. Bearing in mind that learning should focus on the acquisition of values, attitudes and skills required to meet the emerging challenges of contemporary societies, UNESCO contributes to the development of national strategies in human rights education, develops learning materials and works on advocacy and networking. UNESCO continues to have a key role in the implementation of the World Programme for Human Rights Education (2005-ongoing).

UNESCO's work on human rights education was confirmed in the Dakar Framework for Action (2000-2015), a new global priority programme developed at the World Education Forum in 2000. The Framework affirms the need to implement 'quality education' internationally, which is defined as going beyond the traditional school curriculum to include a human rights approach and to address new areas such as cultural diversity, multilingualism in education, peace, non-violence, sustainable development and life skills.[4]

## UNICEF

For sixty years UNICEF has been a global force for children, and today it is present in 191 countries of the world. It works in partnership with a broad coalition of UN agencies, governments, NGOs, and local grassroots organizations to help build a world where the rights of every child are realised. UNICEF's work is guided by the Convention on the Rights of the Child.

In May 2002 a special session of the UN General Assembly produced *A World Fit for Children*, which sets a new agenda for the world's children for the next decade. It recognizes that governments, NGOs

and children and adolescents themselves all have a key role to play to ensure that all children enjoy the rights guaranteed them in the Convention on the Rights of the Child (CRC). To this end educational programmes, materials and the learning environment itself should "reflect fully the protection and promotion of human rights and the values of peace, tolerance and gender equity."[5]

UNICEF has many programmes that contribute to furthering human rights education internationally, regionally and in individual countries. Voices of Youth is a child-friendly website of UNICEF providing information about questions related to children's life on global level and interactive games to promote children's rights.[6] The UNICEF Innocenti Research Centre develops and produces research on children's situation internationally in the belief that awareness and understanding of children's rights improves children's situation everywhere in the world.[7]

# Council of Europe

For the Member States of the Council of Europe human rights are more than just a part of their legal framework; they should be an integral part of education of children, young people and adults. Recommendation No. R (85) 7 of the Committee of Ministers on Teaching and Learning about Human Rights in Schools emphasises that all young people should learn about human rights as part of their preparation for life in a pluralistic democracy; and this approach is slowly being incorporated into different European countries and institutions.[8]

Parliamentary Assembly Recommendation 1346 (1997) on human rights education proposes a whole range of actions for strengthening human rights education in Europe.

> The Assembly further recommends that the Committee of Ministers consider human rights education as a priority for the intergovernmental work of the Council of Europe in the years to come..."[9]

The Council of Europe works closely with the United Nations Office of the High Commissioner for Human Rights (OHCHR), UNESCO, the European Commission and other international organizations in the field of human rights education and education for democratic citizenship. For example the Council of Europe has a special role in monitoring the implementation of the World Programme for Human Rights Education (2005-2007) at the European level. This work includes the development of a concrete framework for action and the strengthening of partnerships and cooperation between the international and grass-roots levels.

In 2007 the Council of Europe initiated a project to design a framework policy document on education for democratic citizenship and human rights education. The acceptance of such a comprehensive document will establish commitment from the member states and will make their efforts measurable. Such a progressive instrument will be a strong recognition of non-formal organizations working in the field and provide standards for a wider international environment.

### Human Rights Education Youth Programme

The Human Rights Education Youth Programme was initiated in 2000 as a priority of the Youth Sector of the Council of Europe. Its main aim has been to bring human rights education into the mainstream of youth work. The first three years served the crucial function of developing educational tools and training possibilities for young people and building a network of partners in national and local level. In the second three-year period, the programme emphasized empowering young people, in particular vulnerable groups, and developing strategies to address racism, xenophobia, discrimination and gender-based violence. Since 2000 several new educational tools have been developed, various long term and advanced training courses implemented, and hundreds of pilot projects funded all over in Europe. 'COM-

PASS – a manual on human rights education with young people', an important educational resource of the Programme, has been translated into some twenty different languages since its publication in 2001. Through a cascading effect the Programme has reached hundreds of NGOs all around Europe that were supported by pilot projects offered by the European Youth Foundation. Human rights education has become key in youth work in Europe and has had fruitful effects on formal education as well. Since 2006 the Programme has also developed a special focus on intercultural dialogue as well.

### Education for Democratic Citizenship (EDC)

Human rights education is a key component in education for democratic citizenship, another approach to give children, youth and adults the knowledge, skills and attitudes that will help them to play an effective role in their communities. Since 1997 the Council of Europe's Programme on Education for Democratic Citizenship has developed concepts, definitions and political strategies and instituted networks to further this work. The Year of Citizenship through Education in 2005 strengthened the commitment of member states to introduce education for democratic citizenship into their educational policies. The Programme now aims to ensure sustainability by supporting these policy developments, research and good practises in teacher training and democratic governance. 'Exploring Children's Rights: lesson sequences for primary schools', a new publication of the Programme, provides concrete ideas on how to elaborate children's rights in the classroom.[10]

### Building a Europe for and with Children

Building a Europe for and with Children (2006-2008) is a programme of the Council that aims to help decision makers and stakeholders establish national strategies and policies to guarantee an integrated approach to promoting children's rights and protecting children from various forms of violence. Under the auspices of the Programme, the Council is revising its existing legal frameworks and instruments and is setting up new standards to better ensure children's rights in Europe. It is also initiating communication campaigns and education and training programmes to help governments and NGOs develop more effective child policies.

## Non-governmental organisations

Non-governmental organisations have an irreplaceable role in the development of a worldwide culture of human rights, particularly at the national and local level, as governments often do not live up to expectations when it comes to the integration of human rights education into the curriculum. As highly committed groups with special expertise, they have contributed to the development of the human rights legislation and are careful watchdogs of the realisation of human rights at the national level. Some global human rights organisations like Amnesty International work systematically on awareness raising on human rights education and produces educational programmes worldwide. People's Decade of Human Rights Education (PDHRE-International) develops programmes and provides a website on human rights education relevant to people's daily lives in the context of their struggles for social and economic justice and democracy.

Some organisations such as the Human Rights Education Associates (HREA), Democracy and Human Rights Education in Europe (DARE) and many youth organisations concentrate on human rights education: they support human rights learning and the training of activists and professionals, develop educational materials and seek to raise the profile of education for democratic citizenship and human rights.

Other organisations concentrate on educating about children's rights. For some such as Save the Children or Fondation Terre des homes (Tdh) this is key to their worldwide mission; others like the Children's Rights Information Network serve hundreds of child-related NGOs by collecting and disseminating information. At the local and national level, many non-governmental organisations in Europe and

worldwide organise human rights education programmes and projects involving children and young people.

Clearly there are many kinds of human rights education and a wide spectrum of institutions and individuals seeking to promote rights learning. However, these diverse efforts have a great deal in common. All are grounded in the international human rights framework of law and seek to empower people to realise human rights in their daily lives in concrete and practical ways. They also share the values and principles of human rights, which are summed up in the preamble to the UDHR: "the inherent dignity and...equal and inalienable rights of all members of the human family."

## Useful Resources

- *ABC: Teaching Human Rights Education:* Office of the High Commissioner for Human Rights, 2004: www.unhchr.ch/html/menu6/2/abc.htm#I.
- Claude, Richard, *The Bells of Freedom*: erc.hrea.org/Library/Bells_of_Freedom/index.html
- *Compendium of good practises in human rights education in the school system, including citizenship education and education for mutual respect and understanding:* www.hrea.org/compendium
- *First Steps: A Manual for Starting Human Rights Education*: Amnesty International, 1996: http:/erc.hrea.org/Library/First_Steps/index.html
- Flowers, Nancy, *The Human Rights Education Handbook:* University of Minnesota Human Rights Center, 2000: www1.umn.edu/humanrts/edumat/hreduseries/hrhandbook/toc.html
- Gollob, Rolf and Kraft, Peter, *Exploring Children's Rights: lesson sequences for primary schools*: Strasbourg, Education for Democratic Citizenship, 2006: www.coe.int/t/dg4/education/edc/ Source/ Pdf/Documents/2006_17_ExploringChildreensRights_En.pdf
- *Play it Right! Human Rights Toolkit for Summer Camps in the City of Montreal*: Equitas, International Centre for Human Rights Education, 2006: www.equitas.org
- Set of drawings to discuss children's rights: www.vormen.org/downloads/ChildrensRightsTextIllustr.pps
- *Vienna Declaration and Programme of Action*: World Conference on Human Rights, United Nations, Vienna, 1993: www.unhchr.ch/huridocda/huridoca.nsf/(Symbol)/A.CONF.157.23. En?OpenDocument

## Useful websites

- Amnesty International: www.amnesty.org
- Building a Europe with and for Children: www.coe.int/children
- Children's Rights Information Network: www.crin.org
- Council of Europe: www.coe.int
- Democracy and Human Rights Education in Europe: www.dare-network.org
- European Children's Network (EURONET): www.europeanchildrensnetwork.org
- Fondation Terre des hommes: www.tdh.ch
- Human Rights Watch: www.hrw.org
- Human Rights Education Associates: www.hrea.org
- Human Rights Education Youth Programme: www.coe.int/compass
- Office of the United Nations High Commissioner for Human Rights: www.ohchr.org
- The People's Decade for Human Rights Education/ International Movement for Human Rights

Learning: www.pdhre.org/index.html

- United Nations CyberSchoolbus: www0.un.org/cyberschoolbus

- UNESCO: www.unesco.org

- UNICEF: www.unicef.org

- UNICEF Innocenti Research Centre: www.unicef-irc.org

- UNICEF Voices of Youth: www.unicef.org/voy

- World Programme for Human Rights Education (2005-ongoing): www.ohchr.org/english/ issues/education/training/programme.htm

. . . . . . . . . . . . . . . . .

### References

1  United Nations World Conference on Human Rights, 1993, *Vienna Declaration and Programme of Action*, para. 33 of Section 1.

2  See www.ohchr.org/english/issues/education/training/programme.htm

3  See http://portal.unesco.org/education/en/ev.php-URL_ID=27234&URL_DO=DO_TOPIC&URL_SECTION=201.html .

4  *The Dakar Framework for Action – Education for All: meeting with our commitments*, World Education Forum, Dakar, Senegal, 26-28 April, 2000: www.unesco.org/education/efa/ed_for_all/framework.shtml

5  See www.unicef.org/specialsession/documentation/ documents/A-S27-19-Rev1E-annex.pdf

6  See www.unicef.org/voy

7  See www.unicef-irc.org

8  *Recommendation No R (85) 7 of the Committee of Ministers*: https://wcd.coe.int/com.instranet.InstraServlet?Command=com. instranet.CmdBlobGet&DocId=686452&SecMode=1&Admin=0&Usage=4&InstranetImage=45239

9  *Council of Europe's Parliamentary Assembly Recommendation 1346 (1997) on human rights education*, point 12.

10  Gollob, Rolf and Kraft, Peter, *Exploring Children's Rights: lesson sequences for primary schools*: Strasbourg, Education for Democratic Citizenship, 2006.

# III. HOW TO USE Compasito

*"No child can learn about human rights in an environment that does not itself respect and promote a culture of human rights. The most important contribution a facilitator can make to a child's understanding of human rights is to create that environment."*

## Getting started with Compasito

This chapter is intended to support you, the facilitator, with practical information about using Compasito. However, do not let so many 'how-to's and 'should's discourage you. No-one knows your context and your children better than you do. Take the information and advice that is helpful to you and run the activities with your group. When you have questions, you may find some helpful answers here. If you create an environment that respects and promotes the human rights of a child, that child is learning about human rights!

Unlike lesson plans for use in a school curriculum, Compasito was designed to be as adaptable as possible to the many settings where children can learn about human rights, from summer camps and out-of-school programmes to youth groups and field trips, as well as the formal school classroom. Although many Compasito activities require some preparation, they can be run almost anywhere and anytime. Finding the moment when children are most receptive to human rights learning – which could be when a conflict occurs in the group, but also when the group is feeling celebratory – is part of the art of facilitation: your art!

**This chapter covers the following topics:**

- The goal of Compasito
- Experiential learning
- Facilitation
- Thinking and leaning styles
- Children' developmental levels
- What is in a Compasito activity?
- The Convention on the Rights of the Child as a foundation
- Selecting activities
- Adapting activities
- Tips for promoting participation
- Tips for facilitation
- Practising human rights education

You will also find further discussion of human rights education in Chapter II, Section 1, p. 25.

# The goal of COMPASITO

COMPASITO seeks to develop in children the knowledge, skills, values and attitudes they need to participate in their society, knowing and protecting their rights and the rights of others. In this way children can actively contribute to building a culture of human rights.

To accomplish this goal, COMPASITO learning activities are designed to

- start from what children already know as a basis for exploring new ideas and perspectives;

- encourage children to participate actively in discussion and to learn from each other as much as possible;

- inspire and enable children to put their learning into simple but meaningful and appropriate action in support of justice, equality and human rights;

- reflect the core values of the **Convention on the Rights of the Child** (CRC) and encourage a culture of human rights among children.

Attitudes and values related to communication, critical thinking, advocacy, responsibility, tolerance and respect for others cannot be taught; they must be learned through experience. For this reason the activities in COMPASITO promote cooperation, participation and active learning. They aim at a holistic engagement of the child's head, heart and hands. Only a child who understands that human rights evolve from basic human needs and feels empathy for other human beings will take personal responsibility to protect the human rights of others.

# Experiential learning

How do we create that understanding and empathy in a child? Human rights education is about education for change, both personal and social. To accomplish this change, the activities of COMPASITO are based on a learning cycle with five phases:

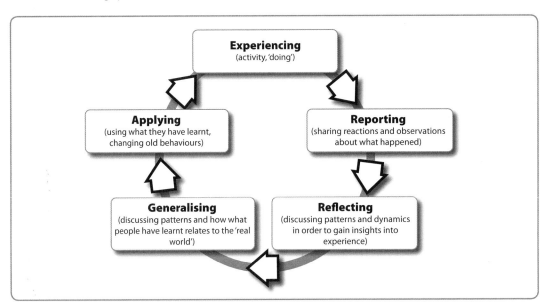

Although all these phases may not always be obvious or occur in this order, they are implicitly present in every COMPASITO activity.

This methodology of experiential learning permits children to develop and change knowledge, skills, attitudes and values in a safe environment that is both challenging and fun. Because it validates the child's

experience and encourages children to take responsibility for their own learning, experiential learning enhances participation, self-reliance and self-confidence. Each phase of this cycle honours children's lived experience while challenging them to articulate, observe, reflect, question and draw conclusions.

## Experiencing

Phase 1 does not aim to generate 'right answers', but to stimulate each child's own opinions, theories and feelings. In most cases these responses are drawn from the child's previous experience rather than school learning. For example, in the activity 'ONCE UPON A TIME...', P. 125, children grasp gender stereotypes from hearing a well-known story with the sex roles reversed. In 'WORLD SUMMER CAMP', P. 205, children confront their unconscious prejudices through the familiar process of selecting playmates.

## Reporting

Phase 2 encourages children to articulate their feelings and reactions. For example, in the 'Debriefing and evaluation' section of each COMPASITO activity, children respond to questions such as "How was this activity for you?", "How did you feel during this experience?" or "What happened during this game?" Such open-ended questions invite a wide range of personal opinions in a non-judgmental context.

The importance of the debriefing stage cannot be overstated. Without adequate time to discuss children's responses and explicitly make a link to human rights, an activity is at best just a game, a period of fun that can be quickly forgotten. At worst, it can reinforce negative attitudes and stereotypes, mislead or confuse children, or even arouse and not deal with painful emotions. If you do not have time for a thorough debriefing, do not run an activity.

## Reflecting

Phase 3 moves children beyond the experience of the activity to its conceptual implications. For example, the discussion that follows a very active game such as 'THE INVISIBLES ARE COMING', P. 171, leads children to consider that the game can be seen as a metaphor for xenophobia. In the activity 'COOKIE MONSTER', P. 95, for example, children experience the value of working cooperatively, but the subsequent discussion asks them to articulate this discovery. Asking questions such as "Have you experienced something like this in your life?" or "Do you know someone like this?" helps children make these connections.

## Generalising

Phase 4 connects the experience of the activity to the 'real world' in general and especially to the way human rights are experienced in everyday life. For example, after a simulation activity such as 'BLINDFOLDED', P. 67, or 'SILENT SPEAKER', P. 160, children discuss how physical disabilities can limit a child's enjoyment of human rights. Phases 3 and 4 are especially effective in eliciting independent thinking and creating opportunities for children to learn from each other. Learning is highly individualized, however: not every child will derive the same learning from participating in the same activity and discussion, and these differences responses need to be respected.

## Applying

In Phase 5 children explore what they themselves can do to address human rights issues. Taking action is not only a logical outcome of the learning process, but also a significant means of reinforcing new knowledge, skills and attitudes which form the basis for the next round of the cycle. It is also a key element in developing active citizenship in a democracy: individuals can make a difference, even as children. For

example, the activity 'A CONSTITUTION FOR OUR GROUP', P. 56, leads the group to develop its own rights and responsibilities, to refer to them to resolve conflicts and to revise them democratically as needed, and 'EVERY VOTE COUNTS', P. 103, challenges children to find democratic methods for making group decisions.

Although the activities in COMPASITO are intended to engage children and be fun, they are also purposeful, offering children a chance to apply what they have learned to their social environments. Most activities have a section of 'Ideas for action'. Such action might be individual and find expression only in the child's private life, such as a new attitude toward siblings. Action might also be collective and result in developing new classroom rules or ways of handling playground conflicts. The Internet also offers new and simple ways for children to 'take action' on global human rights issues. For example, check the websites of human rights and environmental non-governmental organisations for action ideas.

Whatever its level and type, however, the action that children take should be voluntary and self-directed. The facilitator can encourage and assist children to find an appropriate action to achieve their goals. However, the motivation to take action must come from children themselves. Otherwise children are not learning to become active citizens but to follow the directions of an authority figure.

Even in a small group there may be great differences in children's readiness and willingness to take action. Not everyone who wants to do something will want to take the same action. The facilitator needs to help children find a range of options for action that meet the diversity of their abilities and interests.

The facilitator also plays a crucial role in stimulating children to think through their experiences and especially to relate their concerns to human rights. For example, children may decide independently that their school should be more welcoming to newcomers, but they may need the facilitator to connect their action to the human rights principle of non-discrimination.

## Facilitation

COMPASITO uses the word *facilitator* for the people who prepare, present and coordinate the activities and create an environment where children can learn, experience and experiment with human rights. The facilitator sets the stage, creating a setting where human rights are respected but the children are the main actors on this stage. There is, however, no perfect environment for human rights education. Even situations where children violate each other's rights can become learning experiences. The success of any activity, however, depends principally on the tact, skill and experience of the facilitator.

Many people who work with children are unfamiliar with facilitation and find it challenging and even uncomfortable. They take for granted their traditional role as 'leader' or 'teacher'. Most children are also conditioned to depend on an adult to impart information; however, children accept responsibility for their own learning more readily than adults give up their role as authority and expert. Facilitation is not difficult, however, and most facilitators 'learn by doing', provided they understand and accept the shift to a child-centred, experiential approach to learning.

The art of facilitation requires not only a shift in focus, but also a high degree of self-awareness. Because children are powerfully influenced by the behaviour of adults in their lives, facilitators must take care to model the human rights values they wish to convey. An activity on gender stereotyping, for example, will be useless if the facilitator habitually displays gender bias. For this reason, facilitators must recognize, acknowledge and conscientiously address their own prejudices and biases, even more so if they are directed against children in the group.

QUESTION: *Every human being has prejudices! What are yours? Could some of your prejudices affect the children you work with? What can you do to address these prejudices?*

# Thinking and learning styles

To excite the talents and interests of a variety of children, facilitators benefit from a familiarity with the different ways that people think and learn, including themselves. Although everyone uses a mixture of thinking and learning styles, every person has a preferred or dominant style.

## Which is your thinking style?

- **Visual learners** tend to represent the world to themselves in pictures. They may use phrases such as "I see what you mean".
- **Auditory learners** remember more of what they hear and may use phrases like "That sounds such as a good idea".
- **Kinaesthetic learners** tend to remember things through feelings, both physical and emotional. They tend to use terms such as "I love it. Let's go for it".

## Which is your favorite or dominant learning style?

- **Activists** learn best from new experiences, problems and opportunities from experience. They love games, teamwork, task and role-playing exercises. They react against passive learning, solitary activities like reading and independent research, and tasks that require attention to detail.
- **Reflectors** learn best when they can think over an activity. They enjoy research, reviewing what has happened and what they have learned. They react against being forced into the limelight, having insufficient data on which to base a conclusion and having to take short cuts or doing a superficial job.
- **Theorists** learn best when what they are learning about is part of a system, model, concept or theory. They like structured situations with a clear purpose and dealing with interesting ideas and concepts. They often dislike participating in situations that emphasize feelings.
- **Pragmatists** learn best from activities where the subject matter is clearly linked to a real problem and where they are able to implement what they have learned. They react against learning that seems distant from reality and 'all theory and general principles'.

---

QUESTION: *Try to remember a favourite teacher, trainer or facilitator. What was it about the way that person communicated that helped you learn?*

*Is there a correspondence between that person's communication style and your own style of thinking and learning?*

*Most people naturally teach and work with groups in a way that matches their own thinking and learning style. Is that true for you?*

- *With what kinds of learners would you be most effective?*
- *What kinds of learner would have most difficulty learning from you?*
- *How can you adapt your communication style to reach more learners?*

---

In practise everyone uses a combination of ways of thinking and learning. And every group of children presents the facilitator with many different learning needs and styles. Keep this in mind when selecting activities from COMPASITO, balancing the types of activities to match the differing needs and learning styles of the children you work with.

Differences in thinking and learning can also account for the way activities run and how children debrief and evaluate them. You will notice that the same activity produces different levels of participation and different results in different children. Some children are more likely to respond to debriefing questions

than to others. Remember too that thinking and learning styles may account for only part of these differences. Because of a whole range of factors beyond your control, the same children may react quite differently to the same activity on a different day! As you become more familiar with Compasito activities, you will be better able to account for these differences.

# Children's developmental levels

The activities in Compasito are developed for children between the ages of six and thirteen, although many can be easily adapted to younger and older children as well as adults. Childhood is the ideal time to introduce human rights education, for although young children already hold strong values and attitudes, they are also receptive to new perspectives and experiences. Developing values like respect for others and tolerance of difference or skills like empathy and critical thinking requires years. It is never too early to begin!

At the same time children are still very dependent on the guidance and support of adults, especially their families, caregivers and teachers, as well as their peers. Some of the human rights values and attitudes that Compasito endorses may clash with those children encounter in other parts of their lives. Explaining the goals and methods of Compasito to parents, teachers or community leaders can help prevent potential conflict. Facilitators need to be sensitive to such potential conflicts both within the child and with the child's home, school or community environment. In every case, a child at any level of development should not be made the focal point of such conflict.

While each child is unique, the lists below summarize the main characteristics of these age groups. A skilled facilitator needs to understand the developmental level of the group and select and/or adapt activities to match their physical, cognitive, emotional and social development.

## 6 to 7 years olds:

### Physical development

- enjoy outdoor activities with brief but energetic spurts of activity
- prefer simple manual tasks, especially combined with developing a particular physical skill

### Cognitive and emotional development

- like to talk but have a short attention span and have difficulties listening to others
- are very curious
- learn best through physical experiences
- have difficulty making decisions
- can read and write, but these skills are still in the emergent stages
- are highly imaginative and easily become involved in role games and fantasy play
- like stories about friendship and superheroes
- enjoy cartoon figures

### Social development

- are very competitive
- sometimes find cooperation difficult

## 8 to 10 years olds

### Physical development

- seem to have endless physical energy

### Cognitive and emotional development

- like to learn new things, but not necessarily in-depth
- become more aware of differences and inequalities among others
- enjoy problem solving
- enjoy question-answer games
- can be very frustrated if their work does not meet their expectations

### Social development

- enjoy more independence but still need support
- like to talk and discuss things with peers
- can be very critical of both self and others
- are better able to cooperate
- like to belong to a group
- start to idolize real heroes, TV stars and sport figures instead of cartoon figures.

## 11 to 13 years olds

### Physical development

- mature a lot physically although these changes vary greatly among children and may cause self-consciousness and uncomfortable feelings

### Cognitive and emotional development

- mature greatly in their ability to think in a more abstract way
- enjoy arguing and discussing
- find some games predictable and boring; prefer complex activities that involve creating unique strategies and products
- tend toward perfectionism in what they do
- begin to perceive that a story or event can be seen from more than one perspective
- show an increasing interest in social and current events

### Social development

- have a growing interest in a wider social and physical environment
- enjoy testing the limits of self and others
- can combine playfulness and seriousness at the same time
- get more concerned about how they appear to others
- like to learn from role models
- start developing more advanced play in groups and teams
- like to cooperate for common goals
- are strongly influenced by attitudes and behaviour of peers.

ings, not all of which are known to children (e.g. that 'violence' can be both physical and psychological, actual and threatened; that a 'disability' can be physical, mental or psycho-social). Other terms may be only vaguely understood and need concrete examples (e.g. 'exploitation', 'culture,' 'abuse', 'neglect'). Ask the children to provide examples from their own experience.

- Abuse / mistreatment / neglect
- "Accepted everywhere as a person according to law"
- Association
- Cultures/traditions
- "Develop physically, mentally, spiritually, morally and socially"
- Disability
- "Exercise your rights"
- Exploitation
- Government
- "Have your birth registered"
- "Have your situation reviewed"
- Health professionals
- "Honour and reputation"
- Identity

- Juvenile justice
- Leisure
- Loss of liberty
- Media
- Nationality
- Nutritious food
- Pornography
- Privacy
- Prostitution
- Rehabilitation
- Social security
- Trade union, union
- Violence
- Warfare
- War zone

When you are introducing children to the CRC, they do not need this level of detailed information. As they become more familiar with human rights, however, look for opportunities to refine their understanding or correct misunderstandings when you observe them. Keep an eye out for the 'teachable moment'.

# Selecting activities

The facilitator has a variety of factors to consider in determining which activities from COMPASITO to use. Most important of these considerations are –

**1. Your children**: Before selecting activities, the facilitator first needs to know the children involved.

    a. What are their levels of development, interests, concerns and learning styles?

    b. Are there conflicts and problems within the group?

    c. Do these children face particular issues or problems within the community?

    d. How much do the children already know about human rights? Some COMPASITO activities assume prior introduction to the CRC, for example.

However, don't feel you must wait to use COMPASITO activities until you know the answers to all these questions. Often playing activities is the most efficient way to learn about your group!

**2. Your learning objective**: Some activities can be run to increase general understanding of human rights or even just for fun, but most can and should be directed to themes that are close to the children or are an issue in the group, the community or the world. COMPASITO activities focus on these human rights themes:

    a. Citizenship

    b. Democracy

    c. Discrimination

d. Education and leisure

e. Environment

f. Family and alternative care

g. Gender equality

h. Health and welfare

i. Media and Internet

j. Participation

k. Peace and human security

l. Poverty and social exclusion

m. Violence

For a full discussion of COMPASITO's human rights themes, see CHAPTER V., P. 213.

3. **A learning sequence**: Lasting knowledge, skills, values and attitudes are never achieved in a single activity. Select activities that form a series, whether based on a particular human rights theme or the development of certain competencies. This series might extend over a month, a school term or even a whole year. You may want to choose activities that fit into subject areas of the school curriculum or that address current issues in the group or community.

In every case, seek a balance of activity types and make the needs of children your first priority. Methodological diversity not only makes activities more fun, but also enables children to learn through their senses and emotions as well as their minds. For this reason COMPASITO offers you a wide choice of techniques and methodologies (e.g. discussion, debate, story telling, simulation, drama, board games, artistic activities, active group competition).

To further assist selection, a chart showing pertinent information on all the activities in COMPASITO can be found on p. 52.

# Adapting activities

Use COMPASITO as you would a recipe book. Like good cooks, facilitators should feel free to change the 'ingredients' of an activity to fit available time and materials and the size, competence and circumstances of their group. Most activities offer tips on adaptation.

Be aware that every group of children presents you with many different learning styles and different levels of ability. It is easier for you as facilitator to offer children a variety of ways to learn than for a child to adapt to a single method required by you. For example, an activity that is based on real-life problems, such as 'HUMAN RIGHTS IN THE NEWS', P. 110, may delight the 'Pragmatists' but frustrate the 'Theorists.' You could adapt the activity to extend the analytical aspect by comparing how a problem is reported differently in different media. Similarly, many activities can be adapted to accommodate different levels of reading and writing skills. For example, the facilitator could take over all the written aspects of an activity such as 'RABBIT'S RIGHTS', P. 141 or 'WHO'S BEHIND ME?', P. 195. Be creative in providing ways for children to respond to what they have learned. For example, in addition to group discussion, children might draw, mime, write in a journal or share their ideas in pairs.

Careful selection and adaptation of activities is especially important to ensure the inclusion and equal participation of children with special needs, such as homeless, migrant, refugee and institutionalized children. Avoid exposing what may be painful differences amongst the children.

Be especially sensitive to the needs of children with disabilities and avoid putting them in the position of 'agreeing to' an activity in which they cannot participate equally. Instead when you know a child in your group has physical limitations, adapt the activity to the child rather than expecting the

child to accommodate the activity. For example, some adaptations for children with disabilities might include–

- Avoid using red and green in an exercise. Children with daltonism (colour-blindness) have difficulty distinguishing them.
- Include explanations and handouts in Braille for visually impaired children.
- Position non-mobile children to allow them maximum participation.
- Use visual images and written instructions to encourage participation of hearing-impaired children.

## Tips for promoting participation

Skilled facilitators can ensure that every child participates fully, even the shy and disengaged. Here are a few suggestions:

- Rephrase your questions several times to ensure everyone understands.
- Use clear language that children understand; avoid jargon.
- Take responsibility for clear communications (e.g. ask "Did I say that clearly?" rather than "Did you understand?").
- Ask open questions that cannot be answered with a simple 'yes' or 'no' (e.g. not "Did you enjoy that activity?" but "How did you feel about that activity?").
- Establish ground rules for discussion (e.g. no interrupting but raising hands to speak).
- Draw out silent children, asking them to report or share experiences, but never put pressure on a child to participate.
- Create different roles for group work to ensure equal involvement (e.g. time keeper, materials manager, reporter, scribe).
- Emphasize that every child has something to contribute to the activity.
- Summarize regularly or ask children to do this.
- Explain an activity clearly before beginning so that children know what to expect.
- Connect present activity to previous and future activities.
- Be careful that an activity does not expose any child to ridicule, embarrassment or repercussions at home.
- When possible, seek the support of other facilitators, thus increasing the chance for children to connect with facilitators and be exposed to different teaching and learning styles.
- Acknowledge that no facilitator can control everything that happens or be aware of every child at every moment. Just be attentive without being over-concerned.

## Tips for facilitation

Every facilitator needs a repertoire of short techniques and activities for special purposes. These are often helpful to motivate the group, to engage the children in a process, to draw their attention, to break tension or resistance, to gain their confidence and interest or simply to break the ice or to have a bit of fun!

Here are a few proven favorites. A treasury of others can be found on the Internet at sites such as Salto-Youth Support Centre: www.salto-youth.net

## Icebreakers / Warm-ups / Starters

For getting a group started and building solidarity.

- **Group Still Life**: Ask children to bring an object from home that has special significance to them. Each child explains the object as it is added to a group display.

- **Me Too!**[1]: Explain that children must locate others who share the same characteristic. Then call out some categories (e.g. birth month; number of siblings; kind of shoe fastening). Under the right circumstances, use more sensitive categories (e.g. religion, language spoken, skin colour).

- **Musical Chairs:** Arrange chairs in a close circle and ask children to sit down. Stand in the middle of the circle and explain that you are going to state your name and make a statement about yourself. When you do, everyone for whom that statement is also true must change chairs. (e.g. "I am X and am left-handed," "I am X and I have a cat" or "I am X and I dislike eating ___"). Try to get a chair for yourself. The person left without a chair then makes a similar statement about herself or himself. Continue until most children have had a chance to introduce themselves in this way.

- **Portraits**: Divide children into pairs and give each plain paper and a pen. Explain that each person is to draw a quick sketch of the other and to ask some questions (e.g. name, hobby, a surprising fact) that will be incorporated into the portrait. Allow only a short time for this and encourage everyone to make their portraits and names as large as possible. Then ask each child to show his or her portrait and introduce the 'original' to the group. To facilitate learning names, hang the portraits where everyone can see.

- **Teamwork**: Divide children into small teams and allow them time to discover the characteristics they have in common (e.g. culture, appearance, personal tastes, hobbies). Ask each team to give itself a name based on their shared qualities. Each group then introduces themselves to the others and explains their name.

## Energizers

For raising or refocusing the group's energy.

- **The Chain**: Ask children to stand in a circle with their eyes closed. Move them around, attaching their hands to each other so that they make a knot. Then tell them to open their eyes and try to untangle themselves without letting go of their hands.

- **Fireworks**: Assign small groups to make the sounds and gestures of different fireworks. Some are bombs that hiss and explode. Others are firecrackers imitated by handclaps. Some are Catherine Wheels that spin and so on. Call on each group to perform separately, and then the whole group makes a grand display.

- **Group Sit**: Ask children to stand in a circle toe-to-toe. Then ask them to sit down without breaking the connection of their toes. If culturally appropriate, the children could also stand in a circle behind each other with their hands on the shoulders of the child in front. In this way, when they sit down, each one sits on the knees of the child behind them. Of course, neither version is suitable for groups in which any child has physical disabilities.

- **The Rain Forest**: Stand in the centre of children and ask them to mimic you, making different sounds and gestures for aspects of the forest (e.g. birds, insects, leaves rustling, wind blowing, animals calling) by snapping fingers, slapping sides, clapping hands, and imitating animals. The results sound like a rain forest.

- **Silent Calendar**: Ask the whole group to line up in order of the day and month they were born. However, they cannot use words to accomplish this. You could do the same with shoe sizes, number of hours spent watching TV per week, or any other interesting personal data.

- **The Storm**: Assign different sounds and gestures to small groups of children (e.g. wind, rain, lightning,

thunder). Then narrate the soft beginnings of the storm, conducting the various sounds like an orchestra (e.g. "And then the lightning flashes! And the thunder roars!") to the conclusion of the storm.

- **Three Circles:** Ask the children to stand in a circle, and silently to choose one other child in their mind, without telling anyone whom they chose. Explain that when you say, "Go", they will have to run three times around the child they chose. The result will be a complete chaos, but very funny, as everyone is running after someone and being run after at the same time.
- **To the Lifeboats!** – First demonstrate a 'lifeboat': two people hold hands to form the boat; passengers stand inside the circle of their hands. Then explain that everyone is going on a voyage: "At first the sea is calm and everyone is enjoying the trip. Then, suddenly, the ship hits a rock. Everyone must get into a lifeboat in groups of three (or one, or four, etc.)." Children then scramble to form 'lifeboats' and take in the proper number of passages. Usually someone 'drowns.' Then tell children to get back on the ship and take up the narrative again. "Now the ship continues peacefully ... but suddenly a hurricane begins. The ship is sinking. Everyone to the lifeboats in groups of two." Continue like this through several 'shipwrecks'.

## Evaluation and reflection opportunities

For ending a day or a session.

- **Ball Toss**: Children toss a ball from one to another. Each person who catches the ball states one thing she or he learned or can use from the activity.
- **Collective Summary**: Pose a summarizing question (e.g. " What will you especially remember from today's activity?" or an open-ended statement (e.g. "Try to think of a word or phrase that sums up your feelings at the end of today" or "I still wonder..."). Ask children to respond in turn.
- **Group Bulletin Board**: Each child in turn adds one word or picture to a group display and explains why it represents something important he or she is feeling or has learned.
- **Releasing the Dove of Peace**: The facilitator mimes holding a significant object (e.g. bird, newborn baby) and invites each child to say something to it as it is passed from one child to another. After the 'object' has been passed to everyone, they draw into a tight circle and collectively let it go.

## Managing conflict

For addressing conflicts within the group and within individual children.

Conflicting feelings and values are inevitable when dealing with a topic like human rights, especially when engaged in a non-formal activities like those in Compasito that intentionally address children's emotions as well as their intellects. Such conflict, which may arise between children but also within an individual child, is not necessarily negative and with skill facilitation can even be transformed into a constructive experience. Learning to deal with conflict is one of the most important life skills children can acquire and an essential one for developing a culture of human rights in the world around them. Here are some ideas:

- **Anticipate conflict**: When preparing an activity, think about possible conflicts it might evoke in the group or in individual children. Is the topic, the rules or terminology too sensitive for some or all of the children?
- **Do not provoke conflicts but also do not step aside when they arise**.
- **Don't assume conflicts are your fault – or anyone's fault**. They are normal and inevitable within every group. Help children accept that fact and avoid blaming. Focus on managing conflict, not fault finding.
- **Do not ignore bad feelings in the group**. Acknowledge their reality and help children address them.

- **Taking plenty of time for debriefing and discussions** after each activity so that children have a chance to express how they are feeling, both about the activity and each other. This is perhaps your important opportunity to model conflict management.
- **Talk to children individually**: Often a child's feelings are too personal or painful to be discussed within the group. When you sense this, make an opportunity to speak privately about what may be causing this distress. Let the child know you are ready to listen whenever he or she is ready to discuss the problem.

See also the discussion of peace education, CHAPTER V., P. 213.

# Practising human rights education

No child can learn about human rights in an environment that does not itself respect and promote a culture of human rights. The most important contribution a facilitator can make to a child's understanding of human rights is to create that environment.

Model the principle of the child's best interest. For example, deal with the conflicts that inevitably arise among children in a manner that emphasizes everyone's right to participation and to express an opinion, as well as everyone's responsibility for the welfare and harmony of the group. Engage children in actively resolving conflicts.

Practise the non-discrimination you want the children to learn. Be aware that even the with the best intentions, we all reflect the biases of our own culture. These prejudices and stereotypes are especially true in the area of gender equality. Research shows that without knowing or intending to do so, most teachers give boys more attention and encouragement than girls. Make a special effort to see that girls participate equally in all parts of an activity. If necessary, practise positive discrimination.

COMPASITO can only be as effective in promoting human rights as you, the facilitator, are!

**References**

1  All different – All Equal, Education Pack on ideas, resources, methods and activities for informal intercultural education with young people and adults, Council of Europe, 2004. p. 122.

# Summary of activities

| NR | Title | Type of Activity | Complexity | Duration | Themes | Themes | Themes | Page |
|---|---|---|---|---|---|---|---|---|
| 1 | A Body of Knowledge | Making a collage, discussion | 1 | 2x60 | Discrimination | Education and leisure | Health and welfare | 53 |
| 2 | A Constitution for Our Group | Consensus building, rule making | 3 | 90-135 | Citizenship | Democracy | Participation | 56 |
| 3 | A Human Rights Calendar | Drawing, painting, cutting | 2 | 120 | General human rights | | | 60 |
| 4 | Advertising Human Rights | Story telling, drawing, writing | 3 | 120-180 | General human rights | Media and Internet | | 64 |
| 5 | Blindfolded | Simulation, discussion | 1 | 45 | Discrimination | Health and welfare | Participation | 67 |
| 6 | Board Games | Board game | 2 | 45 | General human rights | | | 70 |
| 7 | Boys Don't Cry | Discussion and statement exercise, theatre | 2 | 90 | Discrimination | Gender equality | General human rights | 82 |
| 8 | Bullying Scenes | Discussion with movement | 2 | 60 | Violence | Discrimination | | 85 |
| 9 | Capture the Castle | Active adventure game, experiental learning | 2 | 120 | Peace and human security | | | 89 |
| 10 | COMPASITO Reporter | Photo reportage or other forms of reporting | 2 | 90-120 | Environment | Health and welfare | Participation | 92 |
| 11 | Cookie Monster | Group negotiation, discussion | 2 | 40-60 | Peace and human security | Poverty and social exclusion | | 95 |
| 12 | Dear Diary | Story telling, discussion | 2 | 60 | Discrimination | Health and welfare | Poverty and social exclusion | 99 |
| 13 | Every Vote Counts | Discussion, planning, simulation | 3 | 2x60 | Citizenship | Democracy | | 103 |
| 14 | From Bystander to Helper | Story telling, discussion | 2 | 60 | Peace and human security | Violence | | 108 |
| 15 | Human Rights in the News | Scanning media, making a poster, discussion | 2 | 45 | General human rights | Media and Internet | | 110 |
| 16 | Modern Fairytale | Story telling, discussion | 2 | 60 | Discrimination | Education and leisure | Violence | 113 |
| 17 | Most Important for Whom? | Prioritizing, consensus building, discussion | 3 | 60 | General human rights | | | 118 |
| 18 | My Universe of Rights | Artistic activity | 3 | 2x60 | General human rights | | | 122 |
| 19 | Once Upon a Time | Story telling, discussion | 2 | 40 | Democracy | Discrimination | Gender equality | 125 |
| 20 | Picture Games | Playing with pictures | 2 | 30 | Discrimination | General human rights | Media and Internet | 130 |
| 21 | Picturing Ways Out of Violence | Creating human photos, discussion | 1 | 60 | Violence | | | 133 |
| 22 | Puppets Tell the Story | Dramatization of a story with puppets, discussion | 2 | 120 | General human rights | | | 135 |
| 23 | Putting Rights on the Map | Drawing, analysis, discussion | 2-3 | 60 | General human rights | | | 138 |
| 24 | Rabbit's Rights | Imagining, brainstorming, discussion | 1 | 30 | General human rights | | | 141 |
| 25 | Red Alert | Active outdoor group game | 2 | 60 | General human rights | | | 143 |
| 26 | Rights Mobile | Creative activity | 2 | 120-180 | General human rights | Gender equality | | 148 |
| 27 | Sailing to a New Land | Prioritizing, discussion | 1 | 45 | General human rights | | | 152 |
| 28 | Silent Speaker | Role play, guessing game | 2 | 45 | Discrimination | Health and welfare | Participation | 160 |
| 29 | Take a Step Forward | Role play, simulation, discussion | 2 | 60 | General human rights | Discrimination | Poverty and social exclusion | 163 |
| 30 | The Battle for the Orange | Group competition and discussion | 1 | 30 | Peace and human security | | | 169 |
| 31 | The Invisibles are Coming | Active group competition | 2 | 120-1/2 day | Discrimination | | | 171 |
| 32 | Waterdrops | Playing, discussion | 2 | 60 | Environment | General human rights | | 176 |
| 33 | We are Family | Drawing, discussion | 2 | 60 | Discrimination | Family and alternative care | Gender equality | 180 |
| 34 | What a Wonderful World | Drawing, discussion | 1 | 50 | Discrimination | Environment | Poverty and social exclusion | 182 |
| 35 | What I Like and What I Do | Stating preferences, discussion | 2 | 45 | Discrimination | Family and alternative care | Gender equality | 185 |
| 36 | What if ...? | Analysis, discussion, dramatization | 3 | 60 | General human rights | Education and leisure | Poverty and social exclusion | 187 |
| 37 | Where Do You Stand? | Discussion with some movement | 1 | 30-40 | General human rights | Participation | | 192 |
| 38 | Who's Behind Me? | Playing with pictures, discussion | 2 | 30 | General human rights | Discrimination | Media and Internet | 195 |
| 39 | Who Should Decide? | Decision making, discussion | 2 | 45 | Family and alternative care | Participation | | 198 |
| 40 | Words that Wound | List making, prioritizing, discussion | 2 | 60 | Discrimination | Gender equality | Violence | 202 |
| 41 | World Summer Camp | Prioritizing, negotiation, discussion | 2-3 | 45 -60 | Discrimination | General human rights | | 205 |
| 42 | Zabderfilio | Story telling, reflective activity | 1 | 35 | General human rights | Discrimination | | 209 |

# 1. A Body of Knowledge

I didn't know how much I knew!

| | |
|---|---|
| Themes | Discrimination, Education and leisure, Health and welfare |
| Level of complexity | Level 1 |
| Age | 7-13 years |
| Duration | 2 x 60-minute sessions |
| Group size | 4 – 30 children |
| Type of activity | Making a collage, discussion |
| Overview | Children fill a body outline with knowledge and skills related to the different parts of the body. They discuss how to gain this knowledge, and what happens if you lack the opportunity or right, or if parts of your body are not developed as they should be. |
| Objectives | • To discover one's own and others' abilities and knowledge<br>• To raise awareness of ways and places of learning<br>• To discuss the right to education<br>• To become aware of differently-abled people |
| Preparation | • Collect magazines. |
| Materials | • Large sheets of paper<br>• Markers<br>• Magazines for cutting out pictures<br>• Scissors, glue and other materials for making a collage |

## Instructions

### Session 1:

1. Introduce the topic by reminding the children that they have a human right to be able to learn and develop as much as possible. Observe that they already have a lot of knowledge and skills that they probably don't think about. Ask them, for example, to name some things that they know how to do that they didn't know when they were five or six years old (e.g. read, write, count money, tell time). Explain that this activity will look at the right to learn and develop.

2. Divide the children into groups of four and give each group a sheet of paper large enough to draw the outline of one of the children on it, and materials for making a collage. Explain the activity:

   a. Each group will draw a life-size outline of a child.

   b. Then think about what you know and what you can do best. For each thing you know or can do, think of which part of your body you need for that. Include physical (e.g. singing, riding a bicycle), mental (e.g. doing maths, remembering jokes) and personality skills (e.g. being a friend, keeping a secret).

   c. Then make this knowledge or ability visible: draw, paint, write or paste representations of these things on a part of the body you would use. For example, if you are good at soccer, you might draw a soccer ball on the figure's foot (or head?); if you read well, you might cut out a book and place it near the eyes or head of the figure; if you are a good singer, you might show musical notes coming from the figure's mouth).

   d. Also think of other things you know and can do, not just what you do best.

3. Let the children work on this task until their figure is more or less completely covered with drawings / pictures / slogans, etc.

4. Bring the children together and ask each group to 'introduce' their 'child' to the others, explaining some of the skills and knowledge they have included. If possible leave these figures on the wall until the next session.

**Session 2:**

1. Ask the children to collect their figures and return to their original small groups. Give these instructions:

   a. Think again about the knowledge and abilities you illustrated on your child. How did you get that knowledge and ability? What place or person, institution or situation helped you learn those things? For example, you might have learnt to knit or play cards from a grandparent, you might have learnt a game from children in your neighbourhood, or you might have learnt about the history of your country in school.

   b. When you can identify where you got certain knowledge or skills, draw an arrow from the representation of that skill out to the margin of the paper and write down the name of the source of learning.

2. Bring the children together again and ask them to present their results to the whole group. List the sources of learning as they are mentioned, checking items each time they are mentioned.

**Debriefing and Evaluation**

1. Debrief the activity by asking question such as these:

   a. Was it easy to find things you are able to do?

   b. Are there big differences between the collages?

   c. Did you forget any important ability on the collage?

   d. Do you always remember where you learnt the skills / abilities?

   e. Was it always only one place / person who taught you this?

   f. Why do you think you were asked to remember how you gained your knowledge or skills?

2. Relate the activity to human rights by asking questions such as these:

   a. Do you think that all children can learn the things you have mentioned? Why or why not?

   b. What people and institutions do children need to be able to learn these things?

   c. Are certain people and institutions more important than others (e.g. is a school more important than a sports club)?

   d. What happens if some of these sources of learning are missing?

      i. For example, what if there were no school? How can children learn to write and read? What happens if they don't learn these skills? Is it important? How will it affect the rest of their lives?

      ii. For example, if there were no other children to play with, no family members to learn from, or no youth groups or clubs?

      iii. For example, if a child is disabled and cannot participate in schools and clubs or play with other children?

   e. You related different part of your body to different knowledge and skills. What happens if a child has a disability and cannot use this part of the body? Are there alternative ways to do things and learn things? How could a child with a disability develop other abilities?

   f. Do you know someone who has limited possibilities to learn? How do you think this person copes? Do you support this person?

   g. Why do you think children have a human right to learn and develop?

### Suggestions for follow-up

- Pin the collages to a wall so that the children and others can see them.
- The activities 'Blindfolded', p. 67, and 'Silent Speaker', p. 160, encourage children to consider how they might cope with a disability. 'Dear Diary', p. 99, asks children to consider the same experience through the eyes of three different children, one with a learning disability and another with a chronic illness.

### Ideas for action

- Invite someone with a learning disability or an NGO dealing with this target group to discuss learning disabilities and alternative learning strategies with the children.
- Introduce the concept of learning styles with the children (See Chapter III., p. 37), emphasizing that there are many different kinds of intelligence and ways to learn. Encourage the children to define their own learning styles and those ways which are easier or more challenging for them. Try to develop strategies with the children for how to support each other's learning.

### Tips for the facilitator

- This activity could also be run with the children working on individual figures or working in pairs.
- Encourage children to give their 'person' a name, and to write his or her name on their collage as well as the names of all the members of the group.
- Some children may have difficulty in remembering how they learnt something, especially if they learnt it from a person outside the formal education system. Remind them that they learn a lot from each other as well as family members and other adults in their lives. Help them see that contact with other children is an important source of learning that a disabled child might be denied. It is not necessary to attribute every skill the children have listed! The goal is to enable the children to recognize the importance of many sources of learning and development.
- In the debriefing, help children make the connection between the way they gained knowledge or skills and what happens when a child does not have access to such places, institutions, people or situations.
- Emphasize that everyone has an equal right to learn, although they may not all learn in the same way.

# 2. A Constitution for Our Group

Who has responsibility for my rights?

| | |
|---|---|
| Themes | Citizenship, Democracy, Participation |
| Level of complexity | Level 3 |
| Age | 10-13 years |
| Duration | Phase 1: 60–90 minutes; Phase 2: 30-45 minutes |
| Group size | 10–30 children |
| Type of activity | Discussion, consensus building, rule making |
| Overview | Children develop a group 'constitution' stating their rights and responsibilities |
| Objectives | • To understand the relationship of rights to responsibilities<br>• To connect rights and responsibilities in daily life<br>• To emphasize participation in the creation and protection of rights<br>• To create an agreed set of rules and responsibilities for the group |
| Preparation | None |
| Materials | • Pencil and paper for each participant<br>• Flip chart and markers<br>• Optional: Copies of the simplified CRC |

## Instructions

### Phase One

- Explore children's experience and understanding of rules and responsibilities, starting with some restrictions that they already understand. Ask them to complete sentence such as this: "I don't have the right to ___ because ..." (e.g. I don't have the right to hit people when I am angry because ... / I don't have the right to treat people unfairly.). List these and then ask the children to turn the statements from positive to negative (e.g. I have the right not to be hit / I have the right to be treated fairly.).

- When children understand the process of creating positive rights statements such as these, divide them into small groups of four or five. Give each group paper and markers. Explain that:
  - Each small group should make three or four basic rules for the whole group.
  - They should use the phrase "Everyone has the right to..." (e.g. Everyone has the right to participate.).
  - They can only write this down as a right if everyone in the group agrees.
  - The goal is not to have many rules but rules that everyone accepts.

- Bring the whole group back together and ask each group to present their rules. Record them on a chart such as the one below.
  - First ask for specific rights that groups have identified. Combine similar rights, asking for group approval of any revised language. List these on the flipchart under the 'Rights' column.
  - After listing a right, ask what specific responsibility every individual has to see that everyone enjoys this right. Write this in the 'Responsibilities' column next to the right, using language such as, "I have the responsibility to...", or "I should..."

- Then ask what responsibility each right involves. Write this as a statement next to the right statement, using the first person (e.g. I have the responsibility no t to exclude someone from participating).

| CONSTITUTION | |
| --- | --- |
| *RIGHTS* | *RESPONSIBILITIES* |
| Everyone has the right to be treated fairly.<br>Everyone has the right to express an opinion. | I have the responsibility to treat everyone fairly.<br>I should give everyone the right to express an opinion. |

- After including all the rights and responsibilities listed by the small groups, ask the children to review their draft constitution.
  - Point out that it is better to have a few good rules than too many not-so-good rules. Can any of these rights and responsibilities be combined? Can any be eliminated?
  - Are there other rights and responsibilities that need to be added?
- When the lists of rights and responsibilities are complete, ask the children whether they could use these statements as a kind of 'constitution' for their group.
  - Are they willing to observe these rules that they made themselves?
  - Who is responsible for making sure that everyone follows this 'constitution'?
  - What happens when someone violates one of the rights?
  - Is it necessary to have consequences for not following rules? Why?
- When you have arrived at a final version of the 'constitution', make a clean copy and hang it in a prominent place. Explain that these will be our rules for working and playing together, for both children and adults.
- Conclude the discussion by emphasizing that rules and responsibilities help us to live together in a way that everyone's rights are respected. Rules protect our rights (e.g. to participate, to have an opinion, to learn, to play, etc.), keep us safe and healthy, and also give us responsibilities to respect the rights of others.

## Debriefing and Evaluation

1. Ask the children to discuss their experience of this activity.
   a. Was it easy for your small group to develop a list of rights? Was it easy to draw up the list of responsibilities?
   b. Was it easy to work together in a group? What are some of the advantages and disadvantages of working together in a group?
   c. Were some ideas for rights not agreed on by the whole group? Why?
   d. What did you do with the ideas that were not agreed on? Did anybody try to convince the rest of the group in order to get agreement? Were any ideas reconsidered?
   e. What did you learn about yourself in this activity? What did you learn about rules and responsibilities?
   f. Did you learn anything about democracy?
2. Discuss the purpose of rules and responsibilities by asking questions such as the ones below, and recording their responses.
   a. What rules do you have in your life (e.g. at home, at school, in other settings)? Who made these rules?
   b. What responsibilities do you have? Who gave you these responsibilities?
   c. Do adults have rules and responsibilities too? Where did these come from?
   d. Why do we all have rules and responsibilities? Do we need them?
   e. What happens when somebody doesn't follow the rules? Is it necessary to have consequences for not following rules? Why?

3. Discuss enforcement of rights and responsibilities, asking questions such as these:
   a. Now that you have agreed on rights and responsibilities, how will you make sure that everyone observes them?
   b. Who has the responsibility to see that these rights are respected?
   c. Should there be some consequence for a person who does not observe the rules? Who should decide on the consequences?

**Phase Two**

1. A few days or weeks after making the Constitution, ask the children to reconsider it. Point out that laws often have to be improved, eliminated or added.
   a. Do they still agree on the rights and responsibilities they developed earlier?
   b. Are some responsibilities harder to observe than others? Why
   c. Does anything in their Constitution need to be changed? Eliminated? Added?

2. Discuss enforcement of rules and responsibilities, asking questions such as these:
   a. Are some rights violated more often than others? Why?
   b. Who is taking the responsibility to see that these rights are respected?
   c. Who decides what happens when someone violates one of the group's rules?
   d. Does the group need to work together to establish some consequences for breaking the rules?

### Debriefing and Evaluation

- Discuss what it means to have rules for the group that were made by the group itself. Relate this process to the way laws are made in a democracy.
    - Does it help to have a Constitution for our group?
    - What difference does it make that the group made its own rules?

### Suggestions for follow-up

- You may wish that every child has and keeps a copy of the group's 'constitution'.
- When conflicts or problems arise in the group, try to use the group's constitution to resolve them. Real-life problems often help to bring out needs to revise the 'constitution'.
- You may want to take Phase 2, Step 2 further to enable the children to develop cooperatively some established consequences for breaking the rules.
- Give the children copies of the simplified CRC, p. 296. Ask them to compare their constitution with this document of rights for all the children of the world. Are there rights and corresponding responsibilities in the CRC that they would want to add to their Constitution?
- With older children, discuss why children need a special convention that defines their rights. Do children have different human rights from those of adults? Different responsibilities? Help the children understand the relationship between responsibilities and the CRC principle of evolving capacities.
- 'EVERY VOTE COUNTS', P. 103, which engages children in the process of democratic decision making, makes a good preliminary or follow-up activity.

### Ideas for action

- Ask the children to find out if their school, team, or club has a set of rules or policies and procedures that guard and protect the rights of the children, and if those rules also state their responsibilities. If so, ask them to evaluate these rules:

- Who made them?
- Do you agree with these rules?
- Can they be changed? If so, how?
- What happens when people don't follow these rules?

## Tips for the facilitator

- Some children may not be familiar with the word or concept of 'constitution'. You may decide not to introduce the word (Phase 1, Step 4) and simply call the document 'the rules and responsibilities for our group'. On the other hand, you may want to introduce the concept of a constitution prior to this activity, asking children to find out the answers to the following:
  - Does our country have a constitution?
  - What is in our constitution?
  - Who wrote it? When was it written?
  - Who pays attention to whether it is respected or not?
  - What happens when someone does not follow our constitution?
- Many children have a negative attitude towards rules, seeing them only as restriction on their freedom. You may need to spend some time discussing and giving examples of how we need rules to live together.
- Young children may need help differentiating between responsibilities in terms of personal obligations towards others (e.g. taking turns, respecting differences, refraining from violence) from limitations or tasks placed on them by adults (e.g. brushing teeth, making the bed, raising hands in school, doing homework).
- Stress the connection between the rights and roles/responsibilities of every person, both adults and children. Include the responsibility to enforce rules as well as that of respecting them.

## Adaptations

1. To make this activity less complex for younger children, keep the experience concrete:
   a. Keep the discussion focused on rights and responsibilities.
   b. Don't go into the complications of rules, enforcement, and responsibility for enforcement.
2. For older children you can go further into the abstract relationship between rights, rules, and responsibilities with debriefing questions such as these:
   a. What is the relationship between rights and rules?
   b. What is the difference between rules and responsibilities?

# 3. A Human Rights Calendar

Every day of the year is a human rights day!

| | |
|---|---|
| Themes | General human rights |
| Level of complexity | Level 2 |
| Age | 8-13 years |
| Duration | 120 minutes to create the calendar; additional sessions each month |
| Group size | 2-24 children |
| Type of activity | Drawing, painting, cutting, presenting information graphically |
| Overview | Making a group calendar to mark important human right dates |
| Objectives | • To raise general awareness of the many facets of human rights<br>• To raise awareness of divisions of time (e.g. months, weeks, days of the week) and the time of special occasions<br>• To enhance planning skills<br>• To develop imagination about creating celebrations |
| Preparation | • Prepare one calendar page for each month with days of the week written in columns.<br>• Prepare and copy a list of Special Days to Remember for each group.<br>• A paper square marked 'BIRTHDAY!' for each child and adult member of the group. |
| Materials | • 12 sheets of A4 paper, if possible laminated in plastic or mounted on cardboard<br>• Copies of a handout of special days to remember<br>• Pens, markers or coloured pencils for each group<br>• Sticky tape, glue or Velcro<br>• A paper square marked 'BIRTHDAY!' for each child and facilitator<br>• Optional: additional art supplies, a small calendar, a child-friendly copy of CRC (see Handout) |

## Instructions

1. Explain to the children that they are going to make a calendar that will help them know when special days are coming up, especially those that relate to human rights.

2. Discuss with the children what human rights are and explain (if they don't know already) that there are also children's rights. Ask the children for examples of children's rights and give examples of your own if necessary.

3. Ask the children if they know of any special days that can be linked to children's or human rights. Ask for other holidays and ask them to relate them to children's or human rights (e.g. religious holidays can be linked to Freedom of Thought, Conscience and Belief; national holidays to right to nationality; cultural holidays to right to culture). List all these. Motivate the children to be creative and think of some days that can be linked to human rights. Encourage them to guess. Then distribute the list of 'special days to remember'. Add other holidays mentioned in the discussion. Discuss how these holidays could be celebrated to show their importance to human rights.

Divide the children into four groups and assign each group three months to work on. Give each group three calendar sheets, colouring materials, coloured paper and other supplies needed to complete their calendars.

4. Explain the instructions:

   a. First put in the dates of each month.

   b. Then write in the names of important holidays that come in that month and decorate the

**Source:** Adapted from *COMPASS: A Manual on Human rights education with Young People* (Council of Europe, 2002), p. 263.

square(s) to make the holiday stand out. The decoration should be linked to the theme of the holiday and/or the human right(s) concerned. When a holiday lasts for more than one day, mark every day of that holiday. Include school holidays.

  c. Then make a cover that reads 'HOLIDAY' for these special days so that uncovering them can be a surprise; attach this cover with Velcro or sticky tape.

5. When the pages are complete, put them on the wall or on the floor so everyone can see them. Explain that some very important holidays have been left out.

6. Give every child one square that says 'BIRTHDAY!' Ask each child to go to the calendar page for his or her birthday, write '_____'s Birthday' on the correct day of the calendar and cover it with the square marked 'BIRTHDAY)!' (hinged with sticky tape so it can be lifted and removed). When this task is completed, ask why birthdays are related to human rights and explain that everyone has a human right to life and to a name.

## Debriefing and Evaluation

1. Discuss the activity using questions such as these:
  a. Did you enjoy this activity?
  b. What did you learn about the calendar? About human rights?
  c. Which of these special days do you look forward to? Why?

2. Point out that although we celebrate these special days, we enjoy human rights every day. Ask questions such as these:
  a. What are some human rights you enjoy every day? What human right(s) are you enjoying this minute?
  b. Does every child have these rights? Does every child have the opportunity to enjoy them?
  c. What can we do to make sure that every child's rights are protected? Whose job is this?

3. At the beginning of every month, turn to the new calendar page.
  a. Remove the covers to reveal the events coming up.
  b. Explain the meaning of the holiday, drawing a connection to human rights.
  c. Plan together how to celebrate each one.

## Suggestions for follow-up

During the week of a special human rights day, choose an activity from COMPASITO that addresses issues related to a particular holiday. Use the thematic chart on p. 58 to help with this selection.

## Ideas for action

• Ask the children to plan how to celebrate special days, including birthdays.

• The children may want to make a celebration of some holidays, such as Human Rights Day or Children's Rights Day in the whole community.

## Tips for the facilitator

• Do not reproduce the whole list of special days but select days of relevance to your group, even if the children are not yet familiar with that holiday. The days marked with a star have particular importance to children and/or human rights.

• Move around among the groups while they work on the calendar to make sure the children understand the meaning of each holiday they are working on.

- If you include national or local cultural and religious holidays, be sure to include all those celebrated by the families and communities of children in the group. When in doubt, ask the children to bring a list from home.

- To be sure that each child's birthday is celebrated equally, develop a group ritual with the same privileges, recognition or treats for every birthday child. Depending on the local culture, you may want to use a child's name day rather than their birthday.

- Look for ways to make the calendar lively and decorative. Encourage use of appropriate symbols for each holiday and names in other languages where appropriate.

- Adaptations:
  - For younger children:
    - Let them copy days of the month from a calendar. Call attention to the fact that different months have 28/29, 30 or 31 days and for that reason months don't always start on the same weekday.
    - Give them a calendar with the days added and ask them to add only the special days.
  - For older children: give them copies of the child-friendly version of the CRC and/or UDHR and let them try to connect the holidays on their pages with specific articles of the document..

## HANDOUT: SUGGESTED DAYS TO REMEMBER

| January 1 | World Peace Day |
|---|---|
| March 8 | International Women's Day |
| March 21 | World Forest Day |
| March 22 | World Water Day |
| April 7 | World Health Day |
| April 22 | Earth Day |
| May 1 | International Workers Day |
| May 8 | World Red Cross and Red Crescent Day |
| May 9 | Europe Day |
| May 15 | International Day of Families |
| June 1 | World Children's Day* |
| June 5 | World Environment Day |
| June 21 | World Peace and Prayer Day |
| August 7 | Education Day |
| September 8 | International Literacy Day |
| October 1 | International Music Day |
| October 5 | World Teachers' Day |
| October 16 | World Food Day |
| October 25 | United Nations Day |
| November 9 | Day against Racism |
| November 16 | International Day for Tolerance |
| November 20 | Universal Children's Day |
| December 3 | International Day of Disabled Persons |
| December 10 | Human Rights Day* |

*Children are celebrated on both June 1, International Children's Day, and November 20, Universal Children's Day, the day observed by the UN and UNESCO. In addition many countries observe their own Children's Day.

# HANDOUT: CALENDAR SHEET

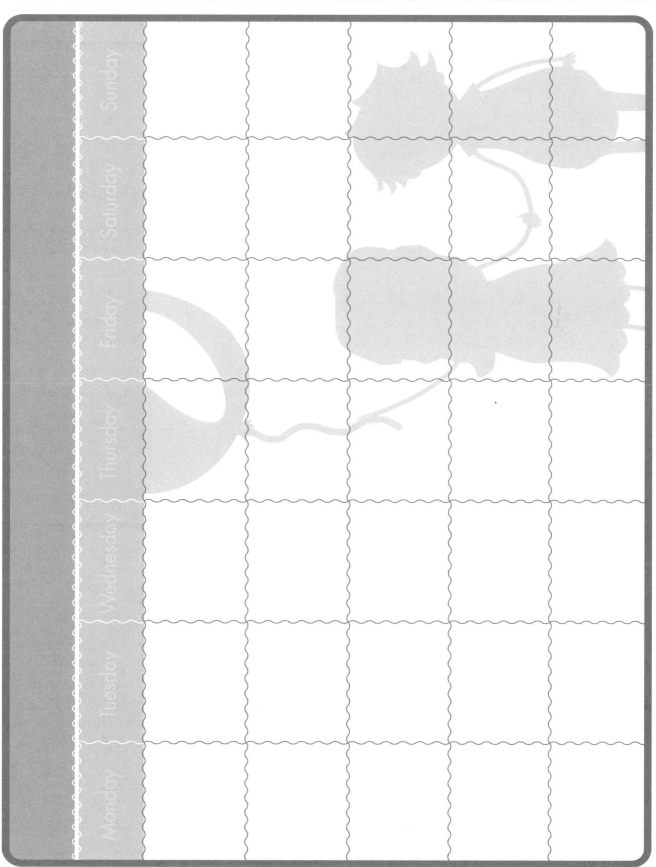

# 4. Advertising Human Rights

Let's tell the world about human rights!

| | |
|---|---|
| Themes | General human rights, adaptable to any theme, Media and Internet |
| Level of complexity | Level 3 |
| Age | 10-13 years |
| Group size | 4-24 children |
| Time | 120-180 min |
| Type of activity | Story telling, drawing, writing |
| Overview | Children develop a TV advertisement for children's human rights |
| Objectives | • To develop critical thinking skills about advertising and the media<br>• To practise creativity and communications skills<br>• To develop ideas on how to promote children's human rights<br>• To deepen understanding about human rights |
| Preparation | • If possible, arrange video equipment to record the advertisements |
| Materials | • Paper and art supplies |

## Instructions

1. Divide children into groups of three or four. Explain that their group has been asked to advertise children's human rights. They will make an advertisement for television that lasts from one to three minutes that makes people aware of and/or understand that right.

2. Ask children to describe some advertisements on TV that have caught their attention. Brainstorm features of good advertisements (e.g. clever phrases, sound effects, music, humour, serious message).

3. Discuss the audience for their advertisement. Is it aimed at children, parents, teachers, the general public or all of these? Discuss ways in which the advertisement can be made attractive to their chosen audience.

4. Explain that each group should choose a right they want to advertise and the audience(s) they want to address. Encourage them to choose a right that they think people really need to know about and the people who really need to know about it. Ask someone from each group to report their right to you, and what audience they have decided upon.

5. Once groups have chosen a right, they should develop an idea to advertise it. Encourage them to consider many different ways to present the right (e.g. a story that they act out, a song they sing, a cartoon for which they draw the storyboard). Remind them that this will be a video for TV so it should be visually interesting and have action, not just 'talking heads'. It should not be too complex to be presented in less than three minutes.

6. Circulate among the groups to monitor their progress. Once a group has completed its advertisement, ask them to give it a title and begin to practise.

7. When all the groups have planned their advertisements, bring the whole group together to share their ideas and get feedback from others. Ask each group to explain their right, their audience, and their ideas. If they are ready, they may try to perform it as well. After each description or performance, encourage constructive suggestions and feedback, asking questions such as:

   a. Will this idea appeal to the chosen audience?

   b. Will it get the idea of the right across clearly?

    c. What do you like about these ideas?

    d. Can you offer any suggestions for improvement?

8. Give the groups time to improve and practise their advertisements.

9. Ask each group to present their advertisement and plans to each other.

## Debriefing and Evaluation

1. Debrief the activity, asking questions such as:

    a. Were any parts of this activity especially challenging? Especially fun?

    b. Did you learn something about how advertisements are made?

    c. Was it hard to think in images rather than just words?

    d. Was it hard to think about how to reach a particular audience?

    e. Are advertisements always positive? Why or why not?

    f. What did you learn from the other storyboards?

    g. Will this activity change the way you look at TV?

2. Relate the activity to human rights, asking questions such as:

    a. Why did your group choose that particular right?

    b. Why did you choose that particular audience?

    c. What kind of reaction or action do you think your advertisement would produce?

    d. Is a TV advertisement a good way to send people a message about human rights? Why or why not?

    e. Did your advertisement involve other rights besides the one you focused on?

    f. Can a right stand alone or is it always connected to other rights?

    g. Can you think of any rights that would be difficult to advertise or represent?

    h. Did any of your characters represent stereotypes? If so, does that have a negative effect? Why or why not?

    i. Why is it important for people to know about their rights?

    j. Who needs education about children's human rights?

## Suggestions and follow up

1. Explain that many advertising campaigns combine TV advertisements with graphic advertisements in print media such as magazines or newspapers or as posters on kiosks, buses and in other public places. Start by asking the children to look through print media or their neighbourhoods to find advertisements they like, and to discuss what makes them attractive. Then ask the children to develop a two-dimensional, graphic advertisement of a right. Where the technology is available, these graphic advertisements could also be created on computer. Make an exhibition of these for the children's centre or school.

2. Point out that many advertising campaigns employ a famous spokesperson. Ask for some examples from their experience. Whom would they like to introduce and/or take part in their advertisement? Why would that person be appropriate for the right or audience they have chosen?

3. Discuss with the children what it would be like to make a longer human rights video that told a story.

    a. How would it be different from an advertisement?

    b. What aspects of the story would be important (e.g. a good story; practical considerations such as expenses; a human rights message)?

    c. What aspects of the proposed video would be important (e.g. requiring actors other than children in the group, lots of props and costumes, unsafe scenes)?

f. What are some things you enjoy doing that would be easy to enjoy even if you had a disability? What about things which might be difficult to do? Would you still enjoy doing them?

2. Draw out stereotypes based on disability, asking questions such as:

   a. What kinds of things do you think children with disabilities like doing? Are they different from the things you like doing? Why or why not?

   b. Do you think children with disabilities have friends? Are all their friends other children with disabilities? What might make it hard to have a disabled child as a friend? What might make it interesting?

   c. What do you think children with disabilities want to be when they grow up? Are they different from you? Why or why not?

   d. This activity helps you understand how children with visual disabilities sometimes need help to do things that are easy for people with good vision. Can you think of other kinds of disability that might need assistance?

   e. Everyone has a right to the things they need to live a full life. What are some things that you need? Do children with disabilities need these things too?

## Suggestions for Follow-up

- Ask children to think of an activity that they could do with everyone blindfolded. For safety reasons select a seated activity (e.g. a guessing game, a puzzle, a role play). Debrief carefully to emphasize both the skills that are lacking and those that remain. How could the activity be adapted to include children with a visual disability?

- To emphasize how the need for assistance also challenges the would-be helper, you might try a short activity such as a 'trust walk', with a blindfolded child being lead around a safe place by another. Then exchange roles. Debrief.

- Give the children the opportunity to experiment with other kinds of disabilities such as limited mobility (e.g. a 'sack race', experimentation with crutches, one arm in a sling) or the inability to speak, read or count.

- Several other activities address children with disabilities. 'SILENT SPEAKER', P. 160, experience of deaf children. 'A BODY OF KNOWLEDGE', P, 53, considers the effects of exclusion on the development of children with disabilities.

## Ideas for action

- Children could evaluate their meeting or living place, school or community: could a person with disabilities live, work or play here with comfort and safety? Could anything be done to make these places more accessible?

- Where do children with disabilities live and go to school in this community? Children could investigate where disabled children with special needs live and learn and why they are or are not among other children.

- Organise an exchange day with a group of disabled or mixed ability children from another school, organisation or children's group.

## Tips for the facilitator

- This activity assumes that none of the children themselves have disabilities. In many groups of children at least some have disabilities, although they may not be immediately obvious (e.g. children who wear glasses could be considered visually impaired). Be sensitive to children and their concept of themselves and their abilities and/or disabilities. Use disabled children in the class as resource peo-

68

ple for explaining answers to some of the debriefing questions, but only after first privately asking if they are comfortable in this role.

- Balance the discussion of need for assistance on the part of people with disabilities with an affirmation of their competence to do many things for themselves. Emphasize that people with disabilities have the same basic need and rights as everyone else.

- Child cut-outs could be mounted with Velcro, sticky tape or drawing pins (or use cardboard or paper mounted on corkboard.)

## Variations

- You could use just one or two paper dolls, asking different children to add articles of clothing. Using at least two allows for both a boy and a girl paper doll, but you could use the single doll twice, once as a boy and once as a girl. You might discuss gender issues and stereotypes related to disability.

- If you have large pieces of paper, you could make an outline of members of the group to use paper dolls.

# 6. Board Games

How well do you know your rights?

| | |
|---|---|
| Themes | General Human Rights |
| Complexity | Level 2 |
| Age | 8-13 years |
| Group Size | 2-6 children per board |
| Duration | 45 minutes |
| Type of Activities | Board games |

This activity contains two different board games with different rules, discussing human rights, that you can play on the same board provided as a handout. The children may play the game by themselves but the facilitator is needed to support them and to run the debriefing.

## 6a, Do You Know Your Rights?

| | |
|---|---|
| Overview: | As in 'Snakes and Ladders', in this activity children move forwards or backwards according to the cards they take. However, in this game they can 'neutralize' a negative card if they can name the children's right that is being violated. |
| Objectives | • To build familiarity with the CRC<br>• To help children relate human rights to everyday life<br>• To raise awareness of human rights issues |
| Preparation | • Check the answers in advance to be sure you are familiar with the issues.<br>• Copy the board provided as a handout.<br>• Copy the instructions and list of 'Neutralizing Rights' on one sheet.<br>• Copy the rights cards and the penalty cards, one set for each group playing.<br>• Copy the child-friendly CRC. |
| Materials | • Game board, pieces and dice<br>• Game cards<br>• Sheet with instructions and list of 'Neutralizing Rights' |

**Instructions**

1. Divide children into groups of two to six and give each group a board, a dice, a set of the rights cards and the penalty cards, a sheet with instructions and a list of 'Neutralizing Rights'. Also give a copy of the child-friendly CRC to each player. In this game, the children should disregard the snakes and ladders on the board but use the coloured squares only. Game cards will inform players about what to do.

2. Explain the game:

   a. Roll the dice. The child with the highest number is the first player.

   b. The first player rolls the dice and moves forward according to the number on the dice.

   c. If a player falls into a coloured square, the player takes a card, reads it aloud and follows the instructions. These could be to go forwards, go backwards, or miss a turn.

   d. However, a card that says to go backwards can be 'neutralized' if the player can name the article of the CRC that is violated. In that case the player gets a bonus step forward.

   e. Continue with next person on the left of the first player.

   f. The first player to reach the end is the winner but the game should continue until every player has reached the end.

## Debriefing and Evaluation

1. Discuss the activity, asking questions such as these:

    a. What did you think of this game?

    b. Did you learn anything new about human rights? About the world around you?

    c. Did some of the situations seem strange or unfamiliar?

    d. Can you think of situations like them, both where human rights are respected and where they are violated?

## Tips for the Facilitator

- The children playing can use the list of neutralising rights and the CRC if they need to, or the facilitator can use the list.

- Adaptation for younger children: Omit identifying articles of the CRC to 'neutralize' backward steps.

- Because the children will have many questions about the cases given, a second facilitator is recommended if several groups are playing this game at once.

- Children might play the game in teams to help each other identify 'neutralizing rights'.

## HANDOUT: RIGHTS CARDS

### RIGHTS CARD 1

Your friend's parents separated this summer but your friend still lives with both of them on alternate weeks because that was his / her choice. Go forward 2 squares.

**CRC Article 12, Respect for the views of the child:**

Children have the right to express their opinion in saying what they think should happen when adults are making decisions that affect them, and to have their opinions taken into account.

### RIGHTS CARD 2

You learned that if you are in serious trouble you can always call for help. If you dial the emergency number and explain the situation, authorities can put you in touch with organizations that try to help children who are abandoned, mistreated or have other problems. Go forward 2 squares.

**CRC Article 19, Protection from all forms of violence, abuse & neglect:**

Governments should ensure that children are properly cared for, and protect them from violence, abuse and neglect by their parents, or anyone else who looks after them.

**CRC Article 36, Protection from other forms of exploitation:**

Children should be protected from any activities that could harm their development and well-being.

### RIGHTS CARD 3

In your friend's class, children who have more difficulties in learning get extra help from teachers. Go forward 2 squares.

**CRC Article 23, Disabled children:**

Children who have any kind of disability should have special care, support, and education so that they can lead full and independent lives to the best of their abilities.

# HANDOUT: RIGHTS CARDS

**RIGHTS CARD 4**

Your school principal learnt that some children in your community didn't come to school because their parents do not have legal permission to live here. The principal managed to get in touch with them and convinced them to send the children to school. Go forward 2 squares.

**CRC Article 28, Right to education:**

Children have a right to education, that is, to go to schools. ... Primary education should be free.

**RIGHTS CARD 5**

You have a right to know your human rights! Go forward 4 squares.

**CRC Article 29, The aims of education:**

Education should develop the child's personality, skills and talents to the full. Education prepares children for life. It should encourage children to respect their parents, and their own and other nations' cultures.

**RIGHTS CARD 6**

Teachers at our school are not allowed to use physical punishment or to insult children, even when they have behaved badly. Go forward 2 squares.

**CRC Article 28, Right to education:**

Discipline in schools should respect children's human dignity; violence (physical and moral) should not be used in discipline.

**RIGHTS CARD 7**

In your school there are many staircases but also elevators and ramps so that people who can't walk well and use wheel chairs can move around. Go forward 3 squares.

**CRC Article 23, Disabled Children:**

Children who have any kind of disability should have special care, support, and education so that they can lead full and independent lives to the best of their abilities.

**RIGHTS CARD 8**

Your friend's father had a bad accident and couldn't work for a long time. While he was recovering, the government helped the family to have enough money to buy food and pay the rent. Go forward 2 squares.

**CRC Article 26, Benefit from social security:**

The society in which a child lives should provide it with benefits of social security (education, culture, nutrition, health, and social welfare) that helps the child develop and live in good conditions. The Government should provide extra money for the children of families in need.

**RIGHTS CARD 9**

You learn that your rights should be protected even during wartime and that there are special agreements to be sure this happens. Go forward 2 squares.

**CRC Article 38, Protection of children affected by armed conflict:**

Governments should not allow children under 15 to join the army or take any direct part in hostilities. Moreover, children in war zones should receive special protection.

**PENALTY CARD 1**

One of your friends lo
not allowed. Go back :

**NEUTRALIZING RIGH**

Children should live ii
who cannot afford to |

**PENALTY CARD 2**

Your classmate's pare:
ent". Go back 4 square

**NEUTRALIZING RIGH**

The rights in the Con
whatever language th

**PENALTY CARD 3**

You learn that in some

**NEUTRALIZING RIGH**

Governments should :
zones should receive s

**PENALTY CARD 4**

A girl in your school i:
have time to do her h(

**NEUTRALIZING RIGH**

The Government shou
might lead to their ex

**PENALTY CARD 5**

We are only allowed
speak their language,

**NEUTRALIZING RIGH**

**CRC Article 29. The**

Education should dev
encourage children tc

OR

**CRC Article 30. Chil**

Children of minoritie
whether these are shɛ
Education should dev
encourage children tc

---

**RIGHTS CARD 10**

In your community there are libraries for children, magazines, films, games and TV shows made especially for children so that you can know and understand what is going on in the world. Go forward 2 squares.

**CRC Article 13, Freedom of expression and information:**

Children have the right to seek, get and share information, in all forms (art, written, broadcast and electronic…) as long as the information is not damaging to them or to others.

**RIGHTS CARD 11**

Bad luck! You have to have an operation. But good luck: you have the right to special protection and care and even to have one of your parents or someone you love stay with you! Go forward 2 squares.

**CRC Article 24, healthcare and health services:**

Children have the right to good quality health care that is medicine, hospitals and doctors when sick. Children also have the right to clean water, nutritious food, and a clean environment, so that they will stay healthy. Rich countries should help poorer countries achieve this.

**PENALTY CARD 1**

One of your friends loses one of his shoes but doesn't have enough money to buy a new pair. The school says barefoot children are not allowed. Go back 2 squares.

**DO YOU KNOW A RIGHT TO NEUTRALIZE THIS PENALTY?**

**PENALTY CARD 2**

Your classmate's parents are Roma. Their family is having trouble finding a place to live in because people say, "They are different". Go back 4 squares.

**DO YOU KNOW A RIGHT TO NEUTRALIZE THIS PENALTY?**

**PENALTY CARD 3**

You learn that in some countries children are forced to war to fight. They are hungry, thirsty and very scared. Go back to Square 1.

**DO YOU KNOW A RIGHT TO NEUTRALIZE THIS PENALTY?**

**PENALTY CARD 4**

A girl in your school is a model. She earns lots of money and has her picture in magazines. But she often misses class and doesn't have time to do her homework or to play with friends. She looks really tired. Go back 2 squares.

**DO YOU KNOW A RIGHT TO NEUTRALIZE THIS PENALTY?**

**PENALTY CARD 5:**

We are only allowed to spea
speak their language, even o
**DO YOU KNOW A RIGHT**

**PENALTY CARD 6**

There is a school in your com
upon. Miss a turn.
**DO YOU KNOW A RIGHT**

**PENALTY CARD 7**

Your friend's parents divorce
misses his dad. Go back 3 sq
**DO YOU KNOW A RIGHT**

**PENALTY CARD 8**

There is a girl in your class wl
ers and sisters. Go back 3 squ
**DO YOU KNOW A RIGHT**

**PENALTY CARD 9**

A boy in your class refuses to
**DO YOU KNOW A RIGHT**

**PENALTY CARD 10**

The boys at your school hav
squares.
**DO YOU KNOW A RIGHT**

### Ideas for action

Relate the cards to the children's experience. Discuss what can they do when violations such as these occur? Who are their allies in claiming their rights?

### Tips for the facilitator

- In the debriefing discussion encourage children to think of real experiences, focusing on violence, bullying, and situations of injustice or unfairness that they have experienced or observed.
- Make copies of the game board and distribute it to the children so that they can play the game with their family and friends.

## HANDOUT: CARDS

**Copy and cut out these cards or make others appropriate to your group.**

**Statement:** Anybody who gets married is no longer a child.

**Answer:** False/ It's a Violation
**CRC Article 1. Who is a child:** Everyone under 18 years of age is considered a child and thus, has all the rights in this convention

**Statement:** All children have the same human rights, no matter whether they or their parents are citizens of a particular country or not.

**Answer:** True/ It's a Right
**CRC Article 2. Non-discrimination:** The rights in the Convention apply to everyone ... wherever they come from and the state must protect the child from any discrimination.

**Statement:** Girls can only play on the football field if the boys are not using it.

**Answer:** False/ It's a Violation
**CRC Article 2., Non-discrimination:** The rights in the CRC apply to everyone whatever their race, colour, religion, sex, abilities, whatever they think or say, whatever language they speak and wherever they come from and the state must protect the child from any discrimination.

**Statement:** If you commit a crime, you could be put in jail with adult criminals.

**Answer:** False/ It's a Violation
**CRC Article 37. Torture, degrading treatment and deprivation of liberty:**
Children who break the law should not be treated cruelly. They should not be put in prison with adults and should be able to keep in contact with their families.

**Statement:** Our school librarian lets me sign out any book I want.

**Answer:** True/ It's a Right
**CRC Article 17. Child's access to appropriate information and media:** Children have the right to reliable information from diverse sources, including mass media. Television, radio, and newspapers should provide information that children can understand, and should not promote materials that could harm children.

**Statement:** A factory nearby puts smelly chemicals into the air that makes people cough.

**Answer:** False/ It's a Violation
**CRC Article 24. Healthcare and health services:** Children have the right to good quality healthcare that is medicine, hospitals and doctors when sick. Children also have the right to clean water, nutritious food, and a clean environment, so that they will stay healthy. Rich countries should help poorer countries achieve this.

# HANDOUT: CARDS

**Statement:** Only your father can decide what is best for you.

**Answer:** False/ It's a Violation
**CRC Article 18. Parents' joint responsibilities:** Both parents share responsibility for bringing up their children, and should always consider what is best for each child. Governments should help parents by providing services to support them, especially if both parents work.

**Statement:** Although I must use a wheelchair, I can go to school with the other kids in my neighbourhood. The school should provide me with a ramp.

**Answer:** True/ It's a Right
**CRC Article 23. Disabled children:** Children who have any kind of disability should have special care, support, and education so that they can lead full and independent lives to the best of their abilities.

**Statement:** Our school computers block some Internet sites.

**Answer:** True/ It's a Right
**CRC Article 17. Child's access to appropriate information and media:** Children have the right to reliable information from diverse sources, including mass media. Information sources should provide information that children can understand, and should not promote materials that could harm children.

**Statement:** In some places children, especially boys, must serve in an army.

**Answer:** False/ It's a Violation
**CRC Article 38. Protection of children affected by armed conflict:** Governments should not allow children under 15 to join the army or take any direct part in hostilities. Moreover, children in war zones should receive special protection.

**Statement:** When a baby is born, the parents must give it a name and officially register its birth.

**Answer:** True/ It's a Right
**CRC Article 7. Birth registration, name, nationality and right to know and be cared for by parents:** All children have the right to a name legally registered in an ID; they have the right to nationality; also the right to know and to be cared for by their parents.

**Statement:** My parents allow my seventeen-year-old brother to watch whatever he likes on TV but they restrict what I can watch because I'm only ten.

**Answer:** True/ It's a Right
**CRC Article 5. Parental guidance and the child's evolving capacities:** The family has the main responsibility for guiding how a child exercises his or her rights, based on growing age and maturity. Governments should respect this right.

**Statement:** Even though I am thirteen my parents read all my mail before they let me see it.

**Answer:** False/ It's a Violation
**CRC Article 16. Privacy, honour, and reputation:** Children have a right to privacy. The law should protect them from attacks against their way of life, their good name, their families, their homes and their letters and mail.

**Statement:** Class 8 produces a weekly magazine and distributes it to the neighbours.

**Answer:** True/ It's a Right
**CRC Article 13. Freedom of expression:** You have the right to think what you want, to say what you like, and nobody should forbid you from doing so. You should be able to share your ideas and opinion, regardless of frontiers.

**Statement:** My mother is working in another country now, but every month either she comes home or my father and I visit her.

**Answer:** True/ It's a Right
**CRC Article 10. Family reunification:** Families who live in different countries should be allowed to move between those countries so aren't and children can stay in contact.

**Statement:** My friends and I are forbidden to speak our native language at school.

**Answer**: False/ It's a Violation
**CRC Article 30. Children of minorities and indigenous people:** Children have a right to learn and use the language and customs of their families, whether these are shared by the majority of people in the country or not.

**Statement:** I have the right to a name, a country and a family.

**Answer**: True/ It's a Right
**CRC Article 8. Preservation of identity:** Governments should respect children's right to a name, a nationality and family ties. The governments have the obligation to protect and to re-establish the child identity.

**Statement:** Children who misbehave at school should not be given physical punishment of any kind.

**Answer**: True/ It's a Right
**CRC Article 28. Right to education:** Children have a right to education, that is, to go to schools. Discipline in schools should respect children's human dignity; violence should not be used in discipline.

**Statement:** My family came here to get away from the war in our country. But refugee children like me are not allowed to go to school here.

**Answer**: False/ It's a Violation
**CRC Article 22. Refugee children**: Special protection is to be given to refugee children. Children who come into a country as refugees should have the same rights as children born in that country.

**Statement:** I have a right to see both my parents, even if they are separated.

**Answer**: True/ It's a Right
**CRC Article 9. Separation from parents**: Children should not be separated from their parents unless it is for their own good, for example, if a parent is mistreating or neglecting a child. Children whose parents have separated have the right to stay in contact with both parents, unless this might hurt the child.

**Statement:** I miss a lot of school because when the baby is sick, I take care of him while my mother is at work.

**Answer**: False/ It's a Violation
**CRC Article 32. Child labour:** The Government should protect children from work that is dangerous, or that might harm their health or their education, or that might lead to their exploitation.

# 7. Boys Don't Cry!

## And Girls Are Smarter…

| | |
|---|---|
| Themes | Discrimination, Gender equality, General human rights |
| Level of complexity | Level 2 |
| Age | 8-13 years |
| Duration | 90 minutes |
| Group size | 8-20 children |
| Type of activity | Discussion, and statement exercise theatrical presentations |
| Overview | Children discuss and present their sketch on provocative statements |
| Objectives | • To discuss gender stereotypes and gender equality<br>• To promote tolerance<br>• To illustrate how stereotypes create discrimination |
| Preparation | • Choose 3 statements from the list or create new ones.<br>• Prepare 4 signs: I agree / I don't know / I am still thinking / I disagree.<br>• Place each in corners of the room.<br>• Choose additional statements to use for the sketch and write out on separate slips of paper. |
| Materials | • Papers for signs, slips of paper for statements |

## Instructions

### Part 1: Taking a Position

1. Explain the first part of the activity to the children:

   a. The room has been divided into four corners. Each corner is marked with a chart: I agree / I don't know / I am still thinking / I disagree.

   b. You will read out three different statements, one by one. The children take a position in a corner according to if they agree, disagree, have no opinion, or need more time to think.

2. Read out the first statement and wait till the children have chosen a position. Then ask children from different corners why they choose this position. Invite children to change positions if they change their mind after hearing others' reasons. Repeat this process for all three statements.

3. Bring children back into one group and discuss this part of the activity:

   a. Did anything about this activity surprise you?

   b. Why do you think people had different opinions about these statements?

   c. Did anyone's reasons lead you to change your position? Why?

   d. How can we know which position is 'right'?

### Part 2: Acting out a Position

4. Divide the children into small groups of no more than five and give each group a different statement. Explain that each group has about fifteen minutes to read their statement, discuss it, and create a short sketch (a mini play) that gives a message about this statement.

5. Ask each group to present their sketch. After each presentation, ask the audience what message they think the presentation was intended to give. Then ask the presenting group what message they wanted to make.

## Debriefing and Evaluation

1. Discuss the effects of gender stereotypes, asking questions such as these:
   a. What was similar about these statements? Do you know of other statements like these?
   b. Are there different rules and expectations for boys or girls in this group? In the classroom or in school? In the family? Does this make sense?
   c. Can you think of other ideas about how boys or girls are supposed to be or what they are supposed to do? Do similar ideas exist in other parts of our country? Of Europe? Of the world?
   d. What happens when a boy or girl doesn't agree with these ideas and wants to be or act differently? Have you ever been in a situation like that? How did you feel? What did you do?
   e. Do ideas about how males and females are expected to be affect adults as well as children?
2. Relate gender stereotypes to discrimination, asking questions such as these:
   a. How do these ideas about males and females limit our choices? Can you give some examples?
   b. How do these limitations affect our human rights?
   c. What can we do in the future so that boys and girls can act more freely the way they want to?

## Suggestions for follow-up

- The activity 'WHAT A WONDERFUL WORLD', P. 182, focuses on appearances and realities.
- The activity 'ONCE UPON A TIME...', P. 125, also deals with gender stereotypes.

## Ideas for action

Develop with the children a kind of personal 'code of conduct' for how people in the group should behave towards each other and how to ensure that girls and boys are treated equally. Mount it on the wall and refer to it when conflicts occur within the group.

## Tips for the facilitator

- Be careful not to reinforce the stereotypes this activity seeks to address. Be aware of your own prejudices and stereotypes relating to gender and how you may convey them to children as a facilitator for the group.
- Choose statements that show how, although girls and boys are physically different, they have equal rights. Choose statements controversial enough to elicit differences of opinions.
- Avoid polarising girls and boys. Depending on the group, you might create single-sex groups or sex-balanced groups for the sketches.
- Parents' attitudes strongly influence those of children. You may hear both positive and negative reactions from parents about this activity.

## Adaptations:

- To shorten the activity run only the part most relevant to your group.
- Rather than creating a sketch, ask the children to make a visual presentation (e.g. a drawing, cartoons, a collage with pictures from magazines, etc).

- Puppets are only for girls.
- Boys don't cry.
- Boys don't wear skirts.
- A girl cannot be the boss.
- Only boys play football.
- Girls are weak and boys are strong.
- Girls help their mothers. Boys help their fathers.
- It is better to be a girl then a boy.
- When something goes wrong, boys are always blamed first.
- Boys can say 'dirty words', but girls can't.
- Girls are smarter then boys.
- Girls win in fights because they fight 'dirty'.
- It is OK for boys to hit each other, but not for girls.
- Boys are lazier then girls.
- Girls are better liars then boys.

# 8. Bullying Scenes

Every bully is a coward in disguise!

| | |
|---|---|
| Themes | Discrimination, Violence |
| Level of complexity | Level 2 |
| Age | 7 - 13 years |
| Duration | 60 minutes |
| Group size | 5 - 20 children |
| Type of activity | Discussion with some movement. |
| Overview | Children discuss bullying and then position themselves to show how they would respond to different bullying scenarios.. |
| Objectives | • To deepen understanding of different kinds of bullying<br>• To identify strategies, people and organisations that can support children being bullied<br>• To analyse different responses to bullying |
| Preparation | Mark the four corners of the room as numbers 1–4. Children should be able to move freely from one corner to another. |
| Materials | • A space that allows the children to sit in circle.<br>• Coloured Paper<br>• Markers<br>• Scissors |

## Instructions

1. Introduce the topic of bullying asking questions such as these:
   - What is bullying?
   - What are the different ways people bully?
   - Why do you think people bully?
   - How does bullying affect people who are bullied? People who bully? The whole community?
2. Ask each child to trace their hand on a coloured piece of paper and cut it out. They should think of one person for each finger whom they can turn to for support if they are being bullied (e.g. friend, parent, teacher, school administrator, police, counselour, sibling). Ask children to explain the supporters they have named.
3. Explain that now you will look at different ways people can respond to situations involving bullying. Demonstrate how it will work:
   a. The facilitator will read a description of bullying. For each situation three possible responses are given. A fourth response is always open if you think of a different response.
   b. Each corner of the room is numbered. After you hear the situation and the responses, go to the corner that represents what you think you would do in this situation.
4. Read out the bullying situation and give the children time to choose their response and go to the corresponding corner of the room. Once the children have taken a position, ask a few in each position why they chose that response and some of its advantages and disadvantages. Allow those children who chose the open corner to explain how they would respond.

## Debriefing and evaluation

1. After responding to five or six bullying scenes, debrief the activity by asking question such as these:
   - How did you feel about the activity?
   - Were some of the scenes difficult to respond to? Which ones and why?

- Can you relate to any of the bullying scenes?
- Do people who are bullied need help and support? Why?
- Where can people who are bullied find help and support?
- What are some of the reasons that people bully others? Are they fair?
- What should you do if you're being bullied and the person you turn to for help and support doesn't do anything about it?
- Is some bullying more often accepted by children and adults? Why or why not?
- Who is responsible to help and support children when they are bullied?
- Can adults experience bullying too? Give some examples.
- Who is responsible to help adults when they are bullied?
- What can be done to help people who bully change their behavior?
- What happens if no one stops people who bully? To the bully? To the community?

2. Relate the activity to human rights by asking questions such as these:
   - Does anyone have the right to bully anyone else? Why or why not?
   - Which human rights can be violated when someone is being bullied?
   - How does ending bullying improve the human rights environment for everyone?

3. At the end of the debriefing, ask the children to look back at their 'hands of support' and add any other person or organisation they can think of whom they could turn to for support when being bullied. Display the 'hands of support' somewhere in the room so that the children can refer to them in the future.

## Suggestions for follow-up

You may like to focus further on violence by running the activity 'PICTURING WAYS OUT OF VIOLENCE', P. 133. The activity 'WORDS THAT WOUND' P. 202 also focuses on verbal bullying and can be run before or after this activity.

## Ideas for action

Discuss ways in which the group can create a 'No Bullying' campaign and ask members of the community to join in the initiative. For example, you might like to organize an exhibition, invite a professional from a child support organization to talk to the children, and/or identify an adult in the school to be the key person people can turn to for help.

Create a theatre performance that shows how children can respond when they're bullied and perform it for other groups of children.

Find out if there is a local children's hotline/helpline that children who are being bullied can call. Find out which services children can turn to for support in the local community. Give this information to children during the activity, and if possible invite someone from that agency to speak to the group.

## Tips for the facilitator

Introduce a magic stick / talking stick or pretend microphone so that people wanting to speak must wait their turn.

Some form of bullying probably exists among children in the group. Bullying affects all children to varying degrees and can take different forms. Be sensitive to the situations that may already exist in the group and try not to focus on any personal situation.

## Adaptations

Write your own bullying scenes that the children in your group can relate to instead of using those that are provided.

Divide children into small groups, give each a bullying situation, and ask them to role play both the bullying and their response. Discuss and debrief eah role play, asking other groups for alternative responses.

# HANDOUT: BULLYING SCENES

Your friends start calling you names, sending you nasty text messages and forcing you to give them things. You don't feel good when these things happen. What should you do?

1. Nothing.You must have done something wrong to make your friends act like that.
2. Start calling them names in return and threaten them..
3. Speak to your parents or teacher and tell them what is happening.
4. Something else (Open corner).

A group of kids in your class are spreading hurtful rumours about you by sending sms messages around. Many kids now won't play with you or even speak to you. Even your friends are starting to think they may be true. What should you do?

1. Nothing. No-one will believe you if everyone thinks the rumours are true.
2. Start spreading bad rumours about the other kids.
3. Tell everyone the rumours are unture.
4. Something else (Open corner).

Your older sister or brother keeps hitting and kicking you when nobody is looking and tells you that if you tell anyone she / he will just hurt you more. What should you do?

1. Tell your parents or teachers about what is happening.
2. Ask your friends at school to help you in fighting her / him.
3. Tell her / him that it hurts and to stop doing it.
4. Something else (Open corner).

Your teacher keeps calling you 'stupid' every time you get an answer wrong in class and says that there's no point in even trying to teach you because you can't learn. Other children have started calling you names too. What should you do?

1. Go straight to the headmaster and tell them what is happening.
2. Start missing class because you don't like going to school.
3. Ask your parents if you can change class or change school.
4. Something else (Open corner).

You notice one of your friends is teasing and making fun of the younger children in the summer camp. Your friend has started taking things from them as well. What should you do?

1. Tell the camp leaders what is happening without letting your friend know.
2. Help your friend in taking things from the younger children in case he/she starts to take things from you.
3. Tell your friend that you think that what he/she's doing is wrong and that they should leave the younger children alone.
4. Something else (Open corner).

A groups of older kids from another school like to pick on younger from your primary school. They wait to catch a child walking home or waiting for the bus alone, surround him or her, and take money, food, or toys. They also throw rocks and threaten to do worse. What should you do?

1. Be very careful to go to and from school in groups
2. Tell adults in your school what is happening and ask for help.
3. Carry rocks or a knife to protect yourself.
4. Something else (Open corner).

A new boy in your class is refugee. Your friends always say racist things to him, make fun of his English and tell him to go back home. What should you do?

1. Join in, he's not your friend so you don't have to worry about him.
2. Tell your teacher that your friends are saying racist things to him.
3. Offer to give him English lessons when you're not playing if your friends to help him fit in.
4. Something else (Open corner)

## HANDOUTS: BULLYING SCENES

You've been teasing one of your friends because he or she is really bad at reading and writing and you noticed that recently he/she has started to sit alone. Once you noticed tears in the child's eyes. What should you do?

1. Nothing, he / she was probably just having a bad day and it has nothing to do with you.
2. Stop teasing your friend and ask him / her about why he / she was crying.
3. Tell you friend that you won't tease him / her in front of anyone anymore but that he / she really is stupid and he / she should get some extra lessons.
4. Something else (Open corner).

You have an older step-brother who's very fond of you. He often wants to kiss you, and hug you, but although you like him, it makes you feel uncomfortable. What should you do?

1. Tell one of your parents, or another brother / sister.
2. Fight against it, and hit him whenever he does it.
3. Avoid him, and try to keep your distance.
4. Something else (Open corner).

# 9. Capture the Castle

*If you don't think, you lose!*

| | |
|---|---|
| Themes | Peace and Human Security |
| Level of complexity | Level 2 |
| Age | 8 – 13 years |
| Duration | 120 minutes |
| Group size | 16 – 30 children, 2-3 facilitators or adults |
| Type of activity | Active adventure game, experiential learning |
| Overview | Children represent different groups in a battle and need to organise themselves in order to win. Afterwards they discuss the different feelings on different sides of a conflict, the reasons and mechanisms behind it. |
| Objectives | • To develop empathy with different sides of a conflict<br>• To cooperate with each other<br>• To become aware of emotions in a conflict<br>• To foster strategic thinking and planning |
| Preparation | • If the game is played outside, examine the area and mark clear boundaries for the activity. Locate any potentially dangerous areas and point them out to the children and group leaders.<br>• Prepare imaginary 'action plans', each on different coloured paper. Cut each one into ten pieces and put each plan into a separate envelope. |
| Materials | • A very large space that allows the children to run and to hide<br>• 6 imaginary 'action plans', each on paper of a different colour, cut into 10 pieces each<br>• 3 different distinguishing signs for the 3 different groups (e.g. colours or face paints or visible ribbons)<br>• Drinks for after the game |

## Instructions

1. Explain there is a beautiful city with a castle at its centre. The city is controlled by the Purple Party, but there are two opposing groups who want to invade and take over the castle, the Blue Party to the south and the Orange Party to the north.

2. Divide the children into 3 groups: 50% Purples, 25% Blues and 25% Oranges. Explain the boundaries of the playing area. Give the Blue Party and the Orange Party three 'action plans' each.

3. Explain the activity carefully so that all the children understand:

    a. Everyone must stay within the boundaries of the activity area.

    b. Each group will establish a camp within the game's boundaries; no other group is allowed to enter another group's camp. The city that the Purple Party is defending should be exactly in the middle, the Blue Party's camp on one side and the Orange Party's camp on the other.

    c. To be able to capture the Castle, the two invading parties must try to exchange their 'action plans' with each other. Each of these groups has three plans on different coloured paper, which are cut in 10 pieces each. Each piece needs to be brought separately by one of the invaders to the other camp. Only one piece at a time can be carried. A Blue is not allowed to transport pieces of the Orange workers or vice versa. Pieces can only be handed over once a Blue or Orange 'courier' reaches the other camp.

    d. To defend the Castle, the Purples must try to prevent the Blues and Oranges from exchanging

**Source:**
Adapted from *"Praxismappe" Bundesjugendwerk der Arbeiterwohlfahrt* (Federal Youth Foundation of the Workers' Welfare Association Germany).

their plans. They try to catch the invaders and take away the pieces of their plans. 'Catching' means just touching lightly on the shoulder or arm.

e. When he or she is caught, the Blue or Orange player has two choices: 1) give their piece of the plan away to the Purples and then be free to rejoin the game; 2) refuse to give the piece away and remain a 'prisoner' in the city until the game is over or the piece is handed over to the Purples. The Blue and Orange Parties can help each other.

f. All pieces of the plans must be carried in a visible way.

g. The two or three facilitators will not take part in the game but supervise to see that the rules are respected.

h. Once the Blue Party or the Orange Party has collected all ten pieces to make a complete action plan, they can take all the pieces the Purple Party are carrying, and they have won! If the Purple Party manage to get all ten pieces of either the Blue Party's or Orange Party's plan, this group is out of the game. However, the remaining Party can still succeed: if it can carry a whole plan to the other camp, they and also the already-eliminated Party win.

i. The game is over when one Party has won or when the set time limit decided by the facilitator has run out.

## Debriefing and evaluation

1. Debrief the activity by asking question such as these:

   a. How do you feel?

   b. What happened with your action plans?

   c. Did you succeed in getting a complete plan? What strategy did you have? How did you make decisions?

   d. Did everyone participate in the game? Were there different roles?

   e. How did you feel about the other two parties?

   f. Did the Blue and Orange Parties team-up or fight each other? How did their relationship affect the outcome of the activity?

   g. Did the Blue and Orange Parties fight against the Purple Party and vice versa? If yes, why? Where did the conflict come from?

   h. Was the situation realistic? Do you know of similar situations in real life? What are some reasons that such conflicts happen in real life?

   i. How do you think this situation could be changed? How could such conflicts be prevented?

   j. Do you know of any other conflicts in your life? What, if anything, are you doing to resolve them? What could be done to change these situations?

   k. How do conflicts arise? What can we do to avoid them, solve them, manage them and/or safeguard peace (depending on the examples discussed)?

2. Relate the activity to human rights by asking questions such as these:

   a. What are some human rights that could be violated when people are in conflict? In an armed conflict?

   b. How are different parties in a conflict affected by having their rights violated? How will this affect their futures?

   c. How are children affected by conflict? How will this affect their futures?

   d. What can be done to prevent conflicts and human rights violations such as these?

   e. Can all conflicts be resolved? If not, how can human rights help people to manage their conflicts?

## Suggestions for follow-up

- Look deeper into some ongoing conflicts in the group in the community, as well as the country, region or world. Try to understand the bases for a conflict and discuss the situation.

## Ideas for action

- If your debriefing discussions focused on armed conflict and peace, try to organise/join a demonstration for peace and/or visit a peace organisation. Help the children find out about how peace organisations understand peace and approach conflict resolution.
- Discuss with the children the ways they deal with conflict among themselves. Help them develop some ground rules for addressing conflicts within their group that reflect human rights standards (e.g. no physical violence, no insulting language, everyone has the right to an opinion and expression, and equal opportunity to participate).

## Tips for the facilitator

- No-one has to fight over anything in this activity. Children in weaker physical conditions can achieve much more through strategy, quickness and cooperation than those who may rely on aggression and strength.
- Prepare the adult facilitators or helpers. Make sure they understand the rules and boundaries and are aware of any potential dangers in the area.
- Explain to the Blue and Orange Parties the importance of having a strategy in order to avoid losing pieces of each plan and therefore never getting one completed.
- Emphasise that 'to catch' means simply touching the person. See some variations below to adapt to differently-abled groups.
- The duration of the game very much depends on the group. Be prepared for the activity to be shorter or longer than expected.
- In the follow-up discussion make a clear distinction between armed conflict and peace, or conflicts in general, such as children experience in everyday life. Both are important but need separate approaches.

## Adaptation:

- If one group or an individual child is weaker than the others, provide some hints on possible strategies (e.g. verify how many pieces of which plan already reached the other camp; risk the loss of some pieces to save the others; don't send pieces of all the plans in the very beginning but save some until you have understood the rhythm of the game).
- Rather than a simple 'catch' someone, include a test after a Purple Party member tags a Blue or Orange Party member (e.g. when they meet, they play 'rock, paper, scissors'; if the Purple wins, then the Blue or Orange gives up the piece; if the Blue or Orange wins he or she goes free). This variation is effective when the children vary in their ages and physical condition, because it gives younger or the weaker children an equal chance.

# 10. Compasito **Reporter**

With their cameras, the Compasitos defend human rights!

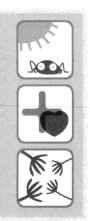

| | |
|---|---|
| Themes | Environment, Health and welfare, Participation |
| Level of complexity | Level 2 |
| Age | 10-13 years |
| Duration | 90-120 minutes |
| Group size | 8-24 children |
| Type of activity | Photo reportage or other forms of reporting |
| Overview | Children report on human rights conditions in their community |
| Objectives | • To develop awareness of human rights in everyday life<br>• To understand how rights can be both violated and defended<br>• To develop collaborative skills for active participation to defend rights and to end violations |
| Preparation | • Choose a few community situations relating to health, safety and the environment (e.g. bathrooms, restaurants, recycling provisions).<br>• Underline relevant articles in the child-friendly version of UDHR and CRC and make copies for each child.<br>• Make copies of maps of the community.<br>• Since this activity involves a critical look at some local institutions, inform in advance relevant officials.<br>• Try to arrange a meeting with relevant local officials to whom the children can present their results and proposals, and discuss possible changes. |
| Materials | • Copies of child-friendly UDHR and CRC for each team, and/or large copies on a flipchart<br>• One digital or Polaroid-type camera for each group<br>• Note pads and pens to take notes and identify pictures<br>• Copies of maps of the community<br>• Optional: Printer for printing digital photographs |

## Instructions

1. Discuss with children what reporters do, both in print media and TV. Explain that they themselves are going become photo reporters and take pictures of how the rights to health, safety and a good environment are experienced in their community. They may find examples where these rights are respected and enjoyed or, on the contrary, where they are violated.

2. Review these rights with children. Give them child-friendly copies of the UDHR and CRC with the relevant articles marked. You might also copy child-friendly versions UDHR Article 25 and CRC Article 3.3, Article 24 and Article 27 on chart paper and discuss their meaning with the children. Explain that these are the rights that they are going to report on, and give some examples of where they might be observed in the community (e.g. fire safety at school, healthy conditions where food is grown, sold, or prepared, clean air, water and environment). Ask the children to discuss how these rights can be observed in the community and ask them to provide other examples.

3. Divide the children into groups of three or four. Give each group a camera and a specific assignment. For example:

   a. Group A might check safety conditions at school and other public places. (e.g. Where are fire extinguishers? Are they in working order? Are emergency doors easily accessible? Do children

know what to do in case of emergency?)

  b. Group B might check safety in relation to traffic. (e.g. Are there safe pavements? Safe places to cross streets? Are the streets and pavements in good repair? Are there controls on drivers' speed? Are there street lights at night?)

  c. Group C might verify eating conditions. (e.g. hygienic conditions of markets and restaurants, information on food menu, nutrition qualities of food and drinks, safety checks on water supply?)

  d. Group D could concentrate on environmental issues. (Are there ways of knowing the quality of the air? Are their green places nearby? Are streets and public places clear? Is rubbish collected regularly? Are bins provided for recycling plastics, paper, glass, etc?)

4. Give the groups time to discuss their topic and plan how they will look for evidence. Make sure they know whom to contact to be able to enter certain areas (e.g. caretaker for school or park). They should all know how to use the camera. Each group should also have at least one child who will take notes and write up captions to identify the photographs, one to relate the photo to specific human rights and another who will write up their suggestions for responses.

5. Ask each group to report on their plans to the whole group. Set a specific deadline for completing their reporting assignments.

6. After groups have taken their photos, give them time to prepare a mini exhibition. Every exhibition should include:

  a. A title

  b. The names of the children in the group

  c. Captions for each picture, stating when and where it was taken and what it shows

  d. Comments on what human right(s) is / are being promoted or violated

  e. Recommendations for addressing the violations observed and commendations for good examples.

7. Invite parents and members of the community to view the exhibition.

8. Try to invite representatives of the local community (e.g. the mayor, school principal, town council members, local associations) to view the exhibition, meet the children to hear their concerns, listen to their proposals, and discuss possible changes.

## Debriefing and Evaluation

1. Debrief the activity by asking questions such as these:

  a. How did you like being a reporter?

  b. Was it difficulty to find the examples you needed?

  c. Was it difficult to 'catch' the situation in a photograph?

  d. Was it difficult to write the captions?

  e. Was it difficult to make commendations? Recommendations?

  f. Did you learn anything about your community? About yourself? Did you see anything in a new way?

  g. Can a camera be a useful tool to reveal situations? Can writing be useful?

  h. Can you think of other tools that could reveal these situations?

  i. What, if anything, does a picture add to something that is written?

2. Relate the activity to human rights by asking questions such as:

  a. What did you learn about human rights in your community?

  b. What were some positive examples where human rights were being protected and enjoyed?

| | GROUP A | GROUP B | FACILITATOR |
|---|---|---|---|
| ROUND 1 | 5 | 5 | |
| ROUND 2 | 0 | 0 | 13 |
| ROUND 3 | 8 | 8 | |
| **TOTAL** | **13** | **13** | **13** |

4. Explain these details regarding the snacks:

    a. Children can eat the snacks they get in the activity after the debriefing.

    b. Snacks cannot be broken into parts.

    c. Snacks eaten by team members during the activity are not replaced.

    d. Reemphasize that when a team cannot agree on the division of snacks, all the snacks will be returned permanently to the facilitator.

### Debriefing and Evaluation

1. To avoid distraction, collect all the snacks and explain that they will be returned for eating after the activity.

2. Discuss the activity using questions such as these:

    a. What happened during the activity?

    b. How did you feel during the activity? What was most exciting? Most frustrating?

    c. Did you have a strategy? How did you develop your strategy?

    d. Did anyone negotiate? Was it successful?

    e. If you played this activity again, would you act differently?

    f. Do you believe that the final result was fair?

3. Discuss the implications of this activity, asking questions such as these:

    a. Did you trust the other team to divide fairly? Why or why not?

    b. What do you mean when you say "fair"? Or the word "share"?

    c. What has trust to do with sharing?

    d. Can you think of situations in life where children need to share? Is it important to share fairly? What happens when sharing is unfair?

    e. Can you think of situations in life where adults need to share? What happens when adults do not share fairly?

    f. Can you think of examples in life where people do not get a "fair share" of things that they need?

    g. What can we do in our daily life to make sure that everybody has a fair share?

4. Relate the activity and discussion to human rights, asking question such as these:

    a. Human rights are based on what everyone needs, not only to survive but also to live a life of dignity with an adequate standard of living. What are some of the things every human being needs? List these things as they are mentioned.

    b. What happens when people don't have these things (e.g. enough food, shelter, education, family)?

    c. Can you see a connection between having a "fair share" of necessities and human rights?

### Suggestions for follow-up:

- The activities 'THE INVISIBLES ARE COMING', P. 171, and 'CAPTURE THE CASTLE', P. 89, also involve cooperation against a common 'enemy'.

- The activities 'SAILING TO A NEW LAND', P. 152, and 'MY UNIVERSE OF RIGHTS', P. 122, distinguish between wants and needs.

## Ideas for action

- Ask for examples of ways the children can improve sharing fairly within their group, at home and in the community (e.g. opportunities to speak, use toys and equipment, have adult attention, act as a leader).
- Contact local or national NGOs working on fair trade. Invite them to explain to your group what they do. Organise activities to support these NGOs.

## Tips for the facilitator

- The relationship between human needs and human rights is fundamental to human rights education. If this concept is not already established, you may wish to precede this activity with another activity such as 'SAILING TO A NEW LAND', P. 152, that focuses on this concept.
- With older children, you may want to relate fair sharing to development. For resources on development education, see page 235.
- This activity can effectively be run a second time. In this case, use different and more desirable snacks to maintain interest.
- You can have several groups playing this activity at the same time. However, be aware that the behaviour of one group can influence another. To encourage this interaction, make a common score board so all groups can see which divisions have been made. Discuss this influence in the debriefing.

|  | TEAM 1, GROUP A | TEAM 1, GROUP B | TEAM 1 FACILITATOR | TEAM 2, GROUP A | TEAM 2, GROUP A | TEAM 2 FACILITATOR |
|---|---|---|---|---|---|---|
| ROUND 1 | 6 | 5 |  | 6 | 5 |  |
| ROUND 2 | 0 | 0 | 13 | 6 | 7 |  |
| ROUND 3 | 8 | 8 |  | 8 | 8 |  |
| TOTAL | 14 | 13 | 13 | 20 | 20 |  |

- If they wish to, allow children to re-divide the snacks after the activity.

## Adaptations

- To lower the level of complexity: The number of snacks to be divided is intentionally uneven in order to challenge the trust and promote negotiation. However, if this strategizing is too complex for your group, make numbers even for both teams in every round.
- To raise the level of complexity: Include an extra rule that puts Team A in a different power position. If Team B refuses a proposal, they get nothing, but Team A gets to keep three snacks anyway. However, if Team B refuses a proposal, they do not get anything.
- To emphasise the relationship of the activity to human rights: If you have more than one facilitator, consider breaking the children into two or more smaller groups for debriefing question 4, the discussion of the relationship between human needs and human rights. The smaller the group, the deeper the discussion is likely to go on this important topic. Conclude by bringing the small groups together to share their discussion. Add another 30 minutes to the activity for this adaptation.

**Group A**

- Your team has 20 snacks that you can divide between you and Team B.
- You will play 3 rounds.
- During each round you have following number of snacks.

| Round 1 | Round 2 | Round 3 |
|---|---|---|
| 6 snacks to divide | 3 snacks to divide | 11 snacks to divide |

In order to keep these snacks, you have to propose how to divide them between your team and Team B. You can propose two solutions in each round. If Team B accepts one of your proposals, then you both get what the number of snacks agreed upon. If Team B rejects both your proposals, then both teams receive nothing.

**Example:**

- Round 1: 6 snacks to be divided by group A
- You propose to give 2 snacks to Team B and keep 4 for yourselves.
- If Team B says, "YES, WE ACCEPT", then they get 2 snacks and you get 4.
- If Team B says, "NO, WE DO NOT ACCEPT", then you can make a second proposal. This proposal can be the same as the first one or a different one.
- If Team B accepts this second proposal, then both groups get the agreed number of snacks.
- If Team B still does not accept, then both teams receive nothing and the snacks are given back to the facilitator.

**Group B**

- Your team has 20 snacks that you can divide between you and Team B.
- You will play 3 rounds.
- During each round you have following number of snacks.

| Round 1 | Round 2 | Round 3 |
|---|---|---|
| 5 snacks to divide | 10 snacks to divide | 5 snacks to divide |

In order to keep these snacks, you have to propose a certain division of these snacks between your group and Team A. You can make 2 proposals each round in order to find a solution.

If Team A accepts your proposed division, then you both get what has been divided.

If Team A does not agree after the second proposal, then you both receive nothing.

**Example:**

- Round 1: 5 snacks to be divided by Team B
- You propose to give 2 snacks to Team A and keep 3 for yourselves.
- If Team A says, "YES, WE ACCEPT", then they get 3 snacks and you get 2.
- If Team A says, "NO, WE DO NOT ACCEPT", then you can make a second proposal. This proposal can be the same as the first one or a different one.
- If Team A accepts this second proposal, then both groups get the agreed number of snacks.
- If Team A still does not accept, then both receive nothing and the snacks are given back to the facilitator.

# 12. Dear Diary

Walk a kilometre in my shoes …

| | |
|---|---|
| Themes | Discrimination, Health and welfare, Poverty and social exclusion |
| Level of complexity | Level 2 |
| Age | 8-13 years |
| Duration | 60 minutes |
| Group size | 6-20 children |
| Type of activity | Story telling, discussion. |
| Overview | Children read three different accounts of the same experience and discuss mistaken judgments about people |
| Objectives | • To practise communication and observation skills<br>• To enhance empathy<br>• To become aware of judgmental attitudes<br>• To understand the subjectivity of individual experience<br>• To discuss the right to education, to play and to health care |
| Preparation | Adapt the stories to the reality of your children and/or your learning objectives. |
| Materials | Copies of the three stories |

## Instructions

1. Explain that three children have permitted us to read their diaries from camp last summer. Divide the children into three groups and give each group one of the stories to read.

2. After they have read the stories, bring the children together and go through the events of the campers' day (e.g. solving puzzles, lunch, playing football, building a raft, crossing the river). Stop at each event ask the children what their character was doing, thinking and feeling at each point. At this point, avoid getting the children to explain the reasons for the campers' different reactions and feelings.

3. Ask members of the group to describe the child whose story they read. Discuss how three children could have such different experience of the same events, asking questions such as:

   a. Why did these children misunderstand each other?

   b. Do you think the children would have behaved differently if they had know more about each other's lives? How?

   c. What misunderstandings did they have about each other?

   d. How did they make these mistakes?

   e. Have you ever made mistakes in your opinion of someone else?

   f. What happens when we misjudge other people?

   g. What can we do to avoid making mistakes about other people?

## Debriefing and Evaluation

1. Debrief the activity by asking question such as:

   a. What do you think about the three stories?

   b. Would you enjoy a day like that? Why or why not?

   c. Are these stories realistic?

   d. Can you identify with any of these children? Which? Why?

99

    e. Can you have friends, even when you are poor or unable to read? Why?

    f. What does friendship mean?

    g. Are there some people who are more disadvantaged than others in your community? Who are they?

    h. What can we do to change this situation?

2. Relate the activity to human rights by asking questions such as these:

    a. What human rights were the children enjoying at camp?

    b. What human rights do they enjoy at home?

    c. Are the rights of any of these children violated?

    d. How are they affected by having their rights violated? How will this affect their futures?

    e. What can be done to prevent rights violations such as these?

### Suggestions for follow-up

- Make drawings of the situations in the stories (e.g. the events of the 'Great adventurous day', each of children in their home environment, etc.)

- The activity 'MOST IMPORTANT FOR WHOM?', P. 118, and 'SAILING TO A NEW LAND', P. 152, focuses on the contrasting responses and priorities in the same situation.

### Ideas for action

In order to avoid similar misunderstandings within your own group, develop with your children a Code of Conduct for being together.

### Tips for the facilitator

- The stories can seem very unrealistic or unfamiliar to some children. Adapt them to reflect your children's reality and concerns without isolating individual children or embarrassing them through stories too close to their personal realities.

- Especially when working with disadvantaged children, be sensitive to the attitudes children have about themselves and others in their community. Allow children to discuss the issues of disadvantaged children but balance this with building confidence in them that all children should have opportunities to live the life they want and to have their rights respected.

- Because some children may identify with the characters in the stories, the activity requires sensitive debriefing. Be aware of stereotypes and judgmental behaviour these stories may provoke in some children, both in assumption about privileged children (e.g. "They don't have any problems"; "They are snobs") and about disadvantaged children (e.g. "They don't have supportive families"; "They are lazy"). The importance of these stories is to encourage children to ask why others act as they do instead of jumping to conclusions based on false assumptions.

- Make a clear distinction in discussion between what the character was doing and what he or she was feeling and thinking.

### Variations:

- Read the stories aloud to the children or ask the children to read them. Then discuss, as in Step 3. You may want to ask the debriefing questions after each story.

- Get the children to act out what the three campers did at each phase of the day. Then ask them to explain how each was feeling at the time. Alternatively ask two children to act the part of each child, one who performs the child's outward words and actions and the other who speaks for the child's inner thoughts and feelings.

**Adaptation:**

- Younger children need some visual materials to remember what happens during the day at camp. Too much information might cause a loss in attention and will make the debriefing very difficult. Make sure the children have understood one story before moving on to the next one.

## HANDOUT: THE STORIES

**During the summer months, many children go to summer camp. The following stories are taken from the diaries of three children who meet for the first time at the same summer camp. They are the same age and involved in the same activities. One day, the youth leaders organised 'The Great Adventurous Day'. That evening all three children wrote the story of that day in their diaries.**

**Margaret wrote under her bedcovers by torchlight.**

Dear Diary,

Oh, what a great day it was. We did many crazy things and I believe it could have been one of the best days in my life. We had exciting activities that were sometimes even dangerous. But I was never afraid. Unlike my friends who did not enjoy everything as I hoped they would. It was a pity Elsa and Ricardo were so strange today.

But to start at the beginning – When we woke up, the leaders divided us into different groups. I was together with Ricardo and Elsa. I like both of them because yesterday we were also in the same group and we laughed so much at all the jokes we were telling each other. The leader gave us 3 messages written in secret codes and we had to find the solutions. I was the first one to find my solution. After a while Ricardo also had his solution, but Elsa was very slow. When I asked her if she needed help, she said she didn't like the activity and that solving the secret code was a boring thing to do. Then I saw that she was holding the paper upside down and I laughed at her saying that she would never find it like this. She gave me an angry look and threw the paper away. "I want to play, not read stuff", she said. I don't think she is very clever. I wonder if she can read at all – strange, because all kids my age can read and write!

Well, we finally managed to discover the meaning of the 3 messages. Then we went down to the river where we played football against another group of children. That was fun. We almost won but it's all Elsa's fault that we lost. Every time the ball came close to her, she touched it with her hands, kicked the other children and made a lot of mistakes. It was like she had never played football before. That seems weird. We all play football after school. Next time I want to be in a different group from Elsa.

After lunch – the meals here are really disgusting – we had to build a raft to cross the river. And that was cool because we had to look for wood and then make all kinds of knots with ropes. Elsa and I were looking for good strong logs, but Ricardo was always bringing in these skinny sticks. I told him that since he was a boy he should work as hard as we were. He said he was dizzy and his back hurt. I think that was just an excuse not to work. When we finished, our raft was the best ever – even the leader said this! Then the leader counted "1, 2 and 3" and then we had to jump on the raft and cross the river together. I jumped first but I fell in the water. Brrr…the water was very, very cold and I screamed at first. Luckily the leader helped me out and then we were all laughing. When I told my friends how cold the water really was, Ricardo said he didn't feel like going anymore. I think he was afraid of the cold water. I didn't know before that Ricardo was such a loser! First the wood and then the water! When I told him he should be braver, he ran away crying. I don't think I want to be in the same group with him anymore! Actually, I will ask the leader to put me in another group next time because Elsa is stupid and Ricardo is just a sissy.

I didn't speak to Elsa and Ricardo again after that and …oops, I think the leaders are coming to our room. Sleep well, my dear diary. Tomorrow I'll give you more news.

Love, Margaret

groups to Situation E, which will later be used as a simulation. Point out the questions to consider at the bottom of the page and explain any terms that may be unfamiliar in the questions.

   a. Alternative: Give all the groups Situation E to emphasize the variety of solutions to the same situation and the negotiation process that follows in Step 5.

4. When the children have had time (about 15-20 minutes) to plan in small groups, ask each group to explain their situation and the decision making process they developed to address it. Call on the groups with Situation E last. After each presentation, ask the other children to critique the plan:

   a. Is it democratic?

   b. Does everyone concerned have a chance to express a choice?

   c. Is it fair?

   d. Is it secret?

   e. Does everyone who votes know who or what they are voting for?

5. When all the situations have been presented, ask the children to turn their attention to Situation E. Explain that they are going to hold a mock vote to decide on this situation. But to do so, they need to agree on one plan for how to decide. Ask them to compare the different plans developed for Situation E:

   a. How are the plans alike? Shall we use these agreements for our mock vote?

   b. How are they different? Which idea will work best? Which should we use?

6. As the children reach agreement on a plan, write down their decisions on chart paper and discuss it, asking questions such as these:

   a. Is anything missing from our new plan for Situation E?

   b. Do you think it will be democratic?

**Session 2:**

1. Remind the children of Session 1 and the facts of Situation E. Reintroduce the plan developed in Session 1 and explain that you will try out their plan with a mock vote on Situation E.

2. Hand out role cards to the children and explain the simulation:

   a. The Election Manager will ask the 3 spokespersons to give their opinion.

   b. The Election Manager will then ask the audience to ask questions and give their opinions as well.

   c. The Election Manager then asks if everyone is ready to vote and explains what it takes to win the vote according to the group's plan (e.g. a simple majority, a proportion of the vote).

   d. The Voting Official will then ask everyone to vote, according to the method in the group's plan. Together the Voting Official and Election Manager will collect and count the votes.

   e. The Voting Official announces the result to the vote. If it qualifies to win, the Election Manager declares the group's decision. If it does not qualify to win, the Election Manager announces that there will have to be a run-off vote.

   f. In the case of a run-off vote, the Voting Official makes new ballots and proceeds as in Step e above.

**Debriefing and evaluation**

1. Debrief the activity by asking questions such as these:

   a. Do you think the vote in the simulation was fair and democratic?

   b. Were you able to recognize real-life situations in this activity?

c. How are decisions like this usually made? Do children get to have an opinion or choice?

d. Are there some decisions that only adults can make?

e. Are decisions in your group usually made democratically? Why or why not?

f. What can you do to ensure that your group makes decisions democratically?

2. Relate the activity to human rights by asking questions such as these:

a. What do we mean when we talk about 'government'?

b. What are some offices in your community that are chosen by election? In your country?

c. Besides holding an elected office, what are some ways that people can participate in their government?

d. How old must you be in your country before you can vote?

e. Are there ways you can participate in government before you can vote?

f. Why do you think the right to participate in government is important enough to be a human right?

g. What would happen if some of the children in your simulation decided not to vote? What happens when people don't exercise their right to participate in their government?

h. Why is it important to use your human rights?

## Suggestions for follow-up

The activity 'A CONSTITUTION FOR OUR GROUP', P. 56 , provides a real-life opportunity to exercise democratic debate about how the group will behave and to practise voting skills.

## Ideas for action

Take every opportunity that arises with your group to model democratic decision making, whether about small matters (e.g. what kind of snacks to have, whether to play inside or outside) or large. Children learn democratic procedures best by practising them. They also benefit from being asked to consider whether everyone concerned in a decision has had a chance to be consulted.

## Tips for the facilitator

- The simplest way to run this fairly complex activity is to have all the children working together on a plan for Situation C. This ensures that everyone understands the situation and emphasizes the need to create a compromise plan, itself an important democratic process.

- If you choose to use several different situations, use at least one situation that involves choosing a person (Situations A and D) and one that involves making a policy decision (Situations D and E). The policy decision situations make for better mock elections because the spokespersons represent points of view rather than themselves.

- This activity contains some terms that may be unfamiliar to children (e.g. nominations, candidates, campaign speeches, debates, run-off election, proportion of the vote, ballot). Once the children are working in small groups, go around to make sure they understand the terms. For younger children proportional representation might be explained simply as 'more than half' or 'a simple majority'.

- The instructions suggest using only Situation E for the simulation, but you can adapt the roles to use any of the situations.

- Make up other situations based on decisions faced by the children in your group.

- For a large group: Add spokespersons with other opinions to the debate.

## Adaptations

To focus on questions of who gets to vote, you can assign some alternate roles such as those below. Read these out at the beginning of the simulation and ask the children to debate whether these children should have a vote. This decision itself might be the basis of a decision by vote.

## Optional Roles

- You are six years old and in the first grade. You can't read yet and don't know much about the group. Should you have a vote?
- You are thirteen but in the fifth class because you have a learning disability. Should you have a vote?
- You have just moved to this community and don't really know anyone yet. Should you have a vote?
- You are a bully. You push younger children around outside and encourage your friends to join you in calling some people nasty names. Should you have a vote?

## HANDOUT: SITUATION SHEET IN SESSION 1

**Situation A:**

Your school has been invited to send someone to represent the school in a city-wide celebration of International Children's Day at the City Hall. The choice is up to the children. There are 500 students. How will you choose a representative democratically?

**Situation B:**

Your sports club needs a president. You have sixty members. How will you decide democratically who the president should be?

The students in your school will choose which drawings in an art contest get first, second and third prize. There were 50 drawings entered in the contest. There are 300 children in the school. How will you decide the winners democratically?

**Situation D:**

Students in your school are debating whether children should be allowed to bring mobile phones to school. Some want to do this. Others think it's distracting and unfair to children who don't own them. The principal of the school says that the children should be allowed to decide themselves. There are 350 children in the school. How can you do this democratically?

**Situation E:**

Your group has been given a gift of about 500 euros. Your group leader says that the group itself should decide how to spend it. Some children want to have a party with nice food. Some want to go on a field trip. Some want to buy new games and art supplies. One person wants to put it aside for emergencies. Another wants to buy an electric keyboard. There are 30 children in your group. How will you decide democratically how to use the money?

**Some things to consider:**

- How will you decide what to vote on? Will you have nominations? If so, how?
- How many candidates will you have? Should the number be limited?
- How will everyone know who or what they are voting for? Will you ask people to make campaign speeches or have debates?
- How will people vote? Will it be secret?
- How will you decide who wins?
- What if there is only a tiny difference in the number of votes between two candidates? Will you have a run-off election? Should a winner need a certain proportion of the votes (e.g. more than 50%)?

# HANDOUT: SITUATION SHEET IN SESSION 2

Roles for Mock Voting on Situation E

You are the **Election Manager**. You organize the debates, explain what it takes for a decision to win and help to count the votes. If there is a run-off, you organize that as well.

You are the **Voting Official**. You make the ballot, organize the voting, count the votes and announce the results. If there is a run-off, you organize the ballot and voting.

You are a **spokesperson** for one point of view. You think the money should be spent on a big party. Give some reasons.

You are a **spokesperson** for one point of view. You think the money should be spent on new games and equipment. Give some reasons.

You are a **spokesperson** for one point of view. You think the money should be spent on a wonderful trip for all the children. Give some reasons.

- Ask children to compare coverage of the same human rights stories in different newspapers and/or different media. What differences can they observe in importance given in the story? In emphasis given in features of the story? Are there different versions of a single event? Did any version of the story explicitly mention human rights?
- Ask participants to watch a news programme on TV and write down the topics covered and the amount of time given to each human rights topic.

## HANDOUT: SAMPLE POSTER

| RIGHTS ENJOYED | | RIGHTS DENIED | | RIGHTS DEFENDED | |
|---|---|---|---|---|---|
| | | | | | |
| Analysis | | Analysis | | Analysis | |
| Right | UDHR Article | Right | UDHR Article | Right | UDHR Article |
| | | | | | |

# 16. Modern Fairytale

Footprints in the sand are not made sitting down!

| | |
|---|---|
| Themes | Discrimination, Education and leisure, Violence |
| Level of complexity | Level 2 |
| Age | 8-13 years |
| Duration | 60 minutes |
| Group size | 5-15 children |
| Type of activity | Story telling, discussion |
| Overview | Children in turns tell a story based on a series of pictures |
| Objectives | • To introduce the issue of child labour and modern-day slavery<br>• To promote active listening<br>• For older children: To introduce the European Court of Human Rights (ECHR) |
| Preparation | • Prepare a smooth wooden stick.<br>• Make copies of the drawings for every two children.<br>• Make copies of the child-friendly CRC for each child. |
| Materials | • Wooden stick<br>• Copies of drawing sequence provided as handout<br>• Copies of the child-friendly CRC |

## Instructions

1. Ask the children to gather in a circle to hear a story in a special way. Try to create a mysterious atmosphere. Show them the wooden stick and explain that this is 'talking stick': only the person holding it may speak. When they have spoken, they should pass on the stick to another person.

2. Lay the pictures out so that the children can see all of them and explain that together they will create a story about a girl named Siwa based on these pictures. Then distribute the pictures, one to each child or pair of children. Explain that this picture represents the part of the story which that child or pair of children will tell. Give the children time to think about what their pictures represent and discuss it together if they are working with a partner.

3. Be the first one to hold the stick and say a little to demonstrate how the story will be told. Then pass the stick to the child who will start the story. Explain that the person who wants to speak next should hold up their picture; if there are several who want to speak, the speaker will decide who gets the talking stick next.

4. When the story has come to an end, ask the children if they would like to hear the real story behind these pictures. Tell or read the story of Siwa.

## Debriefing and Evaluation

1. Debrief the activity by asking questions such as these:
   a. What did you base your story? Did the pictures remind you of something you have experienced or heard about?
   b. Was your story based on the pictures close to the true story?
   c. What did you think of Siwa's story? How did you feel?
   d. Do you have any questions about Siwa's story?

2. Discuss child labour and forms of modern-day slavery by asking questions such as these:

a. What is a slave?

b. In what ways was Siwa's situation like slavery?

c. Do you think that Siwa's story could happen in your country? Do you know of any such incidents?

d. Are there still slaves in the world today?

3. Give children copies of the child-friendly CRC, UDHR or ECHR. Relate Siwa's story to human rights:

a. What happens to children who are forced to work?

b. How does this affect their human rights? Can you name any of Siwa's rights in the CRC that were violated?

c. How does the CRC protect children?

d. Do other human rights documents also offer protection to children?

## Suggestions for follow-up

- An exercise dealing with what might be a frightening subject matter should not stand alone. Follow up with some affirming and positive activity, however brief: For example 'PUTTING RIGHTS ON THE MAP', P. 138 or 'FROM BYSTANDER TO HELPER', P. 108.

- With older children, use the Council of Europe's comic strip on a similar case. Preview for appropriateness: www.hurights.eu/notforsale/fabia/en/01.html

## Ideas for action

- The children can find out what their country's laws are to protect against child labour. How much work are children allowed to do legally? Are children protected from some kinds of work?

- The children can design and conduct a survey to find out how much and what kinds of work children do at home. Is working for and with your family child labour (e.g. child care, housework, helping parents with their work)? Do girls and boys contribute equally to helping their families?

- Plan a campaign with the children to combat child labour and human trafficking, a topic with which children may not be familiar with but which would interest and concern them.

## Tips for the facilitator

- The children may need help telling the story from pictures. You could guide the story closer to the true version by taking part as one of the storytellers. They may also have trouble putting the pictures into a sequence.

- You may need to define trafficking as a concept.

- Be prepared to answer the children's questions about Siwa's story, which may be surprising or upsetting to many of them. You should also be able to explain who and how to get help if they or others are in a similar situation.

- Siwa's story is based on a real-life case settled in the European Court of Human Rights (Siliadin v. France, No. 73316/01). The story in COMPASITO intentionally does not name a specific homeland for Siwa (who was actually from Togo) or the country where she was sent (in fact, France) in order not to suggest that most trafficked children come from Africa or indeed a non-European country, or that France was the only country where such things occur. You may wish to change the story to reflect the situation in your country. However, be mindful not to suggest that trafficking only occurs from outside Europe. Unfortunately, there are many cases from one European country to another.

- Be able to explain other protections of children against child labour besides the CRC. See Chapter V. discussions of child labour, p. 232 , and child trafficking, p. 282.

- Help the children differentiate between work they may do to help their families and inappropriate child labour. Relate this to a child's right to rest and leisure, education and other children's rights.
- Worldwide, girls are given less leisure and expected to do more unpaid work than boys. You may wish to explore the difference in expectations placed on boys and girls and relate it to gender equality.

## Adaptations

- For older children: Relate Siwa's story to the European Court of Human Rights by asking questions such as these:
  - Siwa and her lawyer took her case to the European Court of Human Rights. Have you ever heard of this court? Who or what did Siwa's case try to change?
  - What did the ECHR decide in Siwa's case? What happened as a result?
  - Has your country signed the European Convention of Human Rights?
  - Can you, as a child, apply to the ECHR? What can the ECHR do for you?
- For older children: compare the UDHR and CRC with the European Convention on Human Rights. For a plain-language version on the Convention see www.youthinformation.com/Templates/Internal.asp?NodeID=90847
  - For younger children: Number the pictures and lay them out in order so that children can see the sequence of events.

## Further information

- On the European Court of Human Rights: www.echr.coe.int
- For a video on the ECHR: www.coe.int/t/e/multimedia/defaulten.asp
- On the Council of Europe's campaign to Combat Trafficking in Human Beings: www.coe.int/t/dg2/trafficking/campaign/default_en.asp
- Council of Europe brochure 'Action Against Trafficking in Human Beings', Directorate of Communication – Public Relations Service, in cooperation with the Directorate General of Human Rights – Equality Division, 2006 (also available at www.coe.int/t/dg2/trafficking/campaign/Source/English%20brochure.pdf)
- Council of Europe Convention on Action against Trafficking in Human Beings (also available at www.coe.int/t/dg2/trafficking/campaign)

## Siwa's story

Once upon a time, not so long ago, there was a girl called Siwa. She lived in a very poor country. She lived with her uncle because her parents had died when she was a child.

When she grew older, Siwa realised that the world was much bigger than just her country and that there were other interesting places to visit as well. But like most people in her country, Siwa was poor and didn't have the money to travel.

One day, however, her uncle came up with a plan. He suggested sending Siwa to a rich country to live with Mrs X, an acquaintance of his. Siwa was excited by the idea of travelling and was eager to go. The uncle agreed with Mrs X that she would buy Siwa a plane ticket to her country and that Siwa would live at her house and help the family with the housework until she had earned the price of her plane ticket. So Siwa boarded a plane and flew to this rich country. She was looking forward to all the new things she would be experiencing There, Mrs. X had promised to send her to school and to take care of her legal papers so that she could travel freely and explore this new country.

However, once Siwa arrived at Mrs. X's house, things started to go wrong. Mrs. X was not as friendly as the girl had imagined. She expected Siwa to take care of her children and do all the housework by herself. When Siwa asked about school, Mrs. X said that it could wait.

After a while Mrs. X told Siwa that she was going to live with Mrs. Y for a while. Siwa hoped that now she could finally start going to school and enjoying her stay in this new country. Sadly, however, Mrs. Y was worse than Mrs. X. Life became even harder for Siwa. Now she had to start work early in the morning and could not go to bed until late at night. And even then she couldn't get a good night's sleep as she was sleeping on the floor in the children's room and had to take care of the baby, who woke up crying several times during the night. Besides cleaning, cooking and caring for the children, she was not even allowed to leave the house to walk around in the city. Life was miserable. Siwa regretted ever leaving Africa.

One morning Siwa managed to get permission to go to religious services. But instead of going there, she gathered her courage and knocked on the door of a neighbour's house. She asked the young couple living there for help and told her story. The couple was shocked. They could not imagine someone being treated like a slave in modern times. Siwa's story sounded like an old fairytale, except that in reality there was no fairy to help her, so she had to find a way to help herself.

The couple took Siwa into their house and reported her case to the police. When the police investigated, they charged Mrs. X and Mrs. Y. However, Siwa was not satisfied with having these individuals punished. She wanted to make sure that no other child like her would ever have to face a similar situation. Therefore, with her lawyer's help, she filed a case in the European Court of Human Rights, asking the country where Mrs. X lived to change its laws to protect children from this kind of slavery. The Court agreed with Siwa and that country was forced to take care to prevent similar incidents of forced work in the future. Finally, Siwa was happy. She had not only managed to escape from the imprisonment in Mrs. Y's house, but she had also made sure that no other child in that country would have to experience what she did.

Source: Adapted from the European Court of Human Rights case *Siliadin v. France*, No. 73316/01.

# 17. Most Important for Whom?

Your priorities may not be the same as mine!

| | |
|---|---|
| Themes | General human rights |
| Level of complexity | Level 3 |
| Age | 10-13 years |
| Duration | 60 minutes |
| Group size | 12-24 children |
| Type of activity | Prioritizing, consensus building, discussion |
| Overview | Children decide which CRC articles to eliminate and discuss the consequences and the interdependence of rights |
| Objectives | • To introduce the CRC<br>• To understand how rights are universal, inalienable and interdependent |
| Preparation | Prepare Children's Rights Cards. |
| Materials | • Paper and pens<br>• Flipchart and markers<br>• Enough Children's Rights Cards for half the number of children |

## Instructions

1. Begin the activity by brainstorming children's rights to determine how familiar the group is with the CRC and/or reminding them of what they may previously have learned about children's rights. If the group is unfamiliar with children's rights, begin with the adaptation suggested below.

2. Divide the children into small groups of two to four and give each group two Children's Rights Cards, paper and pen. Explain that each card describes a right in the Convention on the Rights of the Child (CRC). Ask them to read aloud the two articles on the cards and decide which right is more important to children. They should then write down their reasons for choosing one right over the other.

3. Collect the cards for 'less important' rights. Ask each group of four to take their chosen Children's Rights Card and join another group. In this larger group of eight, repeat Step 1, deciding which of the rights on their two Children's Rights Cards is more important for children and writing down their reasons.

4. Again collect cards for the 'less important' rights. List them all on a flipchart, labelled 'Less Important Rights'.

5. When groups have made their final choice, ask someone from each of the groups to read aloud the single Children's Rights Card they have chosen as most important and explain the reasons for their choice. As each is read, list it on a flipchart labelled 'Our Rights'. Only two to four rights will remain, depending on the size of the group.

6. Discuss these choices:

   a. Did you have difficulty making these choices? Why?

   b. What factors made you choose one right over another?

   c. Did your ideas about which rights were most important change during this activity?

   d. Do you agree with the reasons other groups gave for their choices? Why or why not?

7. Give out the cards for the 'less important' rights at random and ask the children to read them aloud. Discuss what would happen if we really rejected these rights.

   a. Choose several specific 'less important' rights and ask the children to imagine what would hap-

pen without them (e.g. right to adoption and alternative care, right to family life, right to play and cultural activity).

    b. How would really losing any of these 'less important' rights affect you personally?

    c. What affect would losing these 'less important' rights have on the chosen rights?

## Debriefing and Evaluation

1. Remind the children of the fundamental principle of universality: everyone has all rights, and discuss:

    a. Why is it important that every human being has the same human rights?

2. Can human rights be taken away from some people? Why?

    a. Discuss the importance of having the full complement of children's rights. Although you need not use terms such as 'inalienability' or 'interdependence', help the children understand that everyone needs all human rights.

    b. Illustrate the interrelation of rights with specific examples (e.g. the right to education and the right to information; the right to family and the right to non-separation from parents).

3. Ask the children for examples of how they need all their rights.

    a. Discuss how choosing one right over another depends on individual priorities (e.g. "I've never been arrested," or "I live with two parents") but the CRC takes into consideration the needs of all children in the world.

    b. Ask the children to think of situations where each of the 'less important' rights might be crucial to the survival or well-being of a particular child.

## Suggestions for follow-up

- The activity 'A CONSTITUTION FOR OUR GROUP', p. 56, relates rights to responsibilities.
- Other activities involving the CRC are 'BOARD GAMES', p. 70, and 'RABBIT'S RIGHTS', p. 141.
- The activity 'SAILING TO A NEW LAND', p. 152, also asks children to prioritise among rights.

## Ideas for action

- Encourage the children to bring in examples in daily life where children enjoy the rights they have discussed.
- Look for and/or research stories about children's rights, either being violated or protected, especially situations such as child labour that may not be familiar to them.

## Tips for the facilitator

- Younger children may need further explanation of some rights.
- The facilitator should accept all group decisions without comment. Any objections to a group's decision should come from other children.
- Children do not need to use legal terms such as 'interdependence' and 'interrelation' to understand the concept.
- In the debriefing discussion, be prepared to give concrete examples of what could happen if a particular right were taken away.
- Be sure children understand that not everything is a right.

## Adaptation

This activity assumes some previous knowledge of the CRC. If children are unfamiliar with the CRC,

# 18. My Universe of Rights

Be a human rights astronaut!

| | |
|---|---|
| Themes | General human rights |
| Level of complexity | Level 3 |
| Age | 8 – 13 years |
| Duration | 2 x 60-minute sessions |
| Group size | Up to 24 children |
| Overview | Children make 'outerspace' shapes labelled with the things they need to be healthy and happy and grow up well. These are then clustered into 'galaxies' representing different children's rights, thereby linking needs to rights. |
| Type of activity | Artistic activity |
| Objectives | • to become acquainted with the CRC<br>• to relate human needs to human rights<br>• to reflect on individual needs and compare them with other's |
| Preparation | • Copy and cut out 'outer space' shapes, approximately 6 shapes per child<br>• Cut out approximately 30 large circles of light blue paper, which will become the 'galaxies' of rights, and about 10 large comet shapes, which will be used for general rights that cover the whole CRC.<br>• Copy the child-friendly CRC; cut out each article as a strip.<br>• Stick or hang the circles, 'the galaxies', on the walls around the room.<br>• Optional: make copies of work sheet for each pair of children. |
| Materials | • Sheets of light blue paper<br>• Construction paper in many colours<br>• Colouring materials<br>• Scissors, sticky tape, glue and other handicraft materials<br>• Optional: work sheet |

## Instructions

### Session 1:

1. Divide the children into pairs and ask them to make a list together of conditions they need a) to be healthy b) to be happy and c) to grow up to be capable adults. Encourage them to have at least four items in each category.

   a. Optional: Give children a work sheet such as the one below.

2. Ask each pair to join up with another pair, and compare their lists, eliminating duplications and adding any new conditions they may think of.

3. Distribute different shapes and colouring materials to each child. Ask the children to write their names and one condition from their list on each shape, and then to colour or decorate the shapes. The partners should each write different conditions from their combined lists.

4. Collect the shapes by topic, i.e. all the conditions for health, for happiness, and for development. Then, divide the children into three groups and give each a category to separate into clusters of similar or identical conditions (e.g. shapes related to leisure, to health care, to education). Younger children may need help to identify the categories.

5. Explain that these clusters represent different categories of human rights and that in the next session they will transform them into galaxies in the universe of rights.

**Session 2:**

1. Remind the children of the clusters of rights they created in Session 1. Divide the children into small groups and give each group some blue circles and rights clusters. Ask the children to glue each cluster to a blue circle, leaving an open place in the centre of each. Mount the circles on the wall or spread them on the floor so that all the children can see them.

2. Introduce the CRC, explaining that it makes up the universe of rights. Their job is to identify the different galaxies that make up this universe. As you read out a right, ask the children to find the galaxy it belongs to and to glue the strip containing the article on it so that that right becomes the centre of each galaxy. Sometimes a galaxy may relate to more than one human right.

3. Point out that some rights (e.g. Article 1, Definition of a child; Article 3, The child's best interest; Article 4, Enjoying the rights in the Convention) run through the whole universe of rights. Ask children to write these articles on comet shapes and to hang them among the galaxies.

4. Make a wall display of these rights galaxies or hang them together from the ceiling.

## Debriefing and evaluation

1. Debrief the activity by asking questions such as these:
    a. What did you like about this activity?
    b. What do you think about the final result?
    c. Is there something you would like to change?
    d. What was the hardest part in this activity?
    e. Did the conditions that you thought were important differ from those of others?

2. Relate the activity to human rights by asking questions such as these:
    a. Which one is the biggest galaxy? Does this mean that this is the most important condition for most of us?
    b. Do you think that these universes are the same for all the children in the world? Why or why not?
    c. What do your rights have to do with your needs? Do you have a right to the things you need to be healthy and happy and develop well?
    d. Do you have a right to everything you think you need to be happy?
    e. What can you do to ensure that the rights of every child are respected in your environment (e.g. group of friends, class, school, organisation, club)?

## Suggestions for follow-up

The activities 'RABBIT'S RIGHTS', P. 141 and 'SAILING TO A NEW LAND', P. 152, also make a link between human needs and human rights, and would combine very well with this activity.

## Ideas for action

• Dress everyone up as astronauts and visit different institutions in your community that symbolize the rights identified by the children. You could do this for each galaxy the children have created.

• Invite another class or group of children to view the wall exhibition; ask the children to explain what it means.

## Tips for the facilitator

• Children like to create a new 'world'. Stimulate their imaginations by showing them images of a galaxy. Use this starting point to make links to existing rights.

- Use 'outer space' shapes (e.g. sun, moon, planets, satellites, spaceships, stars, asteroids) to create the 'galaxy'. Prepare shapes beforehand or make patterns for the children to trace and cut out. The children can also invent these shapes.

- Some of the general articles likely to be identified as 'comets' are these: Articles 1-3, 6-8, 12.

- Children are unlikely to think of some rights (e.g. Article 22, Refugees; Article 35 on Trafficking; Article 39, Rehabilitation of child victims). With younger children you might leave these, as well as Articles 41-54. With older children you might ask them if they are general to the whole treaty and thus 'comets', or if they are just less familiar rights, in which case they should have their own 'galaxy'.

- The children may include some conditions that are not immediately linked to rights. If some represent things they think would make them happy (e.g. toys, vacation trips, special foods), discuss whether these things are necessary to their heath and happiness, helping them to distinguish wants from needs.

### Variation

- Extend the activity by inviting the children to make spaceships and planets using recycled materials. Hang these three-dimensional objects from the ceiling as part of the galaxy exhibition.

### Adaptations

- For a large group: more facilitators are needed for involving all the children and clustering all the children's shapes. Alternatively, you could use fewer shapes.

- For younger children; to facilitate clustering the different papers, copy a simplified version of the child-friendly CRC, cut out the separate articles and attach them to a wall. The children can then place their shapes on the appropriate 'rights galaxy'.

- For older children: Ask them to do the clustering, grouping rights that seem similar. Then give them copies of the child-friendly CRC and ask them to match their clusters to specific articles. When they have completed this process, they can then paste their galaxies and the CRC article together on the blue circles.

## HANDOUT: OPTIONAL WORKSHEET

| THINGS I NEED ... | | |
|---|---|---|
| TO BE HEALTHY | TO BE HAPPY | TO BECOME A CAPABLE ADULT |
| | | |
| | | |
| | | |
| | | |
| | | |

# 19. Once Upon a Time...

See what happens when you reverse the sexes of characters in a well-known story

| | |
|---|---|
| Themes | Democracy, Discrimination, Gender equality |
| Level of complexity | Level 2 |
| Age | 7-13 |
| Duration | 40 minutes |
| Group size | 5-15 children |
| Type of activity | Story telling, discussion |
| Overview | Retelling a familiar story with characters' sexes reversed, leading to discussion of gender stereotypes |
| Objectives | • To recognise stereotypical gender roles and characteristics in stories and everyday life<br>• To discuss traditional and non-traditional gender roles<br>• To encourage gender equality |
| Preparation | Revise / rewrite a well-known story (e.g. novel, fairy tale, film) not longer than 10 minutes, reversing the sex of most characters. If necessary, change their names and other details as well. Choose a story with characters of both sexes who behave in a traditional way. (See example of reversed Cinderella below.) |
| Materials | • Flipchart and pens |

## Instructions

1. Ask the children to sit comfortably in a circle. Explain that you are going to tell them a story; they are to listen carefully and notice anything unusual in the story. Read the modified story to the children. Stop from time to time to ask, "Do you notice anything unusual about this story." Once all the children have understand the role reversals, it may be unnecessary to read the whole story or you may wish to jump to the conclusion.

2. Discuss the story, asking question such as these:

    a. How did you like the story?

    b. Did you find anything unusual in it?

    c. When did you realise that something was unusual? Ask for examples.

3. Point out that something seems unusual to us when it differs from our everyday experience and expectations. Ask the children to think of characteristics and activities that they consider typical of males and females in their everyday life. List their suggestions on a table such as the one below.

### Chart 1, stereotypical gender roles

| | MEN/BOYS | WOMEN/GIRLS |
|---|---|---|
| **USUAL CHARACTERISTICS** | Curious, smart, bold, loud, adventuresome, aggressive, ambitious, have short hair | Polite, sensitive, quiet, thoughtful of others, timid, nosey, obedient, wear dresses, have long hair |
| **USUAL ACTIVITIES** | Like sports, get in fights, go to work, take action, drive trucks | Stay at home, do the housework, cry easily, gossip, like pretty clothes, afraid of bugs |

4. Discuss this chart:

    a. Compare this chart with the familiar version of the story. Do characters have typical char-

**Source:** Adapted from the activity Gender-bender, *ABC Teaching Human Rights, Practical activities for primary and secondary schools*, United Nations, OHCHR, New York, Geneva, 2004, and Myra Sadker Advocates: www.sadker.org

acteristics and activities (e.g. Cinderella stays home, cries, is abused, and gets pretty clothes, while the Prince takes action to find a wife, and executes a clever plan to find Cinderella)?

    b. Ask the children if they can think of other stories where the characters have these typical characteristics and activities? List these stories as they are mentioned and ask the children to explain their suggestions.

5. Are these characteristics and activities typical of real women and men today?

    a. Make a chart such as the one below and ask the children to record their observations of unusual behaviour, first in the story and then in real life.

Chart 2: non-stereotypical gender roles

|  | MEN/BOYS | WOMEN/GIRLS |
|---|---|---|
| **UNUSUAL CHARACTERISTICS** | In the story: Needs help<br>In your experience: | In the story: Commanding, clever<br>In your experience: |
| **UNUSUAL ACTIVITIES** | In the story: Cries, does housework, wants nice clothes, stays at home<br>In your experience: | In the story: Actively pursues a husband, organizes a search<br>In your experience: |

6. Compare and discuss the two charts, asking questions such as these:

    a. Can you think of other stories where the characters have such unusual characteristics and activities? List these stories as they are mentioned and ask the children to explain their suggestions.

    b. Do you know of any real men and women who have non-typical characteristics and activities? Ask the children to describe their unusual characteristics and activities and to explain how they are unusual.

7. Define the word stereotype and give examples.

8. Ask the children to look at their chart of typical characteristics and activities. Ask them to determine which characteristics and activities are biological facts about men or women and which are beliefs, attitudes or stereotypes.

9. Point out that roles such as making money, raising children, and doing housework are common responsibilities of both men and women today.

## Debriefing and Evaluation

1. When the children have understood the concept of stereotypes, ask questions such as these:

    a. How are people treated when they do not conform to stereotypes of how males are females should behave?

    b. Why are stereotypes unfair to men and boys? To women and girls?

    c. How do gender stereotypes create inequality between men and women, boys and girls?

2. What can you do to act against stereotypes?

3. Ask the children if they can see any connection between gender stereotypes and human rights? Help them understand that everyone has a human right to be free from discrimination, including discrimination based on sex or gender stereotypes.

4. Ask the children how they felt about the activity.

## Suggestions for follow-up

- Ask the children to look for other stories or films where girls and boys are more equal and have non-traditional roles and characteristics.

- The activities 'BOYS DON'T CRY', P. 78, and 'WHAT I LIKE AND WHAT I DO', P. 185 also address gender stereotypes and their effects.

## Ideas for action

5. Ask, "Are people in our community discriminated against because they do not act the way people think men/boys or women/girls should?"
   a. Ask for examples, especially from the child's daily life.
   b. Ask the children to role play what they might say or do in such a situation to oppose discrimination.

## Tips for the facilitator

- Your goal in this activity should be to empower gender equality and encourage the children to question their own and others' assumptions about gender roles.

- Point out that expectations for how males and females behave can vary from country to country, community to community and even family to family. Emphasize the equality does not necessarily mean 'the same'.

- When asking the Debriefing and Evaluation questions, be sensitive to the fact that some children may already be teased and excluded for their non-traditional gender behaviour. Do not permit discussion to cause them discomfort.

- You do not need to use terms such as 'gender' or 'gender roles' with young children; however, developmental research shows that even pre-school children already understand different gender expectations.

## Adaptations

- For a large group: Create small groups of four. Give each a copy of Chart 1 and ask them to record the typical activities and characteristics of men and women. Representatives of the groups can present their findings. Discuss traditional and non-traditional roles with the whole group. Then ask the children to go back to their small groups and complete the chart with non-traditional characteristics and activities of men and women in both stories and their everyday life. End the activity with a discussion with the whole group.

- For older children: Instead of a fairy tale choose novel or well-known film. Start the story with sex roles reversed and let the children continue telling it themselves. Some older children may be able to revise and retell a familiar story on their own. Then each small group could share their story with the whole group.

# Cinderella

Once upon a time, there lived an unhappy young **boy**. His **father** had died, and **his mother** had brought home another **man**, a **widower** with two **sons**. His new **stepfather** didn't like the boy one little bit. All the good things, kind words and special privileges were for his own **sons**. They got fashionable clothes, delicious food and special treats. But for the poor unhappy **boy**, there was nothing at all. No nice clothes but only **his stepbrothers'** hand-me downs. No special dishes but only leftovers to eat. No privileges or even rest, for **he** had to work hard all day, grocery shopping, cooking, washing clothes and keeping the whole house clean. Only when evening came was **he** allowed to sit for a while alone by the cinders of the kitchen fire.

During these long evenings alone, he used to cry and talk to the cat. The cat said, "Meow", which really meant, "Cheer up! You have something neither of your **stepbrothers** have, and that is beauty."

What the cat said was quite true. Even dressed in rags with his face grimy from the cinders, he was an attractive young **man**, while no matter how elegant their clothes, **his stepbrothers** were still clumsy and ugly, and always would be.

One day, beautiful new clothes, shoes and jewellery began to arrive at the house. The Queen was holding a ball and the **stepbrothers** were getting ready to attend. They were continually standing in front of the mirror. The **boy** had to help them to dress up in all their finery. He didn't dare ask, "What about me?" for **he** knew very well what the answer to that would be: "You? My dear **boy**, you're staying at home to wash the dishes, scrub the floors and turn down the beds for your **stepbrothers**. They will come home tired and very sleepy."

After the brothers and their father had left for the ball, the poor **boy** brushed away his tears and sighed to the cat. "Oh dear, I'm so unhappy!" and the cat murmured, "Meow".

Just then a flash of light flooded the kitchen and a fairy appeared. "Don't be alarmed, **young boy**," said the fairy. "The wind blew me your sighs. I know you are longing to go to the ball. And so you shall!"

"How can I, dressed in rags?" the poor **boy** replied. "The servants will turn me away!" The fairy smiled. With a flick of his magic wand, the poor **boy** found **himself** wearing the most beautiful clothing, the loveliest ever seen in the realm.

"Now that we have settled the matter of what to wear," said the fairy, "we'll need to get you coach. A real **gentleman** would never go to a ball on foot! Quick! Get me a pumpkin!" **he** ordered.

"Oh, of course," said the poor **boy**, rushing away.

Then the fairy turned to the cat. "You, bring me seven mice!"

The poor boy soon returned with a fine pumpkin and the cat with seven mice **she** had caught in the cellar. "Good!" exclaimed the fairy. With a flick of **his** magic wand – wonder of wonders! – the pumpkin turned into a sparkling coach and the mice became six white horses, while the seventh mouse turned into a **coachwoman**, in a beautiful dress and carrying a whip. The poor **boy** could hardly believe his eyes.

"I shall present you at Court. You will soon see that the **Princess**, in whose honour the ball is being held, will be enchanted by your good looks. But remember! You must leave the ball at midnight and come home. For that is when the spell ends. You will turn back into a pumpkin, the horses will become mice again and the **coachwoman** will turn back into a mouse. And you will be dressed again in rags and wearing clogs instead of these splendid dancing shoes! Do you understand?"

The **boy** smiled and said, "Yes, I understand!"

## SAMPLE REVERSED FAIRYTALE

When the **boy** entered the ballroom at the palace, a hush fell. Everyone stopped in mid-sentence to admire **his** elegance, **his** beauty and grace.

"Who can that be?" people asked each other. The two **stepbrothers** also wondered who the newcomer was, for never in a month of Sundays would they ever have guessed that the beautiful **boy** was really their **stepbrother** who talked to the cat!

Then the **Princess** set eyes on **his** beauty. Walking over to **him**, **she** curtsied and asked **him** to dance. And to the great disappointment of all the **young gentlemen**, **she** danced with the **boy** all evening.

"Who are you, beautiful young **man**?" the Princess kept asking him.

But the poor **boy** only replied: "What does it matter who I am! You will never see me again anyway."

"Oh, but I shall, I'm quite certain!" **she** replied.

The poor **boy** had a wonderful time at the ball, but, all of a sudden, **he** heard the sound of a clock: the first stroke of midnight! **He** remembered what the fairy had said, and without a word of goodbye he slipped from the **Princess'** arms and ran down the steps. As **he** ran he lost one of his dancing shoes, but not for a moment did **he** dream of stopping to pick it up! If the last stroke of midnight were to sound…oh, what a disaster that would be! Out **he** fled and vanished into the night.

The **Princess**, who was now madly in love with **him**, picked up **his** dancing shoe and proclaimed that **she** would marry **the man** whose foot the slipper would fit. **She** said to **her** ministers, "Go and search everywhere for the **boy that** fits this shoe. I will never be content until I find **him**!" So the ministers tried the shoe on the foot of all the **boy**s.

When a minister came to the house where the **boy** lived with his **stepfather** and **stepbrothers**, the minister asked if he could try the shoe on the young **men** in the household. The two **stepbrothers** couldn't even get a toe in the shoe. When the minister asked if there were any other young **men** in the household, the stepfather told **her**. "No". However, just then the cat caught **her** attention, tugging at her **trouser** leg and leading her to the kitchen.

There sat the poor **boy** by the cinders. The minister tried on the slipper and to **her** surprise, it fit him perfectly.

"That awful untidy **boy** simply cannot have been at the ball," snapped the **stepfather**. "Tell the **Princess she** ought to marry one of my two **sons**! Can't you see how ugly the **boy** is! Can't you see?"

Suddenly **he** broke off, for the fairy had appeared.

"That's enough!" **he** exclaimed, raising **his** magic wand. In a flash, the **boy** appeared in a **beautiful** outfit, shining with youth and good looks. **His stepfather and stepbrothers** gaped at **him** in amazement, and the ministers said, "Come with us, handsome young **man**! The **Princess** awaits to present you with her engagement ring!" So the **boy** joyfully went with them. The **Princess** married **him** in a few days later, and they lived happily ever after.

And as for the cat, she just said "Meow!"

Source of the fairytale: Cinderella stories: www.ucalgary.ca/~dkbrown/cinderella.html

# 20. Picture Games

A picture says a thousand words – and more!

| | |
|---|---|
| Themes | Discrimination, General human rights, Media and Internet |
| Level of Complexity | Level 2 |
| Age | 8-13 years |
| Duration | 30 minutes |
| Group size | 2-20 children |
| Type of activity | Playing with pictures |
| Overview | Children work with images to explore stereotypes, different perspectives, and how images inform and misinform. |
| Objectives | • To raise awareness of human rights in everyday life<br>• To develop 'visual literacy', listening and communication skills<br>• To promote empathy and respect for human dignity |

In this activity you will find three different ideas on how to work with pictures on various human rights themes. Try the one that suits your group of children best.

# 20a. Part of the Picture

| | |
|---|---|
| Overview | Children draw conclusions about only part of a picture, then see the whole picture. |
| Preparation | • Find pictures that tell a simple story concerning poverty or an adequate standard of living. Mount pictures on cardboard and cut them into two parts so that the separate pieces suggest a different situation from the whole picture.<br>• Put the picture sets in separate envelopes, one set per child. |
| Materials | • Pictures<br>• Cardboard and glue<br>• Envelopes<br>• Cartoon book downloaded from COE website |

## Instructions

1. Divide children into pairs. Give each pair two envelopes containing a picture set.
2. Explain the activity:
    a. One child opens an envelope and gives the partner one piece of the picture inside.
    b. Let your partner say what they think is going on in the picture (e.g. who is in the picture, what is happening).
    c. Ask your partner if the picture relates to a human right.
    d. Then give your partner the second piece and ask them what they think is happening now that they have the full picture.
    e. Does the complete picture relate to a human right?
    f. Reverse roles.

## Debriefing and Evaluation

1. Debrief the activity by asking question such as these:

**Source:** Adapted from *COMPASS: A Manual on Human rights education with Young People* (Council of Europe, 2002), p. 192.

a. Did anything in this activity surprise you?

b. How did the picture change when you got the second piece?

c. What rights is the complete picture is conveying?

2. Relate the activity to perception by asking question such as these?

a. Can you think of other situations where it's easy to get the wrong idea because you see or hear only part of the situation?

b. How often do people accept what they see and forget that it may not be the 'whole story'?

**Tips for the facilitator**

• You can use this activity as an icebreaker.

• Variations:

■ Develop the activity further by having one pair swap pictures with another pair and repeating the activity. Do people find it easier the second time round? Or is it more challenging? Why?

■ Give the same pictures to two pairs. Then ask them to join in a group of four to compare their answers.

■ Use newspaper photographs, evaluating the picture and then reading the article illustrated by the photograph.

# 20b. Captions

| | |
|---|---|
| Overview | Children make captions for a group of pictures, then compare their different impressions. |
| Preparation | • Select and number 8-10 interesting pictures<br>• Make a work sheet divided into as many strips as you have pictures |
| Materials | • Numbered pictures<br>• Work sheet, paper and a pen for each pair<br>• Glue or tape and scissors for each pair |

**Instructions**

1. Lay the pictures out on a table. Divide the children into pairs and ask them to write captions for each of the pictures. Encourage them to write neatly because others will read what they write.

2. When everyone has finished, hold up the pictures in turn and ask volunteers to read out their captions.

3. Mount each picture on a sheet of paper or bulletin board and ask the children to glue or tape their captions under the picture to make a 'poster'.

**Debriefing and Evaluation**

1. Debrief the activity by asking questions such as these:

a. Was it difficult to write the captions? Why or why not?

b. What makes a good caption?

c. If a picture is worth a thousand words, why do they need captions?

2. Relate the activity to diversity by asking questions such as these:

a. Were there big differences in the way people interpreted the picture? Why?

b. Did you think any of your captions were wrong?

c. Why is it good to have different interpretations of the same thing?

### Tips for the facilitator

- Look for pictures that are both interesting and diverse, perhaps also ambiguous about what is going on.
- Use coloured paper and pens to make the posters more attractive.

# 20c. Speech Bubbles

| | |
|---|---|
| Overview | Children analyse pictures and give the characters cartoon speech bubbles, then they compare their impressions. |
| Preparation | • Copy pictures: 2 or more pairs should get the same picture. You can use the illustrations of the human rights themes in Chapter V..<br>• Make a work sheet with these questions: Who? What? Where? When? How? |
| Materials | • Work sheet, paper and pen for each pair<br>• Glue |

### Instructions

1. Divide the children into pairs. Give each pair a picture, worksheet, paper, pen and glue.
2. Give the children these instructions:
    a. Look at the picture and answer these questions about it on the worksheet: Who? What? Where? When? How?
    b. Then glue the picture onto the worksheet.
    c. Make speech bubbles for the characters in the picture to say something, and write in what they are saying.
3. Ask the pairs to post their pictures on the wall, placing the same pictures side by side for comparison. Ask the children to look at all the pictures and read their speech bubbles.

### Debriefing and Evaluation

1. Debrief the activity by asking question such as these:
    a. How hard was it to answer the questions about the pictures? To write speech bubbles?
    b. How did your analysis of the same picture compare with the analysis of the other pair?
    c. What stereotypes did people find in the pictures? In the speech bubbles?

### Tips for facilitators

In addition to pictures of people, use some with animals. This can be effective in discussing stereotypes. Start out by pointing out how often animals are cast as stereotypes in cartoons and then get the group to look for examples of stereotyping in their pictures and speech bubbles.

# 21. Picturing Ways Out of Violence

Now I see what I could do!

| | |
|---|---|
| Themes | Violence |
| Level of complexity | Level 1 |
| Age | 7 – 13 years |
| Duration | 60 minutes |
| Group size | 4 – 20 children |
| Type of activity | Creating human photos, discussion |
| Overview | Children illustrate a conflict or violent situation with a 'human photo' and then illustrate how it could be resolved without violence. |
| Objectives | • To raise awareness for keys to violence<br>• To develop non-violent ways of conflict resolution<br>• To start discussion on reasons for and behind violence |
| Preparation | None |
| Materials | None |

## Instructions

1. Discuss the topic of 'violence' with the group. What is it? What forms of violence can they think of that exist? Encourage the children to extend their understanding of violence beyond the physical to include verbal and psychological abuse and threats of abuse.

2. Divide the children into groups of 4 – 6. Explain that each group should spend fifteen minutes discussing violent situations they have observed or experienced (e.g. in school, in the family, with friends). The group should choose one violent situation they have discussed and then they should create a 'human photo' to show this situation to the others. The 'human photo' should include all the people in the group and should be a 'still', without any sound or movement. Their pose and facial expression should express their role in the photo (e.g. as a victim, perpetrator or witness).

3. Ask each group to present their 'human photo'. The rest of the group should comment on what they think is going on in the photo. The group presenting, however, should not comment.

4. After all the groups have presented their 'photo', explain that now they should return to their small groups and discuss how the situation or conflict in their presentation could be resolved without any violence. They should then create another human photo to show how the situation was resolved.

5. Ask each group to present their 'conflict resolution photo' to the rest of the group. This time there should be a short discussion after each presentation during which the rest of the group can first comment on what they have seen, and then the presenting group can explain what the situation was and how it was solved. Invite suggestions for other possible resolutions. Ask the children to evaluate these resolutions in terms of their real-life experience, emphasizing that there is usually more than one way to resolve violence.

## Debriefing and evaluation

1. Debrief the activity by asking questions such as these:

    d. Could you identify yourself with the 'human photos' of violence? Have you ever been in violent situations?

    c. How did your group work together as a team?

    d. What method did you use to decide on a story? To assign roles?

    e. How did you feel while playing your role?

2. Relate the activity to human rights by asking question such as these:

    a. Have you ever experienced or observed situations like those in the presentation?

    b. What is the link between these situations and human rights? Were any rights violated? Were any rights defended or enjoyed?

    c. Was the rights violation(s) in the presentation solved? How? Were there other possible ways of solving the problems?

    d. What could you do in real life to address a problem like this?

### Suggestions for follow-up

- The stories, and especially attempts to find solutions, may raise questions about human rights where children need and want more information. Help them find answers to their questions, especially in the CRC. Consider inviting speakers from relevant organisations to talk about their work and suggest ways that children can support it.

### Ideas for action

Perform the plays for other children, parents or other members of the community. Ask the children to explain to the audience the human rights context of their plays and the violation it represents.

### Tips for the facilitator

- Rather than being general, the topic of the stories can be focused on a particular problem or theme being addressed by the group (e.g. bullying, gender discrimination, or verbal abuse).
- The facilitator must be aware of the human rights issues in the stories in order to help the children make the link between the story and human rights.
- The facilitator should not intervene in the group work unless the group is facing difficulties in creating a presentation from a story.
- Younger children may need help in thinking of appropriate solutions. Where several solutions are offered, the children may need to help in deciding which to choose. Help them weigh up the advantages of each and possibly play though several different endings.
- If the children choose a long work such as a novel or film, help them select a single scene to present.
- This activity could easily be run over two or three days.
- If you do not have a puppet theatre, use a large blanket, behind which the children can sit to perform their puppet play.
- Puppets can be made in a variety of ways: use existing puppets, dolls or action figures; decorate socks; make paper cut-outs mounted on a stick; decorate paper tissue tubes or paper cups. Don't spend too much time on the puppets. The presentation is what matters.
- Suggested children's classics: Cinderella, Peter Pan, Hansel and Gretel, The Three Bears, Little Red Riding Hood, The Ugly Duckling.
- Suggested stories in other COMPASITO activities: 'DEAR DIARY', P. 99; 'MODERN FAIRYTALE', P. 113; 'ONCE UPON A TIME...', P. 125; 'ZABDERFILIO', P. 209.

## Variations

- With older children, encourage the creation of stories that involve issues based on the children's personal experiences, or problems being addressed by the group (e.g. bullying, discrimination, violence, or conflict management).

- Ask the children to change some feature of a familiar story (e.g. to make the wolf in 'Little Red Riding Hood' the victim of hurtful gossip; reverse gender roles, as in the activity 'ONCE UPON A TIME...', P. 125).

## Further information

This activity could also be done with families at home.

# 23. Putting Rights on the Map

Where do human rights begin?... In small places close to home!

| | |
|---|---|
| Themes | General human rights |
| Level of complexity | Levels 2-3 |
| Age | 8-13 years |
| Duration | 60 minutes – several days |
| Group size | 2-20 children |
| Type of activity | Drawing, analysis, discussion |
| Overview | Children work cooperatively to create a map of their community and identify the rights associated with major institution. |
| Objectives | • To develop familiarity with human rights<br>• To build association of human rights with places in children's daily life<br>• To encourage evaluation of human rights climate in the community |
| Preparation | • For younger children: prepare map outlines. |
| Materials | • Art supplies, chart paper<br>• Copies of child-friendly UDHR |

## Instructions

1. Divide the children into small groups and give them chart paper and art supplies. Ask them to draw a map of their own neighbourhood (or town, in the case of smaller communities). They should include their homes, major public buildings (e.g. parks, post office, town hall, schools, places of worship) and public services (e.g. hospitals, fire department, police station) and any other places that are important to the community (e.g. grocery stores, cemetery, cinemas, pharmacy, etc.).

2. When the maps are complete, ask the children to analyse their maps from a human rights perspective. What human rights do they associate with different places on their maps? For example, a place of worship with freedom of thought, conscience, and religion; the school with the right to education; the post office with the right to privacy, and to self-expression, the library or Internet café with the right to information. As they identify these rights, they should look up the relevant article(s) in the UDHR and write the article number(s) next to that place on the map.

3. Ask each group to present their map to the whole group and summarize their analysis of human rights exercised in the community.

## Debriefing and Evaluation

1. Debrief the activity by asking questions such as these:
   a. Was it hard to draw the map of our neighbourhood?
   b. Did you learn anything new about the neighbourhood?
   c. Were you surprised to discover human rights in our neighbourhood?
   d. How did your map differ from others?

**Source:**
Adapted from a demonstration by Anette Faye Jacobsen, Danish Intitute for Human Rights.

2. Relate the activity to human rights by asking questions such as these:
   a. Did any parts of your map have a high concentration of rights? How do you explain this?
   b. Did any parts have few or no rights associations? How do you explain this?

c. Are there any articles of the UDHR that seem to be especially exercised in this community? How can this be explained?

d. Are there any articles of the UDHR that no group included on their map? How can this be explained?

e. Are there any places in this community where people's rights are violated?

f. Are there any people in this community whose rights are violated?

g. What happens in this community when someone's human rights are violated?

h. Are there any places in this community where people take action to protect human rights or prevent violations from occurring?

## Suggestion for follow-up

• Use your maps to take a walk around the neighbourhood to observe rights in action.

• The activity 'COMPASITO REPORTER', P. 92, also ask children to evaluate their community through a human rights lens.

## Ideas for action

Invite a neighbourhood social worker, long-time resident or local activist to talk to the group about how they see the neighbourhood, how it is changing and what needs to be done to make it a better place to live. Help the children explore how they can contribute to this change.

## Tips for the facilitator

• This activity assumes that the children are already somewhat familiar with human rights, and helps them to put that conceptual learning into a well-known context. However, the children may still need some assistance in connecting everyday places with rights: e.g. grocery store with the right to health or an adequate standard of living.

• This activity has a very positive message: we enjoy rights everyday in our own neighbourhood. You may want to discuss the presence of violations on a different day to allow for this positive impact to be assimilated.

• Some young children may have little experience in reading a map and may need some time to assimilate the concept. You might begin by mapping the room, playground or building where you meet the children.

## Variations:

▪ Do each part of the activity on a different day, allowing the children time to become accustomed to reading the map and to consider the make-up of the neighbourhood.

▪ Assign each group a particular rights theme to consider when drawing the map.

▪ Use the CRC rather than the UDHR for this activity.

▪ Focus on a single rights theme such as freedom from violence or an adequate standard of living, and see how that theme finds expression in the neighbourhood.

## Adaptations for younger children:

▪ Work with an area that is familiar to the children, such as the immediate neighbourhood, school or home. The younger the children, the smaller the area to be mapped should be.

▪ Create a three-dimensional map using cardboard, boxes and art materials.

▪ To save time and emphasise the map-making process, provide children with a prepared map or

aerial photograph of the area that they can fill in and label. Close-up aerial views of most parts of Europe are available on Google Earth: http://earth.google.com/download-earth.html

- Omit Step 2 where the UDHR articles are matched with the right.

**Adaptations for older children:**

- Draw maps to scale.
- Divide the children into groups and give each group a separate part of one common map to analyse.
- In the debriefing, ask questions about whether the rights they have noted are civil and political rights, and which are economic, social and cultural rights. Did one kind of right predominate on the map? Did one kind of right predominate in certain areas (e.g. more civil and political rights associated with the court house, city hall, or police)?

# 24. Rabbit's Rights

We have a right to be happy, safe and healthy!

| | |
|---|---|
| Themes | General human rights |
| Level of complexity | Level 1 |
| Age | 8 – 10 years |
| Duration | 30 minutes |
| Group size | 5 – 20 children |
| Type of activity | Imagining, brainstorming, discussion |
| Objectives | • To introduce the CRC<br>• To show children that they are instinctively aware of children's rights<br>• To connect human needs with human rights |
| Overview | Children imagine the care a pet rabbit needs and extend that to the needs of children and their right to survive and develop |
| Preparation | • Make a chart, or copies of the CRC. |
| Materials | • Chart paper and markers<br>• Chart, or a copy of the CRC |

## Instructions

1. Ask the children to imagine that they have a pet rabbit to care for, and to give a name to it. They need to think about all the things it needs to be happy, safe and healthy. Ask, "What are all the things the rabbit will need?" They may suggest things such as a hutch, straw, food, water, exercise, attention, love or perhaps another rabbit for company. Write 'RABBIT' (or the given name) at the top of the left-hand column on a chart such as the one below, and record the children's responses.

2. Then ask, "Who is responsible for ensuring that the rabbit gets all the things that it needs?" Note down the children's responses, which may be that they or whoever owns the rabbit is responsible.

3. Confirm the things the rabbit needs to survive and develop, such as food, water, and a hutch. Then ask questions such as these:

    a. If the rabbit really needs these things to survive, then should the rabbit have a right to them?

    b. Who is responsible for ensuring that the rabbit's rights to these things are met?

4. Then write 'CHILDREN' at the top of the right-hand column and ask the group to brainstorm: "What are the things that children need to develop and have for a happy, safe and healthy life?" List the children's responses, helping to elicit such things as home, food, water, family, friends, toys, education, love and attention.

5. Ask, "Who is responsible for ensuring that children get all the things they need to be happy, safe and healthy?" Encourage answers such as adults, parents, family, and caregivers.

6. Ask questions such as these to expand the focus of children's rights, adding additional needs to the chart:

    a. What do children need to be protected, to survive, to develop and to participate?

    b. If children need these things, then should children have a right to them?

    c. Who is responsible for ensuring that children have these rights?

7. Ask the group if they have ever heard of the Convention on the Rights of the Child (CRC). Give them copies of the child-friendly version or use a poster version. Explain that this document states the things to which every child in the world has a right.

**Source:** *DIY guide to improving your community – getting children and young people involved*, Save the Children across Scotland, 2005

### Debriefing and Evaluation

1. Invite the children to compare their list on the chart with those in the CRC. Point out that they have created a list of children's rights. Ask questions such as these:

   a. What needs did you name that are also in the CRC? Mark these on the chart with a star.

   b. Why do you think you were able to think of so many of the rights by yourself?

2. Point out that the group knew from the beginning what children needed to develop and grow, without adults having to tell them. They are experts on their own lives! Explain that the CRC is there to support children's rights, to protect them, to provide for them and to ensure that they can participate in the world around them.

### Suggestions for follow-up

- This is an excellent introduction to children's rights, and it makes a strong connection between needs and rights. It leads directly to other activities that explore children's rights further, such as 'My Universe of Rights', p. 122 and 'Rights Mobile', p. 148.

### Tips for the facilitator

- Because this activity requires no reading skills, it can be run with very young children. However, they only need to have the idea of 'rights' defined, in simple terms. The CRC can be introduced later.

- You could choose to replace 'rabbit' with any other household pet.

- Variations: If appropriate to the group, you might conclude by reading the child-friendly CRC aloud, with each child reading a different article.

- Adaptation for Older Children: When comparing the children's list and the CRC, invite discussion of what they omitted, asking questions such as these:

  - Are there other needs and rights in the CRC that were not on your list?

  - Why do you think they are in the CRC?

  - Why do you think you might have thought of these needs and rights?

## Sample Chart

| RABBIT | CHILDREN |
|---|---|
|  |  |
|  |  |

# 25. Red Alert

*Is half a right better than no right at all?*

| | |
|---|---|
| Themes | General human rights |
| Level of complexity | Level 2 |
| Age | 8 – 13 years |
| Duration | 60 minutes (less for a larger group) |
| Group size | At least 10+ children and 3 facilitators |
| Type of activity | Active outdoor group game |
| Overview | Children try to find the missing half of a right before it is stolen. |
| Objectives | • To promote group dynamics<br>• To create opportunities for discussion of human rights |
| Preparation | • Go over the game instructions and role cards thoroughly so that you understand how the activity works. This is a complicated game with complex roles for all the players. Note that this activity requires a number of facilitators: 10 playing children require a minimum of 3 facilitators (1 coordinator, 1 central post, and 1 hunter) plus 2 Card People, who can be played by children as well.<br>• Copy role cards for facilitators and any children who will play roles.<br>• Brief facilitators and any children who will play roles.<br>• Copy or write the 10 Rights Cards on different pieces of coloured paper in order you have some 50 cards altogether, this is what you need for a group of 10-15 children. For each additional 5 children, add another colour (e.g. for 25 children you need 70 cards in seven colours).<br>• Cut the Rights Cards into strips of individual rights.<br>• Cut Rights Cards in half. Divide the half-cards into two stacks. Give one stack to the Central Post and divide the other at random among the Card People.<br>• Check the location for the game, and define the borders of the playing area. Establish locations for Central Post and the different Card People. |
| Materials | • 50-70 strips of Rights Cards cut in half in different colour copies<br>• Scissors<br>• Sticky tape to glue the cards together<br>• Drawing pins or sticky tape to put up completed Rights Cards<br>• Noisemaker to signal 'hunting season' and end of game (e.g. a whistle)<br>• Signs, hats or other distinguishing clothing for Hunters<br>• Recommended: first aid kit, bottled water |

## Instructions

1. Gather the children at Central Post and introduce the activity: A Red Alert has been given and they have been asked to take action. Ten children's rights have disappeared and seem to be lost forever. However, half of the missing ten rights have been recovered. It will be their challenge to find the missing half and restore the full right. If they can collect all the Rights Cards in a given time they win against the Hunters, who endanger Children Rights.

2. Establish the length of the game (30 minutes for a small group; 20 minutes for groups of 20 or more). Explain the boundaries of the game and agree on an audible sign to indicate the beginning and the end of the game. Explain that you will be outside the game making sure that everyone is safe and follows the rules.

3. The facilitator playing the Central Post gives every child a half-card and keeps the rest of them. Explain to the children that the goal of the game is find the other half of their card in order to make

**143**

a complete Rights Card. The other half cards can be collected from the Card People. It must match in both the number of the right and colour of the card.

4. When you have both halves of the card, they should bring them to Central Post.

5. Introduce and explain the role of the Central Post to the children:

   a. The activity begins and ends at Central Post.

   b. When you have both halves of a Rights Card, you bring it to Central Post. The person there will stick the two halves together and hang up the completed Rights Card.

   c. You will be offered the choice of another card.

6. Introduce and explain the role of the Card People to the children:

   a. The Card People have the missing half cards.

   b. They will be located in different parts of the playing area where players can find them. Most Card People will stay in one place; however, at least one Card Person will walk around.

   c. You will go up to a Card Person and show them your half card. If the Card Person has the other half of that card, he or she will give it to you. You will then take the completed card to Central Post, take another half card and begin again.

   d. If a Card Person doesn't have the other half card, you have to contact another Card Person.

   e. During Hunting Seasons the only safe place is within arms length of the Card People. If you can touch a Card Person, the Hunters cannot catch you. The Card People will now go out and take their positions.

7. Introduce and explain the role of the Hunters and the system of 'hunting seasons':

   a. During hunting seasons Hunters try to catch you and take your rights away.

   b. Each time they catch you, Hunters rip your half-card into two pieces. They give one of the torn pieces back to you and keep the other torn piece to give to the Card People. This means that every time they catch you, it becomes harder to complete your card because it is in smaller pieces.

   c. You will know it is hunting season when you hear a whistle or horn sound once. When hunting season is over, it will be blown twice.

   d. Remember: the only place where the Hunters cannot catch you is within arms length of a Card Person.

8. Start the game. The children start running around in the playing area, looking for the Card People in order to complete the half-card they have.

9. End the game when all the cards have been completed or the time is up.

**Debriefing and evaluation**

1. Debrief the activity by asking questions such as these:

   a. What happened during the game?

   b. What were the most exciting moments?

   c. Did you have a certain strategy?

   d. If you played this game again, would you do anything different?

   e. What do you think of this activity?

2. Relate the activity to human rights by asking questions such as these:

   a. When we say we have "the Right to ...", what does this mean?

   b. Do you think that these Rights are 'universal'? Are they respected all over the world?

   c. In real life, who could the 'hunters' and the 'card-people' be?

d. What can we do in our daily life to make sure that everybody has the same rights?

## Suggestions for follow-up

- The activity 'RIGHTS MOBILE', P. 148, focuses on the same ten rights and links them to gender. It is a calm and creative activity.
- The activities 'MOST IMPORTANT FOR WHOM?', P. 118, and 'SAILING TO A NEW LAND', P. 152, ask children to prioritize among rights, stressing the importance of having the full range of rights.

## Ideas for action

Discuss with the children about which rights they have in their daily life and decide on concrete actions to promote them in their own community.

## Tips for the facilitator

- Note that this activity requires a number of facilitators. At least one facilitator should be outside the game as coordinator. Card People may be facilitators or children, but *only* facilitators should be Central Post or Hunters. The more children there are in the game, the more facilitators you need to play the game safely and smoothly.
    - **Minimum facilitators needed for a small group of children**: 3 facilitators (1 coordinator, 1 central post, and 1 hunter) plus 2 Card People
    - **Minimum for a group up to twenty players**: 4 facilitators (1 coordinator, 1 central post, and 2 hunters) plus 3-4 Card People
    - **Minimum for a group up to twenty-five players**: 5 facilitators (1 coordinator, 1 central post, and 3 hunters) plus 4-5 Card People
- This activity is best run outdoors (e.g. playground, sports field, park, forest). It can also be adapted to a large indoor space.
- Although this activity is quite safe, a first aid kit and bottled water are always advisable for outdoor games away from your school or centre.

# HANDOUT: ROLE CARDS

**ROLE OF COORDINATING FACILITATOR (1 facilitator)**

At the beginning you will explain the game and establish the boundaries. You will also make clear what your signal is to stop the game at the end or in case of emergency, which should be quite different from the signal for the 'hunting season'.

Make sure both children and facilitators understand and maintain their roles. During the activity you will keep watch to see that no-one is playing roughly or doing anything that might endanger a child. Intervene or stop the game if necessary. You will keep the first aid kit and supply of bottled water for use if necessary.

At the end of the time, you will end the game and run the debriefing.

**ROLE OF CENTRAL POST (1 facilitator)**

As the name already implies, this should be a central, fixed location. The activity begins and ends here.

You provide half cards to children and keep the rest of the half-cards that have not been given to the players. The Card-People hold the other halves of all the cards.

- A child who has both halves of a Rights Card will bring it to you. You then let the child choose a new half card from you.
- Stick the completed halves of the Rights Card together. Hang the completed cards on a wall or tree so that the children can easily see their progress.
- Note that as children start choosing new half-cards, they will start developing their own strategy for completing full colour-sets, instead of randomly completing cards. You should encourage but not initiate this strategy building.
- As children withdraw from the game, get them to help you with the tasks at the Central Post.

**ROLE OF THE CARD-PEOPLE (2+ children or facilitators)**

Divide a full set of half-cards among yourselves.

- Find yourselves a position in the playing area. You should not be hidden but spread out. The children should be able to find you.
- All but one Card Person remain in one place. One Card Person walks around during the game, allowing this facilitator to keep an extra eye on the whole game.
- Players will come to you and show you half a card. If you have the other half of this card, give it to the player.
- During Hunting Seasons, there is a safety zone around you as far as you can reach. Within this zone, Hunters cannot catch the players.
- Even when you have no more half cards to give away, stay at your place until the final sound indicates the end of the game. Then go back to Central Post, gathering children along way who may not have heard this sound.

**HUNTERS (1+ facilitators)**

- You role is to catch players and take rights away during hunting seasons. Each time you manage to catch a player, rip the half-card of this player into two pieces. Give one torn piece back to the player and give other torn piece to one of the Card People. This means it becomes harder for the player to complete this card.
- Hunting Season is a very exciting moment for the children. Do it regularly but for short periods. Blow the horn or whistle once when the hunting season starts; twice to announce its ending.
- Hunters should dress alike (e.g. with a sign, hat, coat, or scarf) and be very visible. Make noises during Hunting Season to increase the excitement of the children.
- When 'hunting' children, it is more the purpose to increase excitement than it is to catch them. If you catch too many or the same players, the children may get discouraged.

## HANDOUT: RIGHTS CARDS

After copying the following grid on different coloured papers, cut each right out. When all the rights are cut out, cut them in 2 halves. Each of the rights will then have 2 parts, similar in colour and number. After distributing the half cards to the children the rest of all the rights stay at the Central Post, while the other half are divided amongst the Card People. For a group of 10-15 children copy Rights Cards below on 5 different colours for a total of 50 cards. For each additional 5 children, add another colour (e.g. for 25 children you need 70 cards in seven colours). If it is hard to copy these rights, write them out by hand.

| | | |
|---|---|---|
| 1. | Every child has the Right to protection. | 1. |
| 2. | Every child has the Right to education. | 2. |
| 3. | Every child has the Right to healthcare. | 3. |
| 4. | Every child has the Right to free time activities and playing. | 4. |
| 5. | Every child has the Right to a name and a nationality. | 5. |
| 6. | Every child has the Right to choose his/her own religion. | 6. |
| 7. | Every child has the Right to information. | 7. |
| 8. | Every child has the Right to form an association. | 8. |
| 9. | Every child has the Right to live in a house with his/her family. | 9. |
| 10. | Every child has the Right to a fair trial | 10. |

# 26. Rights Mobile

I'm proud to show my rights for all to see!

| | |
|---|---|
| Themes | General human rights, Gender equality |
| Level of complexity | Level 2 |
| Age | 10-13 years |
| Duration | 120-180 minutes |
| Group size | 1-20 children |
| Type of activity | Creative activity |
| Overview | Children construct hanging mobiles (see example at the end of the activity) showing the rights most important to them. |
| Objectives | • To discuss the content and meaning of basic rights <br> • To discover which rights are respected in your own environment <br> • To explore gender differences in relation rights |
| Preparation | • Practise making a mobile to master the techniques. <br> • Have an example of a mobile to show children what you mean. <br> • Write out the short version of the ten rights on a flipchart or blackboard. <br> • Cut out shapes of people. |
| Materials | • White cardboard paper cut into the shapes of a person <br> • Colouring materials (e.g. wax crayons, paints, markers) <br> • Blue, white and red paper strips, 3 of each colour per child <br> • Flipchart or blackboard for listing rights <br> • Small, light sticks (wooden, plastic or metal), 20 centimetres long <br> • Thin string <br> • Tape, glue or a stapler; drawing pins or small nails <br> • Scissors <br> • Optional: magazine for cut-out pictures |

## Instructions

1. Introduce the activity by showing the children an example of a mobile and explaining that they are going to create a human rights mobile (see the illustration).

2. Ask the children to spend a few minutes in pairs listing all the things that are important to them in their lives (e.g. family, friends, food, home, school, play).

3. Give each child a blank cut-out of a person. Ask them to write their name on the back and decorate the shape, which should symbolize themselves.

4. Begin your explanation by emphasizing that everyone needs all human rights and that we cannot pick and choose among them. However, for their mobiles, they will show the rights that matter the most to them personally. Then give each child three red, three blue and three white paper strips. Explain that red means 'most important', blue 'important' and white 'less important'.

5. Show the children the flipchart with the list of rights. Then read the child-friendly version of the rights and discuss the meaning of each article. Ask the children what they think the article means and elicit specific examples for each right. When you have finished, ask the children to look at the list of rights and decide which are the most important to them and write them out on the red strips; then ask them to write the important ones on the blue strips, and the less important ones on the white strips. Explain that although every child has all these rights, for this activity they must choose the nine rights that are most important to them.

6. Once all the children have written the nine rights on their nine coloured paper strips, explain how to make a mobile. Demonstrate how to create balance in the mobile.

7. Hang the mobiles somewhere clearly visible, for example, from the ceiling.

## Debriefing and Evaluation

1. When all the mobiles have been created, use the grid below to analyse the ranking of rights. Discuss the results by asking questions such as these:

   a. Which rights seem to be the most important to our group? How can you explain this?

   b. Which rights seem to be the least important to our group? How can you explain this?

   c. Which rights are the most important for you? Do your personal priorities different from the group's? How can you explain this?

   d. Is there a difference between the priorities of boys and girls? How can you explain this?

   e. Can you think of other groups who might have different priorities from yours (e.g. disabled children, refugees, ethnic minorities, adults)?

   f. Are all these rights respected in our community?

2. Debrief the activity by asking question such as these:

   a. What do you feel about the activity?

   b. Was it hard to prioritise the rights?

   c. Which part did you enjoy doing most? Why?

   d. Did anything surprise you?

3. Link the activity to general human rights by asking questions such as these:

   a. What is a right?

   b. Why is it important to have all our human rights and not just those that are our favourites?

   c. Do boys and girls have different rights?

   d. Do adults have different rights?

   e. Do you think all the children in the world have the same rights? Why or why not?

   f. What can we do to make sure that all the children in the world have the same reality?

## Suggestions for follow-up

- The activity 'MOST IMPORTANT FOR WHOM?', P. 118 , further develops the concept of the interdependence of rights.

## Ideas for action

- Contact local organizations that work for the most highly rated rights and explore ways to join their activities.

- The children may rate some rights as less important because they are unfamiliar. Learn more about some of these rights and explore how they are important in your community.

- Hang the mobiles along with explanations written by the children about their most important rights as an exhibition in a public place (e.g. library, post office, school corridors). Use the exhibition to celebrate Human Rights Day, December 10, or some other holiday (See the activity 'A HUMAN RIGHTS CALENDAR', P. 60).

## Tips for the facilitator

- Emphasize that neither we nor our government can pick and choose among our human rights. We all

need all our human rights all the time! Clarify that this exercise asks the children only to rank the rights that are most important to them personally. Especially stress this concept of interdependence of rights in Step 3 of the Instructions and Question 1 of the Debriefing and Evaluation section.

- Make a small mobile yourself in advance and experiment with weights and distances to understand how to balance it, and the best ways to connect the papers to the strings and sticks, using tape, glue or staples.
- You may choose other rights from the CRC that you find appropriate for your group.

### Variations:

- Extend this activity over a longer period. Each child could also make a mobile of the community, Europe or the world.
- Give the children nine strips but offer them more than nine rights to choose from.
- Ask the children to design and cut out their own personal shapes.
- Ask the children to decorate the coloured strips with drawings or cut-out pictures that represent that right.
- Make a huge mobile for greater visual impact.
- Depending on the size of your group, the available time and the number of facilitators, the children can work individually or in small groups. If you work in groups, you might divide boys from girls to see what sex differences arise.

### Adaptations:

- For younger children: Facilitators may need help with the manual tasks of this activity.
- For older children: Ask them to make mobiles in small groups where each person has to agree with what is put on the mobile. The debriefing questions would also then have to include questions concerning the group work and process of deciding on the final mobile.

## RIGHTS MOBILE

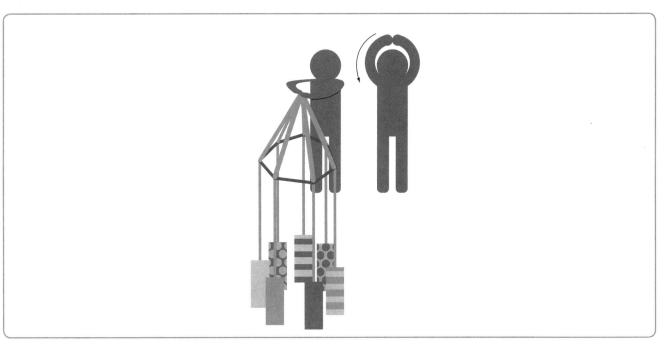

## SAMPLE LIST OF RIGHTS

The following grid can be used to define the total 'score' of each Right. Give 3 points to Red Rights, 2 points to Blue Rights and 1 to the remaining white Rights.

| Some Human Rights | Girls | Boys | Total scores | Final ranking |
|---|---|---|---|---|
| Every child has the right to protection. | | | | |
| Every child has the right to education. | | | | |
| Every child has the right to healthcare. | | | | |
| Every child has the right to free time activities and playing. | | | | |
| Every child has the right to a name and a nationality. | | | | |
| Every child has the right to choose his/her own religion. | | | | |
| Every child has the right to information. | | | | |
| Every child has the right to form an association. | | | | |
| Every child has the right to live in a house with his/her family. | | | | |

# 27. Sailing to a New Land

What will you throw overboard?

| | |
|---|---|
| Themes | General human rights |
| Level of complexity | Level 1 |
| Age | 8 – 13 years |
| Duration | 45 minutes |
| Group size | 8 – 20 children |
| Overview | The children imagine they are sailing to a new continent, but to get there they must choose to cast non-essentials overboard. |
| Type of activity | Prioritising, discussion |
| Objectives | • To evaluate what is essential for survival and development<br>• To separate wants from needs<br>• To connect human needs and human rights |
| Preparation | • Copy and cut out a set of Wants and Needs cards for each group; place in an envelope. |
| Materials | • Envelopes<br>• Copies of Wants and Needs cards<br>• Glue or sticky tape and sheets of paper |

## Instructions

1. Ask the children to imagine that they are about to set sail to a new continent. There are no people living there now, so when they arrive, they will be pioneers establishing a new country.

2. Divide the children into small groups and give each group an envelope with all the Wants and Needs cards in, explaining that these are the things they are packing to take with them for life in the new country. Ask each group to open the envelope, spread out all their cards and examine them.

   **Variation**: Provide a few blank cards and give the children an opportunity to add some additional things they think the might need or like to have.

3. Explain that the boat is setting sail now and begin a narrative like this:

   *At first the trip is very pleasant. The sun is shining and the sea is peaceful. However, a big storm comes up suddenly, and the ship is rocking. In fact, it's about to sink! You must throw three of your cards overboard to keep the boat afloat.*

   Ask every group to decide what to give up. Explain that they won't be able to get these things back later. Collect the cards which have been 'thrown overboard', and put them together in one pile.

4. Return to the narrative:

   *At last the storm is over. Everyone is very relieved. However, a weather report comes that a Category 5 hurricane is heading straight for the ship. If you are going to survive the hurricane, you must throw overboard another three cards! Remember: don't throw away what you may need to survive in your new country.*

   As before, collect these cards and keep them in a separate pile.

5. Return to the narrative:

   *That was a very close shave! However, we are almost at the new continent. Everyone is very*

Adapted from the activity Wants and Needs, developed by Centre for Global Education, York St John University, published in *Our World Our Rights*, Amnesty International, London, 1995. Origin: Pam Pointon, Homerton College, Cambridge

*excited. But just as we sight land on the horizon, a giant whale crashes into the boat and makes a hole in the side. You must make the ship even lighter! Throw away three more cards.*

Collect and put these cards into a pile.

6. Announce that finally they have reached the new continent safely and are ready to build a new country. Ask each group to glue their remaining cards onto a piece of paper so that everyone can remember what they are bringing to the new continent. Have you got all the things you need to survive? To grow and develop well?

7. Ask each group to hang their sheet at the front of the room and explain what they are bringing to the new land. After each description, ask the whole group, "Are they missing anything they will need to survive? To grow and develop?"

## Debriefing and evaluation

1. Debrief the activity by asking questions such as these:
   a. What did you like about this activity?
   b. How did you decide what you could do without? What was essential?
   c. Were some decisions difficult? Which ones?
   d. Were there any disagreements as a group on what to keep and what to throw overboard? How did you solve these disagreements?
   e. Do all people have the same needs? Who may have different needs?
   f. What do you think about your final choices? Will you be able to survive in the new country? Will you be able to grow and develop well?
   g. How did your group decide what to throw away?
   h. Did the final result surprise you?
   i. If you had to do this activity a second time, would you throw away any different things?

2. Emphasise that human rights are based on human needs: the things that every human being needs to survive, grow and develop well and live a life of dignity. Ask questions such as these:
   a. Did you have what you need to survive?
   b. Did you have what you need to grow and develop?
   c. What things did you want to have but decide were not essential?

3. Emphasise that everyone needs all their human rights! Some are necessary to stay alive, such as food, medical care, clean water and shelter. But others are essential for people to live well and develop. It is not enough for anyone just to stay alive. Ask:
   a. Which cards represent things we might want but don't have to have for survival?
   b. Which cards represent things we have to have for physical survival?
   c. Which cards represent things we might need to grow and develop well?
   d. What would happen in this new country if you didn't have _____? (Choose several different examples from the cards.)

## Suggestions for follow-up

- This activity is an excellent follow-up to 'RABBIT'S RIGHTS', P. 141, which introduces human needs as a basis for human rights.
- Follow-up activities can include 'A CONSTITUTION FOR OUR GROUP', P. 56 which discusses democratic rule making with the children.

### Tips for the facilitator

- It is very important that the children do not assume from this activity that some human rights are less important than others and can be eliminated. In the debriefing emphasise the interdependence of rights.

- Emphasise that the things they discard cannot be regained and that the things they keep are needed to build a new country, not just survive until they are 'rescued'.

- Some items are intentionally ambiguous to stimulate debate about what defines an essential item (e.g. a mobile phone might be seen as a luxury by some and a necessity for communication by others).

- Young children may have difficulty distinguishing what they want from what they need. Help them by emphasizing what they will require to survive in a new country.

### Variations

- In the debriefing compare the cards 'thrown overboard' in each crisis. Ask the children what differences they see in people's choices.

opportunities to share my opinion

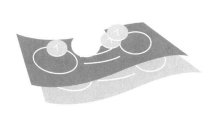

money to spend as I like

clean water

bedroom of my own

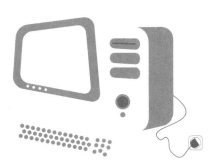

computer and access to the internet

fair treatment and non-discrimination

# HANDOUT: WANTS AND NEEDS CARDS

clean environment

mobile telephone

coke and hamburger

opportunities to rest and play

television and newspaper

opportunities to practise my religion

# HANDOUT: WANTS AND NEEDS CARDS

comfortable home

fashionable clothes

holiday at the beach

nutritious food

protection from abuse

education

**157**

doctors

bicycle

sweets

jewellery

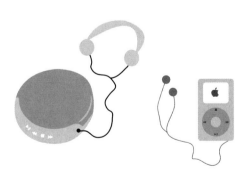

mp3 player or discman

warm clothes

## HANDOUT: WANTS AND NEEDS CARDS

parents

toys and games

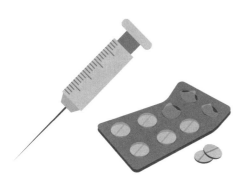

medicine and immunisation
against disease

democratic elections and rules

watch

opportunities to practise my culture
and language

# 28. Silent Speaker

*Read my lips!*

| | |
|---|---|
| Themes | Discrimination, Health, Participation |
| Level of complexity | Level 2 |
| Age | 8–13 years |
| Duration | 45 minutes |
| Group size | 6-21 children |
| Type of activity | Role play, guessing game |
| Overview | Children read an article of the CRC without making a sound; their team members try to identify the article by lip reading. |
| Objectives | • To understand the difficulties people with hearing disability<br>• To understand the skill of lip-reading and the conditions that favour it<br>• To review articles of the CRC<br>• To understand the need for positive discrimination |
| Preparation | • Prepare cards with selected articles of the CRC for each child. Each card should have the name and number of the article and its child-friendly text.<br>• Cut a box to make a frame like a TV screen for the speaker, or use an existing puppet theatre.<br>• Copy the child-friendly CRC for every child. |
| Materials | • Cards with CRC articles<br>• Copies of the child-friendly CRC<br>• Some kind of frame for the speaker<br>• Bag or basket to hold CRC cards |

## Instructions

1. Explain that this activity needs a scorekeeper and ask for a volunteer to play this role. Divide the remaining children into teams of three or four. Give each child a copy of the child-friendly CRC. Review the CRC with them to ensure that everyone is familiar with the document.

2. Explain the activity:

   a. One child from each team will be a 'silent speaker'. The scorekeeper lets that child take a CRC card. The 'silent speaker' then stands in the frame and reads the article, starting with the number and name of the article and continuing to read the whole text without stopping by moving his or her lips but not making a sound. Members of the speaker's team will try to guess which article it is by lip-reading what the 'silent speaker' is reading.

   b. The scorekeeper writes down the score for each team at the end of every turn. Teams can earn the following points:

   c. If a team understands both the name and text of the article, they get three points.

   d. If a team can only guess the name/right of the article, they get one point.

   e. If a team cannot guess the article by the time the reader has finished, they get no points.

3. Start the activity. When one member from each team has been the 'silent speaker', announce the first round's score. The team with the highest score in that round starts first. Continue until each child has had a turn to be the speaker.

## Debriefing and Evaluation

1. Debrief the activity by asking questions such as these:
   a. How did you feel trying to lip-read? Was it difficult? Was it fun? Was it tiring?
   b. What conditions made lip-reading easier? More difficult?
   c. What did you do as the silent reader to help others understand?
   d. Were some people easier to understand than others?
   e. Were some sounds or words easier to understand than others?

2. Put the activity in the context of hearing disability by asking questions such as these:
   a. Some people in our community have to lip-read all the time. Who are they?
   b. Do you know someone who has difficulty hearing?
   c. Because of the position of your mouth when you make sounds, lip-reading only allows for about one third of the information you need to decode a message. What do you think it is like if you have to lip-read all the time? Would it be tiring? Would it be fun?
   d. What are some everyday situations that would be especially difficult for people with hearing disabilities?

3. Put hearing disability into the context of human rights by asking question such as these:
   a. What do people with hearing disabilities have in order to live and work safely and happily in our community? To participate in our community?
   b. Do children with hearing disabilities have special needs? How are they met?
   c. What are some ways in which our community helps people with hearing disabilities? With other disabilities?
   d. What are some ways in which you could help a person with hearing disabilities?
   e. Do people with disabilities have a right to have their needs met? Why?
   f. Explain that Article 23 of the CRC clearly states that children with disabilities have a right to assistance to enjoy their human rights. How could a disability prevent children from enjoying their human rights? What are some kinds of assistance they might need?

## Suggestions for follow-up

- The activity 'BLINDFOLDED', P. 67, deals with the special needs of people with visual disabilities.

## Ideas for action

- The children can conduct a 'soundless survey' of their school and community to assess situations in which children with hearing disabilities would have particular trouble. They can then investigate what could be done to improve these situations.
- The children can learn that there are sign languages that are now recognized as real languages. Introduce them to the sign language used in their country.
- The children can help make materials for deaf children by imagining visual solutions for sound messages (e.g. starting a race use flags instead of a sound), finding cartoons or visual stories and by reading a text at the same time as an interpreter 'says' it in sign language. Check with your local Deaf Association for suggestions of other actions the children can take.

## Tips for the facilitator

- This game should be adjusted to the children's age, reading skills and previous knowledge of human rights. If the children are not skilled readers or have not been introduced to human rights before, you

should simplify the game by asking them to read the names of the rights but not the full articles.

- Keep the emphasis on scorekeeping as low as possible as it may detract from the goal of the activity. Announce the score for a round only at the end of that round and allow the team with the highest score to go first in the next round. Avoid keeping a cumulative score for the activity, although you may get some pressure from the children to do so.

- To get used to the method of the game before starting, you could ask the children to practise by saying the name of another person in the group without making a sound and asking the others to guess which name is being said.

- Clarify whether miming and body gestures are allowed. Younger children may need these extra clues.

# 29. Take a Step Forward

We are all equal – but some are more equal than others.

| | |
|---|---|
| Themes | General human rights, Discrimination, Poverty and social exclusion |
| Complexity | Level 2 |
| Age | 10 – 13 years |
| Group size | 10 – 30 children |
| Type of Activity | Role play, simulation, discussion |
| Time | 60 minutes |
| Overview | Children imagine being someone else and consider inequality as a source of discrimination and exclusion |
| Objectives | • To promote empathy with others who are different |
| | • To raise awareness about the inequality of opportunities in society |
| | • To foster an understanding of possible consequences of belonging to minority groups |
| Preparation | • Adapt the roles and 'situations' to your group. Make a role card for every child. |
| | • Copy the sheet of roles, cut out the strips and fold them over. |
| Materials | Role cards |
| | List of situations |
| | Optional: art materials to make name tags and/or pictures |

## Instructions

1. Introduce the activity by asking the children if they have ever imagined being someone else. Ask for examples. Explain that in this activity they will also imagine that they are someone else, another child who may be quite different from themselves.

2. Explain that everyone will take a slip of paper with their new identity. They should read it silently and not let anyone know who they are. If a child does not understand the meaning of a word in his/her role card, they should silently raise their hand and wait for the facilitator to come and explain.

3. Discourage questions at this point. Explain that even if they don't know much about a person like this, they should just use their imagination. To help children get into role, ask them to do a few specific things to make the role seem real to them. For example:

   a. Give yourself a name. Make a name tag with this name to remind you of who you are imagining yourself to be.

   b. Draw a picture of yourself

   c. Draw a picture of your house, room, or street.

   d. Walk around the room pretending to be this person.

4. To further enhance their imagination, play some quiet music and ask the children to sit down and close their eyes and imagine in silence as you read out a few questions such as these:

   a. Where were you born? What was it like when you were little? What was you family like when you were little? Is it different now?

   b. What is your everyday life like now? Where do you live? Where do you go to school?

   c. What do you do in the morning? In the afternoon? In the evening?

   d. What kind of games do you like playing? Who do you play with?

   e. What sort of work do your parents do? How much money do they earn each month? Do you have a good standard of living?

**Source:** Adapted from *COMPASS: A Manual on Human rights education with Young People* (Council of Europe, 2002), p. 217.

f. What do you do in your holidays? Do you have a pet?

g. What makes you happy? What are you afraid of?

5. Ask the children to remain absolutely silent as they line up beside each other, as if on a starting line. When they have lined up, explain that you are going to describe some things that might happen to a child. If the statement would be true for the person they are imagining themselves to be, then they should take a step forward. Otherwise they should not move.

6. Read out the situations one at a time. Pause between each statement to allow the children time to step forward. Invite them to look around to see where others are.

7. At the end of the activity, invite everyone to sit down in his or her final position. Ask each child in turn to describe their assigned role. After the children have identified themselves, ask them to observe where they are at the end of the activity.

8. Before beginning the debriefing questions, make a clear ending to the role-play. Ask the children to close their eyes and become themselves again. Explain that you will count to three and then they should each shout out their own name. In this way, you conclude the activity and ensure that the children don't stay caught up in the role.

### Debriefing and evaluation

1. Debrief the activity by asking questions such as these:
    a. What happened in this activity?
    b. How easy or difficult was it to play your role?
    c. What did you imagine the person you were playing was like? Do you know anyone like that?
    d. How did you feel, imagining yourself as that person? Was it a person like you at all? Do you know anyone like that person?

2. Relate the activity to issues of discrimination and social and economic inequality asking questions like these:
    a. How did people feel stepping forward – or not?
    b. If you stepped forward often, when did you begin to notice that others were not moving as fast as you were?
    c. Did the person you were imagining move ahead or not? Why?
    d. Did you feel that something was unfair?
    e. Is what happened in this the activity anything like the real world? How?
    f. What gives some people in our community more opportunities than others? Fewer opportunities?

### Suggestions for follow-up

The concept of the stereotypes is not easy for many young children to grasp. Reinforce the learning of this activity with others that also develop this idea, such as 'PICTURE GAMES', P. 130; 'WHO'S BEHIND ME', P. 195; 'WORLD SUMMER CAMP', P. 205; and 'ZABDERFILIO', P. 209.

### Ideas for action

Discuss with the children who in their community has more or fewer opportunities. What first steps could be taken to make opportunities more equal for everyone? Are there inequalities in the group or community that the children can address?

## Tips for the facilitator

- Make your own role cards! Those offered here are meant to serve as samples. The closer your role cards reflect the world in which your children live, the more they will learn from the activity.

- Also adapt the roles to avoid embarrassing any child whose personal situation may too closely mirror that of one of the roles.

- Because the facilitator cannot always be aware of every child's personal life situation, a child may be very disturbed or emotionally caught up in one of the roles. The facilitator needs to be very sensitive in this exercise, and to pay particular attention to children who don't manage to drop the role afterwards or who display unusual behaviour. In such a case, the facilitator should try to speak to the child individually.

- It is very important that the children keep silent as they receive their role, imagine the life of the person they will represent, and move forward according to the life of this person. Not only is suspense created about the children's identities, but keeping silent helps maintain the concentration on the role and avoid distractions, and acting out of roles.

- Make sure every child gets a chance to speak during the debriefing. This activity can call up strong emotions, and the more the children can express themselves and their feelings, the more sense they will get out of it. Spend more time on the debriefing if needed.

- This activity can easily be run outside or in a large room. Keep the children in their final positions when they reveal their roles, as young children need visual reinforcement to recognize the disparity and associate it with the person's role. However, to make sure that the children can hear each other in the debriefing discussion, either draw them into a circle or move inside.

- The power of this activity lies in the impact of actually seeing the distance increasing between the participants, especially at the end. To enhance the impact, choose roles that reflect the realities of the children's own lives. Adjust the roles so that only a few of people can take steps forward (i.e. can answer, "Yes").

- During the Debriefing and Evaluation especially explore how the children knew about lives of the person whose role they had to play. Was it through personal experience or through other sources of information (e.g. other children, adults, books, media, jokes)? Challenge them to question whether their sources of information were reliable. In this way you can introduce how stereotypes and prejudice work.

- Children are generally aware that others have materially more or less than they. However, children are often unable to realize their own privileges. This activity can help the children to put their lives into a larger perspective.

## HANDOUT: ROLE CARDS

**Note to facilitator: Make your own cards! The closer they reflect the experiences of your children, the more effective they will be! These are intended only as samples.**

| | |
|---|---|
| You are eight. You and your two brothers live in a nice house with a big garden and a swimming pool. Your father is the manager of a bank in your town. Your mother takes care of the house and family. | You were born in this town, but your parents moved here from Asia. They run a nice restaurant, and you live in rooms above the restaurant with your sister. You and she help in the restaurant after school. You are thirteen. |
| You are ten years old. You live in a farmhouse in the country. Your father is a farmer and your mother takes care of the cows, geese and chickens. You have three brothers and one sister. | You are an only child. You live alone with your mother in an apartment in the city. Your mother works in a factory. You are very good at music and dancing. You are nine. |
| You are a Roma child of twelve. You live at the edge of a small village in a small house where there is no bathroom. You have six brothers and sisters. | You were born with a disability and have to use a wheelchair. You live in an apartment in the city with your parents and two sisters. Both your parents are teachers. You are twelve. |
| You are eleven. You have lived in an orphanage since you were a baby. You don't know who your parents were. | You are nine years old and have an identical twin. You live in an apartment in the city with your mother, who works in a department store. Your father is in jail. |
| You are nine years old and an only child. You live in an apartment house in a town with your parents. Your father is a construction worker and your mother delivers mail. You are very good at sports. | You and your parents came to this country to find safety from the war going on in your home country in Africa. You are now eleven and have been here for three years, since you were nine. You don't know when you can go home again. |
| You are thirteen, the oldest of six children. Your father drives a truck and is away a lot, and your mother is a waitress who often has to work at night. You have to babysit a lot. | Your parents divorced when you were a baby. Now you are twelve. You live with your mother and her boyfriend. At the weekends you visit your father and his new wife and their two small children. |

# HANDOUT: ROLE CARDS

You are eleven. You have lived with different foster parents since you were a small child because your parents couldn't take care of you. Your foster parents are nice. Four other foster children also live in the same small house as you.

You are eight. You and your sister live with your grandparents in a small town out in the country. Your parents are divorced and your mother works as a secretary in the city. You rarely see your father.

You have a learning disability that makes you two classes behind in school. You are ten and taller than all the other kids, who are only eight. Both your parents work so they don't have much time to help you with homework.

Your mother died when you were born. Your father remarried and you live with him and your stepmother and her two daughters. You are eight and they are teenagers. Your father is a lawyer.

You are eight and the youngest of three children. Your family lives in a small apartment in a big city. Your father is a mechanic but he is out of work right now, so you don't have much money. But your father has more time to play with you.

You immigrated to this country when you were a baby. Now you are ten. Many other immigrants live in your neighbourhood, where your father has a shop. You speak the languages of both your new and old countries and often translate for your mother and grandmother.

You are eleven years old. You live in a village in the country with your parents and a younger brother and sister. Your parents run a bakery. You are sometimes teased because you are rather fat.

You have asthma and have to miss a lot of school because you are sick, especially in winter. You spend a lot of time at home in bed watching TV, surfing on the Internet and playing with Gameboy. It's lonely because both your parents go out to work. You are thirteen.

You are the child of the American ambassador in your country. You go to the international school. You wear thick glasses and stammer a little. You are eleven.

You and your older brother are very talented at mathematics, physics, languages and, in fact, most things. Your parents are university professors. They send you to special courses and training camps all the time to prepare for competitions.

## Situations and events

**Read the following situations out aloud. After reading out each situation, give the children time to step forward and also to look to see where they are, relative to each other.**

1. You and your family always have enough money to meet your needs.

2. You live in a decent place with a telephone and television.

3. You are not teased or excluded because of your different appearance or disability.

4. The people you live with ask your opinion about major decisions that concern you.

5. You go to a good school and belong to after-school clubs and sports.

6. You take extra lessons after school in music and drawing.

7. You are not afraid of being stopped by the police.

8. You live with adults who love you and always have your best interests at heart.

9. You have never felt discriminated against because of your or your parents' origins, background, religion or culture.

10. You have regular medical and dental check-ups, even when you are not sick.

11. You and your family go away on holiday once a year.

12. You can invite friends for dinner or to sleep over at your home.

13. When you are older, you can go to university or choose any job or profession you like.

14. You are not afraid of being teased or attacked in the streets, at school or where you live.

15. You usually see people on TV or in films who look and live as you do.

16. You and your family go on an outing to the cinema, the zoo, a museum, the countryside or other fun places at least once a month.

17. Your parents and grandparents and even great-grandparents were all born in this country.

18. You get new clothes and shoes whenever you need them.

19. You have plenty of time to play and friends to play with.

20. You have access to a computer and can use the Internet.

21. You feel appreciated for what you can do and encouraged to develop all your abilities.

22. You think you are going to have a happy future when you grow up.

# 30. The Battle for the Orange

Can this be a win-win situation?

| | |
|---|---|
| Themes | Peace |
| Level of complexity | Level 1 |
| Age | 8 – 13 years |
| Duration | 30 minutes |
| Group size | 4 – 24 children |
| Type of activity | Group competition and discussion |
| Overview | Children compete for possession of an orange and discuss how to resolve conflicts. |
| Objectives | • To discuss the need for communication in conflict situations<br>• To reflect on strategies for conflict resolution |
| Preparation | • None |
| Materials | • One orange |

## Instructions

1. Explain that the group is going to play 'the Orange Game'. Divide the children into two groups. Ask Group A to go outside and wait for you. Tell Group B that in this activity their goal is to get the orange because they need its juice to make orange juice.

2. Go outside and tell Group A that their goal in this activity is to get the orange because they need the peel of the orange to make an orange cake.

3. Bring both groups together inside and ask each group to sit in a line facing each other.

4. Tell the groups that they have three minutes to get what they need. Emphasise that they should not use violence to get what they want. Then place one orange between the two groups and say, "Go".

   *Usually someone will take the orange and one group will have it and how the groups deal with the situation will be a surprise. Sometimes groups will try to negotiate to divide the orange in half. At other times they will not negotiate at all. Sometimes the groups will communicate further and realize that they both need different parts of the orange; someone from one of the groups will peel the orange, taking the part they need. Do not interfere.*

5. After three minute say, "Stop" or "Time's up".

## Debriefing and evaluation

1. Debrief the activity by asking question such as these:
   a. Did your group get what it wanted before the three minutes were up?
   b. What was your group's goal?
   c. What was the outcome of the conflict over the orange?
   d. What did you do to achieve this outcome?
   e. Why is it important for people to communicate in order to resolve conflicts?
   f. Do people always communicate with each other when they are in a conflict? Why or why not?
   g. Do people always want the same thing in a conflict?
   h. Have you ever experienced similar situations? What was the outcome?

2. Relate the activity to human rights by asking a question such as this:

    a. What are some of the human rights that are violated in a conflict?

### Suggestions for follow-up

• The activity 'PICTURING WAYS OUT OF VIOLENCE', P. 133, also deals with resolving conflict.

• Several activities also require negotiation: 'CAPTURE THE CASTLE', P. 89; 'COOKIE MONSTER', P. 95; 'THE INVISIBLES ARE COMING', P. 171.

### Ideas for action

Develop ideas about how to deal with conflict within the group. List these ideas on a chart and hang it somewhere in the room.

### Tips for the facilitator

• After the three minutes, take the orange, or what is left of it, to avoid distraction during the debriefing.

• During the conflict, you should not try and influence the results but be careful to emphasise to the children that there should be no violence in order to get what they want.

• Adaptation for larger groups: Create four groups instead of two groups and have two 'Orange battles' taking place at the same time. Simply make 2 Group As, and 2 Group Bs and give the same instructions as indicated above. Have 1 Group A sit opposite 1 Group B, and the second Group A sit opposite the second Group B; place one orange between each set of groups. Start and stop the activity at the same time. It may be interesting to discuss the different processes and results in each 'Battle'.

# 31. The Invisibles are Coming

Run for your rights!

| | |
|---|---|
| Themes | Discrimination |
| Level of complexity | Level 2 |
| Age | 8-13 years |
| Duration | 120 minutes – half-day |
| Group size | 30+ children with at least 6 facilitators |
| Type of activity | Active group competition |
| Overview | Teams work together against a common 'enemy' |
| Objectives | • To promote cooperation and solidarity |
| Preparation | • Review the whole activity carefully including the roles of the facilitators and the tips.<br>• Find an appropriate outdoor or large indoor space.<br>• Decide which rights to use.<br>• Gather materials.<br>• Copy the 'passports' for each child that is provided as a handout.<br>• Make copies of the Roles Handout for the facilitators and Invisible(s).<br>• Make signs stating the right each Rights Person represents.<br>• Make signs identifying the Invisible(s).<br>• Before beginning, decide who will be the Invisible(s), ideally adults or older children. There should be a minimum of 1 Invisible, but ideally three for 30 children.<br>• Before the game begins, ask the facilitators to dress up according to their roles: 4 facilitators to put on the 4 team colours (Rights Persons); 1 facilitator puts on all 4 colours (Right to Colours Person); and the 6th (or more) facilitator(s) dress himself/ themselves in a neutral way such as white sheets wrapped around, (Invisible(s)). |
| Materials | • Bottles of juices or yoghurt in 4 colours<br>• 1 unbreakable cup for each child<br>• 1 big pot to collect the Colour Potion<br>• 1 ladle to help serve the Colour Potion<br>• Face paint or other objects in the 4 colours of your juices<br>• Passports for each child plus some extras (handout)<br>• Signs for the Invisibles and Rights People<br>• Markers or pens: 4 black for Invisibles, 4 team colours for Rights People<br>• A first-aid kit in case of accidents<br>• A whistle and horn or other loud noise maker to announce hunting periods and begin and end the game. |

## Instructions

1. Have the facilitators brief the Rights People and the Invisible(s) on their roles and put on their signs and colours. The Invisibles should remain out of sight until the game begins.

2. Introduce the activity to the children with a dramatic description like this:

    a. Life is colourful and that is good. However, a great danger threatens our colourful world. Every 100 years, the Invisibles invade from outer space for a whole day. The Invisibles hate colours. They want to get rid of all the colours in the world and make us all colourless and invisible like themselves.

    b. We must stop them before it is too late! The only way is to repeat an ancient ritual. We must create and drink the powerful 'Colour Potion'. If we can succeed in doing this, the world will be saved again and the Invisibles will disappear for another 100 years. The fight for the Right to Colours has begun.

**Source:** Originally developed for 'Intercultural Week with Children' in Brittany, France, 2005.

3. Divide the children into four teams and assign each a colour to match their team's juice. Give each team face paint or other objects (e.g. hats, fabrics) in their colour and some time to 'decorate' themselves in team colours.

4. Explain how the game works. These are the roles in the game:

    a. 4 Rights People, who are wearing the colours of their team

    b. 'Invisible(s)' who hate colours

    c. 4 teams of children who wear the colours of their team.

5. To make the Colour Potion, you must fill a pot with juices of four different colours. (Give everyone a cup.)

6. To do this, you need to get cupfuls of juice of your own colour, which you can only get from the Rights Person of your colour. Each of them represents a particular human right. (Introduce the four Rights Persons and ask them to explain the right they represent. Then let them leave to establish their hiding places.)

    a. However, before you can get a cupful of juice, you must first get the signatures of all four Rights People. Before filling your cup, your Rights Person will check your passport to see that you have the four required signatures. (Give everyone a passport.)

    b. Once you have juice in your cup, go to the Right to Colours Person who stands at the centre of the space and pour your juice into the pot. (Introduce the Right to Colours Person.)

    c. Then you can start collecting signatures to get a second cupful. This continues till the time is finished or till the minimum level marked on the pot is reached.

    d. Remember: The Colour Potion is the only way to make the Invisibles go away for another hundred years!

    e. Explain how the Invisible(s) attack:

    f. Remember that the Invisible(s) want to prevent you from making the Colour Potion! They can attack suddenly and try to catch you. You will know they are out hunting colours when you hear many short blows on a whistle.

    g. If the Invisible(s) touch you, two things can happen:

        i. They cross out all the signatures you have gathered.

        ii. They drink the cup of juice you are carrying.

    h. However, you can protect yourself from the Invisible(s). They can only catch colours who are alone. If four players from different colours walk together and hold hands, the Invisible(s) are powerless to catch those players.

7. Establish rules for the game:

    a. Announce how long the game will last (e.g. a certain time or when they reach a certain amount of Colour Potion).

    b. Explain the signal to start and stop the game (e.g. 1 long blow on the whistle is the start; 3 long blows announce the end).

    c. Clarify the borders of the play area.

8. Start the game with all the teams standing near the neutral facilitator in the middle of the play space.

    a. Give the signal to end the game and gather all the children at the central post.

    b. Announce victory over the Invisibles: "The battle was hard but together we have succeeded in protecting our right to colours! Together we stand strong!"

    c. Explain that we will celebrate our victory by drinking the Colour Potion we have made together and talking about the battle in small groups.

    d. Divide the children into four groups, combining the four teams. Assign a facilitator and location to each group.

e. Invite everyone to fill their cups from the pot and join their group. The Rights to Colour Person can help by ladling juice into cups.

## Debriefing and Evaluation

1. Debrief the activity, emphasizing cooperation and asking question such as these:
   a. What happened during the game?
   b. What were the most exciting moments?
   c. Did you have a certain strategy?
   d. If you would play this again, would you do something different?
   e. Did you work together with other teams? When did the cooperation start? Why was cooperation a good idea?
   f. 'Cooperation' and 'solidarity': ask if someone can explain these words.
2. Link the activity to discrimination, asking question such as these:
   a. In real life, who could the Invisibles be? What about the Rights People?
   b. Does the right to colours really exist? What could it mean?
   c. What rights did the Rights People represent? Do we need these rights? Do we have others? What if one of these were missing?
   d. Do we have the right to protection? If so, what does this mean?
   e. What can we do in our daily life to make sure that everybody has the same rights?

## Suggestions for follow-up

- Choose a calmer activity as a follow up, for example 'BOYS DON'T CRY', P. 78.

## Ideas for action

The children can research and document diversity in their community (e.g. what languages are spoken at home, what religions are practised, where members of the community or the older generation were born). This research can be the basis of discussion or action based on the benefits of diversity and/or efforts to discourage xenophobia.

## Tips for the facilitator

- Because their concrete actions have an abstract, representational meaning, the debrief section is crucial for the children to get more from this activity than just an exciting game. Some young children may not be able to grasp the game's intended relationship to tolerance and rights, but older children should be challenged to articulate this link in their own words.
- This activity has these roles:
  - At least 5 adults who act as the Rights People
  - At least 1 (ideally 3) Invisibles, ideally played by adults. However, if fewer adults are available, older children can be the Invisibles if they are carefully briefed about their roles. They must know the rules clearly and understand that only a light touch is needed to make a 'catch'.
  - The rest of the participants are children divided into four teams identified by colours. The larger your group, the more Invisibles you need: up to five or six.
- Link the game activity to local customs and traditions (e.g. druids, trolls, vampires, ghosts).
- If possible have different kinds of whistles or noise-makers to differentiate the whistle that begins and ends the game from the sound that signals the attacks of the Invisible(s).

HANDOUT: PASSPORT

## Passport to Fight for the Right to Colours

| | | | | |
|---|---|---|---|---|
| Right 1 | | | | |
| Right 2 | | | | |
| Right 3 | | | | |
| Right 4 | | | | |

# HANDOUT: ROLE CARDS

**Role of the Rights People (4 adults)**

- You represent the Right to _____. Your colour is _____.

- Establish your post in a far corner of the game area and stay there for the whole game. Your post is safe from the Invisibles.

- You have two jobs:

    1. Each player will ask you to write your signature in their passport. When they have a signature from each of the four Rights People, they can obtain a cup of juice for making the Colour Potion from the Rights Person with their own team colour.

    2. Only when someone from your team comes to you with four signatures, can you cross off the signatures and pour out a cupful of juice.

- At your post you need the following: a marker pen in the colour of your team, bottles of juice.

**Role of the Right to Colours Person (1 adult)**

- You represent all human rights. You wear all four colours.

- Establish your post in the centre of the game area and stay there for the whole game. Your post is safe from the Invisibles.

- You have three jobs:

    1. To oversee the collection of juice in the pot.

    2. To encourage the players.

    3. To serve everyone the mixed juices at the end of the game.

- At your post you need the following: a big pot, a ladle.

**Role of the Invisible(s) (1-3 adults or older children**

- You are the evil force in the game, representing intolerance and racism. You do not like the diversity of colours in the world and want to make everything colourless.

- Your job is to prevent the teams from making the Colour Potion. However, you can only catch children when they are alone. If four children of different colours hold hands, you are powerless.

- To make a catch, you need only to touch a child lightly.

- Wear a sign showing you are one of the Invisibles.

- When you touch a child you can do one of three things:

    1. Cross out one of the signatures in this child's passport.

    2. Drink the juice the child has collected.

    3. If the child has neither juice nor any signature on the passport, just let this child go.

- All Invisible(s) go hunting for colours at the same time every five minutes or so. Announce a hunting period by blowing a whistle. If possible each Invisible should have a whistle and continue blowing during the hunt to raise excitement. You can also say threatening things like "I hate blue!" or "No more colours!"

- Your purpose is more to bring excitement to the game than to catch as many children as possible.

- You can also encourage children to cooperate by saying things such as, "Aha, I'm happy you're not walking together because then I wouldn't be able to catch you!"

- For you role you need the following: a whistle, a black marker

# 32. Waterdrops

Water, water everywhere and not a drop to drink

| | |
|---|---|
| Themes | Environment, General human rights |
| Level of complexity | Level 2 |
| Age | 7 - 13 years |
| Duration | 60 minutes |
| Group size | 5-20 children |
| Type of activity | Experiential learning, prioritizing, discussion |
| Overview | Children decide how they can use water so that they do not waste it. They discuss the importance of personal action in order to save one of the most important resources for the environment. |
| Objectives | • To develop awareness of natural resources' sustainable use in everyday life<br>• To discuss ways to protect water and the environment in general<br>• To help children become aware of their rights<br>• To encourage individual action for the sustainable use of resources and water saving. |
| Preparation | • Prepare as many glasses or mugs as children you have in your group.<br>• Prepare a 2-litre bottle and fill it with water. Make sure there is enough water to fill all the glasses. With a bigger group of children, prepare more bottles.<br>• Prepare a bowl or a vessel for water saving.<br>Copy the 'Waterdrop' provided in the Handout for each child. |
| Materials | • 2-litre bottles<br>• Glasses or mugs for each child<br>• A teaspoon for each child<br>• A bowl to hold the common water saved<br>Flipchart<br>Paper and pens |

## Instructions

1. Ask the children to think of as many reasons as possible why water is important (e.g. for plants, animals, human beings, industry, agriculture, recreation), and introduce the idea of water conservation, asking questions such as these:

   - Where can you find water on Earth? (the ocean, icecaps, freshwater)
   - How much of the water on Earth is useful for human beings? (97% oceans, 2% icecaps, only 1% freshwater of all water is useful.)
   - What would life on Earth be like without water? With less water?
   - Is freshwater equally available everywhere on Earth?
   - Which special phenomena today endanger sufficient amounts of freshwater being available in the future?

2. Brainstorm a list of how every child uses water every day (e.g. for cooking, for having a bath or shower, flushing the toilet, washing clothes) and list these on chart paper or the blackboard.

3. Explain that this activity will challenge them to decide how to use water more carefully. Show them one bottle and ask them to imagine that this is all the water that they as a group will have for the period of one day. They must be careful not to waste it.

4. Give every child a glass and fill it with water from the bottle. Explain that this glass represents the amount of water they have individually to use in a day. Make them guess how much water they use a day. (In Europe, the average is approximately 135 litres/day) As they hold their glasses, remind the children of the list they made in Step 2 of the ways they use water.

5. Ask the children to decide how they can make small changes in their daily behaviour so that they can save water. Allow them some time to decide about their choice. Propose that one spoonful of water represents one litre. Then go around the group asking each child to present their decision and pour some spoonfuls of water that they think they could save into the group bowl. Ask children to write their ideas on the 'Waterdrop' provided them as a handout.

6. When every child has spoken, explain that the water that they have decided to save belongs to the whole group. Explain that the bowl will be full as long as each child continues to save some water every day. Otherwise the group will run out of water.

7. Tell them that the group will now have to decide how to use their common resource in their environment. Ask the children to decide as a group how they intend to use the common water they have. Can they recycle some water?

## Debriefing and evaluation

1. Debrief the activity by asking question such as these:
   - Was it easy to think of all the ways you use water every day?
   - Did you notice anything new about the way you use water? About the way their families use water? What about water used in public places (e.g. schools, hospitals, public buildings and parks)?
   - How did you decide to give up a part of your daily water?
   - Which ways of saving water are realistic for your daily life? Which ways of saving water would be hard to maintain every day?
   - Was it hard to decide how to use the 'common water'? Are you satisfied with the group's decision about their common water? Can you think about any other ways to use this water?

2. Lead children to generalize about water conservation:
   - Why is it important to save water?
   - What happens when people do not have access to enough water for their needs?
   - Where does the water our community uses come from? How does it get to us?
   - Does our community waste some of this water?

3. Relate the activity to human rights by asking questions such as these:
   - Water is an essential need for life and survival. What are other resources in the environment which play a key role for life and survival?
   - Do all people get access to these resources, such as clean water, clean air and environment? What happens if the resources are available but not of good quality?
   - Who is responsible for providing these quality resources?
   - Can children also do anything to make sure that everyone gets access to good quality environmental resources?

At the end of the debriefing, ask the children to look back at their 'Waterdrops' and add any other ideas on how to save water and how to use it in their environment. Display the 'Waterdrops' somewhere in the room so that the children can refer to them in the future.

# 33. We are Family

| | |
|---|---|
| Themes | Discrimination, Family, Gender |
| Complexity | Level 2 |
| Age | 8 – 10 years |
| Duration | 60 minutes |
| Group size | 8 – 30 children |
| Type of activity | Drawing, discussion |
| Overview | Using pictures and drawings, children discuss different concepts and structures of 'family' |
| Objectives | • To promote diversity and tolerance towards difference<br>• To make children think of different ways of being brought up and consider the definition of a family<br>• To address discrimination against children with 'unusual' family compositions<br>• To explore the link between family and human rights |
| Preparation | • Prepare a set of illustrations / photos representing different family schemes for each small group (e.g. single parent, classical scheme, same sex couples, patchwork families, adopted children, big families including many generations). |
| Materials | • Copies of all pictures for each small group of children |

## Instructions

1. Introduce the activity by explaining that this activity explores the many different ways that we identify and live with the people we consider our family. Emphasize that not all children live in the same kinds of families.

2. Ask each child to draw the family they live in (i.e. as opposed to family they may be separated from, wish they had, once had, etc.). Encourage them to include details about their family if they want to (e.g. name, age, sex of each person).

3. Ask the children to discuss other types of families they know about. Let them then present their drawings about their own family.

4. Together, brainstorm and list as many types of families as possible. Mention some that have not been spoken about already.

5. Divide the children into small groups of 4 or 5 and give each group a copy of the illustrations / photos you prepared earlier. Ask each group to discuss what the main differences are or what is 'unusual' about each family. Ask the groups to discuss their own family pictures too, and whether they are similar or different to any of the pictures they have been given.

## Debriefing and evaluation

1. Debrief the activity by asking questions such as these:
   a. What happened in this activity?
   b. How easy or difficult was it to draw and present your family?
   c. Were you surprised by other children's drawings? Why?
   d. Were you surprised by any of the other pictures of families? Why?
   e. What did you learn about families?

  f. How do you think children feel when their family is 'different'?

  g. How could you support those children?

2. Relate the activity to human rights by asking questions such as these:

  a. Do all children have the right to live in a family?

  b. Is living in a family important? Why or why not?

  c. Which children perhaps do not live in a family? Where do they live?

  d. Who ensures that all rights of these children are respected?

  e. Do you know any children like this? How can you support these children?

## Suggestions for follow-up

- The activity 'Who Should Decide?', p. 198, addresses questions about how families live together and make decisions.

- Several activities also deal with stereotyped expectations: 'Picture Games', p. 130; 'Who's behind me?', p. 195; 'World Summer Camp', p. 205.

## Ideas for action

- Set up a series of visits to a local orphanage or social care home and create discussion or friendship groups with the children there.

- If there are any 'Adopt a grandparent' or 'Adopt a parent' initiatives in the local community, some children in the group may like to get involved in their activities.

- Some children may like to start their own 'Adopt a brother or sister' initiative, which can be introduced in a local school or community.

## Tips for the facilitator

- Make sure that the children feel comfortable and will not be teased for presenting family styles that are unusual or different. Throughout the exercise, emphasize tolerance, feelings and values which are related to what makes a family.

- It is important to know the family situations of the children in your group and to adapt the activity so as not to embarrass or make any of the children feel uncomfortable about their situation.

- Before running this exercise, read the background information on Family and Alternative Care, p.240. You can also find ideas here on different types of families or family structures that may be useful for this activity.

## Adaptation

To shorten this activity, consider running it without using additional pictures of families. When dividing the children into smaller groups, you can ask them simply to discuss and reflect on their own family drawings without introducing any new ones. However, it remains important to discuss or refer to other types of families that may not be present in the group.

# 34. What a Wonderful World

How do you want to live?

| | |
|---|---|
| Themes | Discrimination, Environment, Poverty and social exclusion |
| Level of complexity | Level 1 |
| Age | 8-13 years |
| Duration | 50 minutes |
| Group size | 1-20 children |
| Type of activity | Drawing, discussion |
| Overview | Children draw contrasting pictures of environments where they would or would not want to live. They discuss what factors make the differences and how to influence their own environment |
| Objectives | • To discuss the concrete and abstract factors of the environment<br>• To evaluate our own and others' environment<br>• To discuss ways to protect and/or change their own environment and that of others |
| Preparation | • Gather colouring materials.<br>• Copy the handout for each child. |
| Materials | • Paper<br>• Colouring materials, e.g. paints, markers, crayons, pencils<br>• Drawing pins or sticky tape to hang drawings |

## Instructions

- Lay out colours of every kind. Ask the children to think about an environment they would like to have – real or imaginary – and to draw it.

- Then ask the children to think about an environment they would not like to have, and to draw it.

- When the drawings are finished, hang them and invite the children to view the mini-exhibition.

## Debriefing and Evaluation

1. Debrief the activity, asking questions such as these:
    a. Was it easy to think of the two different environments?
    b. Which drawing and environment do you like the most? Why?
    c. Which drawing and environment do you like the least? Why?
    d. If there were people living in the environments you have drawn, how do they feel?
    e. Which picture matches your real environment?

2. Relate the activity to human rights, asking questions such as these:
    a. The environment is more than just the physical space. What other factors make up a positive or negative environment? Think of factors such as opportunities, non-violence, non-discrimination, freedom and human rights.
    b. How does our physical environment affect us? How does our rights environment affect us?
    c. How would you describe the rights environment where you live?
    d. What would you like to change about your physical environment? Your rights environment?
    e. What could you do to make your environment more like the one you drew?
    f. Do all the children in the world have an environment they like?

g. Do we have a human right to a good environment?

h. Do you think we should have a right to good environment?

i. What can we do to promote a good environment for all the children in the world?

## Suggestions for follow-up

- The activities 'COMPASITO REPORTER', P. 92, and 'WATERDROPS', P. 176, also engage children in evaluating their community environment.

- In the activity 'DEAR DIARY', P. 99, children see the same experience from different perspectives.

## Ideas for action

- Take a walk through your community and discuss with children the physical environment and what they like and don't like about it. Help the children to develop concrete proposals for changes. Invite municipal officials to discuss the proposals with them and initiate changes.

- To communicate children's ideas about their environment to adults in the community, make an exhibition of their drawings and ideas.

- Build on the children's ideas for changing their environment. What can they do to improve their environment?

- Try to find ongoing projects in which children participate to support other children in more disadvantaged areas than their own. Older children might initiate new projects.

## Tips for the facilitator

- Help children understand that 'environment' is created by both concrete, physical factors as well as abstract ones, such as the degree of rights and freedoms. Emphasize that we need both factors for a good environment. Younger children may have difficulty grasping the abstract concept of environment.

- Before doing the exercise, be clear on which aspects of environment you want to focus. Addressing the entire 'environment' without a clear focus will be too large and abstract.

## Variations

- Use several different colouring techniques for the same drawing, e.g. wax crayons, paint, paper mosaic.

HANDOUT

# 35. What I Like and What I Do

They are not always the same thing!

| | |
|---|---|
| Themes | Discrimination, Family, Gender equality |
| Level of complexity | Level 2 |
| Age | 8 – 13 years |
| Duration | 45 minutes |
| Group size | 8 – 20 children |
| Type of activity | Stating preferences, discussion |
| Overview | Children name things they like, do not like or might like to do that are considered 'appropriate' or 'inappropriate' to their sex. They then discuss gender stereotypes and relate them to human rights. |
| Objectives | • To discover their own and others' abilities and knowledge<br>• To recognize the effects of gender stereotypes |
| Preparation | • Optional: print copies of the questionnaire. |
| Materials | • Paper and pens<br>Optional: printed copies of the questionnaire |

## Instructions

1. Introduce the topic of gender roles by asking, "Are there some behaviours and activities that are considered 'girls' activities' or 'boys' activities'?" and eliciting examples from the children.

2. Give the children slips of paper and pencils. Ask each child to write down the following:

    a. At the top of the paper identify yourself as a boy or girl.

    b. Name four things you do and like doing that are considered activities 'appropriate for your sex'.

    c. Name four things you do but do not like doing that are considered 'appropriate for your sex'.

    d. Name four things you do not do and would not like to do that are considered 'appropriate for the opposite sex'.

    e. Name four things you do not do and but would really like to do that are considered 'appropriate for the opposite sex'.

3. Ask the children to share some of their responses to each question and record them on a chart such as the one below.

| | I do and I like | I do but don't like | I don't do and I don't want to do | I don't do but I would like to do |
|---|---|---|---|---|
| Girls | | | | |
| Boys | | | | |

## Debriefing and evaluation

1. Debrief the activity, asking question such as these:

    a. Were you surprised by some of the things that people like and don't like doing?

b.  Looking at the list of things children would like to do but don't. Do you notice any patterns?

c.  What happens to a girl who does 'boys' things'? To a boy who does 'girls' things'? Why does this happen?

d.  How would adults in your family answer the four questions?

e.  Do members of your family have the same ideas about what is 'appropriate' for men and boys or women and girls?

f.  How do we get our ideas about what is 'appropriate' for men and boys or women and girls?

2.  Relate the activity to human rights by asking questions such as these:

a.  How does limiting what boys and girls can do affect them individually? How could it affect a family? A society?

b.  Do you think gender roles (or stereotypes) are changing? If so, how?

c.  Have you ever tried to challenge gender roles? What happened?

d.  Why do gender roles/stereotypes limit a person's human rights?

e.  What can we do to challenge gender roles in our group?

## Suggestions for follow-up

- Other activities that address gender roles/stereotypes: 'ONCE UPON A TIME...', P. 125 and 'BOYS DON'T CRY', P. 78

- The activity 'WORDS THAT WOUND', P. 202, examines hurtful language based on gender stereotypes, as well as other kinds of insults.

## Ideas for action

- Discuss with the children some of the things they thought of under the category 'Don't do but would like to do'. Help them find opportunities in the group to try out some of these activities in an accepting environment.

## Tips for the facilitator

- Encourage the children to include behavioural expectations and physical appearance among the 'activities appropriate to your sex' (e.g. liking pretty clothes, gossiping, crying easily, using bad language, getting into fights).

- Alternative: Some children may be reluctant or embarrassed to reveal that they like doing things that some consider 'inappropriate'. To avoid this, you could 1) collect the slips, shuffle them and ask the children to read out answers from anonymous children of either sex; 2) divide the children into small, single-sex groups of boys or girls and ask them to answer the questions together as a group; 3) use a printed form with the questions.

- If appropriate for this group, introduce the word 'stereotype' and discuss what this means, eliciting examples from the group. Discuss how stereotypes can limit people's human rights.

- When asking what happens to children who do not conform to gender stereotypes, ask for some of the names these children are called and discuss the implications of those words (e.g. 'sissy', 'tomboy', 'gay').

# 36. What if ...

...the world were flat???

| | |
|---|---|
| Themes | General human rights, Education and leisure, Poverty and social security |
| Level of complexity | Level 3 |
| Age | 8 – 13 years |
| Duration | 60 minutes |
| Group size | 8 – 20 children |
| Type of activity | Analysis, dramatization, discussion |
| Objectives | • To consider the impact and interdependence of rights<br>• To consider rights in our daily life. |
| Overview | Children imagine the consequences that could arise from a particular situation, and then dramatize these results. |
| Preparation | • Choose, adapt or create situations to suit the children's experience and issues.<br>• Copy and cut out the situation cards.<br>• Copy Effects Cascade. |
| Materials | • Situation cards<br>• Paper and pens for presentations<br>• Copies of Effects Cascade |

## Instructions

1. Introduce the activity, explaining that everybody tries to imagine "What if...". Sometimes we imagine good situations (e.g. "What if there were no more wars?") and sometimes bad situations (e.g. "What if a war occurred in my country?"). In this activity they will be given a situation and asked to consider what effects it might have on people's lives.

2. Introduce the Effects Cascade and illustrate how one situation can lead to a chain of events; use a simple, familiar situation (e.g. What if you were not allowed to go to school? > Not learning to read > Not being able to follow written instructions, understand a map, write a letter, use the computer).

3. Divide the children into small groups and give each group a situation and a copy of the Effects Cascade, and pens. Ask them to work together to complete it.

4. When the children have completed the Effects Cascade, explain that they should now prepare a stage presentation that shows what effects that they have imagined could arise from the situation. Give the children time to prepare their presentations.

5. Ask each group in turn to read out their situations and act out their presentation.

6. After each presentation ask for questions and comments, asking questions such as these:

   a. Can you think of other effects that this situation might have?

   b. What human rights are involved in this situation? Does the situation violate a right? Protect and promote a right?

   c. Are other rights involved in the effects on the situation?

## Debriefing and Evaluation

1. Debrief the activity by asking questions such as these:

   a. How do you feel about this activity?

   b. Was it difficult to imagine the situation given?

    c. Was it difficult to think of the effects that could result from this situation?

    d. Do you think these situations are realistic? Why or why not?

    e. Do you believe that these situations exist in the world?

    f. How would you react in this situation?

    g. What could we do to change this situation?

2. Relate the activity to human rights, asking questions such as these:

    a. When one right is violated, how does that affect other rights? Can you think of any examples from the presentations?

    b. When one right is protected and promoted, how does that affect other rights? Can you think of any examples from the presentations?

    c. Why do we need all our human rights?

### Suggestions for follow-up

- The activities 'Sailing to a New Land', p. 152, and 'Most Important for Whom?', p. 118 also deal with the interdependence of rights.

- 'A Body of Knowledge', p. 53, asks children to consider the consequences of not having access sources of learning.

### Ideas for action

The activity 'A Constitution for Our Group', p. 56, engages children in improving the rights environment in which they live. Having a group constitution illustrates the multiple effects of a rights environment in real life.

### Tips for the facilitator

- The effectiveness of this activity depends greatly on the kind of situations you offer the children. Adapt or develop new situations that relate to the children's experience and concerns. Situations could address general human rights or any particular rights theme. For example, you could develop situations that all address social and economic rights or specific themes such as gender equality or the environment. Try to include both positive situations (e.g. What if men and women earned the same amount of money? What if everyone in our town cut their garbage in half by recycling?) and negative situations (e.g. What if only men could own property? What if every adult in our town had a personal car?).

- Be prepared to give some real-life examples of these situations that may actually exist or have existed in the past (e.g. women unable to own property or attend schools; boys and girls forced into military service).

### Variations

- Give the same situation to several or all groups of children. Compare their different ideas about effects.

- Divide children into same-sex groups and compare their different responses to the same gender-related situations.

- To save time, omit the dramatic presentations or present them in mime or as 'tableau' or 'frozen poses'.

### Adaptations

- For younger children: omit the Effects Cascade and go immediately to the presentations.

Younger children may also have difficulty grasping the interdependence of rights; put emphasis instead on the importance of enjoying all our rights.

- For older children: ask them to relate their presentation to specific articles of the UDHR and/ or CRC.

## HANDOUT: EFFECTS CASCADE

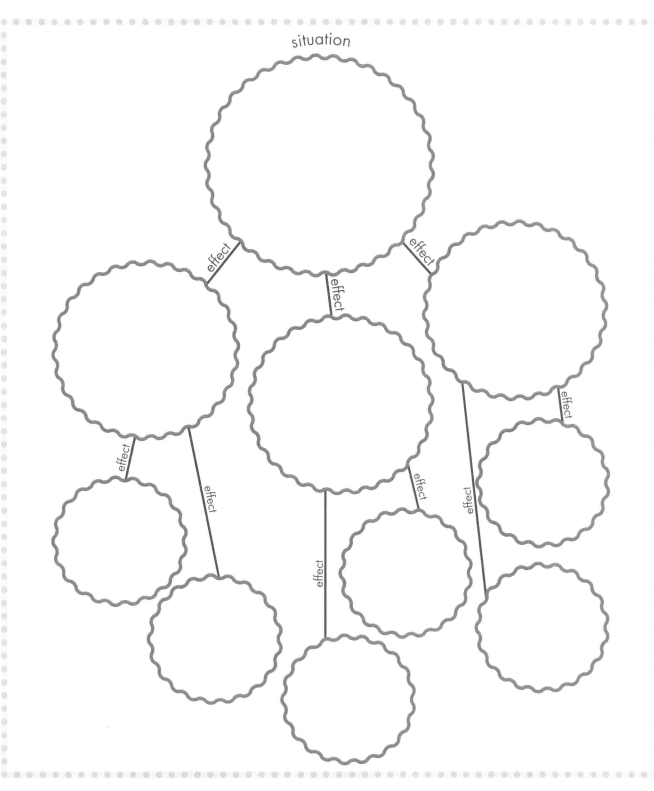

# 37. Where Do You Stand?

Vote with your feet!

| Themes | General human rights, Participation |
|---|---|
| Level of complexity | Level 1 |
| Age | 8-13 years |
| Duration | 30-40 minutes |
| Group size | 6-12 children |
| Type of activity | Discussion with some movement |
| Overview | Children take a physical position in the room and then explain and support their opinions |
| Objectives | • to deepen understanding of participation<br>• to develop listening skills<br>• to develop discussion and argumentation skills |
| Preparation | • Divide the room into two parts and put up signs **AGREE** and **DISAGREE** at either end.<br>• Write discussion statements on a flipchart, each on a separate page, and place them on the line in the middle of the room. |
| Materials | • Flipchart and pens<br>• String or chalk<br>• Paper and markers |

## Instructions

1. Announce to the children that you are interested in their opinion on some important questions. Explain that you will read a statement and individually they have to decide whether they agree or disagree with it and then stand in the part of the room where they see the relevant poster. The goal will be to convince other children to change their opinion and position.

    a. No-one can speak until everyone takes a position.

    b. The more strongly you agree or disagree with the statement, the further away from the centre you will stand.

    c. No-one can stay on the middle line, but if you cannot decide or feel confused about a question, you can stay towards the middle on one side or the other.

2. Show the children the first statement and read it aloud. Then ask them to decide what they think and to take a position.

3. Wait until everyone has taken a position. Then ask individuals from both positions why they stood on the different sides. Let them discuss their views. Encourage many different children to express an opinion.

4. After allowing a reasonable time for discussion, invite any child who wishes to change positions. If several do, ask them what argument made them change their minds. Continue this process for all the statements.

## Debriefing and Evaluation

1. Debrief the activity by asking questions such as these:

    a. How did you like this exercise?

    b. Was it difficult to take a position in some cases? Which ones?

**Source:** Adapted from *The European Convention on Human Rights, Standpoints for Teachers*, Mark Taylor, Council of Europe, 2002.

   c. Did you ever change your position? What made you do so?

   d. Were there some statements which were more complicated than others?

   e. Are there some statements you are still uncertain about?

   f. Would you like to discuss some issues further?

   g. Did you learn something new from this activity? If so, what?

2. Relate the activity to the right to participation by asking questions such as these:

   a. Did you see any connection among these questions?

   b. Are you able to participate in decision making in your family? Your class or school? Your community? Any other situation in your life?

   c. Point out that participation is an important right of every child, and read them Article 12 of the CRC. Can you imagine some new areas in which you could to participate?

   d. Why do you think the right to participation is important for children?

## Suggestions for follow-up

- At the end of the discussion, divide the children into group of three or four and give each group copies of the statements used in the activity. Ask each group to reformulate the statements in a way that they all can agree upon. Compare their restatements.

- The activities 'A CONSTITUTION FOR OUR GROUP', P. 56, or 'EVERY VOTE COUNTS', P. 103, emphasize active participation in democratic processes.

## Ideas for action

- Encourage the children to find ways of participation, e.g. speaking up for their concerns in the school or groups, writing letters to local political figures on local issues that concern them.

- Ask the children to write articles expressing their opinion on situations in their lives (e.g. family, organization, class, school, district). Publish these as a group newspaper or bulletin board display.

## Tips for the facilitator

- Make sure that all the children, even the less outspoken ones, have a chance to express their opinion. You might call on quieter children to express their opinions.

- Discussion time on each statement should be limited so that the activity does not become too long.

- To keep the children alert, encourage stretching or do a quick energizer between questions.

## Adaptation for older children

- Make more gradations of opinion (e.g. Strongly Agree, Somewhat Agree, Somewhat Disagree, Strongly Disagree).

## Variations

- Develop statements relevant to your local situation and familiar to the children.

- Develop statements relating to any other children's rights theme (e.g. right to association, equality, information, environment, family and alternative care).

## SAMPLE STATEMENTS

- All children, even the youngest, have the right to express their opinion on matters affecting them.
- Children have no rights to participate in family decision making. Parents know best what is best for children.
- It can be dangerous for children to express their views on school issues.
- Only outspoken or older children can participate in decision making.
- Every child can participate in the school parliament / student council with equal rights.
- Children who have been in trouble with the law lose their right to participate in any decision making process.
- Not all children have the same right to participate. Poor children cannot participate as much as others.
- To participate at school means to talk a lot in class.
- If one's parents are separated or divorced, children have the right to express their views in the legal process.

# 38. Who's Behind Me?

Who do you think I am?

| | |
|---|---|
| Themes | General human rights, Discrimination, Media and Internet |
| Level of complexity | Level 2 |
| Age | 10-13 years |
| Duration | 30 minutes |
| Group size | 10-20 children |
| Type of activity | Guessing game based on stereotypical responses to photographs; discussion |
| Overview | Children guess the person pictured on their back by the responses of others. |
| Objectives | • To discuss the impact of stereotypes and labelling on individuals and groups of people<br>• To understand the link between stereotyping, prejudice and discrimination<br>• To analyse the role of the media in enhancing stereotypes and prejudice |
| Preparation | Collect a set of 25 pictures showing people in different countries and settings. Mount the pictures on cardboard. Optional: laminate cards with plastic. Number the pictures. |
| Materials | • 25 pictures mounted on cardboard<br>• Pins or sticky tape<br>• Paper and pens<br>• Flipchart and marker |

## Instructions

1. Explain the activity:

   a. Each of you will have a picture of a person taped on your back.

   b. Everyone will walk around the room. When you meet someone, look at the picture and say some words that express the general opinion of society about a person like that. This is not necessarily your personal opinion but the labels or stereotypes that people use about this kind of person. These words might be positive or negative and even unkind.

2. Write down the words used for you and try to guess what kind of person you are.

3. Stick a picture on the back of every child without letting him or her see it. Give each child paper and pencil to record the words used.

4. Start the activity, with the children mingling and giving each other words of description. After about ten minutes, bring the group together.

5. Starting with picture number one, ask each child to guess the identify of the person in the picture based on how others have responded. Ask each child to explain their guess. Then ask each child in turn what words were said about the picture and write these words next to the number of the picture.

   a. After each child has guessed, take off the picture and show it to the group. Discuss each picture briefly:

   b. Where do you think the person in the picture is?

   c. What is the person doing?

   d. Do you see this person enjoying any human rights?

## Debriefing and Evaluation

1. Debrief the activity by asking questions such as these:

a. Was it difficult to find the right words to describe what people say about people like the one in different pictures?

b. How did you feel about saying some harsh or unfair words about the person in the picture?

c. Was it difficult to guess your picture's identity, based on what people said?

d. How did you feel about hearing what people said about the person you represented?

e. Were your ideas about the people represented in the different pictures different from the comments you received?

f. Were some people unable to guess their photos? Why do you think they found it difficult?

2. Discuss the list of descriptive words and make a link to human rights. Making sure you use the words labelling and stereotyping, and ask questions about the list such as these:

a. Do you think most people in this community have ever met people like this?

b. How do you think they form ideas about people like this? Do they ever change their minds?

c. Does anything ever change your mind about a person?

d. Why are labels and stereotyping unfair?

e. How could labels and stereotyping lead to violations of human rights?

f. What do these responses suggest about the way different people see others? Should people all see things the same way?

g. Observe that we get many of our ideas about people we don't know from the media (e.g. radio, television). Discuss the role of the media in stereotyping by asking question such as these:

h. How do the media present people from other cultures and countries? When they live in their country of origin? When they live in your country?

i. How can the media increase labelling and stereotyping?

### Suggestions for follow-up

Several other activities also examine stereotypes:

- 'Picture Games', p. 130 and 'World Summer Camp', p. 205, deal with a variety of stereotypes.
- 'Boys Don't Cry', p. 78, and 'Once Upon a Time...', p. 125, address gender stereotypes.
- 'Blindfolded', p. 67, and 'A Body of Knowledge', p. 53, concern stereotypes about children with disabilities.

### Ideas for action

- The children can develop and carry out a survey of how other people, children and/or adults, in their community respond to the same pictures. Based on their findings, they can decide how to address stereotypes and prejudice.
- Pick an example of a current event, especially involving people from other cultures and countries, and analyse how newspapers, radio and television present the issues and the people involved. Compare how different media deal with the same story. How are the related human rights issues presented?
- If they have access to cameras, the children can create a photo exhibition of 'Views of Human Rights' or 'Faces of Diversity' in your community.

### Tips for the facilitator

- By using different pictures and asking appropriate questions in the debriefing, this activity can be adapted to focus on any human rights theme, e.g. gender equality or poverty and social exclusion.

- The choice of pictures is very important. Collect images from colour magazines, travel brochures, old calendars and post cards. You can also print many from Google images. Be sure that there is no text with any of the pictures, but note the original caption or other information about each picture in order to answer any questions about it.

- To make sure children understand the activity, you may wish to demonstrate with one picture before the activity starts.

- The pictures should show a wide variety of aspects of 'life on earth'; they should include images of individuals and groups, people of different ages, cultures and abilities. There should be pictures in rural and urban settings, of industry and agriculture, people doing different sorts of work and leisure activities, people of different origins, colours, races, and religions. Don't try to put the pictures in any sort of order when you number them.

- Make sure that the pictures that are chosen do not relate too closely to any personal attributes of the children in the group, as this may make them feel uncomfortable or embarrassed.

- Many children will be unable to differentiate between stereotyped responses and their own opinions. Although this activity may challenge them, it may also offer important new perspectives.

## Adaptation

- The children will differ widely in their maturity and sophistication, general knowledge of stereotypes and 'visual literacy' skills. Adapt the level of analysis to the abilities of the group.

# 39. Who Should Decide?

When is 'old enough'?

| | |
|---|---|
| Themes | Family and alternative care, Participation |
| Level of complexity | Level 2 |
| Age | 7 – 10 years |
| Duration | 45 minutes |
| Group size | 4 – 24 children |
| Type of activity | Decision making, small group discussion |
| Overview | Children respond to a list of questions on who should make a decision in each situation. After each question, the children use a colour-coded card to show their response. |
| Objectives | • To reflect on decision making processes in families<br>• To discuss child participation in family life<br>• To introduce the concept of evolving capacities |
| Preparation | • Prepare questions ready to read out.<br>• Make a set of cards for each child. |
| Materials | • 1 x Green, Yellow and Orange card for each child |

## Instructions

1. Ask the group to reflect on what they're wearing and ask them to discuss with a person sitting next to them who decided what they would wear that day. Was it their parent/s? Was it themselves? Was it a joint decision made by the parent/s and child together? Explain that this activity is about making decisions.

2. Give a set of cards to each child (green, yellow and orange). Explain that you will read out a list of decisions that should be made, and after each question you will ask the group to think about who should make the decision. If the child thinks that the parent/s should make the decision, then they should hold up a green card. If they think the child should make the decision, then they should hold up a yellow card. If they think the child and the parent/s should make the decision, then they should hold up an orange card.

3. Read out the questions one by one and after each question wait until everyone in the group has held up their card. Encourage the children to look around at the responses from the rest of the group after each question. Some children in the group will probably make comments, but discourage discussion at this point: hold discussion until the debriefing.

## Debriefing and evaluation

1. Debrief the activity by asking questions such as these:
   a. How did you like this activity?
   b. Was it difficult to respond to some of the questions? Why?
   c. Which ones were easier to respond to and which ones were more difficult? Why?
   d. Why did some people have different answers?
   e. Is there a right answer or a wrong answer to the questions?
   f. Does the age of child make a difference in the role they should have in making decisions concerning themselves? Why or why not?

2. Introduce the phrase 'evolving capacities' and explain that it means that children have more decision making opportunities and responsibilities in personal matters as they mature. For older children, you can refer specifically to Article 5 and 14 of the CRC and discuss this concept further. Ask questions such as these about the children's own role in decision making:

    a. Are you involved in making decisions in your family? Which decisions are they?

    b. Are there some things that you can make a decision about yourself? What decisions are they?

    c. Are there some things that you need help and guidance from your parent/s to make decisions about? What things are they?

    d. What are some ways you can ask for more guidance from your parent/s?

    e. Is it important for you and your parent/s to participate in your family life? Why or why not?

    f. What are some ways you can participate more in your family life?

    g. Do you like the way decisions are made in your family? Are there some decisions you would like to participate in that you do not? What are some things you could do to have a greater role in decision making?

3. Relate the activity to human rights by asking questions such as these:

    a. Why do you think some human rights concern children and their families?

    b. Why do you think participation in decisions that concern them is one of every child's human rights?

    c. Who else makes decisions about children's lives besides themselves and their parents? Why is this important?

## Suggestions for follow-up

- You may like to start focusing on the family by running the activity 'WE ARE FAMILY', P. 180 as a start, before this one.

- The activity 'A CONSTITUTION FOR OUR GROUP', P. 56, also involves children in participatory decision making and negotiation.

## Ideas for action

- Ask each person in the group to develop a family strategy with their parent/s about how each member of the family can participate further in family life.

- Invite parent/s to speak to the group about their views on participation in family life, including how their role in making decisions about children's personal matters changes as the child/children grow and develop.

## Tips for the facilitator

- Some questions may be difficult for some of the children to answer; however, you should encourage them to choose the card or response that is most relevant for them.

- Be sure to know the family situations of the children in the group you are working with. Some children may not live with a parent or parents and may live with a guardian. In these cases, you should also include guardian/s along with parent/s in the activity.

- Some children will want to explain why they have given a certain response straight away but instead of engaging in discussion after each question, remind children that they will have the chance to speak about the activity afterwards.

- You may want to ask children to draw a picture on each coloured card before you read out the questions so that they remember which card represents which response. Alternatively, you can write

this on a chart or board at the front of the room so they can refer to this if they forget which colour responds to who makes the decision.

- Adaptation:
  - For a longer and more in-depth activity, ask the children to discuss their decisions after each set of questions.
  - For older children: ask them to identify which CRC rights the questions refer to.
  - For older children: Ask what human rights protect the participation of children and parent/s in family life? Why are they important?

## QUESTIONS TO READ OUT

Who should decide whether you can stay at home on your own when your family goes shopping:
  At 5 years old?
  At 10 years old?
  At 15 years old?

Who should decide whether you can stay in touch with both your parents after they have separated:
  At 4 years old?
  At 9 years old?
  At 17 years old?

Who should decide whether you can join the military service:
  At 6 years old?
  At 11 years old?
  At 16 years old?

Who should decide whether you should wear a raincoat when going out in the rain:
  At 3 years old?
  At 9 years old?
  At 14 years old?

Who should decide whether you should be a vegetarian or not:
  At 4 years old?
  At 8 years old?
  At 13 years old?

Who should decide whether you can smoke cigarettes:
  At 6 years old?
  At 9 years old?

At 15 years old?

Who should decide whether you can stay up until midnight:

At 5 years old?

At 9 years old?

At 14 years old?

Who should decide whether you can use the Internet without supervision:

At 6 years old?

At 10 years old?

At 16 years old?

Who should decide whether you can choose your own religion:

At 5 years old?

At 9 years old?

At 13 years old?

Who should decide whether you can stop attending school:

At 6 years old?

At 10 years old?

At 15 years old?

Who should decide whether you can join the local choir group:

At 5 years old?

At 9 years old?

At 17 years old?

Who should decide whether you can have your own mobile phone:

At 4 years old?

At 8 years old?

At 14 years old?

Who should decide whether you should be put in foster care:

At 4 years old?

At 10 years old?

At 16 years old?

# 40. Words that Wound

Sticks and stones can break my bones, and words can also hurt me!

| | |
|---|---|
| Themes | Discrimination, Gender equality, Violence |
| Level of complexity | Level 2 |
| Age | 10 – 13 years |
| Duration | 60 minutes |
| Group size | 5-20 children |
| Type of activity | List making, prioritizing, discussion |
| Overview | Children give examples of hurtful language and analyze its motives and effects. |
| Objectives | • To reflect on the causes and effects of hurtful language |
| | • To understand how people may respond differently to different terms |
| | • To understand the limits of freedom of expression |
| | • To practise skills for opposing hurtful language |
| Preparation | Copy CRC Article 13 on chart paper or the blackboard. |
| Materials | • Post-its or slips of paper and sticky tape |
| | • Chart paper and a marker, or blackboard and chalk |
| | • Copy of CRC Article 13 |

## Instructions

1. Write out and/or read CRC Article 13 aloud. Point out that this article of the CRC gives a child the right to freedom of expression but specifically restricts expression that violates the rights and reputations of others. Discuss freedom of expression by asking questions such as these:

    a. Should we always be able to say whatever we like?

    b. Should limits be placed on what we can say about our thoughts and beliefs?

    c. What kind of language would violate the rights of others?

    d. What kind of language would violate the reputation of others?

2. Explain that this activity will explore some of these questions.

3. Give everyone slips of paper and ask them to write down hurtful comments they hear people say about other children or names that children call each other, each one on a separate slip of paper.

4. Make a scale on the wall such as the one below, ranging from 'Teasing / Playful' to 'Extremely Painful / Degrading'. Ask the children to put their words where they think they belong on the scale. Encourage them not to talk during this part of the activity.

| Teasing / Playful / Not painful | A Little Painful / Degrading | Moderately Painful / Degrading | Very Painful / Degrading | Extremely Painful / Degrading |
|---|---|---|---|---|
| | | | | |

5. Then ask everyone to examine the wall silently. Usually the same words will appear several times and are almost always rated at different degrees of severity.

## Debriefing and Evaluation

1. When the children are sitting down again, ask them what they observed, guiding their analysis with questions such as these:
   a. Did some words appear in more than one column?
   b. Why do you think some people thought a word was not hurtful and others though it was painful or degrading?
   c. Does it matter how a word is said? Or by whom?
   d. Why do people use words such as these?
   e. Is hurting others by using words a form of violence? Why?

2. Ask the children if they can see any patterns or categories among these hurtful words. As the children begin to identify and mention these categories (e.g. about physical appearances and abilities, mental characteristics, sexuality, family or ethnic background), write down the categories on the board. Guide their analysis with questions such as these:
   a. Are some words only for girls? For boys?
   b. Why do you think hurtful language falls into these topics?
   c. In what topics or categories do the words considered most hurtful seem to be?
   d. What conclusions can you draw about hurtful language from these categories?

3. Ask the children to remove their slips of paper from the first chart and place them under the topic or category where they best fit. You may want to have one category labelled 'Other'. When the children are re-seated, ask questions such as these:
   a. What categories seem to have the greatest number of slips? How can you explain that?
   b. Do the words considered most hurtful seem to fall into particular categories?
   c. Don't answer aloud but consider: do the words you use yourself fall into a particular category?
   d. Divide the class into small groups and give each group several of the slips containing the words considered most painful. Ask someone in each group to read the first word or phrase. The group should accept that this is a hurtful comment and discuss 1) whether people should be allowed to say such things, and 2) what to do when it happens. Repeat the process for each word or phrase.

4. Ask the children to report back on their conclusions in Step 3. Relate hurtful speech to human rights responsibilities by asking questions such as these:
   a. Do adults have a responsibility to stop hurtful speech? If so, why?
   b. Do children have a responsibility to stop it in their own lives? If so, why?
   c. What can you do in your community to stop hurtful speech?
   d. Why is it important to do so?
   e. In what way is hurtful speech a violation of someone's human rights?

## Suggestions for follow-up

- Further the discussion about what children can do to stop hurtful language. Role-play name-calling situations and let children experiment together with ways to respond.
- The activity 'FROM BYSTANDER TO HELPER', p. 108, helps children consider what they can do individually to intervene in hurtful behaviours.

   b. Were some children chosen many times to share a tent? Why?

   c. Were some children not chosen at all? Why?

   d. How did you decide about the child from a place you had never heard of?

2. How do you feel after this activity?

   a. Did anything funny come up in your group discussion?

   b. Was it hard to agree with your group?

   c. Who is happy about the final result and who is not?

   d. Did you learn anything about yourself? About the way you make choices?

3. Compare this activity with situations in real life:

   a. Was this situation realistic?

   b. Can you think of other situations where you have to choose whom to be with?

   c. How does it feel to choose?

   d. How does it feel in real life to be chosen? Not to be chosen?

   e. What kinds of similar choices do you make in real life?

   f. Do all children have the right to choose? To be chosen?

4. Discuss how we form ideas about others, even those we have never met:

   a. What makes children the same? What makes them different?

   b. How do you get ideas about what children whom you have never met are like?

   c. How do you get ideas about where they come from?

   d. Are there people who have stereotypes about you? About children?

   e. Do you have stereotypes about other people?

   f. What can we do to avoid making unfair opinions based on stereotypes?

   g. Why do stereotypes lead to discrimination?

## Suggestions for follow-up

- The activity 'Dear Diary', p. 99, contrasts perceptions of the same day.
- The activity 'Zabderfilio', p. 209, shows the effects of fear of the unknown.
- The activities 'Blindfolded', p. 67; 'Picture Games', p. 130, and 'Who's Behind Me?', p. 195, deal with stereotypes of different kinds.

## Ideas for action

- The next time the group has to choose partners or teams, take the opportunity to remind the children of this exercise and what they learned about choosing.
- Organize a summer camp yourself: several current European funding programmes already offer possibilities for these kinds of camps. For adolescents from thirteen years on, consult the Youth in Action Programme of the European Commission.

## Tips for the facilitator

- Be careful not to reinforce stereotypes in any way. That would defeat the purpose of this activity!
- The ideal number of children from the small group is four, with each child making a list of three campers. However, the activity can work for small groups of any size who must then negotiate adding or eliminating campers to their list to make 16 children in all.
- Choose and/or adapt the list of campers carefully to shape the activity towards your desired learn-

ing outcomes. Be sure that no child in your group resembles one of the campers. Simplify the description, especially the origins, for younger children. However, do have at least one camper on the list from a fictional place so that children have to decide without knowing anything.

- If summer camp or sharing a tent is not realistic for these children, choose another setting that involves close proximity (e.g. a shared school desk, a youth hostel or dormitory room).

- Avoid answering questions about the list of campers. Explain that the children should decide on the basis of the list alone.

- Some children may be unable to choose and say they don't care with whom they share the tent. In that case, ask them with whom they do not wish to share the tent. The results can still be compared amongst the children in the small group.

- Some members of the group may decide to share a tent with each other and put the 'foreigner campers' in other tents. Do not intervene, for the results will be very revealing. Similarly, do not give the children the impression that it is bad to want to choose people like themselves. Not all choices relate to discrimination.

## Adaptations

- To shorten the activity:
  - Describe smaller tents so that each child must choose only one or two other campers.
  - Reduce the total number of campers to choose from.
  - Leave out the small group work, Step 3.
  - To facilitate small group decision making, make a list of all the campers chosen by members of the group. Then each child in turn chooses one camper until all campers are divided.

- For younger children:
  - Use suggestions above for shortening the activity.
  - Adapt the descriptions of campers to match the experience of the younger children (e.g. Mongolia or a Kung Fu T-shirt may have no connotations for them).

## World summer camp

You and children from all over the world have just arrived at World Summer Camp. Nobody knows each other. The leaders have decided that you can choose with whom you will share a tent for the next two weeks. Each tent sleeps four children. You can choose three other campers to share the tent with you.

## World camp campers

Choose 3 children from this list with whom you would like to share the tent!

1. _____

2. _____

3. _____

1. A child with a broken leg and crutches
2. A Roma child from your own country with golden earrings
3. A child from Australia with red hair and many freckles
4. A Japanese child wearing a Kung Fu T-shirt
5. A fat child from the USA
6. A shy child from Transmarinia
7. An immigrant child from Africa
8. A blind child accompanied by a guide dog
9. A child with thick glasses and a spotty f ace
10. A child from the UK dressed in a school uniform
11. A Turkish child from Germany with a black eye wearing a T-shirt with a skull on it
12. A child from Latin America dressed in traditional clothes
13. A child who uses sign language to communicate
14. A child from Mongolia with very long black hair
15. A child from your country who doesn't seem to be very clever
16. A child from Palestine with only one arm
17. A child with blond hair who speaks very properly
18. A child that seems permanently to have hiccups
19. A child dressed in a jacket just like yours
20. A child who listens to an MP3 all the time

# 42. Zabderfilio

Nobody for one and one for all.

| | |
|---|---|
| Themes | General human rights, Discrimination |
| Level of complexity | Level 1 |
| Age | 7-10 years |
| Duration | 35 minutes |
| Group size | 5-35 |
| Type of activity | Storytelling, reflective activity |
| Objectives | • To discuss the concept of 'All Different – All Equal'<br>• To reflect on the meaning of tolerance and diversity<br>• To discuss violence and conflict management<br>• To understand the principle of universality |
| Preparation | • Practise the puppet show beforehand.<br>• Make a puppet to represent Zabderfilio: an animal that has characteristics of different animals (or you can use the handout). |
| Materials | • A puppet theatre or similar arrangements<br>• Different animal puppets, a hunter puppet, a presenter puppet, and a Zabderfilio puppet, such as in the handout |

## Instructions

1. Gather the children in front of the puppet theatre. Explain that they have to be silent and stay in their seats when the puppet show is running. They should only speak when the characters ask them questions and nobody should try to touch them.

2. Run the puppet show. Ask the children questions regularly to keep their attention and to work towards the learning objectives.

## Debriefing and Evaluation

1. Debrief the activity by asking questions such as these:
   a. How do you feel about the story?
   b. What happened during the story?
   c. What animal do you like the most? The least? Why?
   d. Were the other animals fair towards Zabderfilio?
   e. Why did they act as they did?
   f. Why you think the other animals finally became friends with Zabderfilio? Because he was the strongest? The best looking? Or because he was brave and generous? Or a mixture of different talents?

2. Relate the activity to human rights by asking questions such as these:
   a. Have you ever seen anyone treated the way the animals first treated Zabderfilio?
   b. Why does this happen in real life?
   c. Are we all the same and still different? In what ways are we all alike? And what makes us different?
   d. What can we do to avoid some children feeling as Zabderfilio did when no-one would be his friend?

**Source:** Adapted from a puppet show developed by the Portuguese group 'Animação e Inovacao Social', (MAIS): www.mais.online.pt.

### Suggestions for follow-up

The children can perform this simple story with puppets themselves and put it on for another group of children. They could also make their own puppets and/or develop another story. Other stories in COM-PASITO could also be dramatized as a puppet show (e.g. 'MODERN FAIRYTALE', P. 113; 'ONCE UPON A TIME...', P. 125).

### Ideas for action

Ask the children to think what it would be like if a 'Zabderfilio' joined their group. Help the children develop an internal 'code of conduct' towards each other, respecting each individual and his or her differences. Hang the code in your meeting space and refer to it whenever appropriate.

### Tips for the facilitator

- Instead of having a real puppet theatre, use a blanket to sit behind.
- Use whatever animal puppets you have available. If you do not have the necessary puppets, make the puppets using cut-out cardboard drawings or old socks.
- Adapt your Zabderfilio to fit your imagination. He might have the ears of a rabbit, the horn of a rhino, the nose and whiskers of a mouse, the mane of a lion, the pouch of a kangaroo or any other combination that fits your story. In any case, he should look weird and have at least a conspicuous nose, a loud voice and the ability to move silently. You can also adapt the story to fit any puppet you may have.
- With larger groups, have a second facilitator to help with the process of question and answer between the group and the puppets.

## SCENARIO

**Introduction: (made by a 'presenter puppet' who is not part of the story)**

**Presenter Puppet:** Hello, ladies and gentlemen, boys and girls. I'm happy to see that everybody is ready to listen and watch today's special show!

Well, I can tell you already a little bit of the mystery of today. It all takes place in the world of the animals. And in that world, just like ours, not everything is beautiful and not everything is ugly, not everything is normal and not everything is weird. But – there are always surprises!

And this story is about one of these surprises. It is the story of a very special animal called Zabderfilio. Watch and listen carefully. Please stay where you are, otherwise the animals might run away and we will never know what happens at the end of the story. See you later!

## THE STORY

**Summary:** Zabderfilio meets different existing animals one by one. Each of them considers Zabderfilio a very strange animal. Zabderfilio is looking for friends but none of the animals want to be his friend because he is ... just weird!

**Below is an example of one of his encounters:**

**Giraffe**: *(Comes on the stage and talks to the children)* Hello, everybody. Do you know who I am?

*(Audience: You're a giraffe.)*

**Giraffe**: How do you know? Am I wearing a nametag somewhere?

*(Audience: Because of your long neck, your colours...)*

**Giraffe**: Yes, you are all right. And I have the longest neck of all the animals in the world. I can see a long way, and I can eat from high trees without any great effort!

*(Zabderfilio comes on stage)*

**Zabderfilio**: *(Very friendly and eager)* Hello!

**Giraffe**: WOOEEEHAAA ... you scared me there for a second, sneaking up to me like this. But wait a minute, who are you?

**Zabderfilio**: I am Zabderfilio.

**Giraffe**: Zabberbadderdiloooo-what??

**Zabderfilio**: My name is Zabderfilio and I'm looking for friends. Do you want to be my friend?

**Giraffe**: Er, um... I don't know. You look very strange to me! You are not a mouse, not a lion, not a kangoroo, but you look like all of them. All my friends are one thing or the other and not a mix like you! Excuse me, but I have to go see my friends! Tee hee hee, you are really strange and ugly!

**Zabderfilio**: *(With hurt feelings)* But, but – wait a second ...

*(Giraffe has already disappeared and Zabderfilio talks now to the audience)*

**Zabderfilio**: This makes me sad. Why didn't Giraffe wanted to be my friend? Well, let me walk a little bit longer in the forest and see if I meet any other animals to play with.

None of the animals Zabderfilio meets wants to be his friend. After several encounters, suddenly, a hunter comes on stage. He is hunting animals. Each time one of the animals comes on stage, the hunter tries to grab it, but they all run away, screaming for help.

Then the hunter disappears from the stage, looking in the forest for the animals, and Zabderfilio reappears. He asks the audience what all this noise was about.

After the audience explains the situation, Zabderfilio uses his nose of a mouse to smell the hunter (Aha, with my keen nose I smell a hunter nearby!), his feet of a cat to walk without any noise (I think I can use my cat feet to sneak up on him!) and his lion scream to scare the hunter away (And now I use my huge voice to roar like a lion and frighten him away. ROAR!).

After this heroic deed, the other animals come closer and apologize for their nasty behaviour. They all ask him to be their friend, and Zabderfilio gladly accepts. All the animals say goodbye to the audience and the 'presenting–puppet' appears to make the final comments.

## CONCLUSION

**Presenter Puppet:** Well, boys and girls, ladies and gentlemen. That was the story of Zabderfilio. Did you enjoy it?

He certainly was a funny looking beast! But he was able to help his friends because he combined so many different parts. Next time you see someone who looks a little unusual, I hope you think of Zabderfilio – that person may have talents you never dreamed of and make a wonderful friend.

## HANDOUT: SAMPLE ZABDERFILIO

# V. THEMES

# 1. CITIZENSHIP

*[Children] tend to be either ignored as citizens or regarded in an adult-centric fashion as citizens of the future rather than of the present.*

Brian Howe

## The multiple dimensions of contemporary citizenship

In a strictly legal sense, a citizen is the inhabitant of a state where laws protect people's civic and political rights and where people have reciprocal duties to that state: to obey the laws of the country, to contribute to common expenses and to defend the country if attacked. Citizenship differs from nationality or ethnic identification; in this context these two latter terms are synonymous with a grouping based on a cultural and language community. Most European states are composed of several nationalities. However, people of the same nationality may live in neighbouring states. While the state is a **political** and **geopolitical** entity, the nation is a **cultural** and/or an **ethnic** entity. Citizenship is related to a state and is not dependent on nationality.

Today 'citizenship' goes beyond a simple legal relationship between people and the state. It is understood to have not only a legal dimension, referring to civic and political rights and duties, but also a psychological and social dimension. Being a citizen is part of one's identity. You care for your community because you are part of it, and you expect others to care for it and, with you, to seek the common good of the whole community.

In this broader sense, citizenship is not merely a process of socialisation. It involves feelings of identity, belonging, inclusion, participation and social commitment. As part of the community, the citizen can influence it, participate in its development and contribute to its well-being. Thus the citizen is both a 'receiver' of rights and duties and also an 'actor' who participates within a group of which she or he feels a part. Citizens in this sense are equal in dignity.

QUESTION: *Besides voting in elections, what forms of involvement or participation are possible for ordinary citizens? How can they be encouraged to participate?*

## Historical and contemporary conceptions of citizenship

The historical development of the idea of citizenship helps to explain these multiple dimensions of citizenship.

One of the earliest concept of citizenship can be traced back to ancient Greek city-states, where 'citizens' were those who had a legal right to participate in the affairs of the state. However, only a small percentage of the population were citizens: slaves and women were mere subjects and foreigners were excluded altogether. For those free men who did have the privileged status of being citizens, 'civic virtue' or being a 'good' citizen was an important value. This tradition led to an emphasis on the *duties* that citizenship imposed on citizens.

The association of citizenship with national identity arose in nineteenth century history, when nation states were emerging all over Europe and the legal status of a 'citizen' was often tied to a nation state, even if several ethnicities lived within its territory. The link between citizenship and patriotism became stronger during this period.

**The liberal view of citizenship**, which originated with the French Revolution, emphasized the importance of *rights* for all citizens and a commitment to a constitution rather than an ethnicity. As more people became entitled to vote, justice and political rights also became a reality for an increasing number of people.

In the twentieth century, the supporters of '**social citizenship**' went further to recognize that citizens ought to be able to expect civil and political rights from the state. The rise of the welfare state in the last century owed a great deal to thinkers who argued that the rights of citizens ought to include their livelihood and working conditions.

Citizenship today has various meanings which are interrelated and complementary. '**Active Citizenship**' implies working towards the betterment of one's community through economic participation, public service, volunteer work and other such efforts to improve life for all members of the community.

'**European citizenship**' is understood in many different ways. The Maastricht Treaty of the European Union laid down the concept that citizens of states belonging to the European Union (EU) increasingly have some rights from and duties to the Union as a whole, as well as to their own states. Such rights granted to EU citizens include freedom of movement and the right of residence within the territory of the Member States, and the right to vote and stand as a candidate at elections for the European Parliament. However, a 'European society' cannot be said to exist today in the same way as the Greek or Czech society. European citizenship today lies somewhere between a tangible reality and a distant ideal. "The ideal understanding of European citizenship would be based on the values of Democracy, Human Rights and Social Justice."[1] European citizenship provides a significant sense of belonging to multiple value systems: to human rights, to a nationality, to an ethnicity, to a local community, to a family, to an ideological group and so on. This multiple and dynamic system of belongings involved in European citizenship is not in confrontation with any national identity, but is inclusive and works on the local level.

'**Global citizenship**' is a recent concept that emerged from the idea that everyone is a citizen of the globe. In a legal sense, however, there is no such thing as a global citizen. "Global Citizenship is about understanding the need to tackle injustice and inequality, and having the desire and ability to work actively to do so. It is about valuing the Earth as precious and unique, and safeguarding the future for those coming after us. Global Citizenship lives well together with any other understanding of citizenships; it is a way of thinking and a commitment to make a difference."[2]

As the terms 'citizen' or 'citizenship' have many interpretations, and as nation-state is not necessarily a relevant concept in a multicultural Europe, the Council of Europe uses the term 'citizen' as a 'person co-existing in a society'. Instead of 'nation state', the word 'community' best describes the local, regional and international environment in which an individual lives.

**QUESTION:** *What is your personal understanding of citizenship? What should the criteria be for citizenship in an increasingly mobile and multicultural world? Who in your society should not be entitled to citizenship rights?*

Today, most people's notion of citizenship includes elements of all these concepts, although in different proportions. Some people will emphasize the 'duties' elements of citizenship, while others may give more importance to 'rights'. For some, patriotism has key importance and a relation to one single state, while some people hold a broader understanding of what citizenship means.

## Children as citizens

The law of many countries once considered children to be their parents' property. Although the *patria potestas* that gave a father every right – including that of life and death – over his children is long gone, remnants of this traditional power remain in some countries. The traditional understanding is that children are 'non-citizens' or 'pre-citizens' in a society. While the Convention on the Right of the Child recognizes parents' rights to their children's custody, education and representation (Articles 5 and 18), it also introduces the principle of the child's best interest, which establishes limits to parental rights in the interest of their children (Article 3).

According to Brian Howe, a Canadian children's rights advocate, although children are legally citizens by birth or naturalization, they are often neither recognized nor treated as citizens. "They tend to be either ignored as citizens or regarded in an adult-centric fashion as citizens of the future rather than of the present."[3] Howe identifies two main reasons for this attitude: children's economic dependency and psychological immaturity. He points out that other economically dependent groups such as stay-at-home parents, retired people, university students or adults with disabilities are not denied their citizenship. He concludes that children have a right to citizenship as "citizenship is about inclusion, not economic independence".

**QUESTION:** *Are children really citizens? Or are they just 'pre-citizens' or citizens-to-be?*

Children indeed lack the cognitive development, maturity and self-control of adults. However development is an ongoing, lifelong process, and the cognitive development of children increases when they are treated with respect and provided with age-appropriate opportunities for their autonomy and participation as citizens.

According to national law and to the UDHR, children have rights and responsibilities similar to those of adults. But they also have differentiated citizenship: the CRC recognizes children's need for specific *protection* (e.g. from abuse, neglect, economic and sexual exploitation), *provision* (e.g. of basic needs such as health care, social security or to a quality standard of living, as well as the right to a name, identity and nationality) and to *participation* in all decisions affecting them. These rights are to be exercised in accordance with the **evolving capacities** of the child, as are the child's responsibilities as a citizen. Children, like adults, must respect the rights of others and obey the law, but their level of responsibility and of legal accountability is age-differentiated. For the application of this principle to the right to participate, see the discussion on *Theme 10, Participation* below, p. 262.

**QUESTION:** *What forms of citizen participation are possible and appropriate for children?*

DGIV/EDU/CIT (2006) 17: Council of Europe, 2006. www.unicef-icdc.org/publications

- Howe, Brian, 'Citizenship Education for Child Citizens', *Canadian and International Education Journal*, Vol. 34, no.1: 2005, p. 42-49.
- O'Shea, Karen, Developing a shared understanding, a glossary of terms for education for democratic citizenship, DGIV/EDU/CIT (2003) 29: Strassbourg, Council of Europe, 2003: www.coe.int/t/dg4/education/edc/ Source/Pdf/Documents/2003_29_GlossaryEDC.PDF
- Ramberg, Ingrid, Citizenship Matters: the participation of young women and minorities in Euro-Med youth projects, Seminar report: Council of Europe Publishing, 2005.
- Torney-Purta, Judith et al., *Citizenship and Education in Twenty-Eight Countries: Civic knowledge and engagement at age fourteen*: International Association for the Evaluation of Educational Achievement, Amsterdam, 2001.
- *Under Construction: Citizenship, Youth and Europe,* T-Kit on European Citizenship: Council of Europe, 2003.
- Violence against Children in Europe, A preliminary review of research: UNICEF, Innocenti Research Centre, Florence, 2005.

## Useful Websites

- Droits Partagés: des droits de l'homme aux droits de l'enfant: www.droitspartages.org
- Citizenship Foundation: www.citizenshipfoundation.org.uk
- Oxfam Cool planet for teachers on global citizenship: www.oxfam.org.uk
- Programme 'Building a Europe for and with Children': www.coe.int/children
- UNICEF, Innocenti Research Centre: www.unicef-irc.org/publications/

## References

1 *Under construction, Citizenship, Youth and Europe,* T-kit No 7.Council of Europe, 2003. p.34.
2 *Global Citizenship*, Cool Planet for Teachers: www.oxfam.org.uk/coolplanet/teachers/globciti/index.htm
3 Howe, Brian, *Citizenship Education for Child Citizens*, Canadian and International Education Journal, Vol. 34, no.1: 2005, p. 44.
4 *Recommendation* REC (2002)12 of the Committee of Ministers to member states on education for democratic citizenship.
5 O'Shea, Karen, *Development of a shared understanding*: A glossary of terms for education for democratic citizenship: Council of Europe, GDIV/EDU/CIT (2003)29, p.8.

# 2. DEMOCRACY

*It is vital to promote a culture of democracy and human rights among children and young people, as attitudes and behaviour are shaped at an early stage and can be decisive in determining their future involvement in public affairs.*

Conclusions of the Council of Europe Forum for the Future of Democracy, June 2007

## What is democracy?

Never in the history of Europe has democracy been so widespread and strong in the continent as at the turn of the twenty-first century. Almost all European societies are considered to be democratic if they are founded on the principles of a sovereign citizenship, transparent decision making and accountable government. It is difficult to fully achieve these principles in reality, but nevertheless we can say that in general these are the guidelines for the development of democracy in contemporary Europe.

The word *democracy* comes from the Greek words *demos*, meaning 'people', and *kratos*, meaning 'power'. Accordingly, democracy is often defined as 'the rule of the people': a system of making rules determined by the people who are to obey those rules. In today's world most people and most countries consider democracy to be the only valid and viable system of government.

Democracy rests on two fundamental principles:

- the principle of 'individual autonomy': that no-one should be subject to rules that have been imposed by others;
- the principle of 'equality': that everyone should have the same opportunity to influence the decisions that affect people in society.

Other forms of government violate both these principles, for power is held by a certain person or social class who then take decisions on behalf of the rest of the population. For example, an oligarchy is ruled by a small, privileged group distinguished by some quality such as wealth, family or military powers. In a plutocracy, government is controlled by the wealthy, and in a dictatorship by a single all-powerful individual. In these other forms of government neither individual autonomy nor equality is respected.

Democracy takes many forms. For example, in direct democracy citizens personally participate in decision making. The most widespread form of democracy, however, is liberal or representative democracy, in which citizens elect representatives who create laws and policies and appoint the government officials. In theory, representative democracy involves the free and fair election of a government by a majority vote of the people being represented. A liberal democracy is characterised by the rule of law, separation of powers, protec-

tion of human rights and protection of minorities. The rule of law is the principle that the government and judiciary function only in accordance with written rules. It is closely linked with the principle of separation of power, according to which the legislative (parliament), executive (government) and judiciary (courts) act independently of each other. In a democratic government human rights provide a common value system. Accordingly, underrepresented social group of any kind, such as children, women, migrants, religious or ethnic minorities, are protected from discrimination and their identity and participation are promoted.

The term *democracy* signifies a particular type of society as well as a particular form of government. A democratic society provides the fairest method of governance for most people and the most equality, with the majority of the people playing an active rather than a passive role. It is characterised by a moral imperative to protect and promote the human rights of every individual, every group and every community of society. Because a democratic society is constantly seeking to solve social questions for the benefit of the greatest number of people, these decisions are most likely to be respected by the people. Democracy exist at the local as well the national level.

## Democracy in practise

Democracies are different from each other and none can be considered a model for others. Democratic governments can take several forms, including presidential (as in France, Romania or Russia) or parliamentary (as in the United Kingdom, Slovakia or Spain). Others, such as Germany, have federal governmental structures. Some voting systems are proportional while others are majoritarian. The common principles, however, are the equality of all citizens and the right of every individual to some degree of personal autonomy. However, personal autonomy does not mean that everyone can do whatever she or he likes. It implies that the governmental system allocates an equal vote to each citizen and recognises that each individual is capable of independent choice and entitled to have that choice taken into account. After that, a great deal depends on the initiative and participation of individual citizens.

Democracies differ greatly in the degree to which they respect equality and allow their citizens to influence decisions. People who live in poverty may have a weaker voice. Women, who are less present in the public arena, may have fewer opportunities to influence decisions, even those concerning women specifically. Some social groups, such as children and foreign workers, may not be allowed to vote. At the same time most people believe that rules have been imposed on them by elected officials who do not represent their interests. So where are the basic democratic principles? To what extent can we feel any 'ownership' of the laws and government decisions?

Democracy is never perfect and never complete. Karl Popper has even said, "Democracy is the word for something that does not exist". This may be an exaggeration, but it is true that genuine democracy is an ideal model. It is up to the people to determine how close their society can get to this ideal state.

## Democracy works only if citizens are active

> Democracy is much more than an electoral code. It is a code of behaviour, an attitude and a state of mind.
>
> *Terry Davis, Introductory speech at the Summer University for Democracy, organised by the Council of Europe, 2006*

A democratic society is more than a democratically elected government and a system of national institutions. Strong and independent local authorities, a developed and active civil society at national and local levels, and a democratic ethos in workplaces and schools are also key manifestations of the democratic society. Democracy is a practical process that should be nurtured every day and everywhere.

Democracy can function more effectively and serve the interests of its citizens better if people formulate demands, exert pressure and monitor government's actions continuously. In modern society, non-governmental organisations and the media serve as the key channels for citizens' control. Non-governmental organisations (NGOs) can advocate, educate and mobilise attention around

major public issues and monitor the conduct of government or other governing bodies. Through NGOs, citizens can be the driving force and the principal agents of change for a more democratic world.

The media have a very powerful function in democracies, communicating news and opinions of various social actors and serving as a watchdog on behalf of citizens. But this function exists only if the media are free from governmental or corporate interests and influences, they value public service and take their role seriously.

## What is wrong with democracy?

Now, at the beginning of the twenty-first century there is a universal concern today about the status of democracy. In many European democracies political discontent and scepticism are widespread, and people often believe the political elite can afford to disregard the will of the people. Some contradictory developments of democracy such as acute social inequality and corruption cause frustration and anger that can lead to populism supported by the mass media. Citizens often feel powerless and are discouraged from taking a more active role in their society.

Such concerns about the state of democracy are often based on the levels of citizen participation at elections, which has significantly decreased everywhere in Europe in the last fifteen years. This decline, which appears to indicate a lack of interest and involvement on the part of citizens, undermines the democratic process.

The turnout of young people at elections is especially low, and there is a growing difference in the participation rate between young people and other age groups. While this discrepancy does not necessarily mean that young people will not vote more actively as they get older, their interests are already less represented at elections. All over the world, young people are becoming increasingly removed from democratic institutions and traditional structures of political life, such as political parties, trade unions or formal youth organisations.[1]

Although these are undoubtedly serious problems, other studies[2] indicate that different forms of participation are actually on the increase within pressure groups, campaigns, ad hoc civic initiatives or consultative organs. Global civil society and Internet activism are flexible new forms of civic participation based on the possibilities provided by technological development. Young people can quickly mobilise around single issues, such as, in the United Kingdom, the war in Iraq or the Orange revolution in the Ukraine. Political opinion can also be expressed through arts and sport, voicing environmental concerns, women's rights or consumer boycotts. These forms of participation are just as essential to the effective functioning of democracy as voter turnout at elections. Elections, after all, are a very crude way of ensuring that people's interests are accurately represented. Four or five years between elections is a long time to wait to hold governments to account. Everyday participation is key in democracy, and that starts at the local level. Efforts should always be made to improve participation, especially of young people.

**QUESTION:** *Do you know any non-governmental organisations or citizen's initiative in your community that have successfully influenced a community or government decision in recent years?*

Another serious weakness in European democracies is the representation of minorities, especially those suffering from social exclusion. Thomas Hammarberg, the European Commissioner for Human Rights, said recently that powerlessness is the greatest problem of those millions...

> *"... who are displaced; those who do not have the means to seek legal advice; those who face language barriers when they want help; those who are repressed by their own cultural group or squeezed between two lifestyles; those who are underground and fear exposure; those who are isolated in their disability; those old who have lost everything and are too fragile to start again; those belonging to minorities targeted by xenophobes or homophobes".[3]*

In a society where governments are elected by the majority, and electoral systems work by the 'winner-takes-all' rule, it is especially difficult for minorities to achieve a proper representation. Awareness-raising in favour of the equality and social inclusion of minorities is key to democratic governance.

In the twenty-first century, several economic and social developments have had an effect on the concept and practise of democracy. European integration and global interdependence, technological developments and the growing influence of the media can be positive factors in the development of democracy but can also harm traditional democratic structures. Rapidly changing demographic trends and inter-cultural migration can similarly upset balances in society. It is important to use and build on the opportunities provided by these phenomena in order to develop and make democracy stronger.

**QUESTION:** *Do you think Internet-based technology would provide new techniques for decision makers to consult directly with people on certain local or national issues?*

## Why and how should democracy be taught to children?

For democracy to continue to thrive, children must be taught to value it as a way of life. The necessary skills for building democracy do not develop automatically in children. Teaching democracy means preparing children to become citizens who will preserve and shape democracy in the future. Therefore democracy should be a key aspect in every form of education at the earliest age possible.

As Lianne Singleton, Australian education consultant, argues, educators have to have a conviction that democracy is possible and that the democratic way of life can be lived in society and in children's environments. They should help children understand that no democracy and no government is perfect and no ideology is unquestionably true. In a healthy democracy, citizens question the motives of their leaders and monitor their activities.

> *Teaching for democracy is teaching about an inclusive society. This society recognises all members, regardless... of their situation or status... and recognises diversity among its members, and makes them feel that they are part of the community. ...* [4]

Democracy education is about promoting curiosity, discussion, critical thinking and capacity for constructive criticism. Children should learn about taking responsibility for their action. These educational outcomes are only possible through action. While key concepts of democracy should be understood by children, living and acting in a democratic environment is the only and the best exercise. Schools, institutions, children's clubs and organisations and even families that respect democratic principles and have real democratic structures function as the best models to help children learn what democracy is about. Democratic principles must permeate school structures and the curriculum, and should be standard practise in school relations. Educators should demonstrate respect for children by establishing children's decision making bodies and peer mediation, trusting children to organise their events and empowering children to explore issues, to discuss, to formulate opinion, to debate and to propose strategies to deal with conflict and achieve reasonable goals. Such experiences of participation are especially empowering for children, helping them to understand that participation is a worthwhile effort.

There are plenty of good examples worldwide on how to build successful democratic structures in children's natural environment. The Council of Europe programme 'Education for Democratic Citizenship' has produced guidelines and collected good examples for school democracy building and democratic governance. 'Governance' here demonstrates the openness of educational institutions and organisations, where participants (teachers, children, parents, owners) discuss, negotiate issues and make decisions at the end of the process. 'Democratic' indicates that governance is based on human rights values, empowerment and involvement of all actors: children, adults, parents and staff of the institutions.

# Democracy and Human Rights documents

Human rights and democracy are reciprocal concepts. Human rights form the basis of any democratic system, and states are there to defend and guarantee them. On the other hand, human rights are independent from the states: they are inalienable, belonging to everyone on the sole basis of being human. However, only democratic structures are able to protect people's human rights. Both human rights and democracy are constantly developing.

## Useful resources

- Backman, Elisabeth and Trafford, Bernard, *Democratic Governance of Schools*, Council of Europe, 2007.
- Boman, Julia, *Challenges to Democracy in Today's Europe, Synthesis of plenary sessions and workshops,* Council of Europe, 2006.
- Forbrig, Joerg, *Revisiting youth political participation*, Council of Europe Publishing, 2005: www.youth-knowledge.net/system/galleries/download/research_reports/2005_revisiting_youth_political_participation_coepub.pdf
- *The Future of Democracy in Europe, Trends, analysis and reforms*, Green Paper for the Council of Europe, Council of Europe, 2004: http://edc.unige.ch/download/Schmitter_Trechsel_Green_Paper.pdf
- Gollob, Rolf and Kampf, Peter, *Exploring Children's Rights, Nine projects for primary level,* Council of Europe, 2007.
- Kovacheva, Síyka, 'Will Youth Rejuvenate the Patterns of Political Participation?' Forbrig, Joerg (ed.), in: *Revisiting Youth Political Participation, Challenges for research and democratic practise in Europe*, Council of Europe Publishing, 2005.
- *Revised European Charter on the Participation of Young People in Local and Regional Life*, Adopted by the Congress of Local and Regional Authorities of Europe 2003: www.coe.int/t/e/cultural_cooperation/youth/TXT_charter_participation.pdf
- Singleton, Lianne, *Discovering Democracy, Teaching democracy in the primary school*: www.abc.net.au/civics/democracy/pdf/td_primary.pdf

## Useful Websites

- Discovering Democracy resources: www.civicsandcitizenship.edu.au/cce/default.asp?id=9180
- Electoral Education for Children: http://aceproject.org/electoral-advice/archive/questions/replies/493883939
- Elections in Europe: www.elections-in-europe.org
- Election Resources on the Internet: http://electionresources.org/other.html
- International Institute for Democracy: www.civilsoc.org/elctrnic/ngo-devl/iid.htm
- Voices of Youth: www.unicef.org/voy

## References

1 Forbrig, Joerg, *Revisiting Youth Political Participation, Challenges for research and democratic practise in Europe,* Council of Europe Publishing, 2005, p.134.
2 Kovacheva, Síyka, 'Will Youth Rejuvenate the Patterns of Political Participation?' in Forbrig, Joerg (ed.), in *Revisiting Youth Political Participation: Challenges for research and democratic practise in Europe*: Strasbourg, Council of Europe Publishing, 2005.
3 Thomas Hammarberg's speech at the 1,000[th] session of the Committee of Ministers, Council of Europe, 2007.
4 Singleton, Lianne, *Discovering Democracy, Teaching democracy in the primary school*: www.abc.net.au/civics/democracy/pdf/td_primary.pdf

# 3. DISCRIMINATION

*Discrimination contradicts a fundamental principle of human rights.*

To discriminate against someone is to exclude that person from the full enjoyment of their political, civic, economic, social or cultural rights and freedoms. Discrimination contradicts a basic principle of human rights: that all people are equal in dignity and entitled to the same fundamental rights. This principle is repeated in every fundamental human rights document (e.g. UDHR Article 2, CRC Article 2, ECHR Article 14 and Article 1 of Protocol No. 12). Most national Constitutions also include provisions against discrimination.

Although there is no single definition of 'discrimination' in human rights law, definitions of discrimination in human rights treaties (e.g. UDHR, CRC, ECHR, the **International Convention on the Elimination of All Forms of Racial Discrimination** [CERD] or the **Convention on the Elimination of All Forms of Discrimination against Women** [CEDAW]), all contain certain common elements:

1.  There is a *cause* for discrimination based on a variety of factors. Article 2 of the CRC, for example, specifically names as causes of discrimination "the child's or his or her parent's or legal guardian's race, colour, sex, language, religion, political or other opinion, national, ethnic or social origin, property, disability, birth or other status". The final item, "or other status", allows for many other causes of discrimination such as social class, occupation, sexual orientation or preferred language.

2.  There are *actions* that are qualified as discrimination. These can be rejection, restriction or exclusion of a person or a group of persons. They range from the crudest violations of human rights, such as **genocide**, slavery, ethnic cleansing or religious persecution, to more subtle but also more frequent forms of discrimination, such as hiring and promotion for jobs, housing practises and verbal abuse. Common acts of discrimination among children are exclusion (e.g. refusing to accept a child in a game), bullying and name calling based on difference (e.g. 'sissy', 'fatso', 'dummy'). See also *Theme 13, Violence*, p. 280.

3.  There are *consequences* that can usually prevent individuals from exercising and/or enjoying their human rights and fundamental freedoms. Discrimination also impacts on society as a whole, reinforcing prejudice and racist attitude.

Discrimination is often based on ignorance, prejudices and negative **stereotypes.** Because many people fear what seems strange or unknown, they react with suspicion or even violence to anyone whose appearance, culture or behaviour is unfamiliar.

Attitudes, actions or institutional practises that subordinate or marginalize anyone can be considered discrimination. Racism in particular has historical roots in beliefs in the superiority of one group over another, beliefs that were once used to justify discrimination against 'inferior' groups. Although such beliefs are now widely rejected, racial discrimination nevertheless continues to exist. Other forms of discrimination include sexism, ageism, homophobia, antisemitism and religious intolerance and **xenophobia,** a fear or hatred of foreigners or foreign countries.

**Segregation**, a form of separation of ethnical groups imposed by law or by custom, is an extreme form of discrimination. There have been official forms of segregation in Europe; for example, Jews were once isolated in ghettos. Today many Roma people in several European countries are forced by hostile behaviour or by economic segregation to live in separate communities.

Discrimination may be practised overtly as *direct discrimination,* which is characterized by intentional discrimination against a person or a group. Examples of direct discrimination could be when a child of a certain ethnicity is not admitted to a school or a housing company that does not let flats to immigrants. *Indirect discrimination* focuses on the effect of a policy or measure, which may appear neutral but in fact systematically puts people of a particular minority at a disadvantage compared with others. For example, a fire department that sets a minimum height for fire fighters automatically excludes many female and immigrant applicants, as does a department store that does not hire persons with long skirts or covered heads.

To fight discrimination, particularly that which is more indirect and hidden, some countries have adopted measures of **positive discrimination**, which is also known as **affirmative action**. In some situations positive discrimination means deliberately favouring a certain group or groups who have experienced historic and pervasive discrimination (e.g. giving preference to candidates from groups who seldom attend university, or establishing quotas from minorities, such as women or rural people, for certain public offices. The intended result is to compensate for hidden discriminations as well as to ensure a more balanced social representation. In other situations positive discrimination means creating the conditions for people with difficulties (e.g. physical disabilities) to enjoy the same rights and opportunities. Another form of positive discrimination seeks to 'repair' former injustices. All these measures and practises seek to promote equality 'through inequality'.[1]

Every time we separate people and give different individuals and groups different rights and obligations, we should question why we do this. Is it really necessary? Does it benefit everyone? If not, positive discrimination could itself become a manifestation of prejudice and discrimination.

## Discrimination based on race

**Racism** can be defined as a conscious or unconscious belief in the superiority of one race over other another. This definition presupposes the existence of different biologic 'races', a supposition now dispelled by recent research, especially the human genome project. However, although 'race' is clearly a social construct, racism is nonetheless prevalent throughout the world. Although few people believe any longer in a 'superior race' with an inherent right to exercise power over those considered 'inferior', many people continue to practise cultural racism or **ethnocentrism**, believing that some cultures, usually their own, are superior or that other cultures, traditions, customs and histories are incompatible with theirs.

Racism of any kind is related to power, with people who hold power determining what is 'superior' and discriminating against people with less power. Racism can thus be considered as the practical translation of prejudice into action.

The consequences of racism, both today and in the past, are devastating both for individuals and for society as a whole. Racism has led to mass extermination, genocide and oppression. It has ensured the subjugation of majorities to the whims of tiny minorities who hold wealth and power.

## Discrimination based on ethnicity and culture

As with cultural racism, which holds that certain cultures are superior to others, discrimination based on ethnicity and culture regards some cultures, usually minorities, as inherently inferior or undesirable. Historically, European Jews and Roma have suffered most from this form of discrimination.

Antisemitism, or hostility towards Jews as a religious or ethnic minority, dates from medieval times when Jews were usually the only non-Christian minority living in Christian Europe. Typically prohibited from practising most trades and professions, forced to live in ghettos apart from Christians, penalized with high taxes, stripped of property and even expelled from their countries or killed, Jews struggled for centuries against the injustice and prejudice of Christian societies.

The rise of fascism in the mid-twentieth century, with its ideology of racial superiority, intensified antisemitism in Europe and ultimately resulted in the Holocaust, the systematic extermination of more than six million Jews during the Second World War. In the twenty-first century antisemitism is far from over. Groups claiming their superiority desecrate Jewish cemeteries and neo-Nazi networks openly circulate antisemitic propaganda.

The Roma, also misnamed Gypsies, have lived across Europe for centuries. Without a homeland of their own, Roma people have maintained their language and culture while living mainly nomadic lives as tinkers, craftsmen, musicians and traders. Throughout their existence, the Roma have experienced discrimination, including forced assimilation and outright slavery. During the twentieth century thousands of Roma suffered genocide at the hands of German Nazis, forced socialization under Communist regimes of Eastern Europe, and economic exclusion in high-tech capitalist economies where they lack necessary skills. Today many Roma children grow up in hostile social environments where they are denied many basic rights such as education, health care and housing.

## Discrimination based on xenophobia

In response to growing globalization and diversity of society, some people respond with xenophobia, a fear or aversion to foreigners or foreign countries. In most cases the concept of 'foreign' is based on socially constructed images and ideas that reduces the world to 'us', the normal, 'good ones like me', and 'them', the others who are different: a threat, a disruption, representing a degradation of values and proper behaviour.

**QUESTION:** *Can you think of examples of xenophobia in your country? How does xenophobia affect children? What can you do to address its effects?*

Although most people consider xenophobia morally unacceptable and contrary to a culture of human rights, it is not unusual. Discriminatory actions based on xenophobia, such as verbal abuse and acts of violence, are clearly human rights violations.

## Discrimination based on gender

Although subtle and more or less hidden in Europe, gender discrimination is nonetheless pervasive. Many institutions of society, such as the media, family, childcare institutions or schools, preserve and transmit stereotypes about men and women. Traditional gender traits in Western societies often relate to power: men and their typical activities are characterized as outgoing, strong, productive, brave, important, public-oriented, influential and having high financial rewards and social recognition and value. Women's key characteristics reflect powerlessness: dependent, caring, passive and family-oriented. Women often hold subordinate positions, their work is less valued and it receives less recognition and remuneration. Girls or boys who do not conform to stereotypical expectations can experience criticism, ostracism and even violence. Such conflicts can confuse the development of children's gender identity. See also discussion of *Theme 7, Gender Equality*, p. 245.

## Discrimination based on religion

Freedom of religion is officially respected in Europe, yet discrimination based on religion is nevertheless prevalent, often inextricably linked with racism and xenophobia. Whereas in the past Europe was torn by conflicts and discrimination between Protestant and Catholic Christians, Roman and Eastern Orthodox Catholics and 'official' churches and dissenting sects, today these differences among Christians have become far less important. At the same time many religious communities in minority positions continue to thrive across Europe, including Jews, Hindus, Buddhists, Baha'is, Rastafarians and Muslims. This growing religious diversity is often ignored such as those millions of Europeans who are not religious as well as those who are not Christian.

**QUESTION:** *What minority religions exist in your community? Where do they gather and worship?*

Of particular concern is the rise of Islamophobia, the discrimination, fear and hatred of Islam, which is the most widespread religion in Europe after Christianity and the majority religion in some countries and regions in the Balkans and Caucasus. The hostility towards Islam following the terrorist attacks on targets in the United States, Spain and England in recent years has revealed deep-seated prejudices in most European societies. Some of the most common public expressions of this bias are a lack of official recognition as a religion, the refusal of permission to build mosques, failure to support facilities for Muslim religious groups or communities and restrictions on women and girls wearing the headscarf.

One of the most typical prejudices against Islam is its so-called 'incompatibility' with human rights. The absence of democracy and widespread violations of human rights in many predominantly Muslim countries is cited as evidence, without acknowledging that religion is only one of many factors that may contribute to undemocratic governments.

Much prejudice also results from ignorance about Islam, which many people associate only with terrorism and extremism and politics of certain countries. In fact, Islam, like most religions, preaches tolerance, solidarity and love for one's fellow beings.

## Discrimination based on sexual orientation

Homophobia is an aversion to or hatred of gay, lesbian or homosexual people, or their lifestyle or culture, or generally of people with a different sexual orientation, including bi-sexual and transgendered people. Although legal reforms in Europe have greatly strengthened the human rights of gay and lesbian people, conditions vary greatly, from urban areas where openly homosexual people live and work and form civil unions with relatively little difficulty to rural areas and parts of Eastern and Central Europe where gays may meet with discriminatory laws, harassment and even violence from both the public and authorities. Many people still see homosexuality as a disease, a psychological disorder or even a moral sin. Many others consciously or unconsciously apply heterosexual norms to gay and lesbian people, faulting them for failing to conform to the kinds of behaviour expected of 'normal people'.

**QUESTION:** *Do children you work with use homophobic slurs, even without understanding them? What can you do to address this language?*

## Discrimination based on disability

The term 'person with a disability' may refer to many different conditions: a disability may be physical, intellectual, sensory or psycho-social, temporary or permanent, and result from illness, injury or genetics. People with disabilities have the same human rights as all other people. However, for a number of reasons they often face social, legal and practical barriers in claiming their human rights on an equal basis with others. These reasons usually stem from misperceptions and negative attitudes toward disability itself.

Many people have the misconception that people with disabilities cannot be productive members of society. Chief among negative attitudes are either that people with disabilities are 'broken' or 'sick' and require fixing or healing, or that they are helpless and need to be cared for.

Instead, a positive attitude regards disability as a natural part of human diversity that should be approached with reasonable accommodation, which is any measure designed to promote full participation and access, and to empower a person to act on his or her own behalf (e.g. a wheelchair, or more time to accomplish a task). This positive approach suggests that society has a responsibility to accommodate the person with disabilities.

*The Social Model of Disability*: The barriers created by the social and physical environment that inhibit disabled people's ability to participate in society and exercise their rights should be eliminated. This includes promoting positive attitudes and modifying physical barriers (e.g. buildings with wheelchair access).

In keeping with this social model of disability, children with disabilities are now considered as children 'with special needs'. Social institutions are obliged to take these needs into account and adjust to them. A large proportion of disabled children attend the regular school system today.

The term 'children with special educational needs' also covers those who are failing in school for reasons that are likely to impede their overall development and progress. Schools need to adapt their curriculum, teaching and organisation and/or to provide additional support to help these pupils achieve their potential. These developments are part of the movement toward inclusive education.[2]

**QUESTION:** *How are children with disabilities educated in your country? What provisions are made for children with special educational needs?*

On December 2006 the UN General Assembly adopted the first international treaty addressing the human rights of people with disabilities, the **Convention on The Rights of Persons with Disabilities** (CRPD). The European Union signed it in March of 2007, heralding it as "the first universal HR Convention of the new millennium":

The Convention defines disability as an element of human diversity and praises the contributions of people with disabilities to society. It prohibits obstacles to the participation and promotes the active inclusion of persons with disabilities in society. The long term goal of this Convention is to change the way the public perceives persons with disabilities, thus ultimately changing society as a whole.[3]

## Education for non-discrimination

Educators recognise the need to develop in every child a tolerant, non-discriminatory attitude and create a learning environment that acknowledges and benefits from diversity instead of ignoring or excluding it. As part of this development, those who work with children, as well as children themselves, should become aware of their own and others' discriminatory behaviours. Activities that encourage role-playing and empathy help children to develop awareness and empathy as well as developing resilience and assertiveness in children who experience discrimination.

## European Programmes fighting discrimination

The Council of Europe has established various bodies and programmes to fight discrimination in Europe. The European Commission against Racism and Intolerance (ECRI), which was set up 1993, regularly publishes surveys on the phenomenon of racism and intolerance in Council of Europe member states. It also organises round tables with representatives of civil society and adopts general policy recommendations that are addressed to governments.

The Fundamental Rights Agency, an independent body of the European Union established in 2007, provides expertise to member states implementing law on fundamental rights matters. In addition it seeks to raise public awareness on human rights questions and cooperate with civil society.

Several European countries have established some kind of national equality body to fight discrimination and promote equality and tolerance.

QUESTION: *Does your country have any public authority with the mission to fight discrimination?*

The Council of Europe also works on awareness-raising through different programmes. In 2006-2007, the European Youth Campaign 'All Different – All Equal' highlighted three different values: diversity (celebrating the richness of different cultures and traditions), human rights and participation (allowing everyone to play a part in building a Europe where everyone has the right to be themselves – to be different and equal). Another Council of Europe campaign dealing with discrimination against Roma is 'Dosta!', which is a Romany word meaning 'enough'. This awareness-raising campaign aims at bringing non-Roma closer to Roma citizens.

Nevertheless the struggle against discrimination still goes on and the Council of Europe will continue vigorously to address it.

..........................

### Useful Resources

- Bellamy, Carol, *La Situation des Enfants dans le Monde*: UNICEF, 2004: www.unicef.org/french/sowc04/files/SOWC_04_FR.pdf

- *Children's Etiquette or How to Be Friends with Everybody*: Croatian Union of Physically Disabled Persons Associations (CUPDPA), Zagreb, 2002.
- *The Salamanca Statement and Framework for Action on Special Needs Education*: UNESCO, Salamanca, 1994: http://unesdoc.unesco.org/images/0009/000984/098427eo.pdf
- *Tous les Enfants du Monde ont le Droit* : Editions Fleurus Presse/ UNICEF France, 2007.
- Titley, Gavan, *Youth work with Boys and Young Men as a means to prevent violence in everyday life*, Council of Europe, 2003.

........................

## Useful Websites

- Council of Europe: www.coe.int
- 'All Different – All Equal': http://alldifferent-allequal.info
- Office of the UN High Commissioner for HR: www.ohchr.org/english/
- UNICEF: www.unicef.fr
- Bibliothèque Numérique pour le Handicap : http://bnh.numilog.com
- EU Statement – United Nations: Convention on the Rights of Persons with Disabilities, 2007: www.europa-eu-un.org/articles/fr/article_6914_fr.htm
- International Standard Classification of Education (ISCED): UNESCO, 1997: www.unesco.org/education/information/nfsunesco/doc/isced_1997.htm

.................

## References

1  See Droits Partagés, des droits de l'homme aux droits de l'enfants: www.droitspartages.org
2  See International Standard Classification of Education (ISCED):
    www.unesco.org/education/information/nfsunesco/doc/isced_1997.htm
3  See EU Statement – United Nations: Convention on the Rights of Persons with Disabilities:
    www.europa-eu-un.org/articles/fr/article_6914_fr.htm

# 4. EDUCATION AND LEISURE

*The only way to educate for democracy is to educate democratically. If the link is established, a virtuous circle can be drawn facilitating better and broader access to education and from there, to a wider respect for human rights.*

Speech by Maud de Boer-Buquicchio
Deputy Secretary General of the Council of Europe

Education is a fundamental human right in itself. It is an essential for human development as well as a tool to attain and enjoy other rights. Article 26 of the Universal Declaration of Human Rights (UDHR) establishes that everyone is entitled to education and that education should be provided free at least at the basic level, which should be obligatory. Article 2 of Protocol No.1 of the European Convention on Human Rights (ECHR) guarantees the right to education for all. Secondary schools, professional training and university studies, which in today's Europe are still not accessible to everyone, should be as widely available as possible.

However, free access to basic education alone is no longer considered sufficient to guarantee the right to education. Three other requirements should be met:

1.  **Equal opportunity:** The state should guarantee not only equal access, but also equal opportunities for success. This means that some children may need extra help and special conditions. Deaf children, for example, have a right to reasonable arrangements to help them learn, such as sign language, hearing aids and interpreters whenever needed. Similar adjustments should be made for all children with special needs so that they can be included in the same schools with other children and have an equal opportunity to succeed. For example, some children, such as children of travellers' groups in some European countries, may be deprived of their right to education if special schooling is not provided to accommodate their parents' nomadic way of life.

    Equality in opportunities for success in education also requires attention to other aspects such as the use of a child's mother tongue, homework conditions, access to books, or any learning difficulty. Learning in one's mother tongue not only favours school success, but also constitutes a cultural right. School failure is no solution for learning difficulties. These must be met by well-trained teach-

**231**

## The right to leisure and play

Play is of such importance for a child's health and development that it is recognized as a fundamental right in Article 31 of the CRC. According to the International Association for Children's Right to Play, "playing … is a fundamental activity for the development of every child's potential … because playing is a way to learn to love and to invent life and not merely a way to spend time."[4] At any age a child at play is developing skills, exercising the body and imagination, and engaging in crucial socialisation. The same Article of CRC goes on to state that children have rights "… to participate fully in cultural and artistic life and (States) shall encourage the provision of appropriate and equal opportunities for cultural, artistic, recreational and leisure activities."

Playing, cultural and artistic activities are not simple recreation and joy. These activities contribute to the development of a child's autonomy and promote their interpersonal and intercultural skills. Through play and art children can experience key principles of human rights such as respect, dignity, equality, inclusion, fairness and cooperation.

Sports also convey the social values of participation, cooperation, commitment, effort and positive competition. However, to derive these educational benefits from sports, facilitators and children alike must consciously use them for such purposes and also be aware of the dangers that sports can present, especially when they become predominantly competitive.

## International organisations, human rights and education

### UNESCO Programme 'Education for All'

The World Education Forum held in 2006 accepted the Dakar Framework for Action, the new worldwide strategy on 'Education For All', which is to be implemented by UNESCO and governments in the following decade. This programme focuses on early childhood care, quality education, eliminating gender disparities between girls and boys, and the improvement of life-skills.

### Council of Europe

Council of Europe activities on education are based on the **European Cultural Convention**. There are two main sectors of the Council involved in education, the Directorate of Education School, Out-of-school and Higher Education and the Directorate of Youth and Sport. The activities of the Directorate of Education School, Out-of-school and Higher Education concentrate on quality education, modern education policies, intercultural dialogue through education and education for democratic citizenship.

The Directorate of Youth and Sport elaborates political guidelines and initiates programmes for the development of coherent and effective child and youth policies at local, national and European levels. It provides funding and educational support for international activities aimed at the promotion of child and youth democratic citizenship, participation, human rights education, social cohesion and inclusion of young people. The Youth sector works as a European resource centre on non-formal education.

The Council of Europe also promotes sport as a mean of developing fair play and tolerance among people and encourages healthy lifestyles and participation in sport. For example, in cooperation with the European Union the Council produced the *Clean Sports Guide*, an educational pack for schools and sports organisations.

......................

### Useful Resources

- Delors, Jacques, *Learning: the Treasure Within*: Report to UNESCO of the International Commission on Education for the Twenty-first Century: UNESCO Publishing, 1996: www.unesco.org/delors/delors_e.pdf

- *Recommendation of the European Parliament and of the Council of 18 December 2006 on Key Competencies for Lifelong Learning*, Doc: (2006/962/EC), Official Journal of the European Union, 2006:
  http://eur-lex.europa.eu/LexUriServ/site/en/oj/2006/l_394/l_39420061230en00100018.pdf

## Useful Websites

- Council of Europe: www.coe.int
- Directorate of Youth and Sport, Council of Europe: www.coe.int/youth
- Enabling Education Network: www.eenet.org.uk
- European Paralympic Committee (EPC): www.europaralympic.org
- European Sport Charter: www.coe.int/t/dg4/sport/SportinEurope/charter_en.asp
- Football against Racism in Europe: www.farenet.org
- International Play Association: www.ipaworld.org/home.html
- Let's kick racism out of football: www.kickitout.org
- Right to Education Project: www.right-to-education.org
- UNESCO: portal.unesco.org/education

## References

1  See UNESCO, Peace and Human Rights Education: www.portal.unesco.org/education
2  Delors, Jacques, *Learning: the Treasure Within*: Report to UNESCO of the International Commission on Education for the Twenty-first Century: UNESCO Publishing, 1996, p.16
3  *Recommendation of the European Parliament and of the Council of 18 December 2006 on Key Competencies for Lifelong Learning*, Doc: (2006/962/EC), Official Journal of the European Union, 2006
4  'Declaration' International Play Association,1982

# 5. ENVIRONMENT

*Sustainable development is: development that meets the needs of the present without compromising the ability of future generations to meet their own needs.*

Bruntland Commission, 1987

Human beings are an integral part of their environment and the environment impacts on all aspects of human life, including human rights. The 1972 United Nations Conference on the Human Environment formally recognized the interrelation of environment and human rights, affirming that 'man's environment, the natural and the man-made, are essential to his well-being and to the enjoyment of basic human rights – even the right to life itself'.[1]

Environmental rights belong to the so-called category of **third generation** or **collective rights**. These are rights that affect whole societies or groups of people rather than just individuals, and include those such as the right to peace, to sustainable development, to communication or to share in the common heritage of humankind. Collective rights, such as the right to a healthy environment, acknowledge that human rights exist not only for individuals in a political and social system but for all people united as fellow beings in interdependent systems that transcend nation states. For example, global warming affects all living things, regardless of what country they are in. Just as each individual must respect the intrinsic value of fellow human beings, he or she must also respect the value of all fellow beings: animals, plants and the ecosystems in which we all exist.

The environment impacts on people's human rights both positively and negatively. It plays an essential role in ensuring human life, providing the raw materials for our food, industry and development. However, environmental hazards, such as excess radiation or contaminated drinking water, can also threaten the fundamental right to life. People exposed to pollution of the soil, air or food and water supplies may be subject to human rights violations as well as bad health, genetic damage, loss of livelihood and even death. Many fundamental human rights have significant environmental dimensions: the right to health, to safe and healthy working conditions, to adequate housing and food, to work and to an adequate standard of living.

## Environmental issues in Europe

Europe faces major environmental concerns that may have an impact on future generations:

- **Air pollution** from heavy industry and fossil fuels directly impacts on human health and all living things.
- **Climate changes** resulting from global warming and the greenhouse effect may impact on future generations with drought, severe storms and loss of arable land.
- **Water availability** and quality is a major concern.
- **Modern mass-consumption and domestic waste** has a negative impact on the environmental, e.g. excessive use of private cars, plastic bags, packaging and wrapping.
- **Genetically modified organisms** (GMOs), whose genetic material has been altered by the introduction of a modified gene, can have long term consequences on human health, the environment and sustainable farming.

## Children and the environment

In 2004 European Ministers adopted the Children's Environment and Health Action Plan for Europe (CEHAPE), which addresses the environmental risk factors that most affect the health of European children. This action plan focuses on four regional priority goals for Europe:[2]

- Ensure safe water and adequate sanitation
- Ensure protection from injuries and adequate physical activity
- Ensure clean outdoor and indoor air
- Aim at chemical-free environments.

Critical to achieving these goals is raising children's own awareness and understanding of the environment and how environmental issues relate to human rights.

QUESTION: *What are the major environmental issues in your community? How can children become actively involved in addressing them?*

Children can play an active role in protecting and improving the environment. At the personal level, they can evaluate and change their own lifestyle and how it affects the environment (e.g. preserving resources such as water and electricity, not wasting food). At the local level they can participate in plans to make their homes, schools and youth organisations more environmentally friendly (e.g. use of safe products, disposal of waste, recycling of different materials). Children can evaluate the policies and practises of their local, regional and national communities and make suggestions for improvement. They can join in campaigns and global celebrations such as Earth Day and World Environment Day.

World Environment Day, June 5, was established by the United Nations General Assembly in 1972. It can be celebrated in many ways, including street rallies, bicycle parades, green concerts, essays and poster competitions in schools, tree planting, recycling efforts and clean-up campaigns. Each year World Environment Day has a special theme, such as 'Melting Ice – A Hot Topic?', 'Don't Desert the Dry Lands!' and 'Green Cities: Plan for the Planet!'.[3] Earth Day, April 22, is coordinated by the Earth Day Network, which works together with other environmental and human rights organisations, for example, the Sierra Club and Amnesty International, to generate public action through celebrations and activities in protest against human rights and environmental abuses.[4]

## Sustainable development

We are now living in a Decade of Education for Sustainable Development (DESD), called for by the United Nations General Assembly from 2005-2014. What does 'sustainable development' mean? The Brundtland Commission, which met in the 1980s, defined it as "development that meets the needs of the present without compromising the ability of future generations to meet their own needs."[5] Another key international document for sustainable development is Agenda 21, which was presented at the Earth Summit in Rio de Janeiro in 1992, and has since been accepted by 172 governments. The implementation of this comprehensive action plan is taking place at a global, national and local level by governments, NGOs and international organisations together, and was followed by the World Summit of Sustainable Development in 2002. Sustainability is not just about conserving the environment, but about learning to live in respectful relationships with each other and with our world. So education for sustainable development means learning the values, behaviours and knowledge that will enable us to develop now without robbing future generations of the same possibility.[6]

Children can begin to understand the long term impact of people's actions on the environment by studying their immediate surroundings and then extending what they learn to a global context. If, for example, the city council decides to build a road across a green area in the town, children may lose a place to play and to observe the natural life it contains. Only by caring and thinking about those who come after us can we keep our planet in good health for the future.

The European Environment Bureau, a network of almost 150 environmental non-governmental organisations in Europe, works on raising awareness of issues related to sustainable development in Europe and mobilizes population and governments for continuous improvement.

## Relevant Human Rights Instruments

### Council of Europe

The fact that the **European Convention on Human Rights** does not mention the environment should come as no surprise. It was adopted in 1950, when few people were aware of the far reaching effects of environmental degradation. The ECHR makes many references to 'the *economic* well-being of the country', but not its ecological well-being. Likewise it affirms the importance of and 'the protection of health'. It does not, however, recognize the importance of a healthy environment in creating a healthy population, although efforts are being made to have environmental aspects of human rights recognised by the European Court of Human Rights.[7]

### United Nations

As with the European Convention, early human rights instruments, such as the **Universal Declaration of Human Rights** and the two **Covenants**, precede general awareness of the importance of the environment and consequently make no reference to it. However, the 1989 Convention on the Rights of the Child does make specific reference to the environment in Article 24.c in the context of the child's right to health, urging governments

> *To combat disease and malnutrition, including within the framework of primary health care, through, inter alia, the application of readily available technology and through the provision of adequate nutritious foods and clean drinking water, taking into consideration the dangers and risks of environmental pollution[.]*

Furthermore Article 24.e urges environmental education for parents and children as a part of general health education. Article 29.e includes it among the goals of a quality education to which every child has a right:

> *The development of respect for the natural environment.*

The gradual recognition of the right to a healthy environment illustrates how the **human rights framework** is evolving, with new rights being recognized, defined and ultimately being **codified** in human rights instruments. At present a drafting committee is at work on a convention on environmental rights. This can be a long and contentious process, involving building consensus, consultation with governments, **inter-governmental organisations** and **non-governmental organisations**.

........................

## Useful resources

- *Declaration of the United Nations Conference on the Human Environment*, Report of the United Nations Conference on the Human Environment, Stockholm, 1972: http://un-documents. net/unchedec.htm
- *Fourth Ministerial Conference on Environment and Health: Children's Environment and Health Action Plan for Europe:* World Health Organisation, 2004: www.euro.who.int/document/e83338.pdf
- Garcia San José, Daniel, *Environmental protection and the European Convention on Human Rights*: Council of Europe, 2006.
- *Report of the World Commission on Environment and Development*, Resolution 42/187: United Nations, 1987: www.un.org/documents/ga/res/42/ares42-187.htm
- *Links between the Global Initiatives in Education, Education for sustainable development in action*, Technical Paper N 1: UNESCO, 2005: http://unesdoc.unesco.org/images/0014/001408/140848m.pdf

........................

## Useful websites

- Development Education Program: www.worldbank.org
- Development Education Association: www.dea.org.uk
- Earthday Network Homepage: www.earthday.net
- Epaedia, Environment explained: http://epaedia.eea.europa.eu/
- European Environment Agency: www.eea.europa.eu/
- European Environmental Bureau: www.eeb.org/Index.htm
- European Union Environmental Communication Networks (with best practises from EU countries): http://ec.europa.eu/environment/networks/bestpractise_en.htm
- Green Peace: www.greenpeace.org
- United Nations Division for Sustainable Development: www.un.org/esa/sustdev/
- United Nations Environment Programme: www.unep.org
- Veolia Environment – Tales around the world youth campaign: www.veoliaenvironnement. com/globe/en/

..................

## References

1   *Declaration of the United Nations Conference on the Human Environment*, Report of the United Nations Conference on the Human Environment, Stockholm, 1972.
2   *Fourth Ministerial Conference on Environment and Health: Children's Environment and Health Action Plan for Europe:* World Health Organisation, 2004.
3   See United Nations Environment Programme: www.unep.org
4   See Earthday Network Homepage: www.earthday.net
5   *Report of the World Commission on Environment and Development*: United Nations, 1987.
6   *Links between the Global Initiatives in Education, Education for sustainable development in action*, Technical Paper N.1: UNESCO, 2005.
7   Garcia San José, Daniel, *Environmental protection and the European Convention on Human Rights*: Council of Europe, 2006.

# 6. FAMILY AND ALTERNATIVE CARE

*The family is the natural and fundamental group unit of society and is entitled to protection by society and the State.*

Universal Declaration of Human Rights, Article 16.3

The Convention on the Rights of the Child (CRC) recognizes the family as the natural entity that best protects children and provides the conditions for their healthy development. The child is entitled to care, security and an upbringing that is respectful of his or her person and individuality. Article 3 of the CRC states that parents' guiding consideration should be the child's best interest.

Every child has the right to know and be cared for by his or her parents (Article 7). The CRC allocates responsibilities for the child's well-being to both parents and the state, with states obliged to recognize that primary responsibility for the upbringing and development of the child rest with the parents (Article 5), and to take various positive measures to support parents in performing this duty (Article 18). Parents also have the principal responsibility to ensure the child an adequate standard of living, but if they are unable to provide and care for their child, states have the responsibility to assist or intervene. (Article 27).

Parents should provide appropriate direction and guidance to the child, in a manner consistent with his or her **evolving capacities,** that is, recognising that, as the child grows older, he or she should have a greater say in personal matters (Article 14). In conformity with the CRC, parents have a commitment to view the child as a social actor and rights-bearing entity in itself and not merely as their property.

## What is a family?

In addition to the 'traditional' family of two married parents and their biological children, Europeans live in a variety of family structures such as:

- the multi-generational extended family
- the single-parent family, where one of the parents is absent, whether through divorce, desertion, death or other reasons
- the adoptive or foster family
- the recomposed nuclear family with a step parent and a natural parent and sometimes with both biological and step siblings

- the de facto union when two persons live together without being married
- the family with same-sex parents
- the family composed of children and their grandparents.

Increasingly, children are likely to experience transitions between different family living arrangements and to live with one parent or with stepparents. However, in all European countries at least two-thirds of children still spend the greater part of their childhood living as a family with both their natural parents.

No matter in what family structure the child lives, both parents have the mutual responsibility to support and care for their children, even if they are separated. Article 18 of the CRC recognizes the equal responsibility of both parents for the care and rearing of children. Several European governments are working to improve policies that cater to family and parenting needs, such as paternity leave for fathers and childcare for working couples. The provision of equal opportunities for children, irrespective of gender, status or family economy, is important in supporting the families in the parenting responsibilities.

## Challenges to European families

Families in Europe are facing many challenges:

- **Working parents:** Increasingly both parents are employed. Long working hours and the conflict between work and family responsibilities present many problems. At least 10% of parents in the European Union and 15% in the new European Union member states claim difficulty in fulfilling their family responsibilities due to overwork, with parents of children below three years of age reporting most problems.[1]
- **Single-parent households:** Overall around 80% of children in European countries live with both parents. However, the range varies considerably, from more than 90% in Greece and Italy to less than 70% in the United Kingdom. These figures reflect a strong geographic distribution with less than 9% of children in Belgium, Greece, Italy, Portugal and Spain living with a single parent while it rises to 15% in Denmark, Finland, Norway and Sweden. Between 10 to 15% of children live with single parents in Austria, The Czech Republic, France, Germany, Hungary, the Netherlands, Poland and Switzerland. [2]

The Council of Europe has addressed these challenges extensively. In 2006 the Committee of Ministers issued a recommendation to member states on policy to support positive parenting. It defined positive parenting as "behaviour based on the best interests of the child that is nurturing, empowering, non-violent and provides recognition and guidance which involves setting of boundaries to enable the full development of the child." The recommendation further focused on the importance of:

- positive parenting
- public services to support parents
- services for parents at risk of social exclusion
- work and family life balance
- childcare provision services.[3]

Also in 2006 the Council reported on positive parenting in contemporary Europe, elaborating on the role of parents as well as proper treatment of children and non-violent upbringing. (See *Theme13: Violence*, page 280.) The report highlighted these elements as most important to children:

- **Basic care:** Meeting the child's physical needs (e.g. for food, warmth, shelter, hygiene, appropriate clothing and medical care);
- **Ensuring safety:** Protecting the child from harm both in and outside the home;
- **Emotional warmth:** Ensuring that the child receives emotional support and feels valued;
- **Stimulation**: Stimulating the child's learning and intellectual development through engagement with the child and promoting his or her educational opportunities;
- **Guidance and boundaries:** Setting limits and showing the child how to behave appropriately;

- **Stability:** Consistently providing emotional warmth and response from people who are important to the child.[4]

The report acknowledged that children may be separated from their parents for a variety of reasons: divorce, displacement of family members due to travel or war, death of one or both parents, trafficking or abandonment. Whatever its cause, such separation deeply affects children, jeopardizing their well-being, education and development. For this reason, children have a right to remain with their families except in grave cases where a judicial body deems it in the child's best interest (Article 9).

**QUESTION:** *A fundamental principle of the CRC is the child's best interest. But who decides what is best? For example, who should decide whether it is in a child's best interest to remain with an incompetent parent? Other family members? The child? The state? Who else?*

However, not every parent is capable or willing to provide positive parenting and not all children can benefit from being with their family. CRC Article 20 indicates that,

> *A child temporarily or permanently deprived of his or her family environment, or in whose own best interests cannot be allowed to remain in that environment, shall be entitled to special protection and assistance provide by the State ... [which should] ensure alternative care for such a child.*

These measures are invoked only in extreme cases. In many European countries the child-protection system and childcare institutions provide high quality conditions for children in risk. However, in some countries many children are placed in institutions unnecessarily and for too long. Children who live outside families or without parental care are more vulnerable to discrimination, abuse and exploitation, as well as emotional and social impairment due to neglect.

Provisions for children's alternative care need greater attention, and include informal and formal fostering, kinship care and adoption. Community-based social services, such as day care, parenting education and home support, are also needed to strengthen the capacity of both parents and extended families, as well as communities who care for children whose parents are not available.

Many cities in Europe have street children. They are visible – they live and work in the streets – yet there is no reliable data regarding their identity and numbers, making it extremely hard for authorities to ensure that they receive vital health care or education and are kept safe from harm. They are also invisible because many people choose to ignore these children who represent the physical embodiments of the worst kind of failure in our societies. The problem is global and it is escalating, brought on by poverty, family disintegration, physical and mental abuse, abandonment, neglect and social unrest. Street children are vulnerable. Prostitution, trafficking, crime, drugs, gang violence and even police violence are all real risks for many; for others they are already reality.

## Working with children on family issues

When discussing family questions with children, facilitators should refrain from any stereotypical behaviour or expectation concerning the various family patterns. Children should understand and accept any forms of family and develop empathy and solidarity with each other. It is an important objective that children learn about their rights in the family, such as participation or non-violence.

Discussion of family life may bring up conflicting feelings in some children especially teenagers. Consultation with parents and caretakers may be helpful except in situations where domestic violence has been revealed during the activities. In such cases it is important that children understand they are not the responsible party for abuse, including sexual abuse, and they should be encouraged to communicate problems to friends and helpful adults in their environment. (See *Theme 13: Violence*, p. 280.)

# Relevant human rights instruments

## Council of Europe

Article 8 of the **European Convention on Human Rights** protects everyone's "private and family life, his home and his correspondence" from state interference. This right emphasizes the importance of protecting the family circle, the social unit that nurtures most children to adulthood.

The Revised European Social Charter in its Article 16 protects the rights of children as family members:

> *The family as a fundamental unit of society has the right to appropriate social, legal and economic protection to ensure its full development".*

There are other Council of Europe conventions that protect children's rights if they are born out of wedlock, or when they are adopted. Rights of children and their best interest in legal procedures is guaranteed in the European Convention on the Exercise of Children's Rights

## United Nations

The **Universal Declaration of Human Rights** declares the family to be "the natural and fundamental group unit of society and is entitled to protection by society and the State" (Article16). The Declaration designates the family as one of the particular areas of life in which everyone is entitled to freedom from arbitrary interference (Article 12). It also entitles everyone with the "right to marry and to found a family" (Article 16). The Declaration does not define family, a term that in the twenty-first century can define many different combinations besides the traditional family of two parents and their genetic children.

The **Convention on the Rights of the Child** gives even greater emphasis to the importance of the family, declaring in its Preamble that it is not only the fundamental group of society, but also the "natural environment for the growth and well-being of all its members and particularly children" and recommending the family environment for "the full and harmonious development" of the child's personality.

The Convention makes detailed provisions for the child who is separated from his or her family for a variety of causes, encourages reunification of the family and recognizes that in some cases the child's best interest is to be separated from a family who cannot or will not adequately nurture the child (Articles 9,10, 20, 21 and 22). However, a child's parents are of prime importance. The state is required "to respect the responsibilities, rights and duties of parents or, where applicable, the members of the extended family or community" (Article 5). The importance of the family in defining a child's identity is recognized in Article 7 and in the child's inherent right "to know and be cared for by his or her parents" (Article 7). Parents are given the primary responsibility for the upbringing, development and financial support of the child, following the principle "that both parents have common responsibility for the upbringing and development of the child" (Articles 18 and 27). However, when parents cannot adequately provide for their child, the state is enjoined to assist them (Article 18.2).

As with the UDHR, the Children's Convention bars "interference with the child's privacy, family and home but also from attacks on his or her honour, an affirmation of the child inherent dignity" (Article 16). Furthermore, the child has the right to an education that encourages "respect for the child's parents, his or her own cultural identity, language and values" (Article 29.c).

..........................

## Useful Resources

- *Changes In Parenting: Children Today, Parents Tomorrow*, Conference of European Ministers Responsible for Family Affairs, Final Communique: Lisbon, Council of Europe, May 2006: www.coe.int/t/dg3/youthfamily/source/2006minconFinaldeclaration_en.pdf
- *Child Poverty in Perspective*: An overview of child well-being in rich countries: UNICEF Inno-

*'Sex' refers to the biological and physiological characteristics that define men and women.*
*'Gender' refers to the socially constructed roles, behaviours, activities, and attributes that a given society considers appropriate for men and women.*
*To put it another way:*
*'Male' and 'female' are sex categories, while 'masculine' and 'feminine' are gender categories.*[1]

Some examples of sex characteristics:
- Girls will begin to menstruate while boys do not;
- Boys have testicles while girls do not;
- Women will be able to breastfeed a baby but men cannot;
- After puberty most boys develop greater muscle capacity than girls.

Some examples of gender characteristics:
- In Europe, women earn significantly less money than men for similar work;
- In many countries, girls dance more while boys play more football;
- In the whole world, women and girls do more housework than men and boys;
- Boys more often suffer from corporal punishment than girls.

An important part of one's identity and individuality, gender roles are formed through socialisation. Today, not only the family, school and workplace influence such socialisation, but also the media, including new information technologies, music and films. Both traditional and such new socialising forces serve to preserve and transmit gender stereotypes.

## Gender equality is far from being a reality in Europe

Traditional gender stereotypes remain deeply rooted in European culture and manifest themselves in daily practise. As a result, men and women still have unequal opportunities. Britta Lejon, former Minister for Democracy and Youth in Sweden, illustrated in a presentation how this inequality is a reality amongst young people in Europe:
- Young men earn approximately 20% more than young women;
- When young men and women live together, women do twice as much housework as men;
- Very few young fathers take parental leave in countries where it is possible.[2]

Men continue to take part in many more key decisions than women. In spite of several affirmative measures, women's political participation is still very low: in Europe only 21% of parliamentarians are woman, ranging from 4.4% in Turkey to 45% in Sweden.[3] Because men hold the key roles in politics, in the financial world and in the media, they are able to set the political agenda and the public discourse. In general, men continue to be regarded as the human norm and standard of performance.

## Gender stereotypes

Many institutions of society reinforce traditional gender stereotypes. In the media, for example, women predominantly appear as objects of action, as victims and as caretakers, whereas men are usually portrayed as creative, strong, clever and full of initiative. While the media highlights a man's power and achievement, a woman, even an accomplished woman, is usually first evaluated by her appearance. In these ways the media, which includes television, radio, schoolbooks, children books, magazines, films and many forms of electronic communication, preserve and transmit stereotypes about men and women.

As with the media, the family, schools and leisure centres also have responsibilities for reinforcing gender stereotypes. A recent study shows teachers more often evaluate boys positively if they are dynamic, aggressive, independent, explorative and competitive, while girls often receive positive feedback for being obedient, kind, gentle, passive and positive to the community.[4] Because such gender stereotypes

are principally formed during school years, many girls are discouraged from taking independent action, from competing and from engaging themselves in the public sphere.[5] Girls who do not conform to stereotypical expectations can experience criticism, ostracism and even violence.

Traditional gender stereotypes can hurt boys as well as girls. Stereotypical male expectations of strength and competition often conflict with a boy's daily experiences such as living in atypical family structures, male unemployment or women's growing presence in the public sphere. Such conflicts can confuse the development of boys' gender identity. Boys who do not fit the typical male stereotypes can suffer from bullying, exclusion and discrimination.

QUESTION: *To what extent does our community conform to traditional gender stereotypes? How do these stereotypes affect children's lives? Your life?*

## Gender-based violence

Gender-based violence is a term that can be used to describe any form of violence, be it physical, sexual, psychological, economic or sociocultural, that has a negative impact on the physical or psychological health, development and identity of a person, and that is the result of gendered-power inequities that exploit distinctions between males and females, among males, and among females. Gender-based violence may affect both men and women, but it disproportionately affects women and girls and, therefore, gender-based violence is often simplified to the term 'violence against women'.

Gender-based violence is present in every country and cuts across boundaries of culture, class, education, ethnicity and background. For example, statistics show that 12% to 15% of girls and women in Europe face violence in the home every day[6]. Bullying and sexual harassment towards women are also present in various life settings, including educational institutions and workplaces.

However, of course, gender-based violence affects men as well. For example, boys and men who do not practise traditional 'male virtues' face teasing and violence. Similarly, gays and lesbians are also often subject to physical and verbal violence, particularly in schools where children and young people are discovering sexuality.

Gender-based violence poses a serious obstacle to equality between women and men and is a human rights violation. Acts of gender-based violence are generally committed by individuals often close to the victims. State institutions, however, have a key role and responsibility in responding to the victims and working towards the prevention of all forms of gender-based violence. One of the most important human rights instruments in working towards this goal is the United Nations 'Convention on the Elimination of All Forms of Discrimination Against Women' (CEDAW) which, currently, 185 countries are party to.

According to the United Nations, "The Convention provides the basis for realizing equality between women and men through ensuring women's equal access to, and equal opportunities in, political and public life – including the right to vote and to stand for election – as well as education, health and employment. States parties agree to take all appropriate measures, including legislation and temporary special measures, so that women can enjoy all their human rights and fundamental freedoms."[7]

## What is gender education?

Gender education, especially if it addresses both girls and boys, can be a positive force for creating gender equality in modern society. It seeks to change the roles that girls and boys and women and men play in private and public life. By reducing gender stereotypes, gender education assists children in build-

ing a genuine civic equality where males and females live in relationships of cooperation and in mutual respect.

Gender education starts with building gender awareness. This means recognizing the negative impacts of gender stereotypes and addressing the inequalities that arise from them.[8] The outcome of gender education for girls is greater self-confidence, assertiveness, independence and engagement in the public sphere. The outcome for boys is overcoming fear of failure, learning to be less aggressive, becoming more sociable and responsible and engaging more in the private sphere.

An important function of gender education is to distinguish between facts and beliefs or opinions. By analysing stories or their own activities, children can quickly accept as normal that girls can be boyish and boys can be sensitive and vulnerable. All children need to accept themselves as complex and unique individuals with a wide range of characteristics. Stereotypes and rigid gender expectations can hinder individual development and the realisation of the full potential of both girls and boys.

Gender education is an ongoing process that cannot be limited to specific educational activities. Educators must avoid gender stereotypical activities from early childhood and ensure that girls and boys have the same opportunities for participation and interaction in any activity. Girls should be encouraged to compete in both academics and sports while boys should participate in caring activities. Both sexes should be encouraged to participate in all kinds of activities, e.g. choirs, drama and dance, woodwork, cooking, hiking, and chess. Girls should receive positive feedback on their achievements, and boys for being caring and showing solidarity.

Another important aim of gender education is to help children recognize the social value of traditional female activities, such as motherhood, and characteristics such as caring, attention, cooperation and tolerance. This recognition can lead to genuine partnerships between men and women, which is a key goal of gender education. In this way, children learn that the different contributions of men and women to family and society are equally important and that both men and women have equal rights and responsibilities.

To be effective at gender education, educators must recognize their own gender stereotypes and reflect on their whether their teaching methods, language and interaction with boys and girls reflect the gender equality they are striving to convey.

## Relevant human rights instruments

### Council of Europe

The Council of Europe recognizes equality between women and men as a fundamental human right. Article 14 of the **European Convention of Human Rights** declares that, "the enjoyment of the rights and freedoms shall be secured without discrimination on any ground such as sex, race, colour, language religion political or other opinion...". This article provides the basis for extensive action for the organisation. The responsible body is the **Steering Committee for Equality, between Women and Men** (CDEG), which carries out analyses, studies and evaluations, defines strategies and political measures and, where necessary, decides on appropriate legal instruments.[9]

Through awareness raising efforts and campaign such as the 'Stop Domestic Violence Against Women'[10] campaign, the Council of Europe actively addresses gender-based violence. The Council's programme 'Building Europe for and with Children' targets various forms of child sexual abuse: incest, pornography, prostitution, trafficking in human beings and peer sexual assault.[11]

### United Nations

The first legally binding international document prohibiting discrimination against women and forcing governments to take steps in favour of equality for women and men is the **Convention on the Elimi-**

nation of **All Forms of Discrimination Against Women** (CEDAW)[12]. Since coming into force in 1981, CEDAW comprehensively addresses the fundamental rights of women in politics, health care, education, law, property, marriage and family relations. Countries that have ratified or acceded to the Convention are legally bound to put its provisions into practise. They are also committed to submitting national reports at least every four years on measures they have taken to comply with their treaty obligations. Since 2000, individual women or groups of women have been able to file complaints of rights violations with the Committee on the Elimination of Discrimination Against Women, which can initiate inquiries in case of serious or systematic violations.

**QUESTION:** *Is your country a state party of CEDAW? If so, when did it submit its last report? Did any groups submit a 'shadow report' offering alternative opinions to those of the government? Try to find out!*

In 2000, the United Nation launched the Millennium Development Goals,[13] one aim of which is to "eliminate gender disparity in primary and secondary education preferably by 2005, and at all levels by 2015". This programme has relevance for Europe, where equal access to education and full participation of girls in decision making processes is still not a reality.

## The Convention of the Rights of the Child

Article 2 of the Convention of the Rights of the Child affirms that the rights safeguarded in the convention shall be ensured without any discrimination, including the child's sex. Article 18 aims at a more balanced role of parents in family and childcare stating that, "both parents share responsibility for bringing up their children and should always consider what is best for their child".

## Useful Resources

- Åkerlund, Pia, *Girls' Power: A compilation from the conference on gender equality*: Swedish National Board for Youth Affairs, Stockholm, 2000
- *The Council of Europe Campaign to Combat Violence against Women, Including Domestic Violence*, Fact sheet: Council of Europe, 2006: www.coe.int/t/dg2/equality/domesticviolencecampaign/source/PDF_FS_Violence_Campaign_rev_E.pdf
- *Domestic Violence against Women and Girls*: UNICEF, Innocenti Centre, Florence, 2000: www.unicef-icdc.org/publications/pdf/digest6e.pdf
- *Gender Matters – A manual on addressing gender-based violence with young people*: Council of Europe, 2007
- *Making Rights Reality, Gender awareness workshops*: Amnesty International, 2004: http://web.amnesty.org/library/pdf/ACT770352004ENGLISH/$File/ACT7703504.pdf
- *Promoting Gender Mainstreaming in Schools*, Final Report of the Group of Specialist. EG-S-GS (2004) RAP FIN Council of Europe, 2004: www.coe.int/T/E/Human_Rights/Equality/PDF_EG-S-GS(2004)_E.pdf
- *Sex-Disaggregated Statistics on the Participation of Women and Men in Political and Public Decision making in Council of Europe member states*, Steering Committee for Equality between Women and Men (CDEG): Doc. CDEG (2006) 15 , Council of Europe, 2006: www.coe.int/t/e/human_rights/equality/1PDF_CDEG(2006)15_E.pdf
- Thun, Eva, *Gender Stereotypes in the School*, Hírnők Feminist webportal, Hungary 2002

**Useful websites**

- Building Europe for and with Children:
  www.coe.int/t/transversalprojects/children/violence/sexualAbuse_en.asp
- Equality Between Women and Men: www.coe.int/T/e/human_rights/equality
- Sexual Abuse of Children...hurt for life: Council of Europe:
  www.coe.int/t/transversalprojects/children/violence/sexualAbuse_en.asp
- Stop Domestic Violence against Women:
  www.coe.int/t/dc/campaign/stopviolence/default_en.asp
- Stop Violence against Women: http://web.amnesty.org/actforwomen/index-eng
- UN Convention on the Elimination of All Forms of Discrimination Against Women:
  www.un.org/womenwatch/daw/cedaw
- UN Development Fund for Women: www.unifem.org
- UN Millennium Development Goals: www.un.org/millenniumgoals
- Young Women from Minorities: www.scas.acad.bg/WFM/default.htm
- What Do We Mean by "Sex" and "Gender"? World Health Organisation:
  www.who.int/gender/whatisgender/en

**References**

1  See 'What do we mean by "sex" and "gender"?' www.who.int/gender/whatisgender/en
2  Lejon, Britta quoted in Åkerlund, Pia, *Girls' Power: A compilation from the conference on gender equality*: Swedish National Board for Youth Affairs, Stockholm, 2000
3  *Sex-disaggregated statistics on the participation of women and men in political and public decision making in Council of Europe member states*, Steering Committee for Equality between Women and Men (CDEG), Doc. CDEG (2006) 15: Council of Europe, 2006
4  Thun, Eva, *Gender Stereotypes in the School*, Hírnők Feminist webportal, Hungary, 2002
5  *Promoting Gender Mainstreaming in Schools*, Final Report of Group of Specialists EG-S-GS (2004) RAP FIN, Council of Europe, 2004
6  *The Council of Europe Campaign to Combat Violence against Women, including Domestic Violence,* Fact sheet: Council of Europe, 2006
7  www.un.org/womenwatch/daw/cedaw
8  *Making Rights a Reality: Gender awareness workshops*, Amnesty International, 2004, p. 61
9  See Equality Between Women and Men: www.coe.int/T/e/human_rights/equality
10  See Stop Domestic Violence against Women: www.coe.int/t/dc/campaign/stopviolence/default_en.asp
11  See Sexual Abuse for Children...hurt for life: www.coe.int/t/transversalprojects/children/violence/sexualAbuse_en.asp
12  See Convention on the Elimination of All Forms of Discrimination against Women: www.un.org/womenwatch/daw/cedaw
13  See UN Millenium Development Goals: www.un.org/millenniumgoals

# 8. HEALTH AND WELFARE

*"Health is also an economic and political issue."*

Health is a fundamental human right. The right to health includes equal access for all members of society to health care, medicine, healthy food, clean water, sanitation social services and mental health services. The right to health is fundamentally interrelated to other human rights, including the right to social security, the right to rest and leisure and especially to the right to an adequate standard of living. On the one hand, human rights violations can have serious health consequences (e.g. harmful traditional practises, trafficking, torture and inhuman and degrading treatment, violence). On the other hand, steps to respect, protect and fulfil human rights have a positive effect on people's health (e.g. freedom from discrimination, an adequate standard of living, education).

Health is also an economic and political issue, for inequality and poverty lie at the root of sickness and disease. According to a 2005 World Health Report, extreme poverty is the primary cause of death worldwide.[1] Thus, the goals set in the report, which address poverty in all its forms, are designed to break the existing vicious cycle of poverty and ill health.[2]

---

**QUESTION:** *To what extent does discrimination and poverty affect the health of the children you work with?*

---

Children are entitled to special protection to ensure that they benefit from these rights at this crucial period of their development. Protecting children's right to good health includes preventive care and health education, as well as rehabilitation and protection from abuse and exploitation.

## Health issues for European Children

Several health issues challenge the human rights and well-being of European children and youth:

### Communicable Diseases

Children need protection from diseases of all kinds. This protection starts with maternal and child healthcare, good nutrition and immunization. Other priorities include tuberculosis control, combat-

# Health education

The ultimate aim of health education is to bring about positive attitudes and practises. Children can understand that they are responsible for their health conditions as individuals and member of their families and the wider communities. With better health they can improve their lives and the lives of others.

Effective health education provides children with learning experiences that encourage understanding, positive attitudes and lifelong healthy practises related to critical health issues. These include emotional health and a positive self-image; respect and care for the human body; physical fitness; awareness of harmful addictions like alcohol, tobacco and drug use; positive nutrition, and safe sexual relationships. Sex education is of key importance for teenagers, helping them to develop healthy body awareness and be safe from unwanted pregnancy, sexually transmitted diseases and sexual violence. Peer training is especially appropriate and valuable in health education. The availability of various sports facilities for everyone in schools and the community is a major factor in encouraging children to care for their health throughout their lives. Inclusive and supportive education can provide effective help for children suffering form mental health disorders.

## Relevant human rights instruments

### Council of Europe

The **European Social Charter** (revised) refers to health extensively in Article 11, which ensures that everyone has the right to benefit from any measures enabling them him to enjoy the highest possible standard of health attainable. Article 13 states that "Anyone without adequate resources has the right to social and medical assistance".

### United Nations

Health is a fundamental human right recognized in the Universal Declaration of Human Rights Article 25.1, which relates health to an adequate standard of living:

> Everyone has the right to a standard of living adequate for the health and well-being of himself and of his family, including food, clothing, housing and medical care and necessary social services, and the right to security in the event of unemployment, sickness, disability, widowhood, old age or other lack of livelihood in circumstances beyond his control.

The same article also recognizes the entitlement of children to "special care and assistance". This right is further developed in several international human rights instruments such as Article 12 of the **International Covenant on Economic, Social and Cultural Rights** (ICESCR).

The **Convention on the Rights of the Child** (CRC) details a child's rights to health from many different perspectives.

- Article 3, which establishes the principle of the child's best interest, specifically mentions health and safety in regard to institutions, services and facilities responsible for the care of children.
- Article 13, which states a child's right to "to seek, receive and impart information and ideas of all kinds", has been interpreted by some as including the right to health education, including information about reproduction and sexuality.
- Article 17 recognizes the important role and responsibility of the mass media in promoting children's physical and mental health.
- Article 23, which addresses the rights of children with disabilities, emphasizes the importance of access to health care, preventive measures and social integration for both the physical and mental health of the child.

- Article 24 is the most definitive statement of a child's right to health and the state's obligation to provide it. It affirms

*...the right of the child to the enjoyment of the highest attainable standard of health and to facilities for the treatment of illness and rehabilitation of health. States Parties shall strive to ensure that no child is deprived of his or her right of access to such health care services.*

Article 24 also recognizes the essential factors that contribute to health such as nutritious food, clean drinking water and a wholesome natural environment. It stresses the importance of heath education for both children and their parents.

The **Convention on the Elimination of All Forms of Discrimination Against Women** (CEDAW) recognizes in Article 12 that women and girls have different health needs from men and boys, especially in the area of reproductive health.

Although the **Convention on the Rights of People with Disabilities** (CRPD) creates no new rights, it emphasizes and elaborates on the disabled child's right not only to physical health care but also to reasonable accommodation, participation and education as essential to the child's development and well-being.

..........................
## Useful resources

- *Atlas of Health in Europe*: World Health Organization, 2003: www.euro.who.int/document/E79876.pdf
- *Children and Adolescents' Health in Europe*, Fact Sheet EURO/02/03: World Health Organisation, 2003: www.euro.who.int/document/mediacentre/fs0203e.pdf
- *Children's Health and Environment: Developing National Action Plans,* Fourth Ministerial Conference on Environment and Health, Budapest, 2004: www.euro.who.int/document/eehc/ebakdoc07.pdf
- *Children and Disability in Transition in CEE/CIS*: UNICEF Innocenti Research Centre, Florence, 2004: www.unicef.org/protection/index_28534.html
- *The European Health Report 2005: Public health action for healthier children and populations*: World Health Organization, 2005: www.euro.who.int/document/e87325.pdf
- *European Strategy for Child and Adolescent Health and Development*: World Health Organization, 2005: www.euro.who.int/document/E87710.pdf
- *The Right To Health*: World Health Organization, 2002: www.who.int/bookorders/anglais/detart1.jsp?sesslan=1&codlan=1&codcol=15&codcch=474
- *10 Things You Need to Know about Obesity: Diet and physical activity for health*: WHO European Ministerial Conference on Counteracting Obesity, 2006: www.euro.who.int/Document/NUT/ObesityConf_10things_Eng.pdf

..........................
## Useful Websites

- Child and adolescent health and development: www.euro.who.int/childhealthdev
- European Health for All Database: www.euro.who.int/hfadb
- European Network of Health Promoting Schools: www.euro.who.int/enhps
- Trends in Europe and North America: www.unece.org/stats/trend/register.htm#ch6

..................
**References**

1   *The World Health Report 2005*: World Health Organisation.
2   Ibid.
3   European Forum on Social Cohesion for Mental Well-being among Adolescents, World Health Organisation, Regional Office for Europe: www.euro.who.int/PressRoom/pressnotes/20071002_1
4   Ibid.
5   *The European Health Report 2005*, World Health Organisation, p. 75.
6   *Ten Things You Need to Know about Obesity: Diet and physical activity for health*: World Health Organisation European Ministerial Conference on Counteracting Obesity, 2006.
7   *The European Health Report 2005*, World Health Organisation, p. 82.
8   *The World Health Report 2005*: World Health Organisation.
9   *The European Health Report 2005*, World Health Organisation, p. 82.
10  Ibid
11  *Children and Disability in Transition in CEE/CIS*: UNICEF Innocenti Research Centre, 2004, p.2.

# 9. MEDIA AND INTERNET

*The Council of Europe recommends ... a coherent information literacy and training strategy which is conducive to empowering children and their educators in order for them to make the best possible use of information and communication services and technologies...*
Council of Europe, Committee of Ministers Recommendation REC (2006) 12[1]

The media have become so important in our societies that they are sometimes called 'the fourth power' by analogy with the three traditional powers in a democracy: legislative, executive and judicial. Some people refer to Internet blogs as the fifth power as they increasingly compete with traditional media in raising issues and serving as 'watch dogs'. Although these heightened powers of the media can serve to increase participation and enhance access to information, they also have inherent dangers, particularly for children. The sophisticated technical skills that give children access to information may make them vulnerable to online risks.

Article 19 of the UDHR establishes the freedom of expression to all, including the right to receive and share information and ideas through all means. Article 13 of the CRC extends that rights to children. Other international treaties and most national constitutions develop this right and guarantee freedom of the press, as well as imposing some limits on the press to protect people's right to privacy and reputation. Two further articles of the CRC establish children's rights to get and share information (Article 13) and to obtain safe, reliable and understandable information from the mass media (Article 17). This places a responsibility on the media that information aimed at children should be appropriate and clear.

**QUESTION:** *How does the media influence the children you work with? What are some positive effects? Some negative effects?*

Media, information and communication technology play a central role in the lives of children today. Children sit for hours every day watching television, but they spend even more and more time online, using skills they pick up quickly from their peers. Children use online tools for playing, chatting, blog-

ging, listening to music, posting photos of themselves and searching for other people to communicate with online. Because a real gap exists between children's and adult's media literacy, most adults have little knowledge of what children do online or how they do it.

This virtual world can offer children both opportunities and pitfalls. Using electronic, digital and online media has numerous positive effects on children's development: it is entertaining, educating and socializing. However, it also has the potential to harm children and communities, depending on how it is used. This virtual world can shape children's lives as powerfully as real life, with the same pressures to fit in, to be cool and to have a lot of friends.

Exposure to mass media, particularly television, has negative effects that have preoccupied parents and educators and been the object of many studies:

- **Time spent in front of the television:** there is clear evidence that children who spend more time in front of the television show poorer performance in school, while children whose families use both electronic and print media more carefully tend to do better in school.[2]
- **Violence:** How does violent subject matter affect children, whether from television, films or video games? Does it make them more aggressive? More insensitive? Does it have a cathartic effect? Do these effects happen in all children or only in some more vulnerable children and only in some contexts?
- **Consumerism:** Advertising in its different forms has been blamed for manipulating children, and through them their parents, to buy certain food products (often associated with child obesity epidemics), clothes, and even cleaning products for the home, or cars and trips!
- **Stereotypes:** The media have been blamed for perpetuating social stereotypes, especially gender roles and ethnic characteristics.

In response to these concerns, some countries forbid advertising during children's programming. Some countries have established a 'curfew time' before which violent and pornographic images cannot be shown. Parents in a few countries can buy filters to prevent children from viewing certain programmes. However, in the new technological context of mobile phones, multiple TV channels and the Internet, most of these measures are not effective.

More interactive media, such as the Internet and mobile phones, produce additional dangers for children: children may provide personal data that may be used for unwanted advertising and provide rooms for online predators. Children sometimes use the unsupervised online environment for sending cruel messages and degrading photographs aimed at other kids. 'Cyberbullying' is easy and especially harmful because online mistreatment of this kind is mostly anonymous.

## Right to information versus right to protection

The media raise human rights issues of both children's right to protection and children's right to information. For example:

- **Access and its inequalities.** Access to the Internet is unequal and will probably reinforce inequalities amongst children of different social origins. How can this 'digital divide' be addressed and overcome?
- **Undesirable forms of content and contact.** Recent research show that more than half of young people aged nine to nineteen years old who go online at least once a week have seen pornography online and mostly unintentionally. Some of them are 'disgusted' or 'bothered', as they are also with other unwanted content, such as violent pictures or a site hostile to a group of people. How should we deal with this? To what extent would censoring children's access to the media compromise their right to information? Or another's right to expression?

- **New Internet and media literacy.** Children usually consider themselves – and are considered by adults – to be more expert than their parents in Internet use, thus gaining self-esteem and social status within the family. Nevertheless, most children the lack the experience and judgment for adequately evaluating online content or sources, searching and treating information or using it to communicate. How could educational initiatives address the different media literacy needs of children and adults?[3]

QUESTION: *In what ways have you developed use of the Internet and media so that children have the maximum access to information and learning? How do you protect these children from inappropriate material and exploitation via the Internet?*

## Media education

One answer to these issues is to educate children to become more critical and sophisticated media consumers and communicators. Media education aims at making all children – and all citizens, if possible – aware of the importance and power of the media. Techniques of media education include making children aware of what they see and how that may affect them. For example children might be asked to count the violent acts they watch during a set period, to analyse the persuasive strategies of advertisements or to consider different ways of conveying the same information in order to understand how different senses of reality can be created.

In the last 50 years there have been three significant trends in media education:
- **The 'vaccination' approach,** which aims to make children immune to the effects of the media;
- **The critical mind approach**, which aims at developing children's critical judgement towards the negative content of the media;
- **The decoding approach,** which considers the media indispensable for understanding the contemporary world and tries to help children understand the economic and social context of media production and consumption, and the techniques of message coding.[4]

In the sequence of these approaches one can detect a change in the perception of the child as media consumer, moving from the child as vulnerable subject to the child as participating citizen.

As new information and communication technologies, particularly the Internet, have developed, so have both the benefits and perils of easy access to these media. The Internet is a fantastic means of access to all kinds of information and to communication at a distance. There is no guarantee, however, that the information it provides is true or that a communication has not been made with malicious intentions.

Thus, media education needs to keep pace, developing children's critical skills and understanding of this powerful tool. Media education also aims at making children better communicators of their ideas by providing opportunities to use and learn different media, including desktop publishing, radio and TV programming, websites and blogs. However, media education is also crucial for adults who work with children. Parents, teachers and other educators should invest time and energy to learn about and observe how their children communicate and live together.

The Council of Europe has made the following recommendation with regard to media education:

> *Conscious of the risk of harm from content and behaviour in the new information and communications environment which may not always be illegal but which are capable of adversely affecting the physical, emotional and psychological well-being of children, such as online pornography, the portrayal and glorification of violence and self-harm, demeaning, discriminatory or racist expressions or apologia for such conduct, solicitation (grooming), bullying, stalking and other forms of harassment ... [The Council of Europe] [r]ecommends that member states develop ... a coherent*

*information literacy and training strategy which is conducive to empowering children and their educators in order for them to make the best possible use of information and communication services and technologies...[5]*

The Media Division of the Council of Europe has a project on how children and their parents and educators gain the knowledge and skills necessary for the 'information society'. 'The Internet Literacy Handbook: A guide for parents, teachers and young people', a publication of the Media Division, provides relevant background information and fact sheets on this complex network of information and communication.[6]

## Relevant human rights instruments

### Council of Europe

The **European Convention on Human Rights** guarantees everyone the right to receive and import information and ideas without interference by public authority (Article 10). This right extends to children as well as adults, with the exception that children have a right to be protected from exploitation and exposure to inappropriate kinds of violent and pornographic media. The ECHR recognizes this in including among the duties and responsibilities that go with this right "the protection of health or morals". It does not, however, specify how and by whom 'inappropriate' is determined.

Article 9 of the **Convention on Cybercrime** refers to offences related to child pornography and states that member states shall adopt "legislative and other measures to criminalize the various specified uses of computers involving child pornography".

### United Nations

The right to information is a fundamental human right codified in Article 19 of Universal Declaration of Human Rights:

Everyone has the right to freedom of opinion and expression; this right includes freedom to hold opinions without interference and to seek, receive and impart information and ideas through any media and regardless of frontiers.

Of course, when the Universal Declaration was written in 1948, no-one thought of the Internet as one of the media channels. Even by 1989, when the UN General Assembly adopted the **Convention on the Rights of the Child**, the use of the Internet by the general populace, much less children, was inconceivable. Interestingly, however, the Children's Convention separates freedom of opinion and expression and freedom of information into three separate articles, stressing the importance of each: Article 12 guarantees the child's right to an opinion and to have that opinion taken into consideration; Article 14 guarantees the child's right to thought, conscience and religion.

Article 13 contains the main statement of a child's right to freedom of expression and information:

*The child shall have the right to freedom of expression; this right shall include freedom to seek, receive and impart information and ideas of all kinds, regardless of frontiers, either orally, in writing or in print, in the form of art, or through any other media of the child's choice.*

This article does not, however, give the child unlimited access to information. Balanced against it are safeguards such as protection from exploitation (Articles 19 and 36), specifically sexual exploitation (Articles 19 and 34).

The Convention also recognizes the **evolving capacity** and maturity of the child, so that what may be inappropriate for a child in elementary school may be acceptable for a youth. As with many rights issues, freedoms are often in conflict with protections in this area and require thought and negotiation. In every case, however, the child's best interests should be the deciding consideration.

..........................

## Useful resources

- *Family Guide to the Internet*: Barnardos' National Children's Resource Centres, 2004.
- Gentile, Douglas A. and Walsch, David A., '*A normative study of family media and habits*' in Applied Developmental Psychology 23 (2002) 157-178: National Institute on Media and the Family, 2002: www.mediafamily.org/research/index.shtml
- *Recommendation Rec (2006) 12 of the Committee of Ministers to Member States on Empowering Children in the New Information and Communications Environment*: Council of Europe, 2006: http://wcd.coe.int/ViewDoc.jsp?id=1041181&BackColourInternet=9999CC&BackColourIntranet=FFBB55&BackColourLogged=FFAC75
- Frau-Meigs, Divina, *Council of Europe Pan-European Forum on Human Rights in the Information Society: Empowering children and young people*: Council of Europe, 2006: www.euro.who.int/document/mediacentre/fs0203e.pdf
- Linddal Hansen, Birthe, *Consumer children 2016*, Council of Europe, 2006: www.coe.int/t/e/human_rights/media/links/events/1Forum2006YerevanFuturist_en.asp#TopOfPage
- Livingstone, Sonia and Bober, Magdalena, *UK Children Go Online: Final report of key project findings*: Economic and Social Research Council, 2005: http://news.bbc.co.uk/1/shared/bsp/hi/pdfs/28_04_05_childrenonline.pdf
- Masterman, Len and Mariet, François, *L'éducation aux Média dans l'Europe des Années* 90: *un guide pour les enseignants*: Council of Europe, 1994.
- Piette, Jacques, *Education aux Média et Fonction Critique*: L'Harmattan, Paris, 1996.
- Richardson, Janice, ed., *The Internet Literacy Handbook: A guide for parents, teachers and young people*, 2nd Edition: Strasbourg, Council of Europe, 2006: www.coe.int/T/E/Human_Rights/Media/hbk_en.html
- O'Connell, Rachel and Bryce, Jo, *Young people, well-being and risk on-line*, Council of Europe, 2006: www.echr.coe.int/Library/DIGDOC/DG2/H_INF/COE-2006-EN-H_INF(2006)5.pdf

..........................

## Useful Websites

- European Charter for Media Literacy: www.euromedialiteracy.eu/index.php
- The National Centre for Technology in Education: www.ncte.ie/Internetsafety
- National Institute for Media and the Family: www.mediafamily.org/index.shtml
- Media Wise Trust: www.mediawise.org.uk

.................

## References

1 *Recommendation Rec (2006) 12 of the Committee of Ministers to Member States on Empowering Children in the new Information and Communications Environment*: Council of Europe, 2006.
2 Douglas A. Gentile and David A. Walsch, '*A normative study of family media and habits*, National Institute on Media and the Family', Applied Developmental Psychology 23 (2002), p.174.
3 Livingstone, Sonia and Bober, Magdalena, *UK Children Go Online: Final report of key project findings*: Economic and Social Research Council, 2005
4 Masterman, Len, and Mariet, François, L'éducation aux Média dans l'Europe des Années 90: Council of Europe, 1994.
5 Recommendation Rec (2006) 12 of the Committee of Ministers to Member States on Empowering Children in the New Information and Communications Environment: Council of Europe, 2006: http://wcd.coe.int/ViewDoc.jsp?id=1041181&BackColourInternet=9999CC&BackColourIntranet=FFBB55&BackColourLogged=FFAC75
6 Richardson, Janice, ed., *The Internet Literacy Handbook: A guide for parents, teachers and young people*, 2nd Edition: Strasbourg, Council of Europe, 2006.

# 10. PARTICIPATION

*For both adults and children the development of such a culture of participation can be a very powerful exercise in democracy.*

Participation is both an essential principle of human rights and a working practise of citizenship for all people. The affirmation of the right of children to participate is one of the guiding principles and most progressive innovations of the Convention on the Rights of the Child (See CHAPTER I, P. 21 for a discussion of the Children's Convention).

The Children's Convention articulates several different aspects of children's right to participate:

- **the right to express their views on all matters affecting them** and to have their views given due weight (Article 12)
- **freedom of expression,** including the right to seek and receive impartial information of all kind (Article 13)
- **freedom of thought, conscience and religion** (Article 14)
- **freedom of association** (Article 15)
- **the right of access to information** and material from national and international sources (Article 17)
- **the right to participate in the cultural life of the community** (Article 31).

## Why is children's participation important?

The most important precondition of meaningful participation is that adults respect children's capacities to take part in decisions and recognise them as partners. Rather than traditional relationships built on adults' power and control over children, democratic partnerships result. Otherwise children's participation is merely tokenism: children may give their opinions, but they have no influence on whether or how their contribution is used.

The essence of participation was well explained by the 'Ladder of participation' model[1]. Roger Hart describes an eight-stage Ladder of Participation. The first three stages are manipulation, decoration and tokenism, false means of participation that can compromise the entire process. Real forms of participation include the 'Assigned and informed' stage in which specific roles are given to children, and

# LADDER OF PARTICIPATION

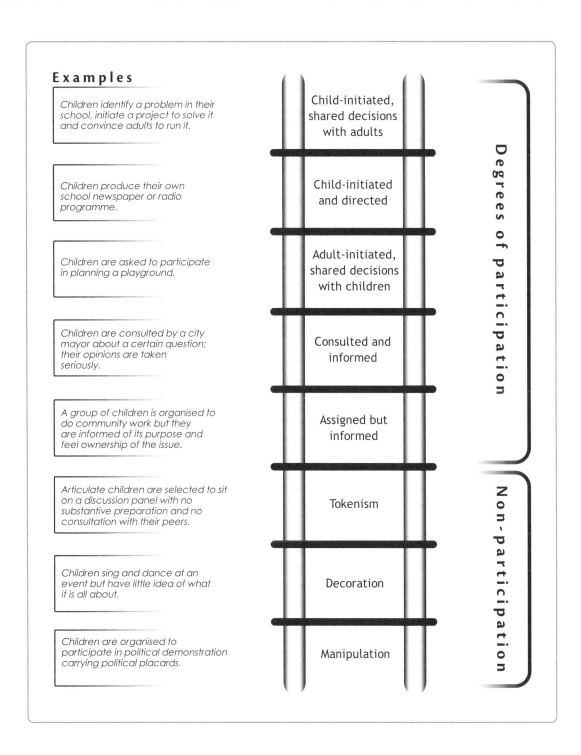

## Examples

Children identify a problem in their school, initiate a project to solve it and convince adults to run it.

Children produce their own school newspaper or radio programme.

Children are asked to participate in planning a playground.

Children are consulted by a city mayor about a certain question; their opinions are taken seriously.

A group of children is organised to do community work but they are informed of its purpose and feel ownership of the issue.

Articulate children are selected to sit on a discussion panel with no substantive preparation and no consultation with their peers.

Children sing and dance at an event but have little idea of what it is all about.

Children are organised to participate in political demonstration carrying political placards.

**Ladder rungs (top to bottom):**
- Child-initiated, shared decisions with adults
- Child-initiated and directed
- Adult-initiated, shared decisions with children
- Consulted and informed
- Assigned but informed
- Tokenism
- Decoration
- Manipulation

**Degrees of participation** (top five rungs) / **Non-participation** (bottom three rungs)

Source: The table was adapted from Hart, Roger: *Children's Participation from Tokenism to Citizenship:* UNICEF Innocenti Research Centre, 1992, Florence.

## Principles for promoting children's participation

UNICEF, the worldwide NGO fighting for children's rights and well-being, has set up principles to ensure children's meaningful participation. These guidelines are useful for any form of participation:

- Children must understand what the project or the process is about, what it is for and their role within it.
- Power relations and decision making structures must be transparent.
- Children should be involved from the earliest possible stage of any initiative.
- All children should be treated with equal respect regardless of their age, situation, ethnicity, abilities or other factors.
- Ground rules should be established with all the children at the beginning.
- Participation should be voluntary and children should be allowed to leave at any stage.
- Children are entitled to respect for their views and experience.[9]

## Relevant human rights instruments

### Council of Europe

Participation is an important area of the Council of Europe's work, especially regarding youth. In a unique manner the Council of Europe has introduced a co-management system into its youth sector, where representatives of European youth organisations and governments decide jointly on the Council's youth programme and budget. In cooperation with the Congress for Local and Regional Authorities, a European Charter on the Participation of Young People in Local and Regional life was produced in 1992 and revised in 2003. This unique tool not only promotes participation of young people, but also presents concrete ideas and instruments that can be used by young people and local authorities. A practical manual with further ideas, 'Have your say!', was produced in 2007.

### United Nations

The rights related to participation are closely linked to those of citizenship, both in the range of freedoms they confer and the responsibilities they impose. (See discussion of *Theme 1, Citizenship*, p. 213) **The Universal Declaration of Human Rights** recognizes in Article 29 the importance of the citizens' participation to both the community and the citizens themselves:

Everyone has duties to the community in which alone the free and full development of his personality is possible.

However, only with the adoption of the **Convention on the Rights of the Child** in 1989 were the rights and benefits of participation recognized as applying to children. Their participation is guaranteed in a wide spectrum of the life of the community:

- Article 9: to participate in proceedings regarding the child's guardianship or custody
- Article 12: to participate in decision making in "all matters affecting the child"
- Article 13: to express opinions and to acquire and give information
- Article 14: to hold views in matters of thought, conscience and religion
- Article 15: to associate with others
- Article 23: the right of a child with disabilities to "active participation in the community"
- Article 30: the right of minority or indigenous children to participate in the community of their own group as well as the larger society
- Article 31: to participate fully in cultural and artistic life.

The Children's Convention defines a child as anyone below the age of eighteen, which necessarily means not every child has the competence or maturity to participate in the same way. To address this fact, the

Convention applies the principle of **evolving capacity**, recommending that both parents and the state recognize and respond to the child based on his growing abilities and maturity. Many adults and institutions continue to be challenged to adapt their long-established attitudes and practises to accommodate the child's right to participation at any age.

........................

## Useful resources

- Backman, Elisabeth, and Trafford, Bernard, *Democratic Governance of Schools*: Council of Europe, 2007:
www.coe.int/t/dg4/education/edc/Source/Pdf/Documents/2007_Tool2demgovschools_en.pdf
- Brocke Hartmut and Karsten, Andreas, *Towards a common culture of cooperation between civil society and local authorities,* Centre Francais de Berlin, Berlin, 2007
- *Building a Europe for and with Children, Children and young people's preparation seminar:* Council of Europe, Monaco, 2006
www.coe.int/t/transversalprojects/children/Source/reports/MonacoPrepSeminar_en.doc
- *Catch Them Young, Recommendations on children's participation,* Ministry of Flemish Community Youth and Sport Division, Benelux, Brussels, 2004: www.wvc.vlaanderen.be/jeugd-beleid/internationaal/documenten/catch%20them%20young.pdf
- *Children and Young People's Participation,* CRIN Newsletter No 16: Child Rights Information Network, October 2002: www.crin.org/docs/resources/publications/crinvol16e.pdf
- *Children, Participation, Projects – How to make it work*: Council of Europe, 2004:
www.bernardvanleer.org/files/crc/3.A.5%20Council_of_Europe.pdf
- *DIY Guide to Improving Your Community – Getting children and young people involved:* Save the Children, Scotland, 2005:
www.savethechildren.org.uk/scuk_cache/scuk/cache/cmsattach/4130_DIY.pdf
- Dürr, Karlheinz, *The School: A democratic learning community, DGIV/EDU/CIT (2003) 23final*: Council of Europe, 2004: www.coe.int/t/dg4/education/edc/Source/Pdf/Documents/2003_23_All-EuropStudyChildrenParticipation_En.PDF
- Gozdik-Ormel, Zaneta, *'Have your say!' Manual on the Revised European Charter on the Participation of Young People in Local and Regional Life*: Council of Europe, 2007.
- Hart, Roger, *Ladder of Participation, Children's Participation: From Tokenism to Citizenship*: UNICEF Innocenti Research Centre, 1992.
- *Learning to Listen, Core Principles for the Involvement of Children and Young People:* Department of Education and Skills, Children's and Young People's Unit, UK, 2001:
www.dfes.gov.uk/listeningtolearn/downloads/LearningtoListen-CorePrinciples.pdf
- *Promoting Children's Participation in Democratic Decision making*: UNICEF Innocenti Research Centre, Florence, 2001: www.asylumsupport.info/publications/unicef/democratic.pdf
- *Recommendation No. R(81)18 of the Committee of Ministers to Member States concerning Participation at Municipal Level,* Council of Europe, 1981:
http://wcd.coe.int/com.instranet.InstraServlet?Command=com.instranet.CmdBlobGet&DocId=673582&SecMode=1&Admin=0&Usage=4&InstranetImage=45568
- *Seven Good Reasons for Building a Europe with and for Children*: Council of Europe, 2006: www.coe.int/t/transversalprojects/children/publications/Default_en.asp
- Sutton, Faye, *The School Council – A Children's Guide*, Save the Children, 1999.
- The United Nations Secretary General's Study on Violence against Children:
www.violencestudy.org

## Useful Websites

- L'Association Themis: www.grainedecitoyen.fr
- Child Rights Information Network: www.crin.org
- Children as Partners Alliance (CAPA): www.crin.org/childrenaspartners
- Children's Rights Alliance for England (CRAE): www.crae.org.uk
- Frequently Asked Questions on Children's Participation: www.everychildmatters.gov.uk/participation/faq
- Save the Children: www.savethechildren.net
- UNICEF: www.unicef.org

..................
## References

1  Originally developed by Arnstein, Sherry R.: *A Ladder of Citizens Participation*, JAIP, Vol 35, No.4, 1969, p. 216-224. http://lithgow-schmidt.dk/sherry-arnstein/ladder-of-citizen-participation.html The model was developed by Hart, Roger: *Children's Participation from Tokenism to Citizenship*: UNICEF Innocenti Research Centre, 1992, Florence.
2  *Building a Europe for and with Children, Children and young people's preparation seminar*, Council of Europe, Monaco 2006, p.16.
3  Dürr, Karlheinz, *The School: A democratic learning Programme Education for Democratic Citizenship* DGIV/EDU/CIT (2003) 23final, Council of Europe, 2004.
4  *Recommendation No. R(81)18 of the Committee of Ministers to Member States concerning Participation at Municipal Level*, Council of Europe, 1981.
5  See Young London Kids: www.london.gov.uk/young-london/kids/have-your-say/index.jsp
6  *DIY Guide to improving your community – Getting children and young people involved*, Save the Children, Scotland, 2005.
7  *Learning to Listen, Core Principles for the Involvement of Children and Young People*, Department of Education and Skills, CYPU, UK, March 2001.
8  See The United Nations Secretary General's Study on Violence against Children.
9  *Promoting Children's Participation in Democratic Decision making*: UNICEF Innocenti Research Centre, 2001.

268

# 11. PEACE

*A culture of peace will be achieved when citizens of the world understand global problems, have the skills to resolve conflicts and struggle for justice non-violently, live by international standards of human rights and equity, appreciate cultural diversity, and respect the Earth and each other. Such learning can only be achieved with systematic education for peace.*

Hague Appeal for Peace Global Campaign for Peace Education

Building such a culture of human rights is a pre-condition to achieving a state of peace. War and violence inevitably result in the denial of human rights, and sustainable, lasting peace and security can only be attained only when all human rights are fulfilled.

Europe in the twenty-first century may be relatively free of war, but it is not free of conflict that directly affects children. Armed conflict threatens some regions of the Balkans and in the Caucasus region. Because the world is interconnected, armed conflict in distant places such as Afghanistan or Iraq has effects in places in Europe such as Madrid and London. Non-military threats to peace and security are also growing: drought, disease, poverty, famine, racism and intolerance are all both sources and consequences of conflict.

In absolute terms the twentieth century was the most violent period in history, with more casualties than all the preceding centuries combined. Some conflicts such as the First and Second World Wars involved the whole planet and left much of Europe in ruins. Others were regional conflicts (e.g. internal conflicts in Spain, Cyprus, Greece and Ireland). In Europe, the twentieth century ended with wars in the former Yugoslavia and the Caucasus.

In our increasingly high-tech, globalised world, the nature of conflict has changed drastically, but still there are too many casualties among civilians, including children. Most of the world refugees are children, many of them are fleeing armed conflict in their home countries. Furthermore, at least half a million girls and boys under 18 have been exploited as participants in war worldwide, either by directly fighting, laying mines or explosives, or by providing support services. The effect of war on children is devastating and total, wounding their bodies and spirits and destroying their families and communities.

## What is human security?

Human security is a relatively new concept that recognizes the interrelation between violence and deprivation of all kinds. It concerns the protection of individuals and communities from both the direct threat of physical violence and the indirect threats that result from poverty and other forms of social, economic or political inequalities, as well as natural disasters and disease. A country may not be under threat of external attack or internal conflict but still be insecure if, for example, it lacks the capacity to maintain the rule of law, if large populations are displaced by famine or decimated by disease or if its people lack the basic necessities of survival.

Human security furthers human rights because it addresses situations that gravely threaten human rights and supports the development of systems that give people the building blocks of survival, dignity and essential freedoms: freedom from want, freedom from fear and freedom to take action on one's own behalf. It uses two general strategies to accomplish this: protection and empowerment. Protection shields people from direct dangers, but also seeks to develop norms, processes and institutions that maintain security. Empowerment enables people to develop their potential and become full participants in decision making. Protection and empowerment are mutually reinforcing, and both are required in most situations.

In 2003 a special UN Commission on Human Security issued *Human Security Now*, a report outlining major areas of concern for establishing and maintaining human security:

* Protecting people in violent conflict, including the proliferation of arms
* Protecting and empowering people on the move, both those migrating to improve their livelihood and those forced to flee to protect themselves from conflicts or serious human rights violations
* Protecting and empowering people in post-conflict situations, including the complex rebuilding of war-torn societies
* Promoting economic security by providing minimum living standards everywhere and enabling people to move out of poverty
* Promoting universal access to basic health care, especially addressing global infections and diseases, poverty-related threats and health problems arising from violence
* Empowering all people with universal basic education
* Clarifying the need for a global human identity while respecting the freedom of individuals to have diverse identities and affiliations.

**QUESTION:** *What factors threaten the security of your community? How do they destabilise society? How does this insecurity affect the children with whom you work?*

## Peace as a human right

Peace is not just the absence of conflict and violence, however: it is a way of living together so that all members of society can accomplish their human rights. Although not formally codified as a human right, peace is recognized as an essential element to the realisation of human rights and belongs to the **third generation** of human rights or so-called **solidarity rights.** These are rights that affect whole societies or groups of people rather than just individuals, such as the right to a healthy environment, to sustainable development, to communication or to share in the common heritage of humankind. Peace is also a product of human rights: the more a society promotes, protects and fulfils the human rights of its people, the greater its chances for curbing violence and resolving conflict peacefully.

Following the lead of UNESCO, in 1999 the UN General Assembly adopted The Declaration on a Culture of Peace. It acknowledges that the responsibility to promote a culture of peace rests with all members of the community, including parents, teachers, politicians, journalists, religious bodies, intellectuals, institutions of civil society, those engaged in scientific, philosophical and creative and artistic activities, health workers, social workers, managers at various levels and non-governmental organisations.

## Intercultural and inter-religious dialogue

*Dialogue between cultures, the oldest and most fundamental mode of democratic conversation, is an antidote to rejection and violence. Its objective is to enable us to live together peacefully and constructively in a multicultural world, to develop a sense of community and belonging.*

Intercultural dialogue and the Council of Europe:
www.coe.int/t/dg4/intercultural/default_en.asp

Growing migration, the effects of globalisation and the advancement of information and communication technologies have made people today increasingly mobile. As a result, cultural diversity has become a main feature of every country in Europe. While this diversity is a rich asset for our societies, it also introduces new social and political challenges. As identity questions become more critical, "stereotyping, racism, xenophobia, intolerance, discrimination and violence can threaten peace and the fabric of national and local communities"[1]. The negative consequences of such phenomena vary from social exclusion in communities to international conflicts.

Intercultural dialogue is a vital tool to combat these developments, learn to live together and develop a sense of community and belonging. "Intercultural dialogue is an open and respectful exchange of views between individuals and groups belonging to different cultures that leads to a deeper understanding of the other's world perception."[2] It is especially important to acknowledge the role religious communities play in this process of developing identity and to stimulate interreligious dialogue to overcome religious-based stereotypes and discrimination at every level of society.

**QUESTION:** *In your community are there different religious communities that effect how people live together? Do conflicts arising from religious difference affect the children you work with?*

## Peace education

Originally focused on eliminating the possibility of global extinction through nuclear war, peace education today addresses the broader objective of building a culture of peace. It seeks to understand and eliminate the causes of conflict such as poverty and all forms of discrimination, as well as to teach the skills of conflict management. Peaceful resolution of conflict is not an innate human quality but a skill that must be learned and practised from childhood. As Mahatma Gandhi observed, "If we are going to bring about peace in the world, we have to begin with the children".[3]

*...education of the child should be directed to ... the preparation of the child for responsible life in a free society, in the spirit of understanding, peace, tolerance, equality of sexes, and friendship among all peoples, ethnic, national and religious groups and persons of indigenous origin.*

Article 29.d of the Convention on the Rights of the Child

Typically a child experiences conflict with other children, parents, teachers and other adults. Conflict is not inherently negative or damaging; it can usually be minimized and resolved. By contrast, violence, the aggressive use of force or abusive exercise of power, always results in injury and destruction. For this reason society has developed many ways of handling conflict using non-violent methods such as negotiations and other cooperative approaches that lead to mutually beneficial agreement ('win–win' solutions) and compromises. Learning to deal with conflict and refrain from violence is an important socialization of every child.

**QUESTION:** *How do the children you work with usually react to conflicts? Are there ways you can help them learn to manage and resolve conflict better?*

Peace education teaches the knowledge, skills, attitudes and values needed to bring about behavioural change that will enable children, youth and adults to prevent conflict and violence, both overt and structural, to resolve conflict peacefully, and to create the conditions conducive to peace, whether at an interpersonal, inter-group, national or international level. Peace education improves children's self-esteem, develops their problem solving skills and avoids unsafe behaviours.

Among UN agencies, UNICEF and UNESCO in particular promote peace education. Unicef describes peace education as schooling and other educational initiatives that:

- Function as 'zones of peace', where children are safe from violent conflict
- Uphold children's basic rights as outlined in the CRC
- Develop a climate that models peaceful and respectful behaviour among all members of the learning community
- Demonstrate the principles of equality and non-discrimination in administrative policies and practises
- Draw on the knowledge of peace-building that exists in the community, including means of dealing with conflict that are effective, non-violent, and rooted in the local culture
- Handle conflicts in ways that respect the rights and dignity of all involved
- Integrate an understanding of peace, human rights, social justice and global issues throughout the curriculum whenever possible
- Provide a forum for the explicit discussion of values of peace and social justice
- Use teaching and learning methods that stress participation, problem solving and respect for differences
- Enable children to put peace-making into practise in the educational setting as well as in the wider community
- Generate opportunities for continuous reflection and professional development of all educators in relation to issues of peace, justice and rights.[4]

Much of the work of UNESCO focuses on promoting education for peace, human rights, and democracy. Since the early 1990s UNESCO has advanced the concept of education for a 'culture of peace' with the aim to "construct a new vision of peace by developing a peace culture based on the universal values of respect for life, liberty, justice, solidarity, tolerance, human rights and equality between women and men" as well as to promote education and research for this vision".[5]

Peace education is an important part of the different educational fields that promote human rights and the culture of peace and democracy. See CHAPTER II., P. 25.

# Relevant human rights instruments

## Council of Europe

The Preamble to the European Convention on Human Rights (ECHR) affirms the essential relationship between peace and human rights, stating that fundamental freedoms are

> *...the foundation of justice and peace in the world and are best maintained on the one hand by an effective political democracy and on the other by a common understanding and observance of the Human Rights upon which they depend.*

Article 5 of the ECHR guarantees everyone security of person, especially against intrusion by the state in the form of arrest and imprisonment.

The Council of Europe has various activities to promote tolerance, peace and mutual understanding among people, including human rights education, education for democratic citizenship, intercultural and interreligious dialogue. In 2007 the Council of Europe published a 'White Paper on Intercultural Dialogue', a coherent policy for the promotion of intercultural dialogue within Europe and between Europe and its neighbouring regions.

## United Nations

The United Nations was established in 1945 to "save succeeding generations from the scourge of war", "to reaffirm faith in the ...dignity and worth of the human person [and] in the equal rights of men and women", "to establish conditions under which justice and respect for the obligations arising from treaties and other sources of international law can be maintained", and "to promote social progress and better standards of life in larger freedom..."[6]

Peace education has developed as a means to achieve these goals. It is education that reflects Article 26 of the Universal Declaration of Human Rights, which includes not simply the right to education but specifies an education "directed to the full development of the human personality and to the strengthening of respect for human rights and fundamental freedoms". It promotes "understanding, tolerance and friendship among all nations, racial or religious groups" and furthers "the activities of the United Nations for the maintenance of peace".

Articles 38 and 39 of the Convention on the Right of the Child concern the rights of children in conditions of armed conflict. Article 38 calls for "all feasible measures to ensure protection and care of children who are affected by an armed conflict". Article 39 calls for the "physical and psychological recovery and social reintegration" of children who have suffered many kinds of abuse, including war. Of particular concern is the protection of the child from service in armed forces. Article 38 bans children under fifteen from participation in direct hostilities, but in 2000 the General Assembly adopted the Optional Protocol on the Involvement of Children in Armed Conflict, which raises the minimum age to eighteen.

..........................

## Useful resources

- Fountain, Susan, *Peace Education in UNICEF*: UNICEF, 1999:
  www.unicef.org/girlseducation/files/PeaceEducation.pdf
- Myers-Walls, Judith A., *Talking to Children about Terrorism and Armed Conflict*: Vol.7, No.1, 2002: North Carolina State Forum for Family and Consumer Issues:
  www.ces.ncsu.edu/depts/fcs/pub/2002w/myers-wall.html

........................

**Useful websites**

- Charter of the United Nations: www.unhchr.ch/html/menu3/b/ch-pream.htm
- Children in armed conflicts: www.crin.org/themes/ViewTheme.asp?id=11
- A Declaration on a Culture of Peace: UNESCO, 2000: www.unesco.org/cpp/uk/declarations/2000.htm
- European Charter for Media Literacy: www.euromedialiteracy.eu/index.php
- The History Guide, Revolutionizing education in the spirit of Socratic wisdom: www.historyguide.org
- Council of Europe White Paper on Intercultural dialogue: www.coe.int/t/dg4/intercultural/default_en.asp
- Manifesto 2000 for a Culture of Peace and Non-violence, International Decade for a Culture of Peace and Non-violence for the Children of the World, 2001 – 2010: UNESCO, 2000: www3.unesco.org/manifesto2000/uk/uk_manifeste.htm
- United Nations Cyberschoolbus: www.un.org/cyberschoolbus/peace/home.asp

.................

**References**

1  Preparing the 'White paper on intercultural dialogue' of the Council of Europe, Consultation document p.3. www.coe.int
2  Ibid., p.6.
3  See Inspiring Quotations: www.peace.ca/inspiringquotations.htm
4  Fountain, Susan, *Peace Education in* UNICEF, 1999. p. 6.
5  *UNESCO and a Culture of Peace*, UNESCO Publishing, 1995.
6  See Charter of the United Nations: www.unhchr.ch/html/menu3/b/ch-pream.htm

# 12. POVERTY AND SOCIAL EXCLUSION

*State Parties recognize the right of every child to a standard of living adequate for the child's physical, mental, spiritual, moral and social development.*

Convention on the Rights of the Child, *Article 27,1*

A person in a state of poverty lacks "an adequate standard of living" such as adequate housing and clothing, nutritious food and clean drinking water, sufficient income, employment and access to health care, education and social services. Poverty may result from particular events, such as war or natural disaster, or be chronic among whole populations, but whatever its cause, poverty is a human rights violation. When people lack the basic requirements for survival, their other human rights are in jeopardy too, even the right to life. The World Bank reports that while in rich countries only one child in a hundred fails to reach its fifth birthday, in poor countries as many as ten in a hundred do not survive.[1] However, living in a prosperous country does not guarantee freedom from poverty. A Unicef report on child poverty shows that from three to over twenty-five percent of children in the world's wealthiest nations live in poverty. The same report states that 47 million children from the 29 members of the Organization for Economic Development (OECD), or one in six, live below the national poverty line, defined as half the average national income.[2]

All societies strive to achieve social cohesion, reinforcing the things that bind people together and fighting the disruptive forces that drive them apart. One of the principal factors of division in any society is an excessive gap between the rich and the poor. Thus, addressing poverty not only enhances the lives of the poor people, but also contributes to a culture of human rights and improves social cohesion for the whole society.[4]

Children experience poverty in a different way from adults. Poverty compromises children's daily lives and has a cumulative and negative impact on their future.[3]

Marta Santos Pais
*Director, UNICEF Innocenti Research Centre*

Article 27 of the Convention on the Rights of the Child recognises children's right to a standard of living adequate to meet their physical, mental, spiritual, moral and social development and exhorts governments to assist families who cannot provide these basic needs of their children, especially with regard to nutrition, clothing and housing. Article 26 of the CRC further highlights the right of the child to benefit from social security benefits that helps the child develop and live in good conditions. However, many governments lack the financial means or the political will to meet the needs

of its children. Even in wealthy countries large numbers of children live in poverty. In the UK, for example, one child in five lives in poverty.[5]

In the European Union child poverty varies from rates above 15% in three Southern European countries (Portugal, Spain and Italy) to under 5% in the four Nordic countries (Denmark, Finland, Norway and Sweden). Nine countries in northern Europe have brought child poverty rates below 10%.[6] However, there is no obvious relationship between levels of child well-being and GDP per capita. The Czech Republic, for example, achieves a higher overall rank for child well-being than several much wealthier countries, including France and Austria. Norway is the only European country where child poverty can be described as very low and continuing to fall.[7]

Significant economic, political, environmental and social changes in the EU directly affect children. The young people in an EU country are more likely to face poverty than the population as a whole (20% for children aged 0-15 and 21% for those aged 16-24, compared to 16% for adults).[8] Children living with poor parents or who cannot live with their parents, as well as children from some ethnic minorities, are particularly exposed to poverty, exclusion and discrimination.[9]

The situation is more serious in Eastern and Southern Europe. Although the absolute number of children living in poverty has declined in the last ten years, one child in four, or approximately 18 million children, are still living in extreme poverty in the countries of south-eastern Europe and the Commonwealth of Independent States. Even though the region's economic recovery has improved conditions for most adults, the *Innocenti Social Monitor 2006*[10] reports that many children are not seeing similar benefits. The report concludes that although there are large disparities among the countries in the region, most governments are not spending enough money on children.

**QUESTION:** *What do you think are the most significant, long term effects of poverty on children?*

Evidence from many countries persistently shows that children who grow up in poverty are generally more vulnerable: they are more likely to be in poor health, to have learning and behavioural difficulties, to underachieve at school, to become pregnant early, to have lower skills and aspirations, to be low-paid, unemployed and dependent on welfare.

People who find themselves in a position of extreme poverty through an accumulation of disadvantages or who suffer from degrading situations can be said to suffer 'social exclusion'.[11] The children of poor parents are especially subject to social exclusion and limited opportunities in education, employment and development. In addition to the right to an adequate standard of living, poverty directly contributes to a denial of poor children's other human rights: it can deprive a child of the right to education, to association, to rest and leisure, to participate in the community, and to other civil and political rights.

The economic, political and social processes that create poverty generally reinforce each other, exacerbating their effects on the lives of poor people. For this reason, a poor child from a minority group may be subject to the combined disadvantages of racial discrimination and the deprivations of poverty. Many immigrants, refugees, and Roma children are subject to poor education, insufficient health services and child labour in addition to social exclusion.

Governments need to address child poverty by ensuring access to social services (education, health, welfare) and providing public services (water, electricity, transportation). Community organizations also play a role in poverty alleviation by providing immediate assistance such as food, clothing, healthcare and education services. Both governments and organizations within civil society can offer income-generating projects, support small business ventures and provide employment opportunities, remedial education and skill-building trainings to poor communities.

Providing poor people with food and shelter is an essential but short term response. However, alleviating poverty in the long run requires strengthening the participation of poor people in decision making

processes, ensuring community based development and removing discrimination based on gender, ethnicity and social status. A key tactic to reducing poverty is stimulating economic growth, making markets work better for poor people, and building up their skills. All these are roles that both individuals and institutions, both governmental and civil society must unite to play.

Because child poverty and growing social exclusion are such endangering processes, in recent years several European countries have formulated government strategies to combat them. These integrated strategies aim not only to improve support measures, such as welfare services, healthcare and early childcare for all, but also to support empowerment and capacity building for families and children as well, such as access to quality education for all children, parent education and the promotion of children's participation in various decision making activities concerning the design of local policies. Combating racism and different forms of discrimination is a key part of such poverty-reduction policies.

## Relevant human rights instruments

### Council of Europe

The European Convention on Human Rights, which guarantees civil and political human rights, is complemented by the European Social Charter (ESC), adopted in 1961 and revised in 1996, which guarantees social and economic human rights. As with most human rights instruments, the European Convention on Human Rights contains a strong statement against discrimination. Although it does not specifically name poverty as a reason for social exclusion, it mentions "property...or other status." Addressing the daily lives of individuals, the European Social Charter covers many of the key components of poverty:

- **Housing:** access to adequate and affordable housing; reduction of homelessness.
- **Health:** accessible, effective health care facilities for the entire population, including preventive illness.
- **Education:** free primary and secondary education and vocational guidance; access to vocational and continuing training.
- **Employment:** an economic and social policy designed to ensure full employment.
- **Legal and social protection:** the right to social security, social welfare and social services; the right to be protected against poverty and social exclusion.

Key among these provisions of the Charter is Article 30, The right to protection against poverty and social exclusion:

With a view to ensuring the effective exercise of the right to protection against poverty and social exclusion, the Parties undertake:

- to take measures within the framework of an overall and coordinated approach to promote the effective access of persons who live or risk living in a situation of social exclusion or poverty, as well as their families, to, in particular, employment, housing, training, education, culture and social and medical assistance;
- to review these measures with a view to their adaptation if necessary.

### United Nations

There are several articles of the **Universal Declaration of Human Rights** which oblige states to provide appropriate services and support its citizens for appropriate living conditions:

- Rights to social security, Article 22
- Right to equal pay for equal work, Article 23
- Right to rest and leisure, Article 24
- Right to education, Article 26

- Right to participate in cultural life, Article 27.

Most directly related to poverty and social exclusion is Article 25:

> *(1) Everyone has the right to a standard of living adequate for the health and well-being of him-self and of his family, including food, clothing, housing and medical care and necessary social services, and the right to security in the event of unemployment, sickness, disability, widowhood, old age or other lack of livelihood in circumstances beyond his control.*

> *(2) Motherhood and childhood are entitled to special care and assistance. All children, whether born in or out of wedlock, shall enjoy the same social protection.*

Not every state has the means to support all the unemployed, sick, disabled, elderly and others unable to obtain an adequate standard living, but states are obliged to give as much support as they are able. Human rights are a direct reflection of human need. Food, clothing, shelter and healthcare are not just necessary for survival; they are also essential to human dignity.

The **Convention on the Rights of the Child** makes extensive provision for the economic well-being of children. While parents are given the principal responsibility for the care, development and support of their child, the state is enjoined to assist parents and guardians if they are unable to adequately care for the child (Article 18). The Convention also entitles all children to:

- the enjoyment of the highest attainable standard of health and to facilities for the treatment of illness and rehabilitation of health (Article 24)
- a standard of living adequate for the child's physical, mental, spiritual, moral and social development (Article 27)
- the right to benefit from social security, including social insurance (Article 26).

If every state had the means and the political will to fully implement the Children's Convention, there would be no homeless or hungry children.

..........................

## Useful Resources

- Bradshaw, Jonathan and Benette, Fran, *Fifth Report on United Kingdom National Action Plan On Social Inclusion 2003-2005*: Social Policy Research Unit, University of York, Heslington, York, 2004: http://ec.europa.eu/employment_social/social_inclusion/docs/3uk_en.pdf
- *Child Poverty in Perspective: An overview of child well-being in rich countries*: UNICEF Innocenti Research Centre, 2007: www.unicef-icdc.org/publications/pdf/rc7_eng.pdf
- *Ending Child Poverty within the EU? A review of the 2006-08 national reports on strategies for social protection and social inclusion:* Eurochild, 2007: www.nabukeuropa.de/fileadmin/user_upload/downloads/Handlungsund_Themenfelder/Jugendsozialarbeit/Final_NAPs_report_January_2007.pdf
- Huster, Ernst U., Benz, Benjamin, and Boeckh, Jurgen, *Implementation of the National Action Plan of Germany against Poverty and Social Exclusion (NAPincl) on the Regional and Local Level: Second report 2004 of the non-governmental experts*: Bochum, 2004: http://ec.europa.eu/employment_social/social_inclusion/docs/3de_en.pdf
- *Innocenti Social Monitor 2006: Understanding Child Poverty in South-eastern Europe and the Commonwealth of Independent States*: UNICEF Innocenti Research Centre, 2006: www.unicef.org/ceecis/SocialMonitor-20061018.pdf
- *Malta National Action Plan on Poverty and Social Exclusion 2004-2006*:
- http://mfss.gov.mt/documents/msp/nap_incl_mt_20040703.pdf
- Minoff, Elisa, *The UK Commitment: Ending Child Poverty by 2020*: Center for Law and Social Policy, Washington DC, 2006: www.clasp.org/publications/uk_childpoverty.pdf

- *A League Table of Child Poverty in Rich Nations*: UNICEF, 2000:
  www.unicef-icdc.org/publications/pdf/repcard1e.pdf
- *Strategy for Social Cohesion*, Council of Europe Document (CDCS (2000) 43):
  www.coe.int/t/dg3/socialpolicies/socialcohesiondev/source/strategy_fr.doc
- *Towards a EU Strategy on the Rights of the Child*: Communication from the Commission COM (2006) 367 final, Brussels, 2006:
  http://eur-lex.europa.eu/LexUriServ/site/en/com/2006/com2006_0367en01.pdf
- *World Development Report 2000/2001: Attacking poverty*, World Bank, 2000:
  http://siteresources.worldbank.org/INTPOVERTY/Resources/WDR/English-Full-Text-Report/ch3.pdf

## Useful website

- European Social Charter: http://conventions.coe.int/treaty/en/Reports/HTML/163.htmv

..............

**References**

1  *World Development Report 2000/2001*: Attacking poverty, World Bank, 2000.
2  *A League Table of Child Poverty in Rich Nations*: UNICEF, 2000, p. 4.
3  Ibid., p. iii.
4  *Strategy for Social Cohesion*, Document (CDCS (2000) 43): Council of Europe, 2000, pp. 7-10.
5  A League Table of Child Poverty in Rich Nations: UNICEF, 2000.
6  *Child Poverty in Perspective: An overview of child well-being in rich countries*: UNICEF Innocenti Research Centre, 2007, p. 5.
7  Ibid., p.6.
8  Ibid.
9  *Towards an EU Strategy on the Rights of the Child*: Communication from the Commission COM (2006) 367 final, Brussels, 2006.
10  Innocenti Social Monitor 2006: *Understanding Child Poverty in South-eastern Europe and the Commonwealth of Independent States*: UNICEF Innocenti Research Centre, 2006.
11  See European Social Charter: http://conventions.coe.int/treaty/en/Reports/HTML/163.htm

# 13. VIOLENCE

*... State Parties shall take all appropriate ... measures to protect the child from all forms of physical or mental violence, injury or abuse, neglect or negligent treatment, maltreatment or exploitation, including sexual abuse, while in the care of parent(s), legal guardian(s) or any other person who has the care of the child.*

Convention on the Rights of the Child, Article 19

Violence is the use or threat of force that can result in injury, harm, deprivation or even death. It may have a purported purpose, such as punishment or forcing someone to act against their will, or it may be an act of random malice. It may be physical, verbal, or psychological. Whatever form it may take, violence is a human rights violation. Although the Convention on the Rights of the Child and many other international and regional treaties guarantee the physical integrity, safety and dignity of the child, violence against children remains widespread. It occurs in every country in Europe, irrespective of people's origin or social stratum.

The maltreatment of children falls into four general categories:

**Emotional Abuse:** This can take the forms of verbal abuse, mental abuse and psychological maltreatment. It includes acts or failures to act by parents or caretakers that cause or could cause serious behavioural, cognitive, emotional or mental disorders.

**Neglect:** The failure to provide for the child's basic needs. Neglect can be physical, educational or emotional. Physical neglect can include failure to provide adequate food or clothing, appropriate medical care, supervision or proper protection from the elements. It may include abandonment. Educational neglect includes failing to provide appropriate schooling or special educational needs and allowing excessive truancies. Psychological neglect includes the lack of love and emotional support and failure to protect the child from abuse, including allowing the child to participate in drug and alcohol use.

**Physical Abuse:** The inflicting of physical injury upon a child. This may include burning, hitting, punching, shaking, kicking, beating or otherwise harming a child. Such injuries are abuse whether the adult intended to do harm or not. For example, an injury may result from over-discipline or physical punishment that is inappropriate to the child's age.

**Sexual Abuse:** Inappropriate sexual behaviour with a child includes fondling a child's genitals, making the child fondle the adult's genitals, intercourse, incest, rape, sodomy, exhibitionism and sexual exploitation. It involves forcing, tricking, bribing, threatening or pressurizing a child into sexual awareness or activity. Sexual abuse occurs when an older or more knowledgeable child or an adult uses a child for sexual pleasure. Sexual abuse is an abuse of power over a child and a violation of a child's right to normal, healthy, trusting relationships.

The effects of such violence on children are devastating. It undermines their well-being and their ability to learn and socialise normally. It leaves physical and emotional scars that can provoke long term traumas. Furthermore, research shows that violence begets violence: an abused child is especially likely to become an abusing parent.

Violence against children must be addressed in all settings. Education, training and capacity building are needed to raise awareness and promote a culture of non-violence. Clear policies and effective reporting mechanisms are necessary, as is advocacy to put non-violence on the political agenda.

## Violence in the family

In many European countries, society tolerates and even approves some recurrent forms of violence against children, in particular corporal punishment inflicted by the family as discipline. Such violence is indirectly sanctioned by law enforcement officials who do not recognize the acts as criminal. Even when states legislate against domestic violence, law enforcement may be selective or nonexistent. Dozen of European children still die each week from maltreatment.[1]

Violence can be hidden and hard to detect when committed by persons who are part of the children's everyday lives in places that should be havens for children, such as the school, the family or residential institutions. Because violence in the families is the least visible form of violence against children, statistics are difficult to obtain and often unreliable. Many children are afraid to speak out against family members, especially in cases of sexual abuse. This silence puts an unqualified burden of responsibility on all those who work with children to know the signs of abuse and report them in every case

One third of Council of Europe member states have abolished corporal punishment (Austria, Bulgaria, Croatia, Cyprus, Denmark, Finland, Germany, Hungary, Iceland, Italy, Latvia, Norway, Portugal, Romania, Sweden, and the Ukraine)[2] and others are committed to legal reform. Despite these positive developments, corporal punishment remains lawful in several countries and is still perceived as an acceptable form of 'discipline'. To end corporal punishment in the home requires an attitude change on the part of parents that leads to more positive, non-violent methods of bringing up children.

## Violence in schools

One in every ten school children faces violence at school, and these figures are rising.[3] The level of violence is linked less to the economic affluence of the country than to the country's attitudes towards children and the political significance of children in society.[4] Although corporal punishment is banned in most European schools, bullying and mobbing is widespread. Children who are slightly different – more clever, bigger or smaller, or with a different skin colour or accent – can find themselves the target of sarcastic humour, rumours, name-calling, intimidating situations and exclusion, as well as physical attacks on their person or belongings.

Bullying in schools may take the form of gang violence or racially motivated attacks especially targeting ethnic minorities or migrants. Today bullying often occurs in the form of 'cyberbullying', in which demeaning photographs or insulting comments about a child are circulated over the Internet. Because this form of bullying is largely anonymous, instantaneous and far reaching, it is especially harmful for affected children. For children who are the victims of such violence, school becomes a place of terror, not a place to

learn. A UN World Report on violence against children showed that girls in Europe are more often bullied than boys and that eighty percent of violence in schools is carried out by the 12-16 age group.[5]

There is a need for public awareness and zero tolerance of school violence. School officials, teachers and parents should be able to detect symptoms of violence and act promptly against it. Every school needs consistent prevention policies to eliminate violence and easy, confidential ways for children to lodge complaints. Involving children in awareness-raising and peer support are effective assets to combating violence in schools.

> The European Observatory on Violence in Schools (EOVS) researches school and urban violence. Based at Victor Ségalen University of Bordeaux in France, it studies violence in Belgium, Germany, Italy, Spain, Switzerland and the United Kingdom, as well some non-European countries, namely Canada, Japan, Mexico and Burkina Faso.
> EOVS studies the problems related to violence and coordinates an international network of collaborators, including UNESCO and the European Parliament.
> *European Observatory of Violence in Schools: www.obsviolence.com/english/presentation/index.html*

## Media and Internet exposure

The Internet and other form of media can expose young people to a wide range of risks. Whether intentional or unintentional, exposure to inappropriate material, such as violent pictures, racist propaganda and pornography, constitutes a form of violence. The Internet also makes a child open to harassment and paedophile activity, even in the safety of the family home.[6] See *Theme 9, Media and Internet* above, p. 257, for a discussion of media education to protect children from such exploitation. In 2006 the Council of Europe's Committee of Ministers adopted a special recommendation on empowering children in the new information and communications environment.[7]

## Sexual abuse of children

Child sexual abuse and exploitation are significant problems in Europe today. It can take many forms including incest, pornography, prostitution, trafficking in human beings and peer sexual assault, all of which can cause serious damage to children's mental and physical health.

It is estimated that between ten and twenty percent of children in Europe are sexually assaulted in childhood.[8] However, most victims do not report the crime perpetrated against them. Many are too young at the time to understand what has happened. Others may have no-one to trust or who will believe them, or they feel too ashamed, guilty and betrayed to tell anyone. Many are threatened and manipulated by the offender, who in the majority of cases is a family member or an adult friend known to the child.

Forced prostitution and organised paedophilia are other forms of sexual abuse where the child is forced to engage in sexual acts with strangers and other adults for money paid to the adult procurer. Children in situations of armed conflicts, displaced, migrant and refugee children, children in institutions, children who lack family support and children in poverty are particularly vulnerable to all forms of sexual exploitation. Parents, teachers, social workers and policy makers all have a role in the protection of children from sexual abuse.

## Child trafficking

Trafficking in human beings is the modern version of the slave trade. Human beings are treated as commodities to be bought and sold and subjected to every form of exploitation. Trafficking is a violation of human rights and an offence to the dignity and integrity of all human beings.

A 'child victim of trafficking' is any person under the age of eighteen who is recruited, transported, transferred, harboured or received for the purpose of exploitation, either within or outside a country. In some cases children are tricked into trafficking with promises of schooling and travel; in others their impoverished families turn them over for a cash reward.

Trafficking exposes children to violence and sexual abuse and deprives children of the right to preserve their identity, to grow up in a family, to education, healthcare, rest and leisure, and to freedom from degrading treatment or punishment. (See also discussion of child labour in *Theme 4: Education and Leisure* above, p. 231)

In Europe, trafficking children is generally for the purpose of sexual exploitation or forced labour. Trafficked children are subjected to prostitution, forced into marriage or illegally adopted; they provide cheap or unpaid labour in agriculture or sweatshops, work as house servants or beggars, and are used for sports. Because they are illegal, trafficked children are usually hidden from public view and difficult to identify. Because they often do not speak the local language and are kept under strict supervision, their opportunities to escape or seek help are severely limited.

## Vulnerable groups of children

Although violence against children is not limited to any group or economic class, some children are especially vulnerable to abuse. These include:

- **Homeless urban children:** 'Street children' face a much higher risk of sexual exploitation, especially girls. UNICEF reports that there are over 100 million children living in the streets of the world today.[9] Thousands of street children can be found in every large city in Europe, and their numbers are growing due to unemployment, poverty and immigration.

- **Children with disabilities:** Although children with disabilities are often the targets of abuse, including violence and sexual assault, child protection services rarely address their needs. Social services may, in fact, perpetuate the abuse of children with disabilities by stigmatizing them as 'special' or 'in need'. In many respects, children with disabilities are taught to be good victims, especially girls who are often valued less than boys. Disabled girls are also less likely than boys to be educated, receive adequate health care and rehabilitation treatment or be permitted to participate in their communities.[10]

- **Refugee and immigrant children:** Refugee and immigrant children may be subject to violence both within the home and in the community from acts of xenophobia. Because their parents are often unfamiliar with its laws and standards, children may be subject to harmful traditional practises such as female genital cutting and male ritual scarification. Family traumas and instability may also lead to child abuse.

- **Child mothers:** Although themselves still children and entitled to all the protections and provisions of the Convention on the Rights of the Child, girls who have babies are widely assumed to have entered adulthood whether they marry or not. They are thus caught in a kind of legal limbo, without the protections offered to children and too young to claim the legal rights of adults.

**What you can do to prevent violence against children**

- Monitor the situation of children and report any violence;
- Monitor government policies and programmes to protect children from violence and pressure authorities for protective legislation;
- Support families through parenting programmes;
- Break the silence! Speak up about violence you experience or witness;
- Challenge the social acceptance of violence;
- Raise awareness about violence against children;
- Recognize signs of violence;
- Mobilize the school and community to prohibit and eliminate bullying and other forms of violence against children;
- Teach children how to protect themselves from abuse and harm;
- Teach children non-violent ways to manage conflict;
- Do not use violence yourself.

# Relevant human rights instruments

### Council of Europe

Article 3 of the **European Convention of Human Rights** states that "No-one shall be subjected to torture or to inhuman or degrading treatment or punishment". To promote and protect this fundamental right, the Council of Europe has addressed many aspects of violence through legal means, awareness raising and campaigns (e.g. trafficking, gender-based violence, child labour, violence in the media).

The Council of Europe has established legal protections against many forms of violence:

- The **European Committee for the Prevention of Torture and Inhuman or Degrading treatment or Punishment (CPT)** develops standards for the protection of juveniles deprived of their liberty, provides non-judicial preventive machinery to protect young detainees and regularly visits young offenders' institutions.[11]
- The **Convention on Action against Trafficking in Human Beings** aims to prevent trafficking, protect the human rights of victims of trafficking and prosecute traffickers.[12] This legally binding treaty, which came into force in 2005, applies to all forms of trafficking, all victims and all forms of exploitation, including sexual, forced labour, slavery, servitude and removal of organs for sale.
- The **Convention on Cybercrime,** which includes offences related to child pornography, states in Article 9 that parties shall adopt "legislative and other measures to criminalize various specified uses of computers involving child pornography".[13]
- The **Convention on the Protection of Children against Sexual Exploitation and Sexual Abuse**, adopted in 2007, is the first treaty to target specifically child abuse. It will fill gaps in European legislation and establish a harmonized legal framework to combat this scourge that affects between 10-20% of all children in Europe.[14]

Many activities and programmes of the Council of Europe also address issues of violence against children:

- In 2006 the Council initiated 'Building Europe with and for Children'. As a follow-up to the UN Report on Violence Against Children in Europe, this three-year programme has among its key purposes that of combating various forms of violence against children, such as corporal punishment, domestic violence, sexual abuse and trafficking. In this area of its mandate,

the programme sets standards, formulates policy guidelines and oversees a strong awareness-raising campaign involving governments, parliaments, municipalities, professionals and NGOs in Europe.

- The **Human Rights Commissioner** systematically addresses children's rights and protection against violence during his monitoring visits to member countries.
- The Council of Europe **Campaign to Combat Trafficking in Human Beings** was launched in 2006 under the slogan 'Human being – not for sale'. The Campaign seeks to raise awareness of the extent of trafficking in human beings in Europe today. It highlights different measures to prevent this new form of slavery, as well as efforts to protect the human rights of victims and to prosecute the traffickers.
- In 2007 the Parliamentary Assembly of the Council of Europe initiated an all-European survey on street children and policy making to address this problem.

## United Nations

The **Universal Declaration of Human Rights** (UDHR, 1948) recognizes freedom from violence as a fundamental human right in Article 5. However, this right is developed much further in the **Convention on the Rights of the Child** (CRC, 1989). Article 19 defines many forms of ill-treatment, including sexual abuse, mental violence and exploitation:

> *States Parties shall take all appropriate legislative, administrative, social and educational measures to protect the child from all forms of physical or mental violence, injury or abuse, neglect or negligent treatment, maltreatment or exploitation, including sexual abuse, while in the care of parent(s), legal guardian(s) or any other person who has the care of the child.*

Both Articles 19 and 37 specifically protect the child from execution, which is still practised in some countries outside Europe.

As the most widely ratified of all UN human rights instruments, the Children's Convention provides a powerful legal basis for the protection of children from violence, whether from the state, from institutions, or individuals. It is invaluable for organisations of all kinds that work for the protection of children.

Domestic violence was long ignored as a 'private matter', except in case of grave bodily harm or death. However, the Vienna Declaration of 1993 recognized violence against women and girls, whether committed by the state or by individuals, as a human rights violation. This recognition was followed the same year by the adoption by the General Assembly of the **Declaration on the Elimination of Violence Against Women** and the appointment of **Special Rapporteur** on Violence against women, an expert appointed to compile information on violence against women and girls. The Declaration specifically calls for programmes in schools at all levels designed to challenge patterns in men's and women's behaviour.[15]

......................

## Useful Resources

- *Action against Trafficking in Human Beings: Prevention, protection and prosecution,* Council of Europe, 2007:
  www.coe.int/t/dg2/trafficking/campaign/Source/eg-thb-sem2_2006_Proceedings.pdf
- *Building a Europe for and with Children: The facts about children and violence,* Fact-pack, Council of Europe: www.coe.int/t/E/Com/Press/Source/Factpack_English.doc
- Campaign to Combat Violence against Women, Fact Sheet: Council of Europe: 2006: www.coe.int/T/E/Human_Rights/Equality/PDF_FS_Violen_E.pdf

- *Declaration on the Elimination of Violence against Women*: General Assembly Resolution 48/104 **of 20: UNESCO, 1993:** http://portal.unesco.org/education/en/file_download.php/7ed3f0d989b575571389ec99fb1bce6bDeclaration-Elimination-Violence-Women.pdf
- *Forced Labour, Child Labour and Human Trafficking in Europe: An ILO Perspective*: International Labour Office, Brussels, 2002: www.belgium.iom.int/STOPConference/Conference%20Papers/06.%20ILO%20-%20Final%20Brussels%20Trafficking%20Paper%20Sept.%202002.pdf
- Frau-Meigs, Divina, *Council of Europe Pan-European Forum on Human Rights in the Information Society: Empowering Children and Young People*: Council of Europe, 2006: www.euro.who.int/document/mediacentre/fs0203e.pdf
- *Gender Matters – A manual on addressing gender-based violence with young people*: Council of Europe, 2007.
- *Handbook for Parliamentarians: The Council of Europe Convention on Action against Trafficking in Human Beings*: Council of Europe, 2007: http://assembly.coe.int/committeedocs/2007/Trafficking-human-beings_E.pdf
- Kennedy, Margaret, 'Rights for Children Who Are Disabled', in *The Handbook of Children's Rights*: Routledge, London, 1995.
- May-Chahal, Corinne and Herczog, Maria, *Child sexual abuse in Europe*: Council of Europe, 2003.
- *Recommendation Rec(2006)12 of the Committee of Ministers to Member States on Empowering Children in the New Information and Communications Environment,* Council of Europe, 2006.
- *Working to Prevent the IT-Related Sexual Exploitation of Children*: Save The Children Denmark, 2005: www.redbarnet.dk/.../DWSDownload.aspx?File=Files%2FFiler%2FSeksuelt_misbrug%2FAarsberetningHotline05_ENG.pdf

..........................

## Useful Websites

- Activist Toolkit, Making rights a reality: http://web.amnesty.org/actforwomen/svaw-toolkit-eng
- Child Rights Information Network: www.crin.org
- Corporal punishment…No punishment is justifiable: www.coe.int/t/transversalprojects/children/violence/corporalPunishment_en.asp
- Council of Europe: www.coe.int/children
- Council of Europe Convention on Action against Trafficking in Human Beings: http://conventions.coe.int/Treaty/EN/Treaties/Html/197.htm
- European Observatory of Violence in Schools: www.obsviolence.com/english/presentation/index.html
- Council of Europe Commissioner for Human Rights: www.coe.int/t/commissioner/default_EN.asp
- Street Children and Homelessness: www.cyc-net.org/cyc-online/cycol-0904-Homelessness.html
- The United Nations Secretary General's Study on Violence against Children: www.violencestudy.org
- UNICEF: www.unicef.org/protection
- End Child Prostitution, Child Pornography and the Trafficking of Children for Sexual Purposes: www.ecpat.net
- International Labour Organization, International Programme for the Elimination of Child Labour (ILO-IPEC): www.ilo.org
- Institute for Research on Working Children (IREWOC): www.childlabour.net
- Coalition to Stop the Use of Child Soldiers (CSC): www.child-soldiers.org

#### References

1 *Corporal Punishment…No violence against children is justifiable*:
     www.coe.int/t/transversalprojects/children/violence/corporalPunishment_en.asp
2 *Building a Europe for and with Children*: The facts about children and violence, Fact-pack, Council of Europe:
     www.coe.int/t/E/Com/Press/Source/Factpack_English.doc
3 *The United Nations Secretary General's Study on Violence against Children*: www.violencestudy.org
4 *Violence Against Children – Europe and Central Asia*, UNICEF, p.9: www.unicef.org/ceecis/sgsvac-eca_04_01-48.pdf
5 *The United Nations Secretary General's Study on Violence against Children*: www.violencestudy.org
6 Working to Prevent the IT- Related Sexual Exploitation of Children: Save the Children Denmark, 2005.
7 Recommendation Rec(2006)12 of the Committee of Ministers to Member States on Empowering Children in the New
     Information and Communications Environment: Council of Europe, 2006.
8 *The United Nations Secretary General's Study on Violence against Children*: www.violencestudy.org
9 See Street Children and Homelessness: www.cyc-net.org/cyc-online/cycol-0904-Homelessness.html
10 Margaret Kennedy, 'Rights for Children Who are Disabled' in *The Handbook of Children's Rights*: London, Routledge, 1995, p.
     149.
11 See www.cpt.coe.int/EN/about.htm
12 Council of Europe Convention on Action against Trafficking in Human Beings:
     http://conventions.coe.int/Treaty/EN/Treaties/Html/197.htm
13 See Council of Europe Convention on Cybercrime: http://conventions.coe.int/Treaty/EN/Treaties/HTML/185.htm
14 *Council of Europe's Convention on the Protection of Children against Sexual Exploitation*, See
     www.coe.int/T/E/Legal_Affairs/Legal_cooperation/Fight_against_sexual_exploitation_of_children
15 *Declaration on the Elimination of Violence against Women*: General Assembly Resolution 48/104 of 20, Art. 4: UNESCO, 1993:
     www.unhchr.ch/huridocda/huridoca.nsf/(Symbol)/A.RES.48.104.Eng

# VI. APPENDICES

## Universal Declaration of Human Rights
## (Child-Friendly Version)

**Article 1, Right to equality:**

You are born free and equal in rights to every other human being. You have the ability to think and to tell right from wrong. You should treat others with friendship.

**Article 2, Freedom from discrimination:**

You have all these human rights no matter what your race, skin colour, sex, language, religion, opinions, family background, social or economic status, birth or nationality.

**Article 3, Right to life, liberty and personal security:**

You have the right to live, to be free and to feel safe.

**Article 4, Freedom from slavery:**

Nobody has the right to treat you as a slave, and you should not make anyone your slave.

**Article 5, Freedom from torture and degrading treatment:**

Nobody has the right to torture, harm or humiliate you.

**Article 6, Right to recognition as a person before the law:**

You have a right to be accepted everywhere as a person according to law.

**Article 7, Right to equality before the law:**

You have a right to be protected and treated equally by the law without discrimination of any kind.

**Article 8, Right to remedy by capable judges:**

If your legal rights are violated, you have the right to fair and capable judges to uphold your rights.

**Article 9, Freedom from arbitrary arrest and exile:**

Nobody has the right to arrest you, put you in prison or to force you out of your country without good reasons.

**Article 10, Right to fair public hearing:**

If you are accused of a crime, you have the right to a fair and public hearing.

**Article 11, Right to be considered innocent until proven guilty:**

1) You should be considered innocent until it can be proved in a fair trial that you are guilty.

2) You cannot be punished for doing something that was not considered a crime at the time you did it.

**Article 12, Freedom from interference with privacy, family, home and correspondence:**

You have the right to be protected if someone tries to harm your good name or enter your house, open your mail or bother you or your family without good reason.

**Article 13, Right to free movement:**

1) You have the right to come and go as you wish within your country.

2) You have the right to leave your country to go to another one, and you should be able to return to your country if you want.

**Article 14, Right to protection in another country:**

1) If someone threatens to hurt you, you have the right to go to another country and ask for protection as a refugee.

2) You lose this right if you have committed a serious crime.

**Article 15, Right to a nationality and the freedom to change it:**

1) You have the right to belong to a country and have a nationality.

2) No-one can take away your nationality without a good reason. You have a right to change your nationality if you wish.

**Article 16, Right to marriage and family:**

1) When you are legally old enough, you have the right to marry and have a family without any limitations based on your race, country or religion. Both partners have the same rights when they are married and also when they are separated.

2) Nobody should force you to marry.

3) The family is the basic unit of society, and government should protect it.

**Article 17, Right to own property:**

1) You have the right to own things.

2) Nobody has the right to take these things from you without a good reason.

**Article 18, Freedom of thought, conscience and religion:**

You have the right to your own thoughts and to believe in any religion. You are free to practise your religion or beliefs and also to change them.

**Article 19, Freedom of opinion and information:**

You have the right to hold and express your own opinions. You should be able to share your opinions with others, including people from other countries, through any ways.

**Article 20, Right to peaceful assembly and association:**

1) You have the right to meet peacefully with other people.

2) No-one can force you to belong to a group.

**Article 21, Right to participate in government and elections:**

1) You have the right participate in your government, either by holding an office or by electing someone to represent you.

2) You and everyone has the right to serve your country.

3) Governments should be elected regularly by fair and secret voting.

**Article 22, Right to social security:**

The society you live in should provide you with social security and the rights necessary for your dignity and development.

**Article 23, Right to desirable work and to join trade unions:**

1) You have the right to work, to choose your work and to work in good conditions.

2) People who do the same work should get the same pay.

3) You should be able to earn a salary that allows you to live and support your family.

4) All people who work have the right to join together in unions to defend their interests.

**Article 24, Right to rest and leisure:**

You have the right to rest and free time. Your workday should not be too long, and you should be able to take regular paid holidays.

**Article 25, Right to adequate living standard:**

1) You have the right to the things you and your family need to have a healthy and comfortable life, including food, clothing, housing, medical care and other social services. You have a right to help if you are out of work or unable to work.

2) Mothers and children should receive special care and help.

**Article 26, Right to education:**

1) You have the right to go to go to school. Primary schooling should be free and required. You should be able to learn a profession or continue your studies as far as you can.

2) At school, you should be able to develop all your talents and learn to respect others, whatever their race, religion or nationality.

3) Your parents should have a say in the kind of education you receive.

**Article 27, Right to participate in the cultural life of community:**

1) You have the right to participate in the traditions and learning of your community, to enjoy the arts and to benefit from scientific progress.

2) If you are an artist, writer or scientist, your work should be protected and you should be able to benefit from it.

**Article 28, Right to a social order:**

You have a right to the kind of world where you and all people can enjoy these rights and freedoms.

**Article 29, Responsibilities to the community**

1) Your personality can only fully develop within your community, and you have responsibilities to that community.

2) The law should guarantee human rights. It should allow everyone to respect others and to be respected.

3) These rights and freedoms should support the purposes and principles of the United Nations.

**Article 30, Freedom from interference in these human rights:**

No person, group or government anywhere in the world should do anything to destroy these rights.

# Universal Declaration of Human Rights

Adopted and proclaimed by General Assembly resolution 217 A (III) of 10 December 1948

On December 10, 1948 the General Assembly of the United Nations adopted and proclaimed the Universal Declaration of Human Rights the full text of which appears in the following pages. Following this historic act the Assembly called upon all Member countries to publicize the text of the Declaration and "to cause it to be disseminated, displayed, read and expounded principally in schools and other educational institutions, without distinction based on the political status of countries or territories."

## PREAMBLE

Whereas recognition of the inherent dignity and of the equal and inalienable rights of all members of the human family is the foundation of freedom, justice and peace in the world,

Whereas disregard and contempt for human rights have resulted in barbarous acts which have outraged the conscience of mankind, and the advent of a world in which human beings shall enjoy freedom of speech and belief and freedom from fear and want has been proclaimed as the highest aspiration of the common people,

Whereas it is essential, if man is not to be compelled to have recourse, as a last resort, to rebellion against tyranny and oppression, that human rights should be protected by the rule of law,

Whereas it is essential to promote the development of friendly relations between nations,

Whereas the peoples of the United Nations have in the Charter reaffirmed their faith in fundamental human rights, in the dignity and worth of the human person and in the equal rights of men and women and have determined to promote social progress and better standards of life in larger freedom,

Whereas Member States have pledged themselves to achieve, in cooperation with the United Nations, the promotion of universal respect for and observance of human rights and fundamental freedoms,

Whereas a common understanding of these rights and freedoms is of the greatest importance for the full realization of this pledge,

Now, Therefore THE GENERAL ASSEMBLY proclaims THIS UNIVERSAL DECLARATION OF HUMAN RIGHTS as a common standard of achievement for all peoples and all nations, to the end that every individual and every organ of society, keeping this Declaration constantly in mind, shall strive by teaching and education to promote respect for these rights and freedoms and by progressive measures, national and international, to secure their universal and effective recognition and observance, both among the peoples of Member States themselves and among the peoples of territories under their jurisdiction.

### Article 1.

All human beings are born free and equal in dignity and rights. They are endowed with reason and conscience and should act towards one another in a spirit of brotherhood.

### Article 2.

Everyone is entitled to all the rights and freedoms set forth in this Declaration, without distinction of any kind, such as race, colour, sex, language, religion, political or other opinion, national or social origin, property, birth or other status. Furthermore, no distinction shall be made on the basis of the political, jurisdictional or international status of the country or territory to which a person belongs, whether it be independent, trust, non-self-governing or under any other limitation of sovereignty.

### Article 3.

Everyone has the right to life, liberty and security of person.

### Article 4.

No-one shall be held in slavery or servitude; slavery and the slave trade shall be prohibited in all their forms.

### Article 5.

No-one shall be subjected to torture or to cruel, inhuman or degrading treatment or punishment.

### Article 6.

Everyone has the right to recognition everywhere as a person before the law.

### Article 7.

All are equal before the law and are entitled without any discrimination to equal protection of the law. All are entitled to equal protection against any discrimination in violation of this Declaration and against any incitement to such discrimination.

### Article 8.

Everyone has the right to an effective remedy by the competent national tribunals for acts violating the fundamental rights granted him by the constitution or by law.

### Article 9.

No-one shall be subjected to arbitrary arrest, detention or exile.

### Article 10.

Everyone is entitled in full equality to a fair and public hearing by an independent and impartial tribunal, in the determination of his rights and obligations and of any criminal charge

against him.

### Article 11.

(1) Everyone charged with a penal offence has the right to be presumed innocent until proved guilty according to law in a public trial at which he has had all the guarantees necessary for his defense.

(2) No-one shall be held guilty of any penal offence on account of any act or omission which did not constitute a penal offence, under national or international law, at the time when it was committed. Nor shall a heavier penalty be imposed than the one that was applicable at the time the penal offence was committed.

### Article 12.

No-one shall be subjected to arbitrary interference with his privacy, family, home or correspondence, nor to attacks upon his honour and reputation. Everyone has the right to the protection of the law against such interference or attacks.

### Article 13.

(1) Everyone has the right to freedom of movement and residence within the borders of each state.

(2) Everyone has the right to leave any country, including his own, and to return to his country.

### Article 14.

(1) Everyone has the right to seek and to enjoy in other countries asylum from persecution.

(2) This right may not be invoked in the case of prosecutions genuinely arising from non-political crimes or from acts contrary to the purposes and principles of the United Nations.

### Article 15.

(1) Everyone has the right to a nationality.

(2) No-one shall be arbitrarily deprived of his nationality nor denied the right to change his nationality.

### Article 16.

(1) Men and women of full age, without any limitation due to race, nationality or religion, have the right to marry and to found a family. They are entitled to equal rights as to marriage, during marriage and at its dissolution.

(2) Marriage shall be entered into only with the free and full consent of the intending spouses.

(3) The family is the natural and fundamental group unit of society and is entitled to protection by society and the State.

### Article 17.

(1) Everyone has the right to own property alone as well as in association with others.

(2) No-one shall be arbitrarily deprived of his property.

### Article 18.

Everyone has the right to freedom of thought, conscience and religion; this right includes freedom to change his religion or belief, and freedom, either alone or in community with others and in public or private, to manifest his religion or belief in teaching, practise, worship and observance.

### Article 19.

Everyone has the right to freedom of opinion and expression; this right includes freedom to hold opinions without interference and to seek, receive and impart information and ideas through any media and regardless of frontiers.

### Article 20.

(1) Everyone has the right to freedom of peaceful assembly and association.

(2) No-one may be compelled to belong to an association.

### Article 21.

(1) Everyone has the right to take part in the government of his country, directly or through freely chosen representatives.

(2) Everyone has the right of equal access to public service in his country.

(3) The will of the people shall be the basis of the authority of government; this will shall be expressed in periodic and genuine elections which shall be by universal and equal suffrage and shall be held by secret vote or by equivalent free voting procedures.

### Article 22.

Everyone, as a member of society, has the right to social security and is entitled to realization, through national effort and international cooperation and in accordance with the organization and resources of each State, of the economic, social and cultural rights indispensable for his dignity and the free development of his personality.

### Article 23.

(1) Everyone has the right to work, to free choice of employment, to just and favourable conditions of work and to protection against unemployment.

(2) Everyone, without any discrimination, has the right to equal pay for equal work.

(3) Everyone who works has the right to just and favourable remuneration ensuring for himself and his family an existence worthy of human dignity, and supplemented, if necessary, by other means of social protection.

(4) Everyone has the right to form and to join trade unions for the protection of his interests.

### Article 24.

Everyone has the right to rest and leisure, including reasonable limitation of working hours and periodic holidays with pay.

### Article 25.

(1) Everyone has the right to a standard of living adequate for the health and well-being of himself and of his family, includ-

ing food, clothing, housing and medical care and necessary social services, and the right to security in the event of unemployment, sickness, disability, widowhood, old age or other lack of livelihood in circumstances beyond his control.

(2) Motherhood and childhood are entitled to special care and assistance. All children, whether born in or out of wedlock, shall enjoy the same social protection.

### Article 26.

(1) Everyone has the right to education. Education shall be free, at least in the elementary and fundamental stages. Elementary education shall be compulsory. Technical and professional education shall be made generally available and higher education shall be equally accessible to all on the basis of merit.

(2) Education shall be directed to the full development of the human personality and to the strengthening of respect for human rights and fundamental freedoms. It shall promote understanding, tolerance and friendship among all nations, racial or religious groups, and shall further the activities of the United Nations for the maintenance of peace.

(3) Parents have a prior right to choose the kind of education that shall be given to their children.

### Article 27.

(1) Everyone has the right freely to participate in the cultural life of the community, to enjoy the arts and to share in scientific advancement and its benefits.

(2) Everyone has the right to the protection of the moral and material interests resulting from any scientific, literary or ar-

tistic production of which he is the author.

### Article 28.

Everyone is entitled to a social and international order in which the rights and freedoms set forth in this Declaration can be fully realized.

### Article 29.

(1) Everyone has duties to the community in which alone the free and full development of his personality is possible.

(2) In the exercise of his rights and freedoms, everyone shall be subject only to such limitations as are determined by law solely for the purpose of securing due recognition and respect for the rights and freedoms of others and of meeting the just requirements of morality, public order and the general welfare in a democratic society.

(3) These rights and freedoms may in no case be exercised contrary to the purposes and principles of the United Nations.

### Article 30.

Nothing in this Declaration may be interpreted as implying for any State, group or person any right to engage in any activity or to perform any act aimed at the destruction of any of the rights and freedoms set forth herein.

..............

**Resource:**

Universal Declaration of Human Rights: www.un.org/Overview/rights.html

# The European Convention on Human Rights
## (Child-Friendly Version)

## Section I: Rights and Freedoms

### Article 1, Obligation to respect human rights:

If you live in a country that has agreed to this convention, you have a right to these basic civil and political rights whether you are a citizen or not.

### Article 2, Right to life:

You have the right to life, and this right is protected by law.[1]

### Article 3, Freedom from torture:

Nobody is allowed to torture, harm or humiliate you.

### Article 4, Freedom from slavery and forced labour:

Nobody is allowed to treat you as a slave, and you should not make anyone your slave. No-one can make you work by force.

### Article 5, Right to liberty and security

You have the right to freedom and safety. No-one is allowed to take away this right except by legal means. If you are arrested, you have many rights, including to understand why you are arrested, to have a prompt hearing and to challenge your arrest,

### Article 6, Right to a fair trial:

If you are accused of a crime, you have the right to a fair and public hearing.

### Article 7, No punishment without law:

You cannot be punished for doing something that was not considered a crime at the time you did it.

### Article 8, Right to respect for private and family life home and correspondence:

You have the right to be protected if someone tries to enter your house, open your letters, or bother you or your family without good reasons.

### Article 9, Freedom of thought, conscience and religion:

You have the right to your own thoughts and to believe in any religion. You are free to practise your religion or beliefs and also to change them.

### Article 10, Freedom of expression:

You have the right to think what you want and responsibly to say what you like. You should be able to share your ideas and opinions in any way including newspapers and magazines, radio, television, and the Internet.

### Article 11, Freedom of assembly and association:

You have the right to meet peacefully with other people, including the right to form and to join trade unions.

### Article 12, Right to marry:

When you are legally old enough, you have the right to marry and to found a family.

### Article 13, Right to an effective remedy:

If your rights are violated by another person or by the government, you have the right to ask for help from the courts or other public bodies to uphold your rights.

### Article 14, Freedom from discrimination:

You have all the rights and freedoms in this convention no matter what your sex, race, colour, language, religion, political or other opinion, national or social background, association with a minority group, economic status, birth or other status.

### Article 15, Derogation in time of emergency:

The government may suspend its duties to uphold these rights and freedoms in time of war. This suspension may not include Article 2, the Right to Life.

### Article 16, Restrictions on political activity of aliens:

The government cannot restrict your political activity simply because you are not a citizen of that country.

---

1  Two additions to the Convention (called protocols) aim at abolishing the death penalty in Europe.

Article 17, Prohibition of abuse of rights:

No person, group or government anywhere in the world may do anything to destroy these rights.

Article 18, Limitation on use of restrictions on rights:

Your rights and freedoms can only be limited in ways set out in this convention.

## Section II: European Court of Human Rights

Articles 19 to 51, The European Court of Human Rights, its mandate and activities:

The Convention establishes a European Court of Human Rights to deal with cases brought to it by individuals and governments. The Judges are entirely independent and are elected by the Parliamentary Assembly of the Council of Europe.

## Section III, Miscellaneous provisions

Articles 52 to 59, Application of rights in this convention

The Committee of Ministers of the Council of Europe oversees how governments respect this convention and fulfill their obligations to promote and protect human rights.

## Protocols to the European Convention on Human Rights

Since the ECHR was adopted in 1950, the Council of Europe has made important additions, known as **protocols**, which add to the human rights of people living in Europe. Among the major rights and freedoms added are these:

### Protocol No. 1:

Article 1, Right to property

You have the right to own property and use your possessions.

Article 2, Right to education

You have the right to go to school.

Article 3, Right to free elections

You have the right to elect the government of your country by secret vote.

### Protocol No. 4:

Article 2, Freedom of movement

If you are in a country legally, you have the right to travel or live wherever you want within it and also to return to your home country.

### Protocols Nos. 6 and 13:

Article 1, Freedom from the death penalty

You cannot be condemned to death or executed by the government either in peace- or wartime.

### Protocol No. 7:

Article 2, Right of appeal in criminal matters

If you have been convicted of a crime, you can appeal to a higher court.

### Protocol No. 12:

Article 1, General protection against discrimination

Public authorities cannot discriminate against you for reasons like your skin colour, sex, language, political or religious beliefs, or origins.

# Convention on the Rights of the Child (CRC)
## (Child-Friendly Version)

Article 1, Definition of a child:

Until you are eighteen, you are considered a child and have all the rights in this convention.

Article 2, Freedom from discrimination:

You should not be discriminated against for any reason, including your race, colour, sex, language, religion, opinion, religion, origin, social or economic status, disability, birth, or any other quality of your or your parents or guardian.

Article 3, The child's best interest:

All actions and decisions that affect children should be based on what is best for you or any child.

Article 4, Enjoying the rights in the Convention:

Governments should make these rights available to you and all children.

Article 5, Parental guidance and the child's growing abillities:

Your family has the main responsibility for guiding you, so that as you grow, you learn to use your rights properly. Governments should respect this right.

Article 6, Right to life and development:

You have the right to live and grow well. Governments should ensure that you survive and develop healthily.

Article 7, Birth registration, name, nationality and parental care:

You have the right to have your birth legally registered, to have a name and nationality and to know and to be cared for by your parents.

Article 8, Preservation of identity:

Governments should respect your right to a name, a nationality and family ties.

Article 9, Separation from parents:

You should not be separated from your parents unless it is for your own good (for example, if a parent mistreats or neglects you). If your parents have separated, you have the right to stay in contact with both of them unless this might hurt you.

Article 10, Family reunification:

If your parents live in different countries, you should be allowed to move between those countries so that you can stay in contact with your parents or get back together as a family.

Article 11, Protection from illegal transfer to another country:

Governments must take steps to stop you being taken out of their own country illegally.

Article 12, Respect for the child's opinion:

When adults are making decisions that affect you, you have the right to say freely what you think should happen and to have your opinions taken into account.

Article 13, Freedom of expression and information:

You have the right to seek, get and share information in all forms (e.g. through writing, art, television, radio and the Internet) as long as the information is not damaging to you or to others.

Article 14, Freedom of thought, conscience and religion:

You have the right to think and believe what you want and to practise your religion as long as you do not stop other people from enjoying their rights. Your parents should guide you on these matters.

Article 15, Freedom of association and peaceful assembly:

You have the right to meet and to join groups and organisations with other children as long as this does not stop other people from enjoying their rights.

Article 16, Privacy, honour and reputation:

You have a right to privacy. No-one should harm your good

name, enter your house, open your letters and emails or bother you or your family without a good reason.

### Article 17, Access to information and media:

You have the right to reliable information from a variety of sources, including books, newspapers and magazines, television, radio and the Internet. Information should be beneficial and understandable to you.

### Article 18, Parents' joint responsibilities:

Both your parents share responsibility for bringing you up and should always consider what is best for you. Governments should provide services to help parents, especially if both parents work.

### Article 19, Protection from all forms of violence, abuse and neglect:

Governments should ensure that you are properly cared for and protect you from violence, abuse and neglect by your parents or anyone else who looks after you.

### Article 20, Alternative care:

If parents and family cannot care for you properly, then you must be looked after by people who respect your religion, traditions and language.

### Article 21, Adoption:

If you are adopted, the first concern must be what is best for you, whether you are adopted in your birth country or if you are taken to live in another country.

### Article 22, Refugee children:

If you have come to a new country because your home country was unsafe, you have a right to protection and support. You have the same rights as children born in that country.

### Article 23, Disabled children:

If you have any kind of disability, you should have special care, support and education so that you can lead a full and independent life and participate in the community to the best of your ability.

### Article 24, Healthcare and health services:

You have the right to good quality health-care (e.g. medicine, hospitals, health professionals). You also have the right to clean water, nutritious food, a clean environment and health education so that you can stay healthy. Rich countries should help poorer countries achieve this.

### Article 25, Periodic review of treatment:

If you are looked after by local authorities or institutions rather than by your parents, you should have your situation reviewed regularly to make sure you have good care and treatment.

### Article 26, Benefit from social security:

The society in which you live should provide you with benefits of social security that help you develop and live in good conditions (e.g. education, culture, nutrition, health, social welfare). The Government should provide extra money for the children of families in need.

### Article 27, Adequate standard of living:

You should live in good conditions that help you develop physically, mentally, spiritually, morally and socially. The Government should help families who cannot afford to provide this.

### Article 28, Right to education:

You have a right to education. Discipline in schools should respect your human dignity. Primary education should be free and required. Rich countries should help poorer countries achieve this.

### Article 29, The aims of education:

Education should develop your personality, talents and mental and physical skills to the fullest. It should prepare you for life and encourage you to respect your parents and your own and other nations and cultures. You have a right to learn about your rights.

### Article 30, Children of minorities and native origin:

You have a right to learn and use the traditions, religion and language of your family, whether or not these are shared by most people in your country.

### Article 31, Leisure, play and culture:

You have a right to relax and play and to join in a wide range of recreational and cultural activities.

### Article 32, Child labour:

The government should protect you from work that is dangerous to your health or development, that inter-

feres with your education or that might lead people to take advantage of you.

### Article 33, Children and drug abuse:

The Government should provide ways of protecting you from using, producing or distributing dangerous drugs.

### Article 34, Protection from sexual exploitation:

The government should protect you from sexual abuse.

### Article 35, Protection from trafficking, sale, and abduction:

The government should make sure that you are not kidnapped, sold or taken to other countries to be exploited.

### Article 36, Protection from other forms of exploitation:

You should be protected from any activities that could harm your development and well-being.

### Article 37, Protection from torture, degrading treatment and loss of liberty:

If you break the law, you should not be treated cruelly. You should not be put in prison with adults and should be able to stay in contact with your family.

### Article 38, Protection of children affected by armed conflict:

If you are under fifteen (under eighteen in most European countries), governments should not allow you to join the army or take any direct part in warfare. Children in war zones should receive special protection.

### Article 39, Rehabilitation of child victims:

If you were neglected, tortured or abused, were a victim of exploitation and warfare, or were put in prison, you should receive special help to regain your physical and mental health and rejoin society.

### Article 40, Juvenile justice:

If you are accused of breaking the law, you must be treated in a way that respects your dignity. You should receive legal help and only be given a prison sentences for the most serious crimes.

### Article 41, Respect for higher human rights standards:

If the laws of your country are better for children than the articles of the Convention, then those laws should be followed.

### Article 42, Making the Convention widely known:

The Government should make the Convention known to all parents, institutions and children.

### Articles 43-54, Duties of Governments:

These articles explain how adults and governments should work together to make sure all children get all their rights

**Note**: The CRC was **adopted** by the UN General Assembly in 1989 and **entered into force** as international law in 1990. The CRC has 54 articles that define the rights of children and how these rights are to be protected and promoted by governments. Almost every country in the world has **ratified** this Convention, promising to recognize all the rights it contains.

# Convention on the Rights of the Child

Adopted and opened for signature, ratification and accession by General Assembly resolution 44/25 of 20 November 1989
entry into force 2 September 1990, in accordance with article 49

## Preamble

### The States Parties to the present Convention,

Considering that, in accordance with the principles proclaimed in the Charter of the United Nations, recognition of the inherent dignity and of the equal and inalienable rights of all members of the human family is the foundation of freedom, justice and peace in the world,

Bearing in mind that the peoples of the United Nations have, in the Charter, reaffirmed their faith in fundamental human rights and in the dignity and worth of the human person, and have determined to promote social progress and better standards of life in larger freedom,

Recognizing that the United Nations has, in the Universal Declaration of Human Rights and in the International Covenants on Human Rights, proclaimed and agreed that everyone is entitled to all the rights and freedoms set forth therein, without distinction of any kind, such as race, colour, sex, language, religion, political or other opinion, national or social origin, property, birth or other status,

Recalling that, in the Universal Declaration of Human Rights, the United Nations has proclaimed that childhood is entitled to special care and assistance,

Convinced that the family, as the fundamental group of society and the natural environment for the growth and well-being of all its members and particularly children, should be afforded the necessary protection and assistance so that it can fully assume its responsibilities within the community,

Recognizing that the child, for the full and harmonious development of his or her personality, should grow up in a family environment, in an atmosphere of happiness, love and understanding,

Considering that the child should be fully prepared to live an individual life in society, and brought up in the spirit of the ideals proclaimed in the Charter of the United Nations, and in particular in the spirit of peace, dignity, tolerance, freedom, equality and solidarity,

Bearing in mind that the need to extend particular care to the child has been stated in the Geneva Declaration of the Rights of the Child of 1924 and in the Declaration of the Rights of the Child adopted by the General Assembly on 20 November 1959 and recognized in the Universal Declaration of Human Rights, in the International Covenant on Civil and Political Rights (in particular in articles 23 and 24), in the International Covenant on Economic, Social and Cultural Rights (in particular in article 10) and in the statutes and relevant instruments of specialized agencies and international organizations concerned with the welfare of children,

Bearing in mind that, as indicated in the Declaration of the Rights of the Child, "the child, by reason of his physical and mental immaturity, needs special safeguards and care, including appropriate legal protection, before as well as after birth",

Recalling the provisions of the Declaration on Social and Legal Principles relating to the Protection and Welfare of Children, with Special Reference to Foster Placement and Adoption Nationally and Internationally; the United Nations Standard Minimum Rules for the Administration of Juvenile Justice (The Beijing Rules) ; and the Declaration on the Protection of Women and Children in Emergency and Armed Conflict, Recognizing that, in all countries in the world, there are children living in exceptionally difficult conditions, and that such children need special consideration,

Taking due account of the importance of the traditions and cultural values of each people for the protection and harmonious development of the child, Recognizing the importance of international cooperation for improving the living conditions of children in every country, in particular in the developing countries,

### Have agreed as follows:

## PART I

### Article 1

For the purposes of the present Convention, a child means every human being below the age of eighteen years unless under the law applicable to the child, majority is attained earlier.

### Article 2

1. States Parties shall respect and ensure the rights set forth in the present Convention to each child within their jurisdiction without discrimination of any kind, irrespective of the child's or his or her parent's or legal guardian's race, colour, sex, language, religion, political or other opinion, national, ethnic or social origin, property, disability, birth or other status.

2. States Parties shall take all appropriate measures to ensure that the child is protected against all forms of discrimination or punishment on the basis of the status, activities, expressed opinions, or beliefs of the child's parents, legal guardians, or family members.

### Article 3

1. In all actions concerning children, whether undertaken by public or private social welfare institutions, courts of law, administrative authorities or legislative bodies, the best interests of the child shall be a primary consideration.

2. States Parties undertake to ensure the child such protection and care as is necessary for his or her well-being, taking into account the rights and duties of his or her parents, legal guardians, or other individuals legally responsible for him or her, and, to this end, shall take all appropriate legislative and administrative measures.

3. States Parties shall ensure that the institutions, services and facilities responsible for the care or protection of children shall conform with the standards established by competent authorities, particularly in the areas of safety, health, in the number and suitability of their staff, as well as competent supervision.

## Article 4

States Parties shall undertake all appropriate legislative, administrative, and other measures for the implementation of the rights recognized in the present Convention. With regard to economic, social and cultural rights, States Parties shall undertake such measures to the maximum extent of their available resources and, where needed, within the framework of international cooperation.

## Article 5

States Parties shall respect the responsibilities, rights and duties of parents or, where applicable, the members of the extended family or community as provided for by local custom, legal guardians or other persons legally responsible for the child, to provide, in a manner consistent with the evolving capacities of the child, appropriate direction and guidance in the exercise by the child of the rights recognized in the present Convention.

## Article 6

1. States Parties recognize that every child has the inherent right to life. States Parties shall ensure to the maximum extent possible the survival and development of the child.

## Article 7

1. The child shall be registered immediately after birth and shall have the right from birth to a name, the right to acquire a nationality and. as far as possible, the right to know and be cared for by his or her parents.

2. States Parties shall ensure the implementation of these rights in accordance with their national law and their obligations under the relevant international instruments in this field, in particular where the child would otherwise be stateless.

## Article 8

1. States Parties undertake to respect the right of the child to preserve his or her identity, including nationality, name and family relations as recognized by law without unlawful interference.

2. Where a child is illegally deprived of some or all of the elements of his or her identity, States Parties shall provide appropriate assistance and protection, with a view to re-establishing speedily his or her identity.

## Article 9

1. States Parties shall ensure that a child shall not be separated from his or her parents against their will, except when competent authorities subject to judicial review determine, in accordance with applicable law and procedures, that such separation is necessary for the best interests of the child.

2. Such determination may be necessary in a particular case such as one involving abuse or neglect of the child by the parents, or one where the parents are living separately and a decision must be made as to the child's place of residence.

3. In any proceedings pursuant to paragraph 1 of the present article, all interested parties shall be given an opportunity to participate in the proceedings and make their views known.

4. States Parties shall respect the right of the child who is separated from one or both parents to maintain personal relations and direct contact with both parents on a regular basis, except if it is contrary to the child's best interests.

5. Where such separation results from any action initiated by a State Party, such as the detention, imprisonment, exile, deportation or death (including death arising from any cause while the person is in the custody of the State) of one or both parents or of the child, that State Party shall, upon request, provide the parents, the child or, if appropriate, another member of the family with the essential information concerning the whereabouts of the absent member(s) of the family unless the provision of the information would be detrimental to the well-being of the child. States Parties shall further ensure that the submission of such a request shall of itself entail no adverse consequences for the person(s) concerned.

## Article 10

1. In accordance with the obligation of States Parties under article 9, paragraph 1, applications by a child or his or her parents to enter or leave a State Party for the purpose of family reunification shall be dealt with by States Parties in a positive, humane and expeditious manner. States Parties shall further ensure that the submission of such a request shall entail no adverse consequences for the applicants and for the members of their family.

2. A child whose parents reside in different States shall have the right to maintain on a regular basis, save in exceptional circumstances personal relations and direct contacts with both parents. Towards that end and in accordance with the obligation of States Parties under article 9, paragraph 1, States Parties shall respect the right of the child and his or her parents to leave any country, including their own, and to enter their own country. The right to leave any country shall be subject only to such restrictions as are prescribed by law and which are necessary to protect the national security, public order (ordre public), public health or morals or the rights and freedoms of others and are consistent with the other rights recognized in the present Convention.

## Article 11

1. States Parties shall take measures to combat the illicit transfer and non-return of children abroad.
2. To this end, States Parties shall promote the conclusion of bilateral or multilateral agreements or accession to existing agreements.

## Article 12

1. States Parties shall assure to the child who is capable of forming his or her own views the right to express those views freely in all matters affecting the child, the views of the child being given due weight in accordance with the age and maturity of the child.
2. For this purpose, the child shall in particular be provided the opportunity to be heard in any judicial and administrative proceedings affecting the child, either directly, or through a representative or an appropriate body, in a manner consistent with the procedural rules of national law.

## Article 13

1. The child shall have the right to freedom of expression; this right shall include freedom to seek, receive and impart information and ideas of all kinds, regardless of frontiers, either orally, in writing or in print, in the form of art, or through any other media of the child's choice.
2. The exercise of this right may be subject to certain restrictions, but these shall only be such as are provided by law and are necessary:
    a. For respect of the rights or reputations of others; or
    b. For the protection of national security or of public order (ordre public), or of public health or morals.

## Article 14

1. States Parties shall respect the right of the child to freedom of thought, conscience and religion.
2. States Parties shall respect the rights and duties of the parents and, when applicable, legal guardians, to provide direction to the child in the exercise of his or her right in a manner consistent with the evolving capacities of the child.
3. Freedom to manifest one's religion or beliefs may be subject only to such limitations as are prescribed by law and are necessary to protect public safety, order, health or morals, or the fundamental rights and freedoms of others.

## Article 15

1. States Parties recognize the rights of the child to freedom of association and to freedom of peaceful assembly.
2. No restrictions may be placed on the exercise of these rights other than those imposed in conformity with the law and which are necessary in a democratic society in the interests of national security or public safety, public order (ordre public), the protection of public health or morals or the protection of the rights and freedoms of others.

## Article 16

1. No child shall be subjected to arbitrary or unlawful interference with his or her privacy, family, home or correspondence, nor to unlawful attacks on his or her honour and reputation.
2. The child has the right to the protection of the law against such interference or attacks.

## Article 17

States Parties recognize the important function performed by the mass media and shall ensure that the child has access to information and material from a diversity of national and international sources, especially those aimed at the promotion of his or her social, spiritual and moral well-being and physical and mental health.

To this end, States Parties shall:

a. Encourage the mass media to disseminate information and material of social and cultural benefit to the child and in accordance with the spirit of article 29;
b. Encourage international cooperation in the production, exchange and dissemination of such information and material from a diversity of cultural, national and international sources;
c. Encourage the production and dissemination of children's books;
d. Encourage the mass media to have particular regard to the linguistic needs of the child who belongs to a minority group or who is indigenous;
e. Encourage the development of appropriate guidelines for the protection of the child from information and material injurious to his or her well-being, bearing in mind the provisions of articles 13 and 18.

## Article 18

1. States Parties shall use their best efforts to ensure recognition of the principle that both parents have common responsibilities for the upbringing and development of the child. Parents or, as the case may be, legal guardians, have the primary responsibility for the upbringing and development of the child. The best interests of the child will be their basic concern.
2. For the purpose of guaranteeing and promoting the rights set forth in the present Convention, States Parties shall render appropriate assistance to parents and legal guardians in the performance of their child-rearing responsibilities and shall ensure the development of institutions, facilities and services for the care of children.
3. States Parties shall take all appropriate measures to ensure that children of working parents have the right to benefit from childcare services and facilities for which they are eligible.

## Article 19

1. States Parties shall take all appropriate legislative, administrative, social and educational measures to protect the child from all forms of physical or mental violence, injury or abuse, neglect or negligent treatment, maltreatment or exploitation, including sexual abuse, while in the care of parent(s), legal guardian(s) or any other person who has the care of the child.

2. Such protective measures should, as appropriate, include effective procedures for the establishment of social programmes to provide necessary support for the child and for those who have the care of the child, as well as for other forms of prevention and for identification, reporting, referral, investigation,treatment and follow-up of instances of child maltreatment described heretofore, and, as appropriate, for judicial involvement.

## Article 20

1. A child temporarily or permanently deprived of his or her family environment, or in whose own best interests cannot be allowed to remain in that environment, shall be entitled to special protection and assistance provided by the State.

2. States Parties shall in accordance with their national laws ensure alternative care for such a child.

3. Such care could include, inter alia, foster placement, kafalah of Islamic law, adoption or if necessary placement in suitable institutions for the care of children. When considering solutions, due regard shall be paid to the desirability of continuity in a child's upbringing and to the child's ethnic, religious, cultural and linguistic background.

## Article 21

States Parties that recognize and/or permit the system of adoption shall ensure that the best interests of the child shall be the paramount consideration and they shall:

a. Ensure that the adoption of a child is authorized only by competent authorities who determine, in accordance with applicable law and procedures and on the basis of all pertinent and reliable information, that the adoption is permissible in view of the child's status concerning parents, relatives and legal guardians and that, if required, the persons concerned have given their informed consent to the adoption on the basis of such counselling as may be necessary;

b. Recognize that inter-country adoption may be considered as an alternative means of child's care, if the child cannot be placed in a foster or an adoptive family or cannot in any suitable manner be cared for in the child's country of origin;

c. Ensure that the child concerned by inter-country adoption enjoys safeguards and standards equivalent to those existing in the case of national adoption;

d. Take all appropriate measures to ensure that, in inter-country adoption, the placement does not result in improper financial gain for those involved in it;

e. Promote, where appropriate, the objectives of the present article by concluding bilateral or multilateral arrangements or agreements, and endeavour, within this framework, to ensure that the placement of the child in another country is carried out by competent authorities or organs.

## Article 22

1. States Parties shall take appropriate measures to ensure that a child who is seeking refugee status or who is considered a refugee in accordance with applicable international or domestic law and procedures shall, whether unaccompanied or accompanied by his or her parents or by any other person, receive appropriate protection and humanitarian assistance in the enjoyment of applicable rights set forth in the present Convention and in other international human rights or humanitarian instruments to which the said States are Parties.

2. For this purpose, States Parties shall provide, as they consider appropriate, cooperation in any efforts by the United Nations and other competent intergovernmental organizations or non-governmental organizations co-operating with the United Nations to protect and assist such a child and to trace the parents or other members of the family of any refugee child in order to obtain information necessary for reunification with his or her family. In cases where no parents or other members of the family can be found, the child shall be accorded the same protection as any other child permanently or temporarily deprived of his or her family environment for any reason , as set forth in the present Convention.

## Article 23

1. States Parties recognize that a mentally or physically disabled child should enjoy a full and decent life, in conditions which ensure dignity, promote self-reliance and facilitate the child's active participation in the community.

2. States Parties recognize the right of the disabled child to special care and shall encourage and ensure the extension, subject to available resources, to the eligible child and those responsible for his or her care, of assistance for which application is made and which is appropriate to the child's condition and to the circumstances of the parents or others caring for the child.

3. Recognizing the special needs of a disabled child, assistance extended in accordance with paragraph

4. 2 of the present article shall be provided free of charge, whenever possible, taking into account the financial resources of the parents or others caring for the child, and shall be designed to ensure that the disabled child has effective access to and receives education, training, health care services, rehabilitation services, preparation for employment and recreation opportunities in a manner conducive to the child's achieving the fullest possible social integration and individual development, including his or her cultural and spiritual development

5. States Parties shall promote, in the spirit of international cooperation, the exchange of appropriate information in the field of preventive health care and of medical, psychological and functional treatment of disabled children, including dissemination of and access to information concerning methods of rehabilitation, education and vocational services, with the aim of enabling States Parties to improve their capabilities and skills and to widen their experience in these areas. In this regard, particular account shall be taken of the needs of developing countries.

### Article 24

1. States Parties recognize the right of the child to the enjoyment of the highest attainable standard of health and to facilities for the treatment of illness and rehabilitation of health. States Parties shall strive to ensure that no child is deprived of his or her right of access to such health care services.

2. States Parties shall pursue full implementation of this right and, in particular, shall take appropriate measures:

    a. To diminish infant and child mortality;

    b. To ensure the provision of necessary medical assistance and health care to all children with emphasis on the development of primary health care;

    c. To combat disease and malnutrition, including within the framework of primary health care, through, inter alia, the application of readily available technology and through the provision of adequate nutritious foods and clean drinking-water, taking into consideration the dangers and risks of environmental pollution;

    d. To ensure appropriate pre-natal and post-natal health care for mothers;

    e. To ensure that all segments of society, in particular parents and children, are informed, have access to education and are supported in the use of basic knowledge of child health and nutrition, the advantages of breastfeeding, hygiene and environmental sanitation and the prevention of accidents;

    f. To develop preventive health care, guidance for parents and family planning education and services.

3. States Parties shall take all effective and appropriate measures with a view to abolishing traditional practises prejudicial to the health of children.

4. States Parties undertake to promote and encourage international cooperation with a view to achieving progressively the full realization of the right recognized in the present article. In this regard, particular account shall be taken of the needs of developing countries.

### Article 25

States Parties recognize the right of a child who has been placed by the competent authorities for the purposes of care, protection or treatment of his or her physical or mental health, to a periodic review of the treatment provided to the child and all other circumstances relevant to his or her placement.

### Article 26

1. States Parties shall recognize for every child the right to benefit from social security, including social insurance, and shall take the necessary measures to achieve the full realization of this right in accordance with their national law.

2. The benefits should, where appropriate, be granted, taking into account the resources and the circumstances of the child and persons having responsibility for the maintenance of the child, as well as any other consideration relevant to an application for benefits made by or on behalf of the child.

### Article 27

1. States Parties recognize the right of every child to a standard of living adequate for the child's physical, mental, spiritual, moral and social development.

2. The parent(s) or others responsible for the child have the primary responsibility to secure, within their abilities and financial capacities, the conditions of living necessary for the child's development.

3. States Parties, in accordance with national conditions and within their means, shall take appropriate measures to assist parents and others responsible for the child to implement this right and shall in case of need provide material assistance and support programmes, particularly with regard to nutrition, clothing and housing.

4. States Parties shall take all appropriate measures to secure the recovery of maintenance for the child from the parents or other persons having financial responsibility for the child, both within the State Party and from abroad. In particular, where the person having financial responsibility for the child lives in a State different from that of the child, States Parties shall promote the accession to international agreements or the conclusion of such agreements, as well as the making of other appropriate arrangements.

### Article 28

1. States Parties recognize the right of the child to education, and with a view to achieving this right progressively and on the basis of equal opportunity, they shall, in particular:

    a. Make primary education compulsory and available free to all;

    b. Encourage the development of different forms of secondary education, including general and vocational education, make them available and accessible to every child, and take appropriate measures such as the introduction of free education and offering financial assistance in case of need;

    c. Make higher education accessible to all on the basis of capacity by every appropriate means;

    d. Make educational and vocational information and guidance available and accessible to all children;

    e. Take measures to encourage regular attendance at schools and the reduction of drop-out rates.

2. States Parties shall take all appropriate measures to ensure that school discipline is administered in a manner consistent with the child's human dignity and in conformity with the present Convention.

3. States Parties shall promote and encourage international cooperation in matters relating to education, in particular with a view to contributing to the elimination of ignorance and illiteracy throughout the world and facilitating access to scientific and technical knowledge and modern teaching methods. In this regard, particular account shall be taken of the needs of developing countries.

### Article 41

Nothing in the present Convention shall affect any provisions which are more conducive to the realization of the rights of the child and which may be contained in:

    a. The law of a State party; or

    b. International law in force for that State.

# PART II

### Article 42

States Parties undertake to make the principles and provisions of the Convention widely known, by appropriate and active means, to adults and children alike.

### Article 43

1. For the purpose of examining the progress made by States Parties in achieving the realization of the obligations undertaken in the present Convention, there shall be established a Committee on the Rights of the Child, which shall carry out the functions hereinafter provided.

2. The Committee shall consist of ten experts of high moral standing and recognized competence in the field covered by this Convention. The members of the Committee shall be elected by States Parties from among their nationals and shall serve in their personal capacity, consideration being given to equitable geographical distribution, as well as to the principal legal systems.

3. The members of the Committee shall be elected by secret ballot from a list of persons nominated by States Parties. Each State Party may nominate one person from among its own nationals.

4. The initial election to the Committee shall be held no later than six months after the date of the entry into force of the present Convention and thereafter every second year. At least four months before the date of each election, the Secretary-General of the United Nations shall address a letter to States Parties inviting them to submit their nominations within two months. The Secretary-General shall subsequently prepare a list in alphabetical order of all persons thus nominated, indicating States Parties which have nominated them, and shall submit it to the States Parties to the present Convention.

5. The elections shall be held at meetings of States Parties convened by the Secretary-General at United Nations Headquarters. At those meetings, for which two thirds of States Parties shall constitute a quorum, the persons elected to the Committee shall be those who obtain the largest number of votes and an absolute majority of the votes of the representatives of States Parties present and voting.

6. The members of the Committee shall be elected for a term of four years. They shall be eligible for re-election if renominated. The term of five of the members elected at the first election shall expire at the end of two years; immediately after the first election, the names of these five members shall be chosen by lot by the Chairman of the meeting.

7. If a member of the Committee dies or resigns or declares that for any other cause he or she can no longer perform the duties of the Committee, the State Party which nominated the member shall appoint another expert from among its nationals to serve for the remainder of the term, subject to the approval of the Committee.

8. The Committee shall establish its own rules of procedure.

9. The Committee shall elect its officers for a period of two years.

10. The meetings of the Committee shall normally be held at United Nations Headquarters or at any other convenient place as determined by the Committee. The Committee shall normally meet annually. The duration of the meetings of the Committee shall be determined, and reviewed, if necessary, by a meeting of the States Parties to the present Convention, subject to the approval of the General Assembly.

11. The Secretary-General of the United Nations shall provide the necessary staff and facilities for the effective performance of the functions of the Committee under the present Convention.

12. With the approval of the General Assembly, the members of the Committee established under the present Convention shall receive emoluments from United Nations resources on such terms and conditions as the Assembly may decide.

### Article 44

1. States Parties undertake to submit to the Committee, through the Secretary-General of the United Nations, reports on the measures they have adopted which give effect to the rights recognized herein and on the progress made on the enjoyment of those rights

    a. Within two years of the entry into force of the Convention for the State Party concerned;

    b. Thereafter every five years.

2. Reports made under the present article shall indicate factors and difficulties, if any, affecting the degree of fulfilment of the obligations under the present Convention. Reports shall also contain sufficient information to provide the Committee with a comprehensive understanding of the implementation of the Convention in the country concerned.

3. A State Party which has submitted a comprehensive initial report to the Committee need not, in its subsequent reports submitted in accordance with paragraph 1 (b) of the present article, repeat basic information previously provided.

4. The Committee may request from States Parties further information relevant to the implementation of the Convention.

5. The Committee shall submit to the General Assembly, through the Economic and Social Council, every two years, reports on its activities.

6. States Parties shall make their reports widely available to the public in their own countries.

### Article 45

In order to foster the effective implementation of the Convention and to encourage international cooperation in the field covered by the Convention:

a. The specialized agencies, the United Nations Children's Fund, and other United Nations organs shall be entitled to be represented at the consideration of the implementation of such provisions of the present Convention as fall within the scope of their mandate. The Committee may invite the specialized agencies, the United Nations Children's Fund and other competent bodies as it may consider appropriate to provide expert advice on the implementation of the Convention in areas falling within the scope of their respective mandates. The Committee may invite the specialized agencies, the

b. United Nations Children's Fund, and other United Nations organs to submit reports on the implementation of the Convention in areas falling within the scope of their activities;

c. The Committee shall transmit, as it consider appropriate, to the specialized agencies, the United Nations Children's Fund and other competent bodies, any reports from States Parties that contain a request, or indicate a need, for technical advice or assistance, along with the Committee's observations and suggestions, if any, on these requests or indications;

d. The Committee may recommend to the General Assembly to request the Secretary-General to undertake on its behalf studies on specific issues relating to the rights of the child;

e. The Committee may make suggestions and general recommendations based on information received pursuant to articles 44 and 45 of the present Convention. Such suggestions and general recommendations shall be transmitted to any State Party concerned and reported to the General Assembly, together with comments, if any, from States Parties.

# PART III

## Article 46

The present Convention shall be open for signature by all States.

## Article 47

The present Convention is subject to ratification. Instruments of ratification shall be deposited with the Secretary-General of the United Nations.

## Article 48

The present Convention shall remain open for accession by any State. The instruments of accession shall be deposited with the Secretary-General of the United Nations.

## Article 49

1. The present Convention shall enter into force on the thirtieth day following the date of deposit with the Secretary-General of the United Nations of the twentieth instrument of ratification or accession.

2. For each State ratifying or acceding to the Convention after the deposit of the twentieth instrument of ratification or accession, the Convention shall enter into force on the thirtieth day after the deposit by such State of its instrument of ratification or accession.

## Article 50

1. Any State Party may propose an amendment and file it with the Secretary-General of the United Nations. The Secretary-General shall thereupon communicate the proposed amendment to States Parties, with a request that they indicate whether they favour a conference of States Parties for the purpose of considering and voting upon the proposals. In the event that, within four months from the date of such communication, at least one third of the States Parties favour such a conference, the Secretary-General shall convene the conference under the auspices of the United Nations. Any amendment adopted by a majority of States Parties present and voting at the conference shall be

2. submitted to the General Assembly for approval.

3. An amendment adopted in accordance with paragraph 1 of the present article shall enter into force when it has been approved by the General Assembly of the United Nations and accepted by a twothirds majority of States Parties.

4. When an amendment enters into force, it shall be binding on those States Parties which have accepted it, other States Parties still being bound by the provisions of the present Convention and any earlier amendments which they have accepted.

## Article 51

1. The Secretary-General of the United Nations shall receive and circulate to all States the text of reservations made by States at the time of ratification or accession.

2. A reservation incompatible with the object and purpose of the present Convention shall not be permitted.

3. Reservations may be withdrawn at any time by notification to that effect addressed to the Secretary-General of the United Nations, who shall then inform all States. Such notification shall take effect on the date on which it is received by the Secretary-General

## Article 52

A State Party may denounce the present Convention by written notification to the Secretary-General of the United Nations. Denunciation becomes effective one year after the date of receipt of the notification by the Secretary-General.

## Article 53

The Secretary-General of the United Nations is designated as the depositary of the present Convention.

## Article 54

The original of the present Convention, of which the Arabic, Chinese, English, French, Russian and Spanish texts are equally authentic, shall be deposited with the Secretary-General of the United Nations. IN WITNESS THEREOF the undersigned plenipotentiaries, being duly authorized thereto by their respective governments, have signed the present Convention.

# Human Rights Glossary

Note: Terms in this glossary are found in bold in the text of COMPASITO.

**Affirmative action:** Action taken by a government or private institution to make up for past discrimination in education or employment.

**African Charter on Human and People's Rights** (African Charter): A Regional human rights treaty for the African continent adopted by the Organisation of Africa Unity (OAU) in 1981.

**American Convention on Human Rights** (American Convention): A human rights treaty adopted by the Organisation for American States (OAS) in 1969. It covers North, Central and South America.

**Codification, Codify:** The process of formalizing law or rights into written instruments.

**Collective rights:** The rights of groups to protect their interests and identities; sometimes referred to as 'third generation rights'.

**Covenant:** Binding agreement between states; used synonymously with **convention** and **treaty**. The major international human rights covenants, both passed in 1966, are the **International Covenant on Civil and Political Rights (ICCPR)** and the **International Covenant on Economic, Social and Cultural Rights (ICESCR)**. Both were adopted in 1966 and **entered into force** in 1976.

**Convention:** Binding agreement between states; used synonymously with **treaty** and **Covenant**. A convention is stronger than a **declaration** because it is legally binding for governments that have **ratified** it. When, for example, the UN General Assembly adopts a convention, it creates international norms and standards. Once the UN General Assembly adopts a convention, **Member States** can then **ratify** the convention, turning it into international law.

**Convention on the Elimination of all Forms of Discrimination Against Women** (Women's Convention, CEDAW) (adopted 1979; **entered into force** 1981): The first legally binding international document prohibiting discrimination against women and obligating governments to take **affirmative action** to advance the equality of women.

**Convention on the Elimination of all Forms of Racial Discrimination** (Race Convention, CERD) (Adopted 1965; **entered into force** 1969): **Convention** defining and prohibiting discrimination based on race.

**Convention on the Prevention and Punishment of the Crime of Genocide** (Genocide Convention, 1951) (Adopted 1948; **entered into force** 1951) : International **convention** defining and prohibiting **genocide**; the first international **treaty** of the United Nations.

**Convention on the Rights of the Child** (Children's Convention, CRC) (adopted 1989; **entered into force** 1990): **Convention** setting forth a full spectrum of civil, cultural, economic, social, and political rights for children.

**Convention on the Rights of Persons with Disabilities** (CRPD) (adopted 2006): the first contention affirming the human rights of people with disabilities of any kind, including physical and psycho-social.

**Council of Europe:** The Council of Europe, founded in 1949, is the first European intergovernmental organisation. Today its 48 members states cover virtually the entire continent of Europe. It seeks to develop common democratic and legal principles based on the European Convention on Human Rights.

**Declaration:** Document stating agreed upon principles and standards but which is not legally binding. UN conferences, like the 1993 UN Conference on Human Rights in Vienna and the 1995 World Conference for Women in Beijing, usually produce two sets of declarations: one written by government representatives and one by **nongovernmental organisations (NGOs).** The UN General Assembly often issues influential but legally non-binding declarations.

**Declaration on the Rights of the Child:** Adopted by the UN General Assembly in 1959, this non-binding instrument sets forth ten general principles, which later formed the basis for the **Convention on the Rights of the Child** (CRC), which was adopted in 1989.

**Entering into force**: the process through which a **treaty** becomes fully binding on the states that have **ratified** it. This happens when the minimum number of **ratifications** called for by the treaty has been achieved.

**European Convention for the Prevention of Torture**: A regional human rights treaty adopted in 1987 by the **Council of Europe** that aims to prevent various violations against people who are detained by a public authority in places like prisons, juvenile detention centres, police stations, refugee camps or psychiatric hospitals.

**European Convention for the Protection of Human Rights and Fundamental Freedoms** (European Convention, European Convention on Human Rights, ECHR): A regional human rights treaty adopted in 1950 by the **Council of Europe**. All Council of Europe member states are party to the ECHR, and new members are expected to ratify the convention at the earliest opportunity.

**European Cultural Convention**: (Adopted by the **Council of Europe, 1954; entered into force 1955**): A regional **treaty** that provides the official framework for the Council of Europe's work on education, culture, heritage, youth and sport. A complement to the **European Convention**, the Cultural Convention seeks to safeguard European culture and to develop mutual understanding and the appreciation of cultural diversity among its various peoples.

**European Social Charter** (Adopted by the **Council of Europe 1962**; revised 1996): A regional **treaty** that guarantees social and economic human rights; it complements the **European Convention**, which principally addresses civil and political rights.

**Evolving capacity:** A principle used in the **Convention on the Rights of the Child** (CRC) that recommends greater exercise of a child's rights in relation to his or her growing cognitive and emotional maturity.

**First-generation rights:** a term referring to all civil and political human rights such as voting, expression, religion, assembly, fair trials, and life. The **International Covenant on Civil and Political Rights** (ICCPR) principally **codifies** these rights. Because the term suggests a hierarchy of civil and political rights over **second generation rights**, or economic and social rights, it is increasingly falling from use.

**Formal education**: the structured education system that runs from primary school to university and includes specialized programmes for technical and professional training.

**Gender**: A social construct that informs roles, attitudes, values and relationships regarding women and men. While sex is determined by biology, gender is determined by society, almost always functioning to subordinate women to men.

**Geneva Conventions**: Four treaties adopted in 1949 under the International Committee of the Red Cross (ICRC) in Geneva, Switzerland. These treaties revise and expanded original treaties adopted in 1864 and 1929. They address the treatment of sick and wounded soldiers and sailors, prisoners of war and civilians under enemy control.

**Genocide**: Acts committed with intent to destroy, in whole or in part, a national, ethnical, racial or religious group.

**Humanitarian law:** the body of law, mainly based on the **Geneva Conventions**, that protects certain persons in times of armed conflict, helps victims and limits the methods and means of combat in order to minimize destruction, loss of life and unnecessary human suffering.

**Human rights framework:** The evolving and interrelated body of international instruments that define human rights and establish mechanisms to promote and protect them.

**Human rights instruments**: any formal, written document of a state or states that sets forth rights as non-binding principles (a **declaration**) or **codifies** rights that are legally binding on those states that **ratify** them (a **covenant**, **treaty**, or **convention**).

**Inalienable**: Refers to rights that belong to every person and cannot be taken from a person under any circumstances.

**Indivisible**: Refers to the equal importance of each human rights law. A person cannot be denied a human right on the grounds that it is 'less important' or 'non-essential'.

**Informal education**: The lifelong process whereby every individual acquires attitudes, values, skills and knowledge from the educational influences and resources in his or her own environment and from daily experience (e.g. with family and neighbours, in the marketplace and library, from the mass media and play).

**Interdependent**: Refers to the complementary framework of human rights law. For example, your ability to participate in your government is directly affected by your right to express yourself, to get an education and even to obtain the necessities of life.

**Intergovernmental organisations** (IGOs): Organisations sponsored by several governments that seek to coordinate their efforts; some are regional (e.g. the **Council of Europe**, the Organisation of African Unity), some are alliances (e.g. the North Atlantic Treaty Organisation, NATO); and some are dedicated to a specific purpose (e.g. the **World Health Organisation** [WHO] and The United Nations Education, Scientific and Cultural Organisation [UNESCO]).

**International Covenant on Civil and Political Rights** (ICCPR)(Adopted1966, and **entered into force** 1976): The ICCPR declares that all people have a broad range of civil and political rights and sets up ways to monitor their respect by the member states.

**International Covenant on Economic, Social, and Cultural Rights** (ICESCR) (Adopted 1966, and **entered into force** 1976): The ICESCR declares that all people have a broad range of economic, social and cultural rights.

**International Labour Organisation** (ILO): Established in 1919 as part of the Versailles Peace Treaty, the ILO became a specialized agency of the UN in 1946. Under its mandate to improve working conditions and promote social justice, the ILO has passed a number of **conventions** pertaining to the human rights of children, especially concerning child labour.

**Member States**: Countries that are members an **intergovernmental organisations** (e.g. the United Nations, the **Council of Europe**).

**Non-formal education:** Any planned programme of personal and social education outside the formal education curriculum that is designed to improve a range of knowledge, skills and competencies.

**Non-governmental Organisations (NGOs)**: Organisations formed by people outside of government. NGOs monitor the proceedings of human rights bodies such as the Human Rights Council of the United Nations and are the 'watchdogs' of the human rights that fall within their mandate. Some are large and international (e.g. the Red Cross, Amnesty Inter-

national, the Scouts); others may be small and local (e.g. an organisation to advocate for people with disabilities in a particular city; a coalition to promote women's rights in one refugee camp). NGOs play a major role in influencing UN policy, and many have official consultative status at the UN.

**Optional Protocol:** A **treaty** that modifies another treaty (e.g. adding additional procedures or provisions). It is called 'optional' because a government that has ratified the original treaty can choose whether or not to ratify the changes made in the protocol.

**Optional Protocol on the Involvement of Children in Armed Conflict**: 2000 Amendment to the **Convention on the Rights of the Child** (CRC) that raises the minimum age for participation in armed conflict from the original fifteen to eighteen years.

**Positive discrimination:** See **affirmative action**.

**Ratification, Ratify**: Process by which the legislative body of a state confirms a government's action in signing a **treaty**; formal procedure by which a state becomes bound to a treaty after acceptance.

**Reservation**: The exceptions that States Parties make to a **treaty** (e.g. provisions that they do not agree to follow). Reservations, however, may not undermine the fundamental meaning of the treaty.

**Second-generation rights:** a term referring to economic, social and cultural rights, such as an adequate standard of living, health care, housing and education. The **International Covenant on Economic, Social, and Cultural Rights** principally **codifies** these rights. Because the term suggests a hierarchy of civil and political rights over economic and social rights, it is increasingly falling from usage.

**Shadow report:** An unofficial report prepared by institutes or individuals representing civil society submitted to a committee monitoring a human rights **treaty**. Such reports usually contradict or add to the official report on treaty compliance and implementation submitted by a government as part of its treaty obligations.

**Solidarity rights:** See **collective rights**.

**Special Rapporteur:** A person chosen by a UN human rights body to report on a particular theme (e.g. on the sale of chil-

dren, child prostitution and child pornography; on violence against women) or on the human rights situation in a particular country.

**Stereotype:** An oversimplified, generalised and often unconscious preconception about people or ideas that may lead to prejudice and discrimination.

**Third generation rights**: See **collective rights**.

**Treaty**: Formal agreement between states that defines and modifies their mutual duties and obligations; used synonymously with **convention** and **covenant**. When **Member States** ratify a treaty that has been adopted by the UN General Assembly, the articles of that treaty become part of its domestic legal obligations.

**UNICEF** (the United Nations Children's Fund): Mandated by the United Nations General Assembly, UNICEF advocates for the protection of children's rights, to help meet their basic needs and to expand their opportunities to reach their full potential. UNICEF is guided by the **Convention on the Rights of the Child** and strives to establish it as enduring ethical principles and international standards of behaviour towards children.

**Universality:** A principle that all human rights are held by all persons in all states and societies in the world.

**Universal Declaration of Human Rights** (Universal Declaration, UDHR): Adopted by the general assembly on December 10, 1948. Primary UN document establishing human rights standards and norms. All member states have agreed to uphold the UDHR. Although the declaration was intended to be non-binding, through time its various provisions have become so widely recognized that it can now be said to be customary international law.

**World Health Organisation** (WHO): an **intergovernmental organisation** under the auspices of the United Nations that works to promote health worldwide.

**Xenophobia:** A fear of foreigners, of persons from other countries or of things foreign generally. Xenophobia can lead to discrimination, racism, violence and even armed conflict against foreigners.

# Useful Resources

Note: The following provide general information on the children's rights. This is not, however, a comprehensive list. See Chapter V., Selected Human Rights Themes, for resources on specific topics.

Action Aid: www.actionaid.org

Amnesty International: http://web.amnesty.org

Bernard van Leer Foundation (BVLF): www.bernardvanleer.org

Coalition to Stop the Use of Child Soldiers (CSC): www.child-soldiers.org

Child Rights Information Network (CRIN): www.crin.org

- Children as Partners Alliance: www.crin.org/childrenaspartners/
- Focal Point on Sexual Exploitation of Children: www.crin.org/organisations/vieworg.asp?id=725
- NGO Group for the Convention on the Rights of the Child: www.crin.org/NGOGroupforCRC

Children's House: http://child-abuse.com/childhouse/

Clearinghouse on International Developments in Child, Youth and Family Policies: www.childpolicyintl.org

Childnet International: www.childnet-int.org

Child Soldiers: www.childsoldiers.org/home/

Child Workers in Asia (CWA): www.cwa.tnet.co.th

Coalition to Stop the Use of Child Soldiers: www.child-soldiers.org

Compendium of Good Practises in Human Rights Education: www.hrea.org/compendium

Council of Europe: www.coe.int

- Building Europe with and for Children: www.coe.int/children
- Directorate of Youth and Sport: www.coe.int/youth
- Education for Democratic Citizenship: www.coe.int/t/dg4/education/edc/default_EN.asp?
- Human Rights Education Youth Resources: www.coe.int/compass

Concerned for Working Children (CWC): www.workingchild.org

Defence for Children International (DCI): www.dci-is.org

Enabling Education Network: www.eenet.org.uk/

Eurobarometer: www.gesis.org/en/data_service/eurobarometer/

Euronet, The European Children's Network: www.europeanchildrensnetwork.org

European Forum for Child Welfare: www.efcw.org

End Child Prostitution, Child Pornography and the Trafficking of Children for Sexual Purposes: www.ecpat.net

Handicap International: www.handicap-international.org/index.html

Human Rights Education Associates: www.hrea.org/

Human Rights Internet: www.hri.ca/children/ThematicIndex.shtml

Human Rights Information and Documentation System: www.huridocs.org/

Human Rights Watch: http://hrw.org

Human Rights Web: www.hrweb.org

Institute for Research on Working Children (IREWOC): www.childlabour.net

International Catholic Child Bureau (BICE): www.bice.org

International Labour Organization, International Programme for the

Elimination of Child Labour (ILO-IPEC): www.ilo.org

International Federation Terre des Hommes (IFTDH): www.terredeshommes.org

International Clearinghouse on Children, Youth and Media: www.nordicom.gu.se/clearinghouse.php

Media Wise Trust: www.mediawise.org.uk

Minority Rights Group International (MRG): www.minorityrights.org

Ombudsman for Children in Norway: www.barneombudet.no

Open Society Institute: www.osi.hu/

Organisation Mondiale Contre la Torture (OMCT): www.omct.org

Oxfam International Secretariat: www.oxfaminternational.org

People's Movement for Human Rights Education: www.pdhre.org/

Plan International Website: www.plan-international.org

Right to Education Project: www.right-to-education.org

Safe On Line Outreach (SOLO): www.safeonlineoutreach.com

Save the Children Alliance: www.savethechildren.net
- Save the Children Europe Group: www.savethechildren.net/alliance/where_we_work/europegrp_who.html
- Save the Children Norway: www.reddbarna.no
- Save the Children Sweden www.rb.se
- Save the Children UK (SCUK): www.savethechildren.org.uk

South East European Child Rights Network (SEECRAN): www.seecran.org

Understanding Children's Work: www.ucw-project.org

UNICEF: www.unicef.org
- UNICEF CEE/CIS and Baltics Regional Website: www.unicef.org/programme/highlights/cee
- UNICEF Child trafficking Research Hub: www.childtrafficking.org/
- UNICEF Innocenti Research Centre: www.unicef-icdc.org
- UNICEF Magic: www.unicef.org/magic/
- UNICEF Voices of Youth: www.unicef.org/voy/
- UNICEF Young People's Media Network: http://ypmn.blogspot.com/2006_07_23_archive.html

United Nations
- UN Committee on the Rights of the Child: http://193.194.138.190/html/menu2/6/crc/
- UN Committee on the Elimination of Racial Discrimination (CERD): www.ohchr.org/english/bodies/cerd/index.htm
- UN CyberSchoolbus Global Teaching and Learing Project: http://cyberschoolbus.un.org/
- UN Office of the High Commissioner for Human Rights: www.unhchr.ch
- UN Special Rapporteur on the sale of children, child prostitution and child pornography: www.ohchr.org/english/issues/children/rapporteur/index.htm

War Child: www.warchild.org

World Bank:
- Europe and Central Asia: http://lnweb18.worldbank.org/eca/eca.nsf
- World Bank Youthink!: www.worldbank.org/html/schools/
- World Bank Group Global Child Labour Programme:

World Health Organization (WHO): www.who.int/en/

World Vision International (WVI) Website: www.wvi.org/home.shtml

# Status of Ratification of Major International Human Rights Instruments

| COUNTRIES | UNITED NATIONS | | | COUNCIL OF EUROPE | | | |
|---|---|---|---|---|---|---|---|
| | International Covenant on Economic, Social and Cultural Rights – CESCR | International Covenant on Civil and Political Rights – CCPR | Convention on Rights of the Child | European Convention on Human Rights – ECHR | European Social Charter – ESC | European Social Charter Revised – ESCR | European Convention for the Prevention of Torture and Inhuman or Degrading Treatment or Punishment |
| *Status at* | 19.04.2007 | 19.04.2007 | 03.06.2005 | 27.02.2006 | 15.06.2006 | 02.07.2007 | 27.02.2006 |
| *Entry into force* | 03.01.1976 | 23.03.1976 | 02.09.1990 | 03.09.1953 | 26.02.1965 | 01.07.1999 | 01.02.1989 |
| Albania | ✓ | ✓ | ✓ | ✓ | | ✓ | ✓ |
| Andorra | | ✓ | ✓ | ✓ | | ✓ | ✓ |
| Armenia | ✓ | ✓ | ✓ | ✓ | | ✓ | ✓ |
| Austria | ✓ | ✓ | ✓ | ✓ | ✓ | | ✓ |
| Azerbaijan | ✓ | ✓ | ✓ | ✓ | | ✓ | ✓ |
| Belarus | ✓ | ✓ | ✓ | | | | |
| Belgium | ✓ | ✓ | ✓ | ✓ | ✓ | ✓ | ✓ |
| Bosnia and Herzegovina | ✓ | ✓ | ✓ | ✓ | | | ✓ |
| Bulgaria | ✓ | ✓ | ✓ | ✓ | | ✓ | ✓ |
| Croatia | ✓ | ✓ | ✓ | ✓ | ✓ | | ✓ |
| Cyprus | ✓ | ✓ | ✓ | ✓ | ✓ | ✓ | ✓ |
| Czech Republic | ✓ | ✓ | ✓ | ✓ | ✓ | | ✓ |
| Denmark | ✓ | ✓ | ✓ | ✓ | ✓ | | ✓ |
| Estonia | ✓ | ✓ | ✓ | ✓ | | ✓ | ✓ |
| Finland | ✓ | ✓ | ✓ | ✓ | ✓ | ✓ | ✓ |
| France | ✓ | ✓ | ✓ | ✓ | ✓ | ✓ | ✓ |
| Georgia | ✓ | ✓ | ✓ | ✓ | | ✓ | ✓ |
| Germany | ✓ | ✓ | ✓ | ✓ | ✓ | | ✓ |
| Greece | ✓ | ✓ | ✓ | ✓ | ✓ | | ✓ |
| Hungary | ✓ | ✓ | ✓ | ✓ | ✓ | | ✓ |
| Iceland | ✓ | ✓ | ✓ | ✓ | ✓ | | ✓ |
| Ireland | ✓ | ✓ | ✓ | ✓ | ✓ | ✓ | ✓ |
| Italy | ✓ | ✓ | ✓ | ✓ | ✓ | ✓ | ✓ |
| Latvia | ✓ | ✓ | ✓ | ✓ | ✓ | | ✓ |
| Liechtenstein | ✓ | ✓ | ✓ | ✓ | | | ✓ |
| Lithuania | ✓ | ✓ | ✓ | ✓ | | ✓ | ✓ |
| Luxembourg | ✓ | ✓ | ✓ | ✓ | ✓ | | ✓ |
| Malta | ✓ | ✓ | ✓ | ✓ | ✓ | ✓ | ✓ |
| Moldova | ✓ | ✓ | ✓ | ✓ | | ✓ | ✓ |
| Monaco | ✓ | ✓ | ✓ | ✓ | | | ✓ |
| Montenegro | ✓ | ✓ | ✓ | | | | ✓ |
| Netherlands | ✓ | ✓ | ✓ | ✓ | ✓ | ✓ | ✓ |
| Norway | ✓ | ✓ | ✓ | ✓ | ✓ | ✓ | ✓ |
| Poland | ✓ | ✓ | ✓ | ✓ | ✓ | | ✓ |
| Portugal | ✓ | ✓ | ✓ | ✓ | ✓ | ✓ | ✓ |
| Romania | ✓ | ✓ | ✓ | ✓ | | ✓ | ✓ |

| COUNTRIES | UNITED NATIONS | | | COUNCIL OF EUROPE | | | |
|---|---|---|---|---|---|---|---|
| | International Covenant on Economic, Social and Cultural Rights – CESCR | International Covenant on Civil and Political Rights – CCPR | Convention on Rights of the Child | European Convention on Human Rights – ECHR | European Social Charter – ESC | European Social Charter Revised – ESCR | European Convention for the Prevention of Torture and Inhuman or Degrading Treatment or Punishment |
| *Status at* | *19.04.2007* | *19.04.2007* | *03.06.2005* | *27.02.2006* | *15.06.2006* | *02.07.2007* | *27.02.2006* |
| *Entry into force* | *03.01.1976* | *23.03.1976* | *02.09.1990* | *03.09.1953* | *26.02.1965* | *01.07.1999* | *01.02.1989* |
| Russian Federation | ✓ | ✓ | ✓ | ✓ | | | ✓ |
| San Marino | ✓ | ✓ | ✓ | ✓ | | | ✓ |
| Serbia | ✓ | ✓ | ✓ | ✓ | | | ✓ |
| Slovakia | ✓ | ✓ | ✓ | ✓ | ✓ | | ✓ |
| Slovenia | ✓ | ✓ | ✓ | ✓ | | ✓ | ✓ |
| Spain | ✓ | ✓ | ✓ | ✓ | ✓ | | ✓ |
| Sweden | ✓ | ✓ | ✓ | ✓ | ✓ | ✓ | ✓ |
| Switzerland | ✓ | ✓ | ✓ | ✓ | | | ✓ |
| "the Former Yugoslav Republic of Macedonia" | ✓ | ✓ | ✓ | ✓ | ✓ | | ✓ |
| Turkey | ✓ | ✓ | ✓ | ✓ | ✓ | | ✓ |
| Ukraine | ✓ | ✓ | ✓ | ✓ | | ✓ | ✓ |
| United Kingdom | ✓ | ✓ | ✓ | ✓ | ✓ | | ✓ |

# Sales agents for publications of the Council of Europe
# Agents de vente des publications du Conseil de l'Europe

**BELGIUM/BELGIQUE**
La Librairie Européenne -
The European Bookshop
Rue de l'Orme, 1
B-1040 BRUXELLES
Tel.: +32 (0)2 231 04 35
Fax: +32 (0)2 735 08 60
E-mail: order@libeurop.be
http://www.libeurop.be

Jean De Lannoy
Avenue du Roi 202 Koningslaan
B-1190 BRUXELLES
Tel.: +32 (0)2 538 43 08
Fax: +32 (0)2 538 08 41
E-mail: jean.de.lannoy@dl-servi.com
http://www.jean-de-lannoy.be

**CANADA**
Renouf Publishing Co. Ltd.
1-5369 Canotek Road
OTTAWA, Ontario K1J 9J3, Canada
Tel.: +1 613 745 2665
Fax: +1 613 745 7660
Toll-Free Tel.: (866) 767-6766
E-mail: order.dept@renoufbooks.com
http://www.renoufbooks.com

**CZECH REPUBLIC/**
**RÉPUBLIQUE TCHÈQUE**
Suweco CZ, s.r.o.
Klecakova 347
CZ-180 21 PRAHA 9
Tel.: +420 2 424 59 204
Fax: +420 2 848 21 646
E-mail: import@suweco.cz
http://www.suweco.cz

**DENMARK/DANEMARK**
GAD
Vimmelskaftet 32
DK-1161 KØBENHAVN K
Tel.: +45 77 66 60 00
Fax: +45 77 66 60 01
E-mail: gad@gad.dk
http://www.gad.dk

**FINLAND/FINLANDE**
Akateeminen Kirjakauppa
PO Box 128
Keskuskatu 1
FIN-00100 HELSINKI
Tel.: +358 (0)9 121 4430
Fax: +358 (0)9 121 4242
E-mail: akatilaus@akateeminen.com
http://www.akateeminen.com

**FRANCE**
La Documentation française
(diffusion/distribution France entière)
124, rue Henri Barbusse
F-93308 AUBERVILLIERS CEDEX
Tél.: +33 (0)1 40 15 70 00
Fax: +33 (0)1 40 15 68 00
E-mail: commande@ladocumentationfrancaise.fr
http://www.ladocumentationfrancaise.fr

Librairie Kléber
1 rue des Francs Bourgeois
F-67000 STRASBOURG
Tel.: +33 (0)3 88 15 78 88
Fax: +33 (0)3 88 15 78 80
E-mail: francois.wolfermann@librairie-kleber.fr
http://www.librairie-kleber.com

**GERMANY/ALLEMAGNE**
**AUSTRIA/AUTRICHE**
UNO Verlag GmbH
August-Bebel-Allee 6
D-53175 BONN
Tel.: +49 (0)228 94 90 20
Fax: +49 (0)228 94 90 222
E-mail: bestellung@uno-verlag.de
http://www.uno-verlag.de

**GREECE/GRÈCE**
Librairie Kauffmann s.a.
Stadiou 28
GR-105 64 ATHINAI
Tel.: +30 210 32 55 321
Fax.: +30 210 32 30 320
E-mail: ord@otenet.gr
http://www.kauffmann.gr

**HUNGARY/HONGRIE**
Euro Info Service kft.
1137 Bp. Szent István krt. 12.
H-1137 BUDAPEST
Tel.: +36 (06)1 329 2170
Fax: +36 (06)1 349 2053
E-mail: euroinfo@euroinfo.hu
http://www.euroinfo.hu

**ITALY/ITALIE**
Licosa SpA
Via Duca di Calabria, 1/1
I-50125 FIRENZE
Tel.: +39 0556 483215
Fax: +39 0556 41257
E-mail: licosa@licosa.com
http://www.licosa.com

**MEXICO/MEXIQUE**
Mundi-Prensa México, S.A. De C.V.
Río Pánuco, 141 Delegacíon Cuauhtémoc
06500 MÉXICO, D.F.
Tel.: +52 (01)55 55 33 56 58
Fax: +52 (01)55 55 14 67 99
E-mail: mundiprensa@mundiprensa.com.mx
http://www.mundiprensa.com.mx

**NETHERLANDS/PAYS-BAS**
De Lindeboom Internationale Publicaties b.v.
M.A. de Ruyterstraat 20 A
NL-7482 BZ HAAKSBERGEN
Tel.: +31 (0)53 5740004
Fax: +31 (0)53 5729296
E-mail: books@delindeboom.com
http://www.delindeboom.com

**NORWAY/NORVÈGE**
Akademika
Postboks 84 Blindern
N-0314 OSLO
Tel.: +47 2 218 8100
Fax: +47 2 218 8103
E-mail: support@akademika.no
http://www.akademika.no

**POLAND/POLOGNE**
Ars Polona JSC
25 Obroncow Street
PL-03-933 WARSZAWA
Tel.: +48 (0)22 509 86 00
Fax: +48 (0)22 509 86 10
E-mail: arspolona@arspolona.com.pl
http://www.arspolona.com.pl

**PORTUGAL**
Livraria Portugal
(Dias & Andrade, Lda.)
Rua do Carmo, 70
P-1200-094 LISBOA
Tel.: +351 21 347 42 82 / 85
Fax: +351 21 347 02 64
E-mail: info@livrariaportugal.pt
http://www.livrariaportugal.pt

**RUSSIAN FEDERATION/**
**FÉDÉRATION DE RUSSIE**
Ves Mir
9a, Kolpacnhyi per.
RU-101000 MOSCOW
Tel.: +7 (8)495 623 6839
Fax: +7 (8)495 625 4269
E-mail: orders@vesmirbooks.ru
http://www.vesmirbooks.ru

**SPAIN/ESPAGNE**
Mundi-Prensa Libros, s.a.
Castelló, 37
E-28001 MADRID
Tel.: +34 914 36 37 00
Fax: +34 915 75 39 98
E-mail: libreria@mundiprensa.es
http://www.mundiprensa.com

**SWITZERLAND/SUISSE**
Van Diermen Editions – ADECO
Chemin du Lacuez 41
CH-1807 BLONAY
Tel.: +41 (0)21 943 26 73
Fax: +41 (0)21 943 36 05
E-mail: info@adeco.org
http://www.adeco.org

**UNITED KINGDOM/ROYAUME-UNI**
The Stationery Office Ltd
PO Box 29
GB-NORWICH NR3 1GN
Tel.: +44 (0)870 600 5522
Fax: +44 (0)870 600 5533
E-mail: book.enquiries@tso.co.uk
http://www.tsoshop.co.uk

**UNITED STATES and CANADA/**
**ÉTATS-UNIS et CANADA**
Manhattan Publishing Company
468 Albany Post Road
CROTTON-ON-HUDSON, NY 10520, USA
Tel.: +1 914 271 5194
Fax: +1 914 271 5856
E-mail: Info@manhattanpublishing.com
http://www.manhattanpublishing.com

**Council of Europe Publishing/Editions du Conseil de l'Europe**
F-67075 Strasbourg Cedex
Tel.: +33 (0)3 88 41 25 81 – Fax: +33 (0)3 88 41 39 10 – E-mail: publishing@coe.int – Website: http://book.coe.int